World

FRANCE

Steve Fallon
Michael Rothschild

WORLD FOOD France
1st edition

Published by
Lonely Planet Publications Pty Ltd ABN 36 005 607 983
192 Burwood Rd, Hawthorn, Victoria 3122, Australia

Lonely Planet Offices
Australia PO Box 617, Hawthorn, Victoria 3122
USA 150 Linden Street, Oakland CA 94607
UK 10a Spring Place, London NW5 3BH
France 1 rue du Dahomey, 75011 Paris

Photography
All of the images in this guide are available
for licensing from Lonely Planet Images.
email: lpi@lonelyplanet.com.au

Published
September 2000

ISBN 1 86450 021 2

Printed by
The Bookmaker International Ltd.
Printed in China.

About the Authors

Steve Fallon was born in Boston and received a Bachelor of Sciences degree in modern languages from Georgetown University in Washington DC. He has worked as a journalist (and sometime bookseller) in the USA, Hong Kong, Budapest and London and has written and/or contributed to a number of other Lonely Planet titles.

Michael Rothschild, who wrote the Wine & Champagne chapter, was born in Philadelphia and earned his degree in Asian studies at McGill University in Montreal. He has lived and worked in all the same places as Steve and is currently employed as a financial journalist at the London bureau of Bloomberg News. Mike and Steve met in a laundrette in Philadelphia on a wintry afternoon in early 1977. They have been eating and travelling – and washing their dirty laundry – together ever since.

About the Photographer

A predilection for playing with knives and fire led Greg Elms to a lukewarm vocation in catering. His life changed when he saw a black & white photograph of a pepper – now others cook while he eats the props.

He is a fine art graduate (VCA), has a Bachelor of Arts and works out of a disused church in Melbourne where he produces blasphemous Christmas cards – when he's not freelancing for various Australian and international magazines.

From the Publisher

This first edition of *World Food France* was edited by Patrick Witton and designed by Brendan Dempsey of Lonely Planet's Melbourne office. Martin Hughes oversaw the book's production. Natasha Velleley mapped, and Kristin Odijk proofed. Patrick Witton and Tim Uden indexed.

The language section was compiled by Sophie Le Mao & Sandrine Dupain, and was coordinated in the French Office by Caroline Guilleminot & Zahia Hafs and in Australia by Karin Vidstrup Monk & Peter D'Onghia. Olivier Breton edited and worked on transliterations, Karin Vidstrup Monk co-edited, Joanne Adams laid it out, Michael Janes proofed and Fabrice Rocher & Kerrie Hickin provided assistance.

Valerie Tellini, of Lonely Planet Images, coordinated the supply of photographs and Brett Pascoe managed the pre-press work on the images.

Sally Steward, publisher, developed the series and Martin Hughes, series editor, nurtured each book from the seeds of ideas through to fruition, with inimitable flair.

Acknowledgements

From the author: I would like to thank my partner, copain de table and now co-author, Mike Rothschild, for writing the wine and Champagne sections of the Drinks chapter. As always Zahia Hafs and Rob Flynn were hospitable, helpful and great fun at home in Paris as were Nicola Williams and Matthias Lüfkens chez eux in Lyon. Emma Bland, marketeer par excellence, was kind enough to cover Paris' markets, and I am once again in debt to the staff at Lonely Planet's Paris office, especially Bénédicte Houdré, for correcting some of my sillier mistakes at the 11th hour. Thanks, too, to fellow Lonely Planet author, Daniel Robinson of Tel Aviv, for some of the inspired prose, and to fellow gourmand (in every sense), Sue Girdwood of Sydney, for vetting the manuscript and offering useful comments and criticisms. Merci mille fois à tous!

Warning & Request

Things change; markets give way to supermarkets, prices go up, good places go bad and not much stays the same. Please tell us if you've discovered changes and help make the next edition even more useful. We value all your feedback, and strive to improve our books accordingly. We have a well-travelled, well-fed team that reads and acknowledges every letter, postcard and email and ensures that every morsel of information finds its way to the appropriate people.

Each correspondent will receive the latest issue of Planet Talk, our quarterly printed newsletter, or Comet, our monthly email newsletter. Subscriptions to both are free. The newsletters might even feature your letter so let us know if you don't want it published.

If you have an interesting anecdote or story to do with your culinary travels, we'd love to hear it. If we publish it in the next edition, we'll send you a free Lonely Planet book of your choice.

Send your correspondence to the nearest Lonely Planet office:
Australia: PO Box 617, Hawthorn, Victoria 3122
UK: 10a Spring Place, London NW5 3BH
USA: 150 Linden St, Oakland CA 94607
France: 1 rue du Dahomey, Paris 75011

Or email us at: talk2us@lonelyplanet.com

contents

FRANCE

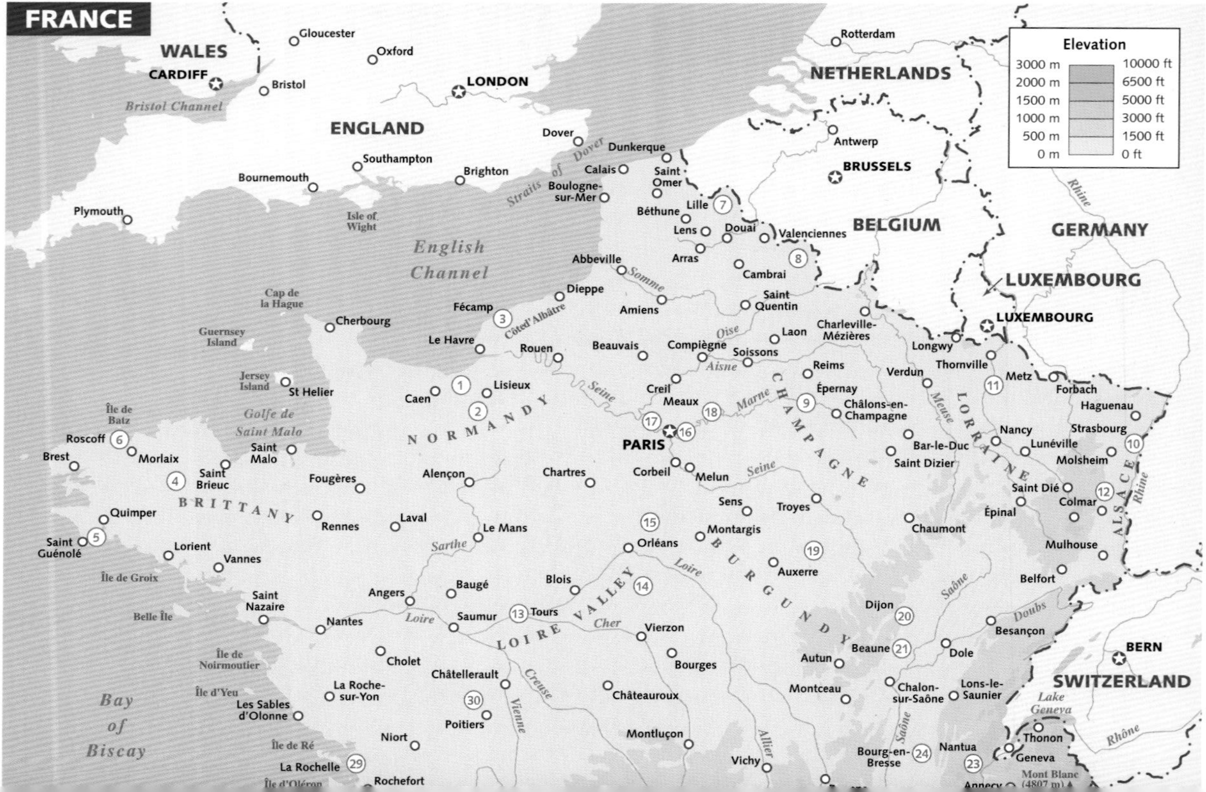
Elevation
3000 m 10000 ft
2000 m 6500 ft
1500 m 5000 ft
1000 m 3000 ft
500 m 1500 ft
0 m 0 ft
WALES
CARDIFF
Gloucester
Oxford
Bristol
LONDON
Bristol Channel
ENGLAND
Southampton
Bournemouth
Brighton
Plymouth
Isle of Wight
Dover
Straits of Dover
English Channel
Dunkerque
Calais
Boulogne-sur-Mer
Saint Omer
Béthune
Lille
Lens
Douai
Arras
Valenciennes
Cambrai
Abbeville
Somme
Dieppe
Amiens
Saint Quentin
Cap de la Hague
Guernsey Island
Jersey Island
St Helier
Cherbourg
Fécamp
Côte d'Albâtre
Le Havre
Rouen
Beauvais
Compiègne
Oise
Laon
Soissons
Aisne
Charleville-Mézières
Reims
Épernay
Châlons-en-Champagne
Caen
Lisieux
Seine
Creil
Meaux
Marne
PARIS
NORMANDY
CHAMPAGNE
Île de Batz
Roscoff
Brest
Morlaix
Golfe de Saint Malo
Saint Malo
Saint Brieuc
BRITTANY
Fougères
Alençon
Chartres
Corbeil
Melun
Quimper
Rennes
Laval
Le Mans
Sens
Troyes
Saint Guénolé
Lorient
Vannes
Île de Groix
Sarthe
Orléans
Montargis
BURGUNDY
Auxerre
Belle Île
Saint Nazaire
Angers
Baugé
Blois
Loire
LOIRE VALLEY
Nantes
Saumur
Tours
Cher
Vierzon
Cholet
Bourges
Île de Noirmoutier
Châtellerault
Creuse
Vienne
Châteauroux
Île d'Yeu
La Roche-sur-Yon
Les Sables d'Olonne
Poitiers
Bay of Biscay
Niort
Île de Ré
La Rochelle
Île d'Oléron
Rochefort
Montluçon
Allier
Vichy
Rotterdam
NETHERLANDS
Antwerp
BRUSSELS
BELGIUM
GERMANY
Rhine
LUXEMBOURG
LUXEMBOURG
Longwy
Thornville
Metz
Forbach
Verdun
Meuse
LORRAINE
Haguenau
Strasbourg
Nancy
Lunéville
Molsheim
Bar-le-Duc
Saint Dizier
Saint Dié
Colmar
ALSACE
Épinal
Chaumont
Mulhouse
Belfort
Saône
Dijon
Doubs
Besançon
Beaune
Dole
Autun
BERN
SWITZERLAND
Montceau
Chalon-sur-Saône
Lons-le-Saunier
Lake Geneva
Thonon
Geneva
Rhône
Bourg-en-Bresse
Nantua
Mont Blanc (4807 m)
Annecy
1
2
3
4
5
6
7
8
9
10
11
12
13
14
15
16
17
18
19
20
21
23
24
29
30

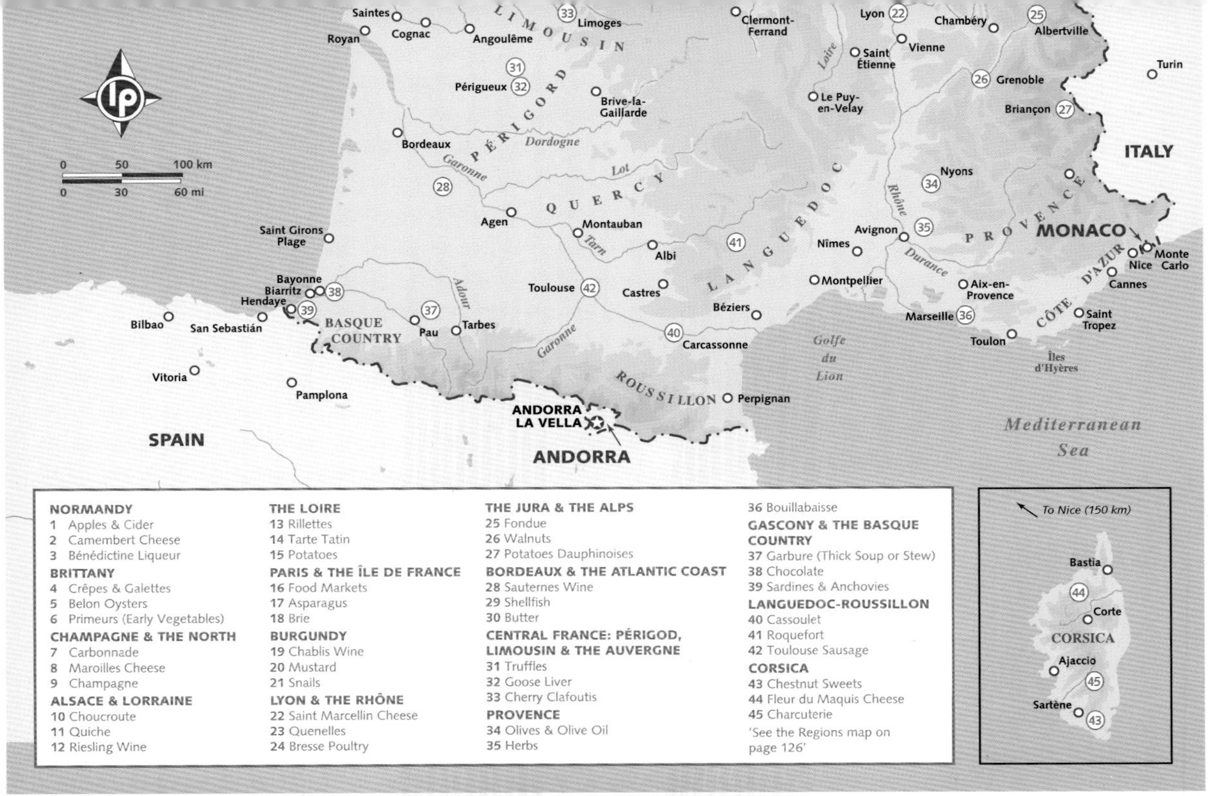
Saintes
Royan
Cognac
Angoulême
LIMOUSIN
Limoges
Clermont-Ferrand
Lyon
Chambéry
Albertville
Turin
Saint Étienne
Vienne
Loire
Le Puy-en-Velay
Grenoble
Briançon
ITALY
Périgueux
PÉRIGORD
Brive-la-Gaillarde
Bordeaux
Garonne
Dordogne
Lot
QUERCY
Agen
Montauban
Tarn
Albi
LANGUEDOC
Nyons
Rhône
Avignon
Nîmes
PROVENCE
MONACO
Monte Carlo
Nice
Cannes
CÔTE D'AZUR
Saint Tropez
Saint Girons Plage
Bayonne
Biarritz
Hendaye
Bilbao
San Sebastián
BASQUE COUNTRY
Pau
Tarbes
Adour
Toulouse
Castres
Béziers
Montpellier
Durance
Aix-en-Provence
Marseille
Toulon
Îles d'Hyères
Carcassonne
Golfe du Lion
Vitoria
Pamplona
ROUSSILLON
Perpignan
ANDORRA LA VELLA
ANDORRA
SPAIN
Mediterranean Sea
0 50 100 km
0 30 60 mi
NORMANDY
1 Apples & Cider
2 Camembert Cheese
3 Bénédictine Liqueur
BRITTANY
4 Crêpes & Galettes
5 Belon Oysters
6 Primeurs (Early Vegetables)
CHAMPAGNE & THE NORTH
7 Carbonnade
8 Maroilles Cheese
9 Champagne
ALSACE & LORRAINE
10 Choucroute
11 Quiche
12 Riesling Wine
THE LOIRE
13 Rillettes
14 Tarte Tatin
15 Potatoes
PARIS & THE ÎLE DE FRANCE
16 Food Markets
17 Asparagus
18 Brie
BURGUNDY
19 Chablis Wine
20 Mustard
21 Snails
LYON & THE RHÔNE
22 Saint Marcellin Cheese
23 Quenelles
24 Bresse Poultry
THE JURA & THE ALPS
25 Fondue
26 Walnuts
27 Potatoes Dauphinoises
BORDEAUX & THE ATLANTIC COAST
28 Sauternes Wine
29 Shellfish
30 Butter
CENTRAL FRANCE: PÉRIGOD, LIMOUSIN & THE AUVERGNE
31 Truffles
32 Goose Liver
33 Cherry Clafoutis
PROVENCE
34 Olives & Olive Oil
35 Herbs
36 Bouillabaisse
GASCONY & THE BASQUE COUNTRY
37 Garbure (Thick Soup or Stew)
38 Chocolate
39 Sardines & Anchovies
LANGUEDOC-ROUSSILLON
40 Cassoulet
41 Roquefort
42 Toulouse Sausage
CORSICA
43 Chestnut Sweets
44 Fleur du Maquis Cheese
45 Charcuterie
'See the Regions map on page 126'
To Nice (150 km)
Bastia
Corte
CORSICA
Ajaccio
Sartène

"The French think mainly about two things – their two main meals", a well-fed bon vivant friend in Paris once told us. "Everything else is in parentheses." And it's true. While not every French man, woman and child is a walking *Larousse Gastronomique*, eating well is still of prime importance to most people here, and they continue to spend an inordinate amount of time thinking about, talking about and consuming food.

No other cuisine in the world – apart from the Chinese on the other side of the world, perhaps – comes close to that of the French for freshness of ingredients, natural flavours, regional variety and refined, often complex, cooking methods. French cuisine is indisputably the western world's most important and seminal style of cooking and has been for centuries. Indeed, the very word 'cuisine' was borrowed from the French because the English phrase 'cooking style' just couldn't handle all the nuances.

Don't think for a moment, though, that this national obsession with all things culinary means that eating out or dining in a private home in France has to be a ceremonious occasion, full of pitfalls for the uninitiated. Indeed, contrary to a commonly held Anglo-Saxon belief, the French can be among the kindest, most generous and open people anywhere. Approach French food and wine with half the enthusiasm les français themselves do, and you will be warmly received, tutored, encouraged and fed. But do not try to sanctify food here as is so often the case elsewhere nowadays. Most French people find this silly, boring and ultimately pointless.

This book will take you on a culinary tour of each of the regions of France, walk you through its liveliest markets, invite you to a celebratory dinner in a private home and even help you prepare and cook your own French banquet. But first things first … you must know your basic ingredients and we've done the homework for you. Here you'll learn about France's most celebrated lentils and prunes, how to choose the perfect croissant, the difference between a saucepan and a casserole (nothing – it's the same thing in French) and how to tell a Burgundy from a Bordeaux.

What we set out to do from the start was to separate the wheat from the chaff, choosing favourite dishes, wines and sweets from across France and offering a taste of how and when and why the French enjoy them so. It's up to you to fill in the gaps by helping yourself and tucking in. Bon voyage and a very bon appétit.

"Tell me what you eat, and I shall tell you what you are."

Jean-Anthelme Brillat-Savarin, *The Physiology of Taste* (1826)

the culture of french cuisine

French cuisine is indisputably the yardstick by which the world measures and compares all other western styles of cooking. But what does 'French cuisine' mean exactly? Is it a national cooking style, or is it a term used to encompass the distinct cuisines of France's regions? At the risk of sounding equivocal, we believe it's a bit of both.

The cuisine of France is indeed remarkably varied, with many differences based on the produce and gastronomy of the country's regions. But many dishes such as quiche, onion soup, **escargots** (snails) and **crêpes** (thin pancakes) shed their provincial robes long ago and have joined the panoply that the world now knows as 'French dishes'. Remember, though, that these dishes did originate in a particular place and ideally should be enjoyed there still. That quiche will be much tastier in Lorraine, those snails plumper and more tasty in Burgundy, a crêpe lighter and thinner (and more authentically made with nutty-tasting buckwheat) in Brittany.

Geese in Basse-Normandy

On the other hand, while many dishes have become favourites across France and even abroad, they've managed to retain their strong regional associations and flavours; Alsatian **choucroute** (pickled cabbage with juniper berries, sausages, bacon and pork) and **bouillabaisse** (soup of fish stewed in a broth flavoured with garlic, orange peel, fennel, tomatoes and saffron) from Marseille spring to mind. Still others remain firmly rooted in their birthplace: **brandade de morue** (salt cod purée) still conjures up (and tastes of) the sun-bathed coastline of Provence; a **friture** (fry-up) of smelts and whitebait recalls the languid rivers of the Loire region; and **piperade** (scrambled eggs cooked with ham and vegetables) will forever be Basque.

SILVER LININGS

Even disasters have been kind to France and ultimately helped to bring new gastronomic wealth. When the *phylloxera* lice from the USA destroyed most of France's vineyards in the 19th century, for example, some growers in Burgundy planted **cassis** (blackcurrants) while the slopes of Deux-Sèvres in Poitou-Charentes on the Atlantic coast were laid to grass and cows brought down from Normandy. As a result we now have **crème de cassis** one of the tastiest liqueurs made in France, and **beurre de Charente**, the finest butter in the country.

Lunchtime picnickers in the Trocadéro gardens, Paris

Culinary traditions that have been developed and perfected over the centuries have made French cooking a highly refined art. But while even simple peasant dishes require careful preparation and great attention to detail, the secret to success in French cooking remains not so much elaborate techniques as the use of the freshest local and seasonal ingredients.

Will all this continue in the 21st century? Can small growers and makers of artisan products compete with the mass production of attractive but generally tasteless (and even genetically modified) fruit and vegetables? Can bistros and neighbourhood restaurants compete with fast-food outlets, which many French despise primarily because they have removed that time-honoured aperitif, the smell of food cooking? Will the younger generation pick up the saucepan when grand-mère and maman move on to that great fiery kitchen in the sky?

Fruit and vegetable stall in Nice, Provence

These have been matters of concern and debate at least since the early 20th century, when for the first time most French people were able to afford a great variety and quality of foodstuffs (and the free time to prepare them). Of course, things have changed and will continue to do so based on the demands of modern life and new tastes. But a visit to a **fromagerie** (cheese shop) will convince you that young people can and will choose a piece of **chèvre** (goat's milk cheese) or a **tomme** (semi-hard cheese) from Savoy with skill and alacrity. And so what if people now eat Thai or Vietnamese noodles instead of French **pâtes fraîches** (fresh pasta) once a week? Like anything organic, French cuisine has to borrow and change to nourish itself. As history shows, this has always been the case. **Plus ça change, plus c'est la même chose** (the more it changes, the more it stays the same).

History

The development and refinement of French cuisine and the French dining experience as we know it can be traced historically to conscious efforts by certain individuals to clean up the mess.

The Celtic Gauls, France's original settlers and under the authority of Rome from the middle of the 1st century BC, were immoderate in their eating habits even by their conquerors' orgiastic standards, consuming "bread in a very small quantity with a great deal of meat either boiled, roasted or grilled", according to the peripatetic Greek geographer, Strabo. Along with game (animals were not domesticated for consumption at this time), the Gauls favoured such 'oddities' as cranes, herons, hedgehogs and dormice highly spiced with cumin, coriander, mint and pepper. As they would be for centuries, seasonings were more a necessity than a preference; the main object of cooking was to disguise the flavour of food, much of which was tainted or spoiled.

Painted tiles inside the Cochon A L'Oreille Restaurant, Paris

A stone farm house, Basse-Normandy

Despite what you're told, tastes in food – like fashion – have not ceased changing over the centuries. According to Jean-Louis Flandrin, France's foremost food historian and author of *Histoire de l'alimentation* (The History of Food), "we would be incapable of swallowing even a teaspoon of the **sauce verte** (green sauce) that accompanied most meat dishes between the 14th and 16th centuries". Today, about one teaspoon of vinegar goes into every 10 of oil; at that time the proportion was reversed and green sauce was essentially pure vinegar or green grape juice that had been lightly seasoned. As for spices, recipes from the 14th century recommend the equivalent of 80g of cloves for cooking a single chicken. Since it takes about 15 cloves to make one gram that would mean a bird studded with some 1200 cloves. The taste is inconceivable today.

Dining – for the wealthier classes at least – essentially meant sitting around a large table, sawing off hunks of meat with small knives. Peasants subsisted on bread or dumplings made of rye flour, water or weak ale, and whatever *companaticum* (Latin for 'that which goes with bread') was available in the cauldron forever on the boil over the hearth. In good times a family could nourish themselves from this **pot-au-feu** (literally, pot on the fire and today an actual French dish) stocked with a hare, pigeon or even a chicken. But when times were lean – much less during the frequent famines – the cauldron generally contained salt pork or just the stock left over from previous meals.

The Franks, successors to the Gauls, introduced a certain amount of refinement but only at the table itself – not much was changed on the menu. Emperor Charlemagne had banquet tables laid with silver and gold goblets and plates, but the food remained coarse and primarily meat based. Even by the time the first French-language cookbook was published by Guillaume Tirel (or Taillevent) in about 1375, menus consisted almost entirely of 'soups' (actually sodden pieces of bread, or sops, boiled in a thickened stock) and meat and poultry heavy with the taste of herbs and spices, including new ones like ginger, cinnamon and cloves first introduced via Spain by the Moors. The book's very title, *Le Viander de Taillevent*, suggests a carnivorous diet; at that time **viande** (meat) simply meant 'food'.

Sheep grazing, Normandy

The Middle Ages saw some important changes in the structure of the French kitchen and its equipment. Until about the 12th century, food was cooked on andirons over a roaring fire, obviating the preparation of anything that had to be stirred frequently or fried quickly in small quantities. When hearths were enlarged, cauldrons could be suspended at the correct height for things like sauces. Ovens brought ways of cooking meat beyond just spit-roasting or boiling it, and they allowed chefs to concentrate on dishes that required more care and attention. Many of these innovations were first tested in the kitchens of monasteries, convents and at the châteaux of the Loire Valley.

The 16th century was a watershed for French cuisine. The culture of the Italian Renaissance (French for 'rebirth') arrived full swing during the reign of François I (1515-47), partly because of a series of indecisive French military operations in Italy. For the first time, the French aristocracy was exposed to new ideas of scientific and geographic scholarship and the arts, including gastronomy.

When Catherine de Médicis, future consort to François' son, Henri II, arrived in Paris in 1533, she brought with her a team of Florentine chefs and pastry cooks adept in the subtleties of Italian Renaissance cooking. They introduced such delicacies as aspic, truffles, **quenelles** (dumplings), artichokes, macaroons and puddings to the French court. One of Catherine's cousins, Marie de Médicis, imported even more chefs into France when she married Henry IV in 1600. The French cooks, increasingly aware of their rising social status, took the Italians' recipes and sophisticated cooking styles on board, and the rest – to the eternal gratitude of epicures everywhere – is history.

Saint Cirq Lapopie, Quercy

France enjoyed an era of order and prosperity in the 17th century under the rule of Henri IV (1589-1610), who is famously credited with having wished all of his subjects to have a **poule au pot** (literally, chicken in the pot) every Sunday – an ambition echoed by American President Herbert Hoover in the early days of the Great Depression. Later in the century the sweet tooth of Louis XIV (1643-1715) launched the custom of eating desserts, once reserved for feast days and other celebrations, at the end of a meal.

Perhaps the most decisive influence on French cuisine at this time was the work of chef François-Pierre de la Varenne, who learned his trade in Marie de Médicis' kitchens. La Varenne's cookery book, *Le Cuisinier françois* (1652), was a gastronomic landmark for many reasons. It was the first to give instructions for preparing vegetables; it introduced soups in the modern sense, with the 'soup' being more important than the sops it contained; and it discarded bread and breadcrumbs as thickening agents in favour of **roux**, a much more versatile mixture of flour and fat. Most importantly, La Varenne downplayed the use of spices, preferring to serve meat in its natural juices sharpened with vinegar or lemon juice. A basic tenet of French cuisine was thus born: to enhance the natural flavours of food in cooking and not to disguise it with heavy seasonings.

WORDS GOOD ENOUGH TO EAT

While English is not short of metaphors and colloquialisms to do with food – working for his bread and butter for the apple of his eye is no longer his cup of tea – they often sound like a list of the Seven Basic Foods. French, on the other hand, is a bit more adventurous.

In matters of the heart, meat words figure prominently. You can address your beloved as **mon poussin** (my young chicken) or **petit canard** (little duck). If you're summoning him or her jocularly you can say **amène ta viande**! (get your meat over here!).

Vegetables and fruit also figure in phrases. Your **petit chou** (little cabbage) may have a **cœur d'artichaut** (artichoke heart; be fickle), and may make you **faire le poireau** (make like the leek; stand you up) and **aller aux fraises** (go to the strawberries; go off with someone). It's all over, mate – **les carottes sont cuites** (the carrots are cooked), in which case you'll most likely **tomber dans les pommes** (fall into the apples; faint). **Une bonne poire** (a good pear) is a sucker who doesn't use his **citron** (lemon; head). And if the brain in that head is going a bit, well, doddery he might start **sucrer les fraises** (sugaring the strawberries), an unnecessary act when it comes to the sweet berries grown in France.

La vie est douce (life is sweet) and so are many French expressions: **c'est du nougat** is something 'dead easy' while **du flan** is 'hogwash'. Life can be savoury too; **le gratin parisien** is not a 'crumb-topped dish baked in Paris' but the high society of the capital.

And even business vocabulary gets the occasional bite to eat. When you **vendre sa salade** (sell your lettuce) you make your sales pitch. And if there is nothing more to be gained in the business, well, **il n'y a rien à grignoter dans cette affaire**, there's just nothing to nibble on.

The 18th century, the **Grand Siècle** (great century) of reason, brought little enlightenment to the French menu apart from dishes and sauces named after great lords and royalty by their sycophantic chefs. This era gave us dishes such as **sauce Béchamel** (a milk-based sauce that is thickened with a roux) and **bouchée à la reine** (round puff filled with poultry, sweetbread, or veal dumplings and mushrooms, in white cream sauce). For the most part, the reigns of both Louis XV (1715-74) and Louis XVI (1774-93) were marked by extreme opulence and unbridled extravagance, but changes in how and where people dined went though something of a metamorphosis.

This was the century when newfangled foodstuffs from the New World – the tomato, corn, bean, red pepper and especially the potato so integral today in French cuisine – gained currency, when the fork became a standard part of the table setting, and when the first restaurant opened (see the boxed text The Birth of Restoration). Perhaps most important was the new trend to serve dishes in a logical order rather than heaping them on the table all at the same time.

THE BIRTH OF RESTORATION

In 1765 Monsieur A Boulanger opened a small business in Rue Bailleul just off Rue de Rivoli in Paris, selling soups, broths and later sheep's feet in a white sauce. Above the door he hung a sign advertising these **restaurants** (restoratives, from the verb *se restaurer,* to feed oneself). The world had its first restaurant as we know it today – and a new name for a place to eat.

Hostelries and inns existed before, but they only served guests set meals at set times and prices from the **table d'hôte** (host's table), while cafés only offered drinks. Boulanger's restaurant was the first public establishment where diners could order a meal from a menu offering a range of dishes.

Other restaurants opened in following decades, including a luxury one in Paris called La Grande Taverne de Londres in 1782. The 1789 Revolution at first stemmed the tide of new restaurants but when corporations and privileges were abolished in the 1790s, restaurant numbers multiplied. By 1804 Paris alone counted some 500 restaurants, providing employment for many of the chefs and cooks who had once worked in the kitchens of the aristocracy. A typical menu at that time might include 12 soups, two dozen hors d'œuvre, up to 30 entrées of beef, veal, mutton, fowl and game, 24 fish dishes, 12 types of **pâtisseries** (pastries) and 50 desserts.

Poireaux
8F,90 le Kg
Courgette
2Kg

Fresh produce for sale, Provence

The French Revolution and the Reign of Terror that followed was a period as austere as some Communist regimes of the last century. The ovens in the kitchens of the great aristocratic households went cold, and their chefs were driven in tumbrels to the guillotine. But a new avenue soon opened to those who managed to escape the Terror: employment in the kitchens of restaurants open to the public. This development put the country's most talented chefs in charge of both safeguarding and developing la cuisine française; many made outstanding contributions to gastronomy that endure to this day.

The first and most important of these chefs was Marie-Antoine Carême (1784-1833), who started his career working as an apprentice in a fashionable **pâtisserie** (pastry shop) and moved on to become personal chef to such luminaries as French statesmen Talleyrand, England's Prince Regent and Tsar Alexander I. Marie-Antoine Carême designed and built elaborate table decorations from confectionery that he called **pièces montées**, precursors of the modern wedding cake, but he is primarily remembered for writing several literary masterpieces, including *L'Art de la cuisine française au XIXe siècle* (The Art of French Cooking in the 19th Century; 1833). This 'culinary charter', in which Carême set out to establish 'order and taste' in French gastronomy, included hundreds of recipes, daily menus, guidelines for serving courses, tips on marketing and organising the kitchen and, of course, sketches of his sumptuous pièces montées.

To most English speakers, however, the name Georges-August Escoffier (1846-1935) is more synonymous with **haute cuisine** (high cuisine). Escoffier was a reformer who simplified or discarded decorations and garnishes, shortened menus and streamlined food preparation in kitchens, having taken his cue from Prosper Montagné, one of the great French chefs of all times and author of *Larousse Gastronomique* (1938), the seminal encyclopaedia of French gastronomy. Escoffier, known as 'the king of chefs and the chef of kings', reached the apex of his career directing the kitchens of the Savoy and Carlton Hotels in London between 1890 and 1922. Though he too left several books behind, including *Le Livre des menus* (The Book of Menus; 1912) and *Ma Cuisine* (My Cuisine; 1934), Escoffier is best remembered for creating exquisite dishes named after contemporary personalities, such as **pêche melba** and **tournedos Rossini**, a tradition established by French chefs before him.

The most important development in French gastronomy in the 20th century was the arrival of so-called **nouvelle cuisine**, a reaction against the grande cuisine of Escoffier. The low-fat 'new cuisine' eliminated many sauces in favour of stock reductions, prepared dishes in such a way as to emphasise the inherent textures and colours of the ingredients, and served them artistically on large plates. Nouvelle cuisine made a big splash at home and abroad in the diet conscious 1970s and 80s, when it was also know as **cuisine minceur** (lean cuisine), and its proponents, including chefs Paul Bocuse, Jean and Pierre Troisgros and Michel Guérard, became the new saints of the grazing faithful from Paris to Perth.

BLESS THE CHEF

The French custom of canonising chefs has existed at least since the time of Carême. The following verse by the poet and composer Marc Antoine Désaugiers (1772-1827) rings as true – and, depending on how you read them, mocking – today as they did when penned in the early 19th century:

Un cusinier, quand je dîne,	When I dine, a cook,
Me semble un être divin	Seems to me a divine being
Qui, du fond de sa cuisine,	Who, from deep within his kitchen,
Gouverne le genre humain.	Rules the human race.
Qu'ici bas, on le contemple	Those below consider him
Comme un ministre du ciel,	A minister of heaven,
Car sa cuisine est un temple	Because his kitchen is a church
Dont les fourneaux sont l'autel.	In which the ovens are the altar.

How the French Eat

The French don't eat in the clutter-clatter style of the Chinese or with the exuberance and gusto of, say, the Italians. A meal is an artistic and sensual delight, something to be savoured and enjoyed with finesse. Even Luigi Barzini had to admit in his seminal book, *The Italians*, almost four decades ago that "Italian cuisine merely presents Nature at its best. French cuisine is a challenge to Nature, it subverts Nature, it creates a new Nature of its own. French cuisine is an art".

FOOTBALL
Zidane :
« Ce ne sera pas
si facile »

Baguette and cheese for breakfast, Paris

Breakfast

In France **petit déjeuner** (breakfast) is not every Anglo-Saxon's cup of tea; masters of the kitchen throughout the rest of the day, chefs here don't seem up to it in the morning. The whole idea is probably not to fill up – petit déjeuner literally means 'little lunch' and the real **déjeuner** (lunch) is just around the corner!

Country-style breakfast with thick toast, jam and coffee

In the continental style, the French traditionally start the day with a bread roll or a bit of baguette left over from the night before, eaten with butter and jam and followed by a **café au lait** (coffee with lots of hot milk), a small black coffee or even a hot chocolate. Some people also eat cereal, toast, fruit and even yoghurt in the morning – something they never did before. City dwellers will often eschew breakfast at home altogether, opting for a quick coffee and a sweet roll at a train station café.

Contrary to what many foreigners think, the French do not eat croissants every day. They are usually reserved as a weekend morning treat, when they may also choose **brioches** (roll or cake made of yeast, flour, eggs and butter), **pains au chocolat** (a flat croissant filled with chocolate) or other **viennoiserie** (baked goods). People generally know where the best croissants are sold in their neighbourhood and will go out of their way to buy them there.

Lunch & Dinner

For many French people, especially those in the provinces, **déjeuner** (lunch) is still the main meal of the day, but with both members of a couple now usually employed and often working some distance from home, lunch is usually taken at a restaurant. This being France, people rarely eat at their desks and use the lunch hour to socialise and enjoy the food.

Retired people and families engaged in more traditional activities – farming, say, or fishing – still eat their main meal at home and it will inevitably be composed of three courses: a soup or other starter; a main course of meat, poultry, fish (or a 'one pot' meal like bouillabaisse if in Provence or cassoulet in Languedoc); and a dessert or some seasonal fruit. In general the fare served at a traditional lunch, usually begun around 1pm, is largely indistinguishable from that served at dinner, which starts at around 8.30pm, no matter who cooks it and where.

Restaurants generally serve lunch between noon and 2.30pm and **dîner** (dinner or supper) from 7pm until about 11pm. Very few restaurants are open between lunch and dinner, with the exception of brasseries, cafés and fast-food places. In many cities and towns, the vast majority of restaurants close on Sunday. In cities such as Paris, from where locals flee for the beaches in August, many restaurateurs lock up and leave town along with their clients. But this is changing rapidly and you'll find considerably more places open in summer than even a decade ago.

ORDERLY COURSES

The courses of a traditional home-cooked French meal are served in the following order:

Apéritif	aperitif; a predinner drink
Hors d'œuvre	appetisers; cold and/or warm snacks taken before the start of the meal
Entrée	first course or starter
Plat principal	main course
Salade	a relatively simple green salad with dressing
Fromage	cheese
Dessert	dessert
Fruit	fruit (sometimes instead of dessert)
Café	coffee
Digestif	digestive or after dinner drink

Les Deux Magots

As the pace of French life is as hectic as it is elsewhere in the industrialised world nowadays, the two hour midday meal has become increasingly rare, at least on weekdays and in big cities. Dinners, however, are still elaborate affairs whenever time and finances permit. A traditional French meal at home is an awesome event, often comprising six **plats** (courses). They are always served with wine – red, white or rosé (or a combination of two or all three), depending on what you're eating. A meal in a restaurant almost never consists of more than three courses: the **entrée** (first course), **plat principal** (main course) and **dessert** (dessert).

A CUISINE FOR EVERY KITCHEN

There are several general types of French cuisine:

Haute cuisine (high cuisine) – also known as **grande cuisine** (great cuisine) – is the classic cooking style of France and is typified by rich, elaborately prepared and beautifully presented multicourse meals. The aim is harmony and an appearance of artfulness and order.

Cuisine bourgeoise is French home cooking of the highest quality in which the goals are bold, earthy tastes and textures.

Cuisine des provinces (provincial cuisine), also known as **cuisine campagnarde** (country cooking), uses the best local ingredients and most refined techniques to prepare traditional rural dishes.

Nouvelle cuisine (new cuisine), characterised by rather small portions served with light sauces and artistically arranged, was a very popular cooking style in the late 20th century but has since fallen out of favour. Nevertheless, nouvelle cuisine has had a great influence on cooking techniques and the presentation of food here and abroad.

Not everyone has the time, inclination or ability to cook elaborate meals even at the weekend, and this is where **traiteurs** (caterers or delicatessens) come in with their takeaway dishes. In recent years the supermarket sections of national department stores have done a roaring trade in such 'convenience foods', and you'll see people – generally younger ones – lining up to buy **plats cuisinés** (ready-made meals), branded by famous chefs or food critics, such as Paul Bocuse à la Carte's **canard au poivre vert** (duck with green peppercorns), Gault Millau's **choucroute d'Alsace au Riesling** (Alsatian sauerkraut in Riesling with meats), or the store's own variety such as Monoprix's **dos de saumon, sauce à l'óseille** (salmon in sorrel sauce).

Relaxing at an outdoor café, Paris

Snacks & Street Food

Though French people may snack or eat between meals, they do not seem to relish the types of street food popular elsewhere; hot dog stands and noodle carts are just not for them. You may encounter a crêpe maker on a busy (and touristed) corner of a city or someone selling roasted **châtaignes** (chestnuts) in autumn, but generally people will stop in a café for **un truc à grignoter** (something to nibble on) or a pâtisserie for a slice of something sweet to be eaten on the trot. Food shop window displays in France, among the most attractive and tempting in the world, certainly have something to do with this; pâtisseries, traiteurs and **confiseries** (sweet shops) arrange their wares in such a way as to pull in the crowds – and they do.

WELLS OF GOOD EATING

We won't say we weren't awed by the whole matter. When you're meeting your idol for the first time – be it Leonardo DiCaprio, Madonna or Patricia Wells – well, you're a bit apprehensive. And we were doing what ours does best: lunch.

Patricia Wells, an American who "gave up vegetarianism for my career" is the food critic for the Paris-based *International Herald Tribune* and also contributes to the *New York Times*. We'd been reading her reviews for years and always admired her crisp, clear no-nonsense style of writing. We also envied her for the mouth-watering dishes she got to sample. Today Wells divides her time between Paris and her country home in northern Provence, where she writes (she's already got a half-dozen books under her belt, including *The Food Lover's Guide to Paris)*, gives cooking courses and tends her garden. The lady doesn't muck about.

We were like kids in a candy store, trying to focus on the delightful dishes set before us at this little bistro (and called just that – Le Troquet) and all the things we wanted to ask. What was her favourite regional cuisine? What did France do best? And, most importantly, would it continue to do so?

"Food in France is going in two directions", she said. "The quality and availability has never been better, and more efforts are being made to produce perfect fruit and vegetables. But it's beginning to unravel and I am fearful."

We mentioned that we could remember – barely – when French men came home for lunch even in cities and she agreed. "Today many of the younger generation have no memories of food – grandma's chicken, mum's soups. They exist on McDonald's hamburgers and Coke."

nutella
Making crêpes, Paris

Pastries at a pâtisserie, Paris

But, according to Wells, it's not just the fault of the young. "Consumers are lazy", she said, pointing out that 80% of all food bought today in France is processed in some way or another. "Some 5000 people live in my village in Provence, which has six or seven butchers' shops, five bakeries and one of the top 10 cheese shops in France. People should patronise these places, not just supermarkets."

Is this affecting restaurants and what they offering? "A lot of new restaurants are not about food but 'the scene'", she said, adding that the catering trade, notorious for its long hours and hard physical work, isn't attracting young people today. "Still, new restaurants that are in for the long haul make an effort."

The cuisine of Provence is obviously on the top of her list – she digs her own truffles and makes her own wine in the Midi sun for a good part of every year – but she has her 'other' favourite areas as well: Brittany for its abundance of fresh fish, and the food of the southwest. In fact, she says that she likes all styles of cooking that, like Thai cuisine (her favourite 'foreign' one), make good use of fresh produce: mushrooms, truffles, shellfish, poultry, fruit and vegetables.

Invoking the litany of what France grows and raises best seemed to brighten her up. "There will always be great stuff around, and wherever I go these days it seems all people want to talk about is food."

At the end of the meal Wells placed a name card face down on the table and pushed it towards us; we remembered that she'd booked the table under a pseudonym to ensure her anonymity. "You never know", she said. Indeed, when you're Patricia Wells – the doyenne of dining and muse to the masses who love good food and restaurants, you can never be too careful.

You can visit Patricia Wells' Web site at **www.patriciawells.com.**

Etiquette

It's not easy to cause offence at a French table, and while there are some distinctions, manners have more to do with common sense than learned behaviour. If you are invited to someone's home for a meal, always bring some sort of gift, such as good wine – not a cheap **vin de table** (table wine). Flowers are another good standby, although you should eschew **œillets** (carnations), which bring bad luck, and **chrysanthèmes** (chrysanthemums), which are only brought to cemeteries. You can also offer to provide the dessert course.

When greeting one another it is customary for people who know each other to exchange **bises** (kisses on the cheek). Close male friends and relations have always done this in the south, but it is becoming increasingly common nowadays among younger and educated northerners who don't give a hoot that older males consider it **pédérastique** (queer or poofy). The usual ritual is one glancing peck on each cheek, but some people go for three or even four kisses. People who don't kiss each other will almost always shake hands when meeting up.

A French table will be set for all courses at restaurants (not always at home), with two forks, two knives and a large spoon for soup or dessert. When they finish each course, diners cross their knife and fork (not lay

SMOKED OUT

By their very nature, French people dismiss laws they consider stupid or intrusive; whether others feel the same is another matter. Laws banning smoking in public places and in certain sections of restaurants do exist, for example, but no one seems to pay much attention to them. The French smoke a lot – from Broyards filled with pungent black tobacco to Gitanes rolled in thick yellow-coloured corn paper – and diners will often smoke in the **espace non-fumeur** (non-smoking section) of restaurants. The waiter will happily bring them a **cendrier** (ashtray) if requested. French people smoke between courses both at home and when dining out, and those who complain will probably be received with a Gallic shrug.

A café in Pigalle, Paris

them side by side) face down on the plate to be cleared away. If there's only one knife and fork at your setting, you should place the cutlery back on the table after each course. You should always wait for the host to be seated or your fellow diners to be served before starting to eat. (For more on restaurant etiquette see the Where to Eat & Drink chapter.)

Like other Europeans, the French hold their fork in their left hand and their knife in the right while eating; they don't cut their food and then switch the fork to the right hand as is the custom in North America. If you find it difficult eating with your left hand, just do what comes naturally. The French understand this cultural difference and no offence will be taken. It's considered polite to rest your hands to either side of the plate during a meal, and you never cut the bread but break it.

At a dinner party, courses may not be served in the order to which you are accustomed; salad may follow the main course and cheese always precedes dessert (see the boxed text Orderly Courses earlier in this chapter). A separate plate for bread may or may not be provided. If it is missing, rest the slice on the edge of the main plate or on the tablecloth. It is quite acceptable – in fact, encouraged – to sop up sauces and juices with bread.

You will not be expected to know the intricacies of cutting different types of cheese but at least try to remember three cardinal rules: never cut off the tip of pie-shaped soft cheeses, such as Brie or Camembert; cut cheeses whose middle is the best part (eg, the blues) in such a way as to take your fair share of the crust; and at very formal dinners, diners *never* go back for seconds at the cheese course (see the boxed text A Cheesy Lay-Away Plan in the Staples & Specialities chapter).

Do not be intimidated by table settings in restaurants. If there are wine glasses of varying sizes at each place setting, the larger one (or ones) will be for red wine (and water), the smaller one for white wine. If in doubt, just follow the lead. In general it's better for you to wait for the host to pour the wine rather than helping yourself, but this depends on your relationship and the tone of the evening. Serving the wine at home and tasting it in restaurants have traditionally been male tasks, but these days many women will happily pour and more enlightened **sommeliers** (wine waiters) will ask which one of a male/female couple would prefer to try the wine.

A polite way of getting rid of guests, by the way, is to serve them all a glass of orange juice, a sign recognised by most that it's time to say **bonne nuit** (good night). The idea is that the vitamin C will dilute the alcohol for those driving – or staggering – home.

Noisette

staples
& specialities

The cuisine of any nation is dictated first and foremost by climate and geography, and with such a diverse landscape, France's staples are high in both quality and quantity. For centuries the country's fertile farmlands, sloping vineyards and mountain pastures as well as the wealth available in the Mediterranean Sea and Atlantic Ocean have presented chefs with an enviable supply of raw materials.

COSTE-COSTE
COSTE-COSTE

France is both the largest agricultural producer and exporter in the European Union (EU) and largely self-sufficient in food, except for products such as bananas and coffee. Its production of wheat, barley, maize (corn) and cheese is particularly significant.

Every nation or culture has its own staples dictated by climate, geography and tradition. France has long stood apart for its variety of foods available. Among its innumerable staples are beef, lamb, pork, poultry, fish and shellfish, cereals, vegetables, legumes and herbs. As for both regional and national specialities, well, **tout est possible** (the sky's the limit).

LETTERS & LABELS

SELLES
APPELLATION D'ORIGINE CONTRÔLÉE
SUR CHER
INAO

The French are furiously protective of their agricultural produce, which they safeguard through three systems. The first is the **Appellation d'Origine Contrôlée** (AOC; literally, label of inspected origin), a guarantee usually associated with wine (see the boxed text Assurances of Wine Quality in the Drinks chapter) but one that is also bestowed on foodstuffs as diverse as Bresse poultry, Le Puy lentils and Grenoble walnuts. The system, which dates back to the vine-destroying *phylloxera* epidemic of the 19th century, recognises the unique qualities of certain foodstuffs along with the skills, geography, climate and local conditions necessary to produce them. An AOC label usually means top quality.

The **Label Rouge**, separate from AOC but sometimes shared by one type of food, has been bestowed upon more than 100 products, including Bintje potatoes from the north and Créances carrots from Normandy, but it is mostly associated with poultry. The label – and it is actually a red one – is filled with information about how the animal was raised, how long the cheese was ripened, when the vegetables or fruits were harvested and so on. Label Rouge products can be even more expensive than AOC ones but are almost always worth the extra money.

The newest safeguard in France is the Label **Agriculture Biologique** (AB). If you see any foodstuffs on sale bearing a label with these two white letters on a green background, you can be sure that they are either 70% or 95% organic as stated.

Cutting cantal cheese in a Les Halles boucherie, Paris

Bread

Nothing is more French than **pain** (bread). The peasants were demanding bread on the eve of the French Revolution when Queen Marie-Antoinette famously suggested they "eat cake". More than 80% of all people here eat it at every meal, and it comes in an infinite variety. French **boulangeries** (bakeries) offer many types of breads; one smallish boulangerie we happened upon in Bayonne, for example, listed no fewer than 28 different varieties. All boulangeries have **baguettes** (or **flûtes**), which are long and thin, as well as wider loaves simply known as **pain** (bread), both of which are at their best if eaten within four hours of baking. You can store them for longer in a plastic bag, but the crust becomes soft and chewy; if you leave them out, they'll soon be hard – which is the way many French people like them at breakfast the next day. The pain is softer on the inside, has a less crispy crust than the baguette, and is slightly cheaper by weight. If you're not very hungry, ask for a **demi baguette** (half a loaf) or a **demi pain**.

Bread has experienced a renaissance in France in recent years, and most boulangeries also carry heavier, more expensive varieties made with all sorts of grains and cereals; you will also find loaves studded with nuts, raisins or herbs. Other types of bread, which come in a wide range of sizes and shapes, vary from shop to shop and region to region, but since they are all on display, making a selection is easy. These heavier breads keep much longer than baguettes and standard white-flour breads. To extend the life of them, do like the French and wrap the loaf snugly in a slightly moist tea towel or dish cloth.

Olive bread at Carpentras Market, Provence

THE STAFF OF LIFE

The following are just some of the breads you'll find at a boulangerie.

Baguette	the standard long, crispy French loaf weighing 250g
Ficelle	a thinner, crustier 200g version of the baguette (really like a very thick breadstick)
Flûte	similar to, though often heavier than, a baguette
Pain	a wider, less crispy version of a baguette weighing 400g
Pain d'avoine	oat bread
Pain azyme	a flat unleavened loaf
Pain aux cinq/six/ sept céréales	five/six/seven-grain bread
Pain biologique (pain bio)	organic bread
Pain de campagne	country loaf
Pain complet	wholemeal bread
Pain cuit au feu de bois	bread baked in a woodfire oven
Pain de froment	wheat bread
Pain de gruau	fine wheaten bread
Pain au levain	traditionally made yeast bread that is usually a bit chewy
Pain au pavot	bread with poppy seeds
Pain de seigle	rye bread
Pain de seigle noir	dark rye bread (pumpernickel)
Pain de son	bread with bran

Along with bread, bakeries usually sell baked goods that are lumped together under the term **viennoiserie**.

Brioche	bun; a small roll or cake made of yeast, flour, eggs and butter, sometimes flavoured with nuts, currants or candied fruits, baked in many shapes and usually served at breakfast
Croissant	flaky crescent-shaped roll, usually served for breakfast
Pain au chocolat	a flat 'croissant' filled with chocolate

Cereals, Grains & Pulses

France produces more **grains** and **céréales** than any other country in Europe. What is not exported is turned into the flour that feeds the ovens of boulangeries and pâtisseries throughout the country.

The most important cereal crop in France is **blé** (wheat), produced largely in Picardy. The flat plain of Beauce near Orléans, used by Émile Zola as a setting for his novel about the greed for fertile land, *La Terre* (The Soil; 1888), produces some of the best quality wheat flour. Burgundy grows and harvests three times as much wheat as it consumes. The area around Honfleur in Normandy is also wheat country.

Wheat has been the basis for most of the nation's breads, pastries and other baked goods ever since France weaned itself off rye in the Middle Ages. It is also goes into making fresh pasta, stuffed **ravioles** (distant cousins of Italian ravioli introduced by Catherine de Médecis that are a speciality of the Rhône), and the roux used to thicken sauces. But wheat is not the whole grain story. Other important cereal crops include **seigle** (rye), **avoine** (oats) and **son** (bran), which are also used in bread, and **orge** (barley), which goes into the barley sugar made at Moret-sur Loing in the Île de France, and the **Grain d'Orge** beer from the north. The flour or meal made from **maïs** (maize or corn) grown in Périgord and the southwest is the key component of corn oil, **cannelés** (caramelised brioche-like pastries eaten in Bordeaux), and **millas** and **miques** (cornflour and goose-fat cakes).

The production of **riz** (rice) in the Camargue delta provides France with about one-third of its requirements and is harvested in mid-August. In recent years its **riz rouge** (red rice) has become a gourmet favourite and is available in supermarkets throughout Europe (see the boxed text opposite).

LE HARICOT
TARBAIS
LENTILLES
LENTILLES
VERTES

Legumes at an épicerie, Paris

Légumes secs (pulses) such as **haricots blancs** (kidney beans) are cooked with lamb or ham in the Loire region and near the Atlantic coast, and are a key ingredient in the casseroles of Languedoc. The humble **fève** (broad bean) is grown everywhere, but a real treat from Brittany is the chestnut-flavoured **coco de Paimpol**, which is the first haricot to get an AOC guarantee (see the boxed text Letters & Labels earlier in this chapter). The blue-green **lentilles de Puy** (Puy lentils) are heralded as the best in the world, though excellent lentils are also grown in the Berry region of the Loire.

ZAKIA
SURES DE RIZ
A1 SUPER
POIDS NET
S' FERICO
BASMATI
COUSCOUS
LE
RENARD
Rice and couscous for sale, Provence

THE RED RICE OF CAMARGUE

The southern part of the Camargue delta on the border between Provence and Languedoc is made up of shallow salt marshes, inland lakes and lagoons while the northern part is dry. After WWII huge tracts of the north were desalinated to make the area suitable for large-scale agriculture, especially the cultivation of rice. Rice production has dropped since the 1960s, but it is still a very important part of the Camarguais economy.

In recent years, a new variety of rice has come on the scene and is now the darling of cooks both in France and abroad. And apparently it was an accidental birth (as so many other culinary success stories seem to have been). Camargue farmers had never been able to harvest the indigenous red-grained wild rice that grew in profusion on the delta; once it ripened it dropped its grains. Then sometime in the early 1980s one of them noticed that – oooh la la – the wild rice had cross-pollinated with the cultivated white rice, ripened and was holding its grains on the stalk. Riz rouge de Camargue was born.

Camargue red rice has a nutty, almost earthy taste with a pleasant, chewy texture and is like a cross between American wild rice, actually an aquatic grass, and brown rice. It goes well with most meats but especially lamb in our experience.

Vegetables

Légumes (vegetables) were a relative latecomer to the French table; the first recorded appearance was in the form of **choux** (cabbage) at a banquet prepared by Taillevent for the king in the late 14th century. But when they did arrive, the French welcomed them with a relish that continues today.

France abounds in vegetables of all types and, depending on the season, you'll find everything from the tiny purple **artichauts** (artichokes) of Provence and the celebrated **Rose de Roscoff**, the pink onion grown in Brittany (see the boxed text Les Johnnies in the Regional Variations chapter), to the humble **potiron** (pumpkin) and **courge** (marrow or squash).

The climate in the northwest is perfect for growing vegetables, and Brittany's tender **primeurs** (early spring vegetables) and the sheer variety and quantity of vegetables grown in Normandy are celebrated throughout France. Normandy alone produces some 130,000 tonnes of **carottes** (carrots) a year, the best ones are from the town of Créances. Many of the vegetables grown in Brittany – **haricots verts** (green beans), **petits pois**

MONSIEUR POTATO HEAD

From the time of its introduction from the New World in about 1540, the **pomme de terre** (potato; literally, earth apple) had been viewed with suspicion; it was popular as an ornamental plant but scorned as a foodstuff. In 1771 Antoine-Auguste Parmentier (1737-1817), an agronomist, wrote a thesis in which he listed the potato, along with horse chestnuts (conkers), acorns and gladioli bulbs, as a vegetable that could be eaten during shortages or famine. During just such a time just before the Revolution, Louis XVI granted Parmentier about 20 hectares of poor land in the Gironde to grow an experimental crop. The cultivation proved enormously successful, and within two decades the potato had become a French staple. Nowadays the potato is an important component of many dishes. The best varieties are grown in the north (**Bintje**, **Roseval**, **Picardine**), in Brittany (**Noirmoutier**), the Loire region (**Fine de Ratte de Loire**) and the Île de Ré (**Alcmaria**, **Starlette**, **Roseval**, **Charlotte** and **Amandine**). Among the more unusual types is **La Vitelotte**, a tiny 'black' or purple potato from Loiret in the Loire.

As Americans credit John 'Johnny Appleseed' Chapman with sowing the first seeds of the apple orchards in the Midwest, the French pay homage to Parmentier for bringing the potato into fashion in France. He is honoured in the typically French 'name-as-dish' manner: **Parmentier** means any dish with potatoes (for example **potage Parmentier**, a thick potato soup, and **hachis Parmentier**, mincemeat cooked with potatoes.

(peas), **épinard** (spinach) and **choux de Bruxelles** (Brussels sprouts) – are destined for canning and bottling.

With its warm summers, Provence and the lower Rhône region is well suited for growing artichokes, aubergine, peppers and all of the salad vegetables. The pharmaceutical-sounding **mesclun** is a mixture of salad greens, including rocket, lamb's lettuce and endive, that is very popular in the south. And of course Provence has its olives: La Picholine **olives vertes** (green olives) and the AOC **olives noires** (black olives) of La Vallée des Baux and Nyons (see Oils & Fats later in this chapter).

Among vegetables not commonly seen outside France are **crosnes**, a small tuber vegetable imported from Japan in the 19th century that tastes vaguely of Jerusalem artichokes. Another root vegetable, **salsifis** (salsify or oyster plant), is eaten fried or cooked in cream. You may also come across unfamiliar bitter greens like **oseille** (sorrel), used in salads and soups, and the mysteriously named **pissenlits** (dandelion greens; literally, piss in bed), often served with salt pork. Vegetables once considered common fare – such as **rutabaga** (swede or rutabaga), **topinambour** (Jerusalem artichoke) and **chou-rave** (kohlrabi) – are now being cooked in new and different ways.

Vegetarian meal at Le Totem Restaurant, Trocadéro, Paris

Fruit & Nuts

The amount and choice of **fruit** available in France is as great as the variety of its vegetables. Spring brings **fruits rouges** (red or berry fruits), such as **fromboises** (raspberries) and **fraises** (strawberries), for which the French have a particular fondness. These are followed by stone and pitted fruits such as **cerises** (cherries), **pêches** (peaches) and **prunes** (plums), as well as the wonderful little yellow **mirabelle** plums, and later soft fruits like **groseilles** (red currants), **cassis** (blackcurrants) and **groseilles à maquereau** (gooseberries). Late summer and autumn bring **pommes** (apples) and **poires** (pears) as well as **amandes** (almonds), **noix** (walnuts), **noisettes** (hazelnuts) and **châtaignes** and **marrons**, two kinds of chestnuts that can be ground into flour for baking pastries and cakes.

Berries for sale at Rue Mouffetard Market, Paris

As with vegetables, certain regions and even towns are known for certain fruit. Normandy produces more apples than any other place in France and makes good use of them in its **tartes** (pies), **cidre** (cider) and **Calvados** (apple brandy). But the finest apple, the little green **Reine de Reinettes**, grows primarily in the Loire region. Normandy also has pears, cherries and some soft fruits. Pears and apples from Picardy, especially the **Belle de Boskoop** and **Reinette de Picardy**, go into making apple cider and **poiré** (perry or pear cider).

Walnuts at an épicerie, Paris

Arguably the most famous fruit in France is not eaten fresh but dried. **Pruneaux d'Agen** (Agen prunes) start life as a deep purple **prune** (plum) grafted onto a mature Ente plum tree. The plums are picked, often by hand, between 25 August and 25 September, and the drying process begins. Within 24 hours some 40,000 tonnes of plums, which will become 12,000 tonnes of prunes, pass through a series of drying chambers, are sterilised and then preserved. Most of them end up as whole, juicy **pruneaux demi-secs** to be eaten plain or cooked in poultry, pork or veal dishes. The rest will be made into delicious and popular **pruneaux fourrés**, prunes stuffed with prune cream, almond paste or even chocolate.

The peaches and pears of the Touraine, the cherries of Auxerre in Burgundy and Céret in Roussillon (which ripen in late April, the first available in France), the melons of Poitou-Charentes, the sweet chestnuts of the Cévennes in Languedoc and the Ardèche in the Rhône region, and the black walnuts of Grenoble and Périgord are all eagerly awaited by fruit lovers across the country. **Bluets** (blueberries) were introduced to the Vosges, the mountains separating Alsace and Lorraine, from North America in the early 20th century and are the only real blueberries in France, distantly related to **myrtilles sauvages** (wild bilberries or European blueberries).

Pears at Carpentras Market, Provence

Meat & Game

Viande (meat) originally meant 'food' – the first French-language cookbook was called *Le Viander de Taillevent* (1375) – and in some regards that definition remains valid today: a meal in France is not complete without meat, and vegetarianism and vegetarian restaurants have been very slow to catch on (see the Where to Eat & Drink chapter).

The most popular meats in France are **porc** (pork), **veau** (veal), **bœuf** (beef), **agneau** (lamb) and **mouton** (mutton) – in that order. There are niche markets for other meats as well, including **cheval** (horse; see the boxed text), **chèvre** (goat) and even **âne** (donkey), which usually ends up as an air-dried sausage.

It's not that the French consume meat in vast quantities at one sitting like Texans and Argentines do; meat is primarily used in charcuterie, casseroles and stews. Indeed, most uninitiated Anglophones will recognise very few cuts at a French **boucherie** (butcher); T-bone steaks and roasts are nowhere to be seen.

HORSE D'ŒUVRE

That cute gilded horsy head above the shop entrance is not telling the kids that rocking horses are on sale inside; it's a **boucherie chevaline**, a butcher selling horsemeat. In France, they eat horses, don't they?

Indeed they do. Predictably, the taste for horsemeat in France developed during troubled times – the 1789 Revolution and the Napoleonic Wars of the early 19th century. However, fearing an outbreak of diseases "which such meat cannot fail to induce", the city of Paris banned the sale of horsemeat for human consumption, but the ordinance was lifted in 1830. A campaign in favour of horsemeat was launched, culminating in a ceremonious horsemeat banquet at the Grand Hôtel in 1865.

Today people of all ages and walks of life dine on horsemeat – not just children and the infirm, whose doctors often recommend it for their cardiopulmonary systems. They like the taste (it's sweeter than beef or mutton), the low fat and the deep, almost ruby-red colour. Horsemeat almost never appears on restaurant menus in France but is cooked at home, usually following a recipe for beef.

When we were poor starving students in Paris, back when the prehistoric Lascaux cave paintings in Périgord were still wet, we used to buy ground horsemeat for hamburgers from a boucherie chevaline on the Rue du Commerce. There was almost no fat to bind them but cheese on the top held the burgers together rather nicely. Cheese-val burgers, we called them – our own little culinary invention.

At the same time, those used to buying their flesh shrink-wrapped in an antiseptic supermarket might find a boucherie here to be a vision of hell itself, with entire pigs' heads, skinned rabbits (furry ears and vacant eyes very much intact) and heifers' hearts the size of basketballs on full, bloody display. **Abats de boucherie** and **organes** (offal and organ meats) including liver, kidneys, tripe, heart, brains and even lung, are especially popular (see the boxed text Offal Time in a Lyon Bouchon in the Regional Variations chapter).

The best beef comes from cattle raised in Limousin, Bazas in the Gironde near Bordeaux and, in particular, Charolles in Burgundy. A **pavé charolais**, a thick-cut steak of Charolles beef, is synonymous with good-quality meat in France. The meat should be tender and almost soft to the touch, veined with fat and dark red in colour.

Cows in Charolles

Ovines that graze on salty tidal marshes by the sea produce the best meat; look for lamb and mutton from Pauillac, the Cotentin peninsula in Normandy, and the Vendée and Touraine regions of the Loire. The pigs in Alsace, Brittany and the Cantal in the Auvergne produce the best pork, and Le Mans in the Loire region is known for its excellent veal.

Gibier (game) is neither as abundant nor as popular as it once was, and much game is now artificially reared, especially in the Loire region, which was once a royal hunting ground. Even so, **lièvre** (hare) and **lapin de garenne** (wild rabbit) often appear on menus. In season and particularly in Alsace, you might encounter **cerf** (stag), **chevreuil** (roe buck), **sanglier** (boar) or even **marcassin** (young boar).

Poultry

Volaille (poultry) is the French term used to describe all types of winged creatures, including **volaille de la basse-cour** (barnyard fowl). Of these, the most popular is **poulet** (chicken), a term that encompasses any number of variations: **poussin** (very young chicken), **poule** (boiling hen), **poulet de grain** (corn-fed chicken), **poulet de fermier** (free-range chicken), **poularde** (pullet or fatted hen used for roasting), **coq** (cock or rooster) and **chapon** (a castrated rooster).

The choicest chicken available is that bred in Bresse in Franche-Comté (see the boxed text Bresse of Chicken). These AOC **poulets de Bresse** (Bresse chickens) are the delight of both amateur cooks and prize-winning chefs. Easily recognised by their distinctive white plumage, bright red wattle and blue-grey legs, Bresse chickens – and not their eggs, of course – are coddled in ways unfamiliar to most barnyard animals. Raised in the open for 12 weeks where they scratch and peck on insects and grass, the birds spend their last fortnight in a 'finishing off' process where they are fed on corn and milk to fatten them up. They are ready for the oven in 3½ months, though the **poulardes de Bresse** and the highly prized (and expensive) **chapons de Bresse** take around two or three months longer. **Dindons** (turkeys) are raised here too for the holidays.

Geese in Périgord

Canards (ducks) and **oies** (geese) are widely consumed but are especially popular in Normandy and Périgord (see the Regional Variations chapter). **Dindon**, **dinde** and **dindonneau**, all words for turkey depending on whether the bird is male, female or young, are not so popular, but eating the **dinde de Noël** (Christmas turkey) remains a strong tradition. The best turkeys are bred in Bresse, Pauillac and at Licques in the north, where the dumb clucker (and turkeys are *really* stupid) is fêted with a festival in its honour every September.

BIRDS FOR A SONG

Out of preference or necessity the French have always liked **oiseaux** (birds) on their plate, and the people of Provence have had a taste for **petits oiseaux** (little birds) like larks and sparrows roasted or cooked on skewers. While their hunting and consumption is now banned by the EU, such birds live on in common expressions. The equivalent of 'better than nothing' is **faute de grives, on mange des merles** (when there are no thrushes, you eat blackbirds). And to describe lean times, people make reference to the **ortolan**, a small garden bunting said to be the most delicately flavoured of all wild birds: **à l'époque, on ne se nourrissait pas d'ortolans** (in those days, we weren't living on ortolans).

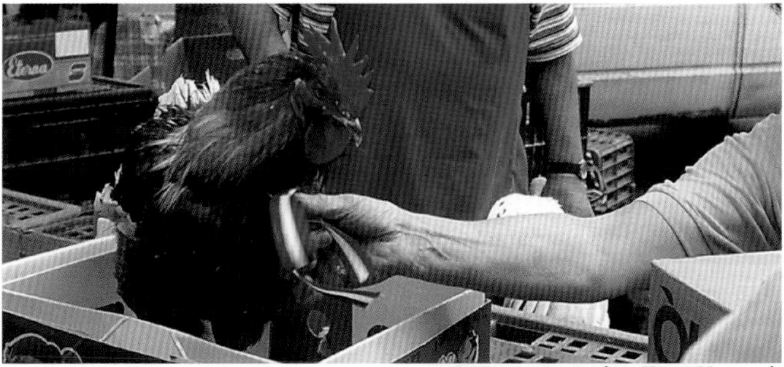

Prize-winning poultry, Haute-Normandy

BRESSE OF CHICKEN

Fraud in trading Bresse chickens is not unknown – how many restaurateurs serve chicken with their feathers, wattle, legs and AOC tag all intact? – and some places pass off more common varieties as the real McCoy. Rapacious chicken farmers in the past have engaged in even more complicated scams, importing eggs and chicks from other areas and giving them a send-off in Bresse. So be on your guard when forking out that extra cash for a Bresse chicken – you might be buying poultry that started life as an egg in Brittany. But if you do and it did, at least you will have solved that age-old riddle: the egg definitely came before your poulet de Bresse.

Charcuterie

Trying to compile a list of French **charcuterie** is like attempting to determine the length of a piece of string – it can just go on and on and on. Strictly speaking, charcuterie (from the verb **charcuter**, 'to hack' or 'to butcher'; the word encompassing sausages, blood puddings, hams and other cured and salted meats) is made only from pork, though a number of other meats (beef, veal, chicken, goose) are used. The all-encompassing **cochonailles** (pig or pork products) now does the job that charcuterie used to do.

Charcuterie at Carpentras Market, Provence

A CHARCUTERIE PRIMER

While every region produces standard charcuterie favourites as well as its own specialities, some – notably Alsace, Brittany and the Auvergne – do it better than others (see the Regional Variations chapter). Nevertheless there are basic types of charcuterie available everywhere. The definitions are not, well, cut and dried – the **saucisson de Lyon** can be both an air-dried sausage (sliced and eaten as is) or boiled, at which point it becomes **saucisson chaud** (hot sausage). But these general terms will at least be able to help you find your way.

Andouille	large smoked tripe (chitterling) sausage cooked and ready to eat (usually cold) when you buy it
Andouillette	soft raw sausage made from the pig's small intestines that is grilled and usually eaten with onions and potatoes

Andouillette

Saucisson de Lyon with potatoes

Ballotine	essentially a **galantine** served hot or lukewarm
Boudin blanc	smooth white sausage made from poultry, veal, pork or even rabbit, which is cooked and can be served with, say, haricot beans or apples
Boudin noir	blood sausage or pudding made with pig's blood, onions and spices and usually eaten hot with stewed apples and potatoes
Fromage de tête	brawn or head cheese; also called **hure**
Galantine	boned, stuffed and pressed or rolled poultry or pork served cold in aspic; **ballotine** is the warm equivalent
Jambon	ham; usually smoked or salt-cured pork made from a pig's hindquarters, but can also be prepared with poultry, such as **jambon de canard**
Saucisse	usually a small fresh sausage that is boiled or grilled
Saucisson	generally a large salami eaten cold
Saucisson sec	air-dried salami or saucisson

Pâtés & Terrines

Pâtés, terrines and rillettes are essentially charcuterie, but they are prepared in so many different ways nowadays and are so widespread that we have given them a separate section. These three are as French as wine and cheese; in fact, one could almost say that they make up something of a trinity in the French kitchen (though whoever is entering the kitchen might have to bring along a loaf of bread as well).

Pâté is essentially mincemeat that has been spiced and baked in a mould and can be served hot or cold. Strictly speaking, the term pâté should only be used to describe mixtures baked in a **pâte** (pastry or crust), but it now refers to any preparation in a baking dish or earthenware **terrine**.

The difference between a pâté and a terrine is academic: a pâté is removed from its container and sliced before it is served while a terrine is sliced from the container itself. **Rillettes**, on the other hand, is potted meat that is not ground, chopped or sliced but shredded with two forks, seasoned, mixed with fat and spread cold like pâté over bread.

Mixed pâté with foie gras

Rillettes de Tours

Pâtés, terrines and rillettes can be made of just about any type of meat or fish, but the most celebrated of them of all is **pâté de foie gras**, the sublime, unctuous 'butter' of fattened goose or duck liver (see the boxed text). Perhaps the area most celebrated for all three types is the Loire region, the birthplace of rillettes, but other important centres are Alsace, the Auvergne and Périgord. The north is a major centre for commercially produced pâtés and terrines, including the undistinguished **pâté d'Ardennes**.

The way in which goose and duck livers have been traditionally, well, overcharged is through a process called **gavage**, from the verb **gaver** meaning 'to cram' or 'to fill up'. This meant restricting and force-feeding the birds a rich diet of cereal gruel and, in Alsace, even noodles. More humane methods of gavage are now proscribed by law, but some people still feel uncomfortable with the process and avoid foie gras altogether.

LIVER: DUCKS & GEESE

The key component of pâté de foie gras is, of course, the liver of fattened ducks and geese. It was first prepared around 1780 as **pâté en croûte à la Clause** by one Jean-Pierre Clause, chef to the military governor of Alsace, who was impressed enough to send a batch to the king at Versailles.

Goose and duck liver have been enjoyed since time immemorial – the 1st century AD Roman scholar Pliny the Younger mentioned it in his writings and François Rabelais (1494-1553) praised those who "take care to fatten their geese". But it wasn't until the 18th century in Strasbourg that it was introduced on a large scale. Jews escaping the pogroms of Eastern Europe and forbidden by Talmudic law to cook food with most animal fats, with the exception of poultry fat, raised and plumped up their geese and ducks for the rich **schmaltz** (Yiddish and Alsatian for 'fat'). The livers were, well, a kind of afterthought.

Afterthought, schmafterthought – foie gras is big business now, with 30,000 people involved in the yearly production of 13,000 tonnes of the stuff. France raises 25 million ducks, which breed all year and whose livers go for around 200FF a kilo, while the livers of the 600,000 geese raised here, which reproduce only once a year, sell for 1900FF a kilo in the best food shops of Paris. So the goose liver is superior to duck liver, right?

That ain't necessarily so. It's true that goose liver is more delicate and less gamey tasting than its duck equivalent, but many chefs prefer the latter because goose liver has a tendency to explode and break down into a pool of liquid fat while being cooked. But we know which side of the pen we sit on. Stuff the ducks (with chestnuts or forcemeat, perhaps) and pan-fry us a goose liver with peaches and a splash-ette of peach eau-de-vie as we once had in Périgueux. Move over God, we're in heaven too.

Fish & Shellfish

The wealth of **poisson** (fish) and **coquillage** (shellfish) of France's coast and waterways is for many the crowning glory of French cuisine. The rivers, streams and lakes of areas such as the Loire, Alsace and the mountains provide the **brochet** (pike), **sandre** (pike-perch), **tanche** (tench), **carpe** (carp), **truite** (trout) and **anguille** (eel) that go into any number of freshwater fish dishes and stews. The Mediterranean surrenders its bounty of **crustacés** (crustaceans), **poissons de rocher** (rockfish) and the prehistoric-looking **rascasse** (scorpion fish) so integral in bouillabaisse. But in term of freshness, quality and quantity of sea life, nowhere is better than the briny, frigid waters of the Atlantic.

The French have demanded fresh ocean fish for centuries; indeed in the Middle Ages fishermen from Boulogne and their draught horses could reach Paris some 300km away in less than 24 hours with their supply of fresh fish and shellfish. Today Atlantic fare is available everywhere, from Paris to Périgueux, in markets, supermarkets and, of course, **poissoneries** (fishmongers or fish shops).

The Atlantic Ocean provides France with its **morue** (cod), **loup de mer** (sea bass) and dozens of other types of fish, as well as shellfish like **coques** (cockles), **bulots** (whelks), **palourdes** (clams), **pétoncles** (queen scallops) and **moules** (mussels), which can be fished wild but are usually **moules de bouchot**, tiny mussels cultivated on pilings stuck into the ocean floor around La Rochelle.

A meal of mussels, Basse-Normandy

Perhaps the Atlantic's greatest contribution to the shellfish-eating world, however, is the **huître** (oyster). Oysters can also be fished on the open sea, but they are usually cultivated in oyster beds though a lucky few make it to **claires**, clear water ponds created from old salt marshes, where they feed on the algae that gives their shells a distinctive green colour. The popularity of oysters here can be seen in the wide variety available. Native flat or plate oysters are called **belons**, while **creuses** with their crinkly shells, and **gigas** were imported from Asia. The list goes on. **Claires** is also the name for oysters that have been raised in a bed for two years and then moved to a crowded claire for a month before harvesting, while **fines de claires** spend the same amount of time in a claire but with only 20 of the bivalves per sq metre. **Spéciales de claire** spend two months in a claire with only nine neighbours per sq metre, and **pousses in claire** eight months with no more than five other oysters.

Brittany produces some excellent oysters at Cancale, Quiberon and the Morbihan Gulf coast, but the best oysters are raised farther down the Atlantic around La Rochelle, especially those from Marennes, the Île d'Oléron and Arachon.

Oysters and mussels prepared in a seafood restaurant, Provence

Trout for sale at a street market, Paris

While not exactly fish, frogs live in the water and snails have shells, and both are consumed with relish by the French (see Alsace & Lorraine, Bordeaux and Burgundy in the Regional Variations chapter).

Cheese

The story of French **fromage** is an epic tale full of plots, subplots, twists and innumerable characters. General Charles de Gaulle, expostulating on the inability of anyone to unite the French on a single issue after WWII, famously grumbled "you cannot easily bring together a country that has 265 kinds of cheese". But le bon Charlie's comments are well out of date; today France counts upwards of 500.

The complexities of cheese production cannot be overstated; entire volumes have been written about just a single type. There are, however, several generalities that can be applied to all French cheeses. French cheese is made from cow's, goat's or ewe's milk. The milk can be raw, pasteurised or **petit-lait** (the whey left over after the milk fats and solids have been curdled with rennet). Vegetarians should note that most French cheeses are made with rennet, which is an enzyme derived from the stomach of a calf or young goat. Some plant extracts can have the same curdling effect as rennet and are used to produce **fromage végétal** (vegetarian cheese).

PHONY FROMAGE

This cave at the Societe Roquefort holds 23,000 rounds of cheese. The cheeses here are actually fakes placed for tourists and removed during the production months of December to July.

In terms of texture, the **pâte** (effectively what's in between the rind) of a French cheese can be soft – uncooked and unpressed – and simply shaped in a mould; soft with its rind washed in brine, beer, eau-de-vie or marc, or covered with mould, ashes or leaves; streaked with greenish or blue veins; semi-hard and pressed but not cooked; or hard after being both cooked and pressed. Cheese can also take on a multitude of sizes and forms – from small and round and long and cylindrical to the shape of pyramids, hearts, bricks and large wheels. The taste of France's cheeses are as complex as its wines: sweet, nutty, earthy, salty, acid, metallic and so on. But all cheeses have one thing in common: they all undergo a process of ripening or curing (see the boxed text A Cheesy Lay-Away Plan later in this chapter).

The goats of Lyon

The choice on offer at a **fromagerie** (cheese shop) can be overwhelming – even to the initiated. But don't be daunted. **Fromagers** (cheese merchants) always allow you to sample before you buy (see Fromagerie in the Shopping chapter). In the meantime, we've done some of the homework for you. The following list divides French cheeses into five main groups as they might be divided in a fromagerie and recommends several types to try. It's a very subjective list admittedly, but it will introduce you to the complex world of French cheese, one that exists well beyond the commercially produced cheeses like Bombel, La Vache qui Rit and Bonjura. Get in there and have a taste. As the French like to say: a meal without cheese is like a day without sunshine. (For more on cheese see the Regional Variations chapter.)

A PLATTER OF CHEESES

Fromage de Chèvre (Goat's Milk Cheese)

Goat's milk cheese is usually creamy and both sweet and a little salty when fresh but hardens and gets much saltier as it matures.

Sainte Maure de Touraine (AOC) is a creamy, mild cheese from the Loire region but isn't the most flavoursome of goat's milk cheeses, nevertheless it's a good introduction to the goat family. It has a salted ash rind and a distinctive straw running through the centre to ventilate and hold it together.

Crottin de Chavignol (AOC) from Burgundy is the classic goat's milk cheese. It can get very salty after a maturation period lasting more than two weeks.

Cabécou de Rocamadour (AOC) comes from the Midi-Pyrenées and is excellent in spring when the cheese is fresh and tastes of grass and milk. Cabécou de Rocamadour is often served warm with salad or marinated in oil and rosemary.

Other recommendations include: **Clacbitou**, an oblong-shaped goat's milk cheese from the Charolles region of Burgundy; **Saint Marcellin**, a soft white goat's milk cheese and a favourite in Lyon; and **tomme de chèvre**, a harder variety and best from the Pyrenees.

Fromage à Pâte Persillée (Veined or Blue Cheese)

Blue (blue) cheese is also called **persillé** because the veins often resemble parsley. **Fourme**, which now denotes a type of blue-veined cheese, was once the catch-all word for cheese and the origin of the word, **fromage**.

Fourme d'Ambert (AOC) is a very mild cow's milk cheese from Rhône-Alpes; it is to veined cheese what Sainte Maure is to goat's milk cheese, but again a good introduction for newcomers. The consistency lies somewhere between Gorgonzola and Roquefort.

Roquefort (AOC), an ewe's milk cheese, is to many the king of French cheese (see the boxed text The King of Cheeses in the Regional Variations chapter).

Bresse Bleu is a pasteurised cow's milk cheese from Rhône-Alpes and has a soft rind of white mould and is creamier than most blues.

Other recommendations include: **Bleu du Haut Jura** (AOC), a mild blue-vein mountain cheese (also called **Bleu de Gex** and **Bleu de Septmoncel**), and **Bleu de Termignon**, an excellent blue made in very limited quantities in the Alps.

Fromage à Pâte Molle (Soft Cheese)

The first two on the list are moulded, the last is rind-washed.

Camembert de Normandie is the classic moulded AOC cheese from Normandy; some say camembert is synonymous with the phrase 'French cheese'. It's made all over Normandy from raw cow's milk.

Brie de Meaux (AOC) is a refined Brie made from raw cow's milk and moulded in the Île de France.

Munster is a rind-washed Alsatian cheese, which shares its AOC with the Lorraine version called Géromé. Munster is very pungent and has a very soft centre. Eat it as the locals do, with caraway seeds.

Other recommendations include: **Brie de Melun**, earthier and more robust than Brie de Meaux, and **Époisses de Bourgogne**, a strong-smelling, fine-textured cheese washed in marc during ripening.

Fromage à Pâte Demi-Dure (Semi-Hard Cheese)

These are all uncooked pressed cheeses.

Tomme de Savoie is an outstanding cheese made from either raw or pasteurised cow's milk.

Cantal (AOC) is a large cow's milk cheese from Auvergne that tastes something like Cheddar.

Saint Nectaire (AOC) is a pressed cheese of pink or reddish colour that has a strong smell and a complex taste.

Other recommendations include: **Ossau-Iraty**, a ewe's milk cheese made in the Basque Country, and **Abbaye de Cîteaux**, a mild cheese made by Cistercian monks in Burgundy.

Fromage à Pâte Dure (Hard Cheese)

Hard cheeses in France are always cooked and pressed.

Beaufort (AOC) is a grainy cow's milk cheese with a slightly fruity taste from Rhône-Alpes; one of the largest-selling cheeses in France.

Comté (AOC) is a a yellowish, pressed and cooked cow's milk cheese from Franche-Comté.

Emmental is a cow's milk cheese made all over France, but **Emmental Grand Cru**, arguably the best, comes from the mountains in the east.

Other recommendations include: **Mimolette** (or **Boule de Lille**), an Edam-like bright orange cheese that can be aged up to 36 months, and **Brebis des Pyrénées**, made with ewe's milk in the Basque Country.

A CHEESY LAY-AWAY PLAN

Philippe Alléosse is a man who takes his time – seriously. He has to. Philippe is a cheese seller and a ripener, and he knows that as fickle a union as time and love is that of time and cheese.

Cheese is made at farms, dairies, mountain huts and even monasteries. Some of the producers do their own ripening while others send their cheese to an **affineur** (ripener), who takes the trouble of turning each cheese over as required or washing the rinds with brine, marc or beer as they cure. All the while he watches the thermostat *and* the clock like a hawk, knowing precisely what temperature will produce an incomparable Brie or a Camembert 'without white' (that chalky bit in the middle) and – most crucially – when. Time is of the essence with cheese.

While Alléosse sometimes helps the staff or handles the till at his cheese shop on Rue Poncelet in Paris, he spends an equal amount of time at the **affinage**, a series of four cellars a couple of kilometres to the northeast. The cellars, with specially sealed ceilings and walls to prevent condensation, are each of a different temperature, feel and smell. The first is the cellar where the rind-washed cheeses like **Livarot** and **Maroilles** mature. The smell is damp and sweet, perhaps from the marc that has just been sprayed on the **Langres**, a smooth, pungent cheese from Champagne. The next is the pungent cellar full of goat's milk cheese that could be a child's playroom with all the strange shapes: oblong **Sainte Maure de Touraine** covered in ash; the truncated pyramid of a **Valençay**; or the square **Brin d'Amour** from Corsica with its pretty topping of herbs and berries.

The third cellar is reserved for the **pâtes cuites**, cheeses whose pâte – effectively what's in between the rind – is cooked. The cheeses are all large and heavy, from the wheel-like **tommes** to the fiery-orange **Mimolettes** the size of a baby's head. The last cellar is for the soft cheeses like Camembert and Brie with bloomy white rinds. You can also imagine these elegant little rounds giggling and flirting with the tommes when you shut the door.

As a native of Brittany, the French region with the least tradition of cheese making, Alléosse is something of a maverick, and his enthusiasm for his product is boundless as he feeds visitors another sliver of 'solid cream'. He is happy with the direction cheese is taking, saying that young people know and buy quality cheese – at least at his shop.

He reserves his main criticism for restaurateurs who put cheese very low on their list of priorities. They'll rub their hands together when diners order an expensive bottle, he says, but couldn't be bothered with the correct care, handling and storage of cheese. When he recommends that they buy a special refrigerated chest for storing more fragile cheeses, they scoff and say there are more important things to spend money on.

Storage and Serving Cheese

There are some tips to follow that will produce a perfect cheese every time. The ideal place to store cheese is a cool, dark, well-ventilated room. The refrigerator is a second choice as it is usually airless, but that's where most people in France keep it these days.

Most cheese should be wrapped in foil – or waxed paper and then foil – before being placed in the refrigerator. This prevents goat's milk cheese from drying out, keeps the mould on veined cheese from sweating, protects the bloomy rind on soft cheeses like Camembert and Brie, and preserves the moist crust of rind-washed cheeses like Munster and Époisses de Bourgogne. Goat's milk cheese can also be put on a small plate and then inside a loose paper bag for protection. To protect hard cheeses, place a sheet of cling film on the pâte to allow the rind to breathe. Uncovered cheeses should never be placed in the fridge with other raw foods as they will absorb other aromas and may spoil.

Allow cheese removed from the fridge to warm up for a half-hour to allow the flavour to develop. Some cheeses can be freshened up by scraping their pâte with a sharp knife to remove any dried or discoloured bits, but wash the knife in hot water after each cheese to prevent cross contamination.

When cutting cheese at the table as either the host or guest, remember that a small circular cheese like a Camembert is cut in slices like a pie. If a large round cheese has been bought already sliced (eg, Brie), never cut off the tip; instead cut from the tip to the rind. Slice cheeses whose middle is the best part (eg, the blues) in such a way as to take your fair share of the rind. A flat piece of semi-hard cheese like Emmental is usually just cut horizontally in hunks.

Serving a cheese platter, Honfleur, Basse-Normandy

Other Dairy Products

Traditionally the region of Normandy had the sweetest **beurre** (butter) in the land, particularly its **beurre d'Isigny** made in Calvados. Times have changed, however, and the Norman cows that took up residence in the Deux-Sèvres **département** (administrative division) of Poitou-Charentes now produce an even fuller, waxier butter than their bovine cousins up north; look for the names **beurre des Deux-Sèvres, beurre d'Échiré** or **beurre des Charentes.**

Crème (cream) comes in a number of guises. **Crème crue** is unpasteurised like the milk used in many of the best cheeses. Also keep an eye out for **crème fraîche** (literally, fresh cream), actually a mature cream with a slightly sour tang that comes from the days before refrigeration. The best is the AOC stuff from Isigny in Normandy.

Of prepared dairy products, the most popular is **yaourt** (yoghurt). Once eaten only as a snack or at the end of a meal, yoghurt is now widely eaten at breakfast. **Yaourt à boire** (drinking yoghurt) is very popular as are the sweet commercial yoghurt-based drinks like Yop and Dan'up, which are similar to Indian lassis.

Other dairy delicacies to try include **fromage frais** (literally, fresh cheese), a fermented dairy product similar to curds or cottage cheese, and **fromage blanc** (literally, white cheese), similar to (though softer than) cream cheese. Popular commercial brands are Petit-Suisse and Gervais. **Lait fermenté** (sour milk) is not just used in cooking but eaten as a snack or with a meal. Fjord, a great favourite of ours, is a popular brand.

CHÂTEAU DE WHIPPED CREAM

Like every self-respecting château of the 18th century, the Château de Chantilly had its own **hameau** (hamlet), a mock rural village on the grounds complete with **laitier** (dairy) where the lady of the household and her guests could play at being milkmaids as Marie-Antoinette did at Versailles. But the cows at Chantilly took their job rather seriously, and news of the sweet cream served at the hamlet's teas became the talk (and envy) of aristocratic Europe. The future Hapsburg Emperor Joseph II visited this 'marble temple' incognito in 1777, and when the Baroness of Oberkirch tasted the goods she cried "never have I eaten such good cream, so appetising, so well prepared". Château de Chantilly and its hamlet were demolished after the Revolution, but were rebuilt in the late 1870s and can be visited today.

Chantilly (or more properly **crème Chantilly**) is whipped unpasteurised cream with a twist. It is beaten with icing sugar and vanilla sugar to the consistency of a mousse. We'd like to bathe in it but usually settle for just having it dolloped on berries.

Soup

Soupes and **potages**, both of which mean 'soup', are an integral part of French cuisine. What could be more French than **soupe à l'oignon** (onion soup)? The word potage comes from the Latin *potare* (to drink) – the Romans 'drank' not 'ate' liquid foods – and is related to such one-dish meals in France as **potée** (meat and vegetables cooked in an earthenware pot). But soup started off as an altogether different kettle of fish.

In the Middle Ages soups were closer to what we would call porridge and the word 'soupe' referred to a piece of bread (or sop) boiled in a broth or stock. The sop was originally the focus of the dish, but as the bouillon became more important, the terms were reversed and the broth became the soup. The latest trend in Paris restaurants is to place a somewhat more refined 'sop' – perhaps a **quenelle** (meat or fish dumpling) – at the bottom of a soup bowl and then ladle out the broth at the table.

IN THE SOUP

In the 19th century, it was not uncommon to encounter a dozen choices for soup on a Parisian menu. Nowadays expect two or three in most restaurants, but you may find more. The following are a dozen soups of various classifications that you're likely to come across; not everything is here – it's just a whiff of what to expect.

Bisque d'écrevisses	thick soup made with freshwater crayfish
Bisque de homard	similar to bisque d'écrevisses but made with lobster
Consommé printanier	clear broth with spring vegetables
Consommé à la madrilène	'Madrid-style consommé'; cold consommé with tomatoes
Crème d'asperges blanches	(or **potage Argenteuil**), white asparagus cream soup; excellent in season, but usually this is to soup what vanilla is to ice cream
Crème de volaille	cream of chicken soup
Potage Parmentier	thick soup based on potatoes and leeks; when served cold it becomes **vichyssoise**
Potage Saint-Germain	thick green pea soup; a speciality of Paris
Soupe à l'oignon gratinée	the classic onion soup sprinkled with grated cheese and then browned in the oven
Soupe au pistou	a Provençal soup of vegetables, noodles, beans and basil
Velouté de perdrix	a classic thickened partridge soup

Soupe à l'oignon Gratinée (Onion Soup)

Nothing is more Parisian than onion soup with a crust of oven-browned grated cheese.

Ingredients

225g/7oz	onions, thinly sliced
60g/2oz	butter
1 tablespoon	flour
1½L/6 cups	water
	salt and pepper
	thin rounds of bread
	thin slices of Gruyère cheese

Cook the sliced onions in the butter. When they are golden, sprinkle with flour. Mix well with a wooden spoon and gradually blend in the water. Season with salt and pepper and simmer for 15 minutes. Slice the bread thinly and brown in butter. Ladle the soup into individual earthenware bowls, top with **croûtons** (toasted bread cubes) and cheese and heat in the oven until the cheese begins to brown.

Serves 6

Serving vegetable soup from the tureen, Périgord

France's **haute cuisine** (high cuisine) is said to be the only truly organised system of gastronomy in the world, with such relatively simple dishes as soupe and potage divided into several categories and subcategories, depending on their base, thickness and what is added to them.

The most basic of all soups is **consommé**, a clear meat broth or fish stock that becomes a **consommé garni** when a 'garnish' such as meat, game, fish or pasta is added. Consommés can be served either hot or cold.

There are several broad categories of thick soup. A **potage purée** is a thick pulp of strained vegetables, meat or fish thinned with a little consommé; when Béchamel and/or cream is folded in, it becomes a **potage crème** (cream soup). A soup with a shellfish purée as its key ingredient is a **bisque**. A **potage velouté** is purée combined with **velouté** (veal, chicken or fish stock thickened with roux) as well as egg yolks and cream.

Fungi

Champignon is a general term for 'mushroom', both cultivated and wild. The ordinary **champignons de Paris** (button mushrooms) that you'll see everywhere are grown in the Île de France as well as in the Loire region. They go into soups and sauces and are cooked with meats. In recent years the French have developed a taste for Asian mushrooms like Japanese shiitakes and Chinese black mushrooms.

No cultivated mushroom can come close in fragrance, flavour and texture to the wild variety, and **aller aux champignons** (to go mushrooming) in any wood close by in autumn is a well-established tradition. There are literally dozens of edible types that all fall in line below the king of all fungi in France, the **truffe** (truffle). Never attempt to gather mushrooms yourself if you are not familiar with the varieties that grow in France. Tag along with an expert (some tourist offices in France offer tours) and never place all your mushrooms in one basket; even a little poisonous one will spoil the lot. Staff at pharmacies are able to separate the delicious from the potentially deadly.

KNOW YOUR MUSHROOM

Cèpe	boletus mushroom; a large orange-coloured fan-shaped fungi with thick stems and caps
Chanterelle	a pale orange or yellow mushroom with forking gills and funnel-shaped cap (also known as **girolle**)
Morille	morel; a dark brown, cone-shaped mushroom usually gathered in spring
Mousseron	blewit; a very small, oval-shaped beige or grey mushroom
Pied bleu	literally, blue foot; a blue and white, medium-sized mushroom
Pied de mouton	literally, sheep's foot; a meaty, cream-coloured mushroom
Pleurote	oyster mushroom; a soft, feather-edged brownish mushroom
Trompette de la mort	literally, trumpet of death; a delicious dark brown (almost black) mushroom in the shape of a horn with vein-like gills and frilled edges; also known as **corne d'abondance** (literally, horn of plenty)

THE BLACK DIAMONDS OF THE SOUTHWEST

While truffles are found in Burgundy and Provence, the **diamants noirs** (black diamonds) of Périgord are the finest, and most expensive. Hunted by specially trained pigs (or more commonly dogs nowadays) between November and March, the aromatic Périgord truffle is black, rough in texture and can range in size from that of a pea to an orange but is usually the size of a walnut weighing 15-20g. It is traditionally added to a variety of sauces, pâtés and other dishes but is also delicious in simple meals like pastas. Truffles are at their best when eaten fresh – they only keep for a week and lose some of their flavour when preserved. According to the experts, the best way to extend the lives of raw truffles is to freeze them whole or, better yet, put them in a container filled with oil and place that in the freezer; you get the flavour but sacrifice the texture. You can also store truffles in an air-tight container cushioned by rice or covered with eggs, from which you can make an omelette fit for the gods.

A truffle hunter and a faithful friend, Périgord

Oils & Fats

Huiles (oils) and **graisses animales** (animal fats) have always been integral parts of French cuisine as cooking agents, additives and flavourings, and so they remain today. In his seminal book, *The Food of France*, Waverley Root divides France into three regions: the domain of butter, the domain of fat and the domain of oil. At first glance the division seems obvious enough – butter in the north where all the cows graze, animal fats in the central regions where they breed all those pigs, geese and ducks, and oil to the south, abundant in olive trees. But oils and fats don't necessarily keep to this geographical order. Alsace traditionally relies primarily on pork fat though it borders the butter land of Champagne. The mountainous Dauphiné, sharing frontiers with Provence and Italy, uses butter. The regions that follow the Pyrenees from coast to coast – the Basque Country all the way to Roussillon – use a combination of all three. While those divisions still hold true, times have changed and many people prefer lighter and healthier **graisses végétales** (vegetable fats). Out go the **graisse de porc** (lard), the **graisse d'oie** (goose fat) and the **beurre** (butter), and in come the oils.

A grove of olive trees, Provence

By and large France does not make a lot of **huile d'olive** (olive oil) – a mere 0.02% of world production, in fact – but what it does press is lighter, more fruity and easier to digest than the olive oils of Spain, Italy or Greece. French olive oils are rated according to their acid content: by law **huile vierge extra** has an acidity of no more than 1%; **vierge fine** of less than 1.5%; and **vierge** or **vierge semi-fine** of up to 3%. Organic shops often stock **huile d'olive vierge extra nonfiltrée** (extra virgin unfiltered olive oil), a cloudy but healthy variety.

Tasting olive oil, Provence

There are two AOC olive oils in France, both from Provence: **Les Beaux-de-Provence** and **Nyons**. These oils are usually cold-pressed first; anything above 27°C affects the flavour. But most French cooks would hardly 'waste' such fine oil when preparing **frites** (chips or French fries). Like cooks everywhere they reach for the cheaper variety, saving the expensive French brands for salad dressings, mayonnaise or making **aïoli** (garlic mayonnaise). Edible oils commonly used in modern French kitchens include **huile d'arachide** (peanut or groundnut oil), **huile de colza** (rapeseed oil), **huile de mäis** (corn oil) and **huile de table** (salad oil).

Keep an eye out for unusual flavoured oils on sale in speciality shops, including **huile d'olive au bergamot**, olive oil pressed with bergamot orange. Périgord produces oils flavoured with walnuts, hazelnuts, mushrooms and truffles.

Herbs, Spices & Seasonings

Once used to mask the taste of spoiled or tainted meat, **herbes** (herbs), **épices** (spices) and **assaisonnements** (seasonings) are now added to bring out the natural flavours, textures and colours of foods. Some may find the abundant use of **ail** (garlic) south of the Loire a bit too much though.

Every French kitchen has a spice rack with the usual array – **muscade** (nutmeg), **cumin** (cumin) and **cannelle** (cinnamon), for example – as well as **basilic** (basil), **romarin** (rosemary), **coriandre** (coriander) and **marjolaine** (marjoram) either dried or growing in little pots on the windowsill. **Fines herbes** is a mixture of 'sweet herbs', usually parsley, chives and tarragon or chervil. A **bouquet garni** can be any herbs tied together and stuck into a stew or casserole during cooking but it usually means parsley, bay leaf and thyme.

The **maquis** (underbrush) of Corsica is peppered with fragrant herbs used in local dishes, but the most important region for herbs is Provence. Herbs farmed here include coriander, marjoram, basil, chervil, tarragon, fennel, oregano, parsley and sage. Herbs that grow wild here include rosemary, wild thyme, juniper and savory. But Provence doesn't hold the title to all herbs

VINEGAR – THE SOUR SEASONING

The first commercial vinegar product in France was probably wine vinegar (the name comes from the French **vin aigre**, 'sour wine'). In the 13th century vendors rolled their barrels through the streets calling "good and beautiful vinegars!", and in 1657 King Charles IX issued an edict allowing vintners to sell vinegar in Paris by the **pot** (half-litre mug).

Having little wine of its own but lying conveniently between the vineyards of the Loire Valley and Paris, Orléans has always been associated with the production of wine vinegar. Though it once produced up to half of all vinegar consumed in France, Orléans now counts only one producer, Martin Pouret, making vinegar according to the 'Orléans method'. This process is now known as **vinaigre à l'ancienne** and was studied by Louis Pasteur, whose career began with finding a solution to preventing wine from spoiling.

In the Orléans process, oaken barrels filled three-quarters up with wine are laid on their sides, small air holes are drilled in the top and the temperature is maintained at 21°C. A thick, sticky skin called the 'vinegar mother' then forms on the surface, turning the alcohol into acetic acid, which moves to the bottom. Vinegar can then be drawn off from the bottom of the cask and more wine added to replace it, with care taken not to break the mother. Vinegars produced and aged according to the **vinaigre à l'ancienne** method are labelled accordingly.

and spices grown in France; you'll find saffron grown in the Gâtinais region of the Loire, for example. Other herbs used primarily in the north include sorrel, dill and chives.

Flowers are also used to flavour or colour dishes. Jam made of **églantine** (wild rose) goes into doughnuts, **hélianthe** (sunflower) root may be used to flavour a vegetable mousse served with fish, and snails are sometimes cooked with **hysope** (hyssop), an aromatic blue-flowered member of the mint family. **Violettes** (violets) are candied in Toulouse, and the **lavande** (lavender) of Provence is made into sweets and liqueurs.

That most essential of seasonings, **sel** (salt), is mined in the Meurthe-et-Moselle département of Lorraine, but better cooks prefer to use sea salt from the Île de Ré off La Rochelle on the Atlantic coast or, better still, the incomparable Fleur de Sel de Guérande from Brittany (see the boxed text). You'll always find ground **poivre noir** (black pepper) on a French table but, oddly, not always salt. If it's absent, it's usually a statement from the chef or cook heard loud and clear by most diners.

Rue Mouffetard Market, Paris

SALT OF THE SEA

Sea salt is prized for its stronger and more pleasant taste than mined salt, which can be somewhat metallic. Many cooks consider the salt of Guérande from the marshes of the Guérande peninsula in Brittany to be the finest sea salt in the world. It certainly is among the most natural. On warm and dry days, the wind blows a thin layer of salt off the beds, which settles in a mound in the water. Using a long-handled rake salt-makers collect the salt and allow it to drain and dry in the sun, paying special attention to the weather conditions; rain and wind can wipe out an entire harvest. The result of all this time and effort is a delicate, violet-coloured salt with a slight iodine taste called **fleur de sel**, ideal for cooking or sprinkling on food. A coarser, moister salt called **sel gris** is also produced here, which can also be used in cooking and is often flavoured with herbs.

Jam & Honey

Confiture (jam) and **miel** (honey) are so ubiquitous and of such high quality here that they demand special attention. French jams are usually looser and less sweet than the ones you may be used to; they're often just reduced fruits with little or no sugar added and closer to what we call conserves. **Gelées** (fruit jellies) such as **gelée de mûres** (blackberry jelly) and **gelée de pommes** (apple jelly) are often eaten with meat and game as we serve mint jelly with lamb.

Along with being a process for preserving meats and glazing fruit, **confit** is also a jelly served with savoury dishes. The **confit de vin blanc** (white wine jelly) made on the Île de Ré, for example, is wonderful with white meats, especially veal. **Marmelade** can mean stewed fruit (or compote) as well as 'marmalade'. **Coings** (quince) is a favourite local ingredient and is sold sliced from a cheese-like block as **pâte de coings** (quince paste).

Honey and lavender for sale, Provence

Be on the lookout for small 'boutique' producers especially in Alsace, where vast quantities of soft fruits, assorted plums and apricots end up as sticky, scrumptious confitures. Among the best we've ever had are Confitures Extra de Christine Ferber made at Niedermorschwihr in Alsace, but you'll find conserves of blackcurrants in Burgundy, bilberries in the mountains and cherries in the Basque Country. **Purée de marrons** (chestnut purée) is not a jam, but combine it with meringue and crème Chantilly and you'll be on top of the world with a dessert called **Mont Blanc.**

Miel (honey) is eaten with yoghurt or spread on buttered bread. It is also a prime ingredient in such cakes and sweets as **gâteau de miel aux noisettes** (honey cake with hazelnuts) from Limousin and **nougat de miel** (honey nougat) from Champagne. **Miel de Corse** (or *mele di Corsica* in Corsican) is the delicious honey made from nectar collected from Corsica's fragrant maquis in summer. Other honeys available are: **miel de lavande**, a thin lavender honey from Provence; **miel de châtaignes**, thick and dark chestnut honey from the Cévennes in Languedoc; **miel de Savoie**, very thick wild flower honey from the Alps; and **miel de sapin des Vosges**, a dark pine honey from the Vosges.

Goat's milk cheese and cherry jam at Le Bascou Restaurant, Paris

STAPLES

Pâtisserie

The French love sweet things and judging from the eye-catching and drool-inducing window displays at pastry shops throughout the land, they can't get enough of them. Most people usually eat a sweet or some sort of dessert at the end of both lunch and dinner – cooks at home, who slave over the entrées and plats principaux, have never balked at procuring their sweet course from a pâtisserie – and they often have a slice of something at a café in the afternoon.

Flans for sale at a street market, Paris

Pâtisserie is a general term for 'pastry' and usually includes **tartes** (pies), **flans** (custard pies), **gâteaux** (cakes), **biscuits** (cookies or biscuits), **macarons** (macaroons) and so on in all their varieties. Although often sweet (or sweetish), such baked goods as croissants and brioches are classified as **viennoiserie** (baked goods) and are normally sold at bakeries.

A TARTE IS BORN

Among the tales of dishes being snatched from the flames of disaster and then rising, phoenix-like to join the panoply of culinary immortals, the one about **tarte Tatin**, an upside-down caramelised apple pie, has few peers. It goes something like this. It's 1888 just before midday and the two Tatin sisters, Caroline and Stéphanie, are getting ready for the lunchtime scramble at their hotel restaurant in the village of Lamotte-Beuvron in the Loire region. Stéphanie, who commands the kitchen, is readying a **tarte aux pommes** (apple pie), for which she has gained a certain reputation, but in her haste puts the apples cooked in butter and sugar in a tin not yet lined with pastry. Flustered, she attempts to control the damage by placing the dough on top of the fruit mixture, bakes it and turns it upside down. A star – **la tarte des demoiselles Tatin** – is born.

Another story has the sisters flirting with clients and burning the tarte. It is only when they go to throw it into the bin upside down that they realise what a treat they've created. But does it matter? Tarte Tatin is now one of France's most popular desserts, usually served warm with ice cream.

KNOW YOUR PÂTISSERIE

Each region of France has its own specialities and trying to compile a list of generic pâtisserie is like counting charcuterie – it's an endless (though hardly thankless) task.

Baba au rhum	a sponge cake soaked in rum syrup
Beignet	a doughnut often filled with confiture
Flan	both baked custard in a pastry shell and a tart with various fillings
Florentine	a flat cookie or biscuit with glazed fruit and a chocolate coating
Jalousie	a latticed flaky pastry filled with almond paste and jam
Macaron	a macaroon made with egg white, almonds and sugar
Madeleine	a small scallop-shaped cake flavoured with lemon
Merveille	fried dough sprinkled with sugar
Mille-feuille	literally, 1000 leaves; flaky pastry layered with custard or thick cream filling
Religieuse	an eclair with one cream puff perched on top of another to resemble a nun's habit
Sablé	a shortbread biscuit
Tarte aux fruits	a fruit tart, the ultimate French pâtisserie
Tarte Tatin	an upside-down caramelised apple pie (see overleaf)
Tuile	fragile, wing-like almond cookies

A pâtisserie display, Alsace

Tarte Tatin

When preparing a tarte Tatin, use the best apples available (ideally **Reine de Reinettes**) but Granny Smith or Golden Delicious will do.

Crust Ingredients

210g/1¾ cups	flour
1	egg
100g/3½oz	butter
1 tablespoon	sugar
1 tablespoon	water
	pinch of salt

Filling Ingredients

120g/4oz	butter
180g/¾ cup	icing sugar
1¼kg/2½lb	apples, peeled and quartered

Put the flour into a large bowl, make a well in the centre and break the egg into it. Add the butter, sugar and salt and mix together with a wooden spoon. Sprinkle some of the water to moisten the mixture and form into a ball.

Melt the butter in a high-sided skillet and sprinkle in the icing sugar. Add the apples and stir to combine. Cook for 20 minutes and then turn up the heat for 10 minutes more, or until the apples turn golden brown. Do not let the mixture burn.

Place the apples in a 24cm glass baking dish, filling in any gaps with large slices. Roll out the dough and place it on top of the apples, tucking the dough around the edge into the dish. Bake the pie at 180°C (350°F) for 20 minutes, then remove from the oven and allow to stand for a few minutes. Place a serving platter over the baking dish and flip it over quickly. Serve plain or with ice cream.

Serves 8

Confectionery

France has a predilection for confection, known as **confisserie** or **friandise**. Every region produces several of its own sweet specialities – from the unpretentious **bêtises de Cambrai** (mint-flavoured hard candy) of the north and the **dragées de Verdun** (Verdun sugar-coated almonds) of Lorraine, to the delectable **marrons glacés** (candied chestnuts) of Ardèche and **Anis de l'Abbaye de Flavigny** of Burgundy (see the Regional Variations chapter). But nothing, absolutely nothing, can touch **chocolat** (chocolate) in terms of consumption and quality.

A confectionery display, Paris

Chocolate is a veritable religion in France and its temple is the Valhrona factory at Tain-l'Hermitage, south of Lyon, producing what many say is the finest chocolate in the world. Other chocolate shrines are Strasbourg, which owes its superb chocolate to Jews who introduced it to eastern France from Germany in the 18th century, and Bayonne, the first place in France to manufacture the sweet, dark and unctuous stuff after it was brought up from Spain in the 17th century.

Valhrona is to chocolate what Château Lafite Rothschild is to wine. That comparison with wine is not a facile one: the Valhrona factory is set amid vineyards on the Rhône and much of the terminology used in viniculture is applied here, such as describing one of its cocoa bean varieties as a **grand cru amer-doux** (grand cru bitter-sweet).

Valhrona is almost always dark (not milk) chocolate and made from a single type of cocoa bean. The process from bean to chocolate is long and painstaking. The beans are roasted, mixed with sugar and perhaps vanilla, then ground. After it has been mixed with the fat from cocoa butter (never vegetable fat), the chocolate is 'conched' (a crucial process in which the emulsified substance is turned in a machine resembling a cement mixer) and finally 'tempered'. This involves heating the chocolate to melting point and cooling it down rapidly to start the process of crystallisation, giving the chocolate its colour, texture and – the sure sign of quality – its clean snap when you break it.

Val de Rance
Cru Breton
Cidre Bouché Brut
non pasteurisé
Breton

drinks

France's wines and liqueurs are loved the world over, but the birthplace of Château d'Yquem, Champagne and Grand Marnier is home to many other fine tipples. Beers from the north and Alsace complement local dishes perfectly, Bretons take pride in their cider, and there's delicious kir, Cognac and a range of flavoursome eaux-de-vie. Even if you're avoiding alcohol there's no lack of choice. Take yourself to a café for café, quench your thirst with lemon squash, or sample some of France's famous mineral waters.

A BASIC GUIDE TO WINE TASTING

Wine tasting is a complex process that can take years to fully appreciate and employs an extensive and – to the uninitiated – often obscure vocabulary of adjectives describing bouquet, nose and taste. But that's no reason to be intimidated; taste is subjective and you are entitled to your own opinion. Just follow the guide below and you'll be on your way.

Colour Look through the wine towards a source of light, holding the glass by the stem. Then tilt the glass slightly and look through it towards a white or at least pale background. What you're looking for here is clarity and colour. Clarity is obvious, but colour is a more complex issue. A deep colour indicates a strong wine. The colour can also reveal the types of grapes used as well as the wine's age (for example, in red wines a bluish hue around the ring of the surface indicates a young wine whereas an orange one suggests an aged wine).

Smell Swirl the wine around and smell it in one inhalation. The agitation will release the wine's full bouquet. Close your eyes and concentrate. What do you smell? There are 11 main groups of smells associated with wine, ranging from fruits, herbs and spices to leather and even stone.

Taste Take a sip, swill it around in your mouth and then (here's the tough part) draw in some air to bring out the flavour. Our tastebuds can identify four sensations: bitter, acid, salty and sweet. After doing this swallow the wine. A fine wine should leave an aftertaste. Be aware that acidity makes the mouth water while tannin dries it. Length is the duration of taste on your palate after swallowing. The following descriptions will give you an indication of what to expect and enjoy.

Wine

The **vignoble** (vineyard) has always been an integral feature on France's culinary map, and no other nation makes wines like France. Is there anything comparable to an expertly blended Bordeaux or a Burgundy made from a single grape variety? When it comes to a celebration, the bubbles of Dom Perignon are what really makes an event special. And Château d'Yquem is so popular that this sweet, liquid gold is virtually impossible to find.

Your average Jean or Marianne, with thousands of wines to choose from, rarely tipple **les grands vins** (great or grand wines). As wine is actually an everyday staple in France, there are favourite wines for all budgets and occasions, with local varieties generally preferred for everyday meals. But although Jean or Marianne might not regularly buy top-shelf wines, they are probably just as knowledgeable about vintages from across France as they are about cheeses. If anything, French wine drinkers are becoming more discriminating. They may be drinking less wine in favour of mineral water, juice or soft drinks, but the demand for better-quality products has increased. Cheap Algerian imports are out; recognised labels are in.

History

The French thirst for wine goes back to Roman times, when techniques to grow grapes and process wine were introduced. Wine got a real boost in the Middle Ages when vineyards developed around monasteries; priests needed wine to celebrate Mass and no doubt the monks wanted to enjoy themselves in the process. Large-scale wine production later moved closer to the coast, from where wine could be exported out of such ports as Bordeaux.

France nearly became a nation of beer drinkers in the 19th century when the *phylloxera* lice chomped its way through grapevines from France to Hungary, decimating entire crops, and Chablis was almost wiped out. It looked like wine production was doomed until cuttings resistant to the pest were brought from California and grafted on to what roots remained.

A vineyard in Gascony

A TASTE OF FRENCH WINES

Chablis is one of the leanest and driest of French wines. Underpinning the wine's rich butteriness, ripe melon and citrus notes is a bone dryness and steely acidity. It's a wine just made for food.

For a rich, weighty Chardonnay, try Mersault with its intense hints of over-ripe melon, treacle, honey, butter and vanilla, and its long finish. It's lovely young, but a five to eight-year wait will deliver even more.

The refreshing Loire twins, Sancerre and Pouilly Fumé, transcend their lemon zest and gooseberry Sauvignon Blanc origins and give forth more sophisticated nuances. Pouilly Fumé has smoky, flinty overtones, while Sancerre is fruitier.

Beaujolais' winemaking techniques give their wines maximum fruitiness. The **crus** (growths or vineyards) offer a perfumed nose and spice, red fruits and damson plums on the palate. They team well with white and red meats. The lighter styles are scrumptious served chilled.

Elegance and finesse are the bywords for the reds from the Côte d'Or. Don't let a mouldy vegetable or farmyardy nose put you off; once you sip these silky textured wines, seduction is complete. Concentrated mocha, vegetal, red fruits with balanced acidity and tanning sum up Nuits Saint George. Coffee beans, a touch of spice, buttered vegetables and hints of liquorice bring to mind Gevrey Chambertin. Prices are high but worth it.

With the macho Châteuneuf-du-Pape, some 13 grape varieties are permitted in the blend. The result is a rich, warming, fragrant wine with red and black fruits, spices, herbs (eg thyme, lavender, rosemary), high alcohol and a long finish. Its northern Rhône counterpart is the wonderful Côte Rotie. A Syrah-based wine displaying full-bodied, concentrated black fruits, spearmint, chocolate, coffee and velvet smoothness, and culminating in a lingering finish. It's lively young but delicious aged for 10 years.

Dependable and gorgeous are Bordeaux reds. Flavours can range from young, fruity, stalky wines to the more mature, rich and opulent ones with complex cigar box, cedarwood and subtle blackcurrants. Château Batailley has a smoky, vanilla nose and abundant blackcurrants, red fruits and vanilla on the palate, ending on a vegetal tone. Château Soutard is a delicious wine with harmonious spices, black fruits, oak and vanilla.

London-based Jacqueline Graves is an accredited Wine & Spirit Educational Trust Lecturer

Production

Grape juice differs from wine in one way: fermentation – the chemical process caused by the reaction of yeast with sugar. As yeast is found in grape skins and the fruit contains sugar, grapes have both the ingredients required.

After the grapes are carefully picked and sorted, they are pressed. This was traditionally done by naked men stomping around in large troughs but is now accomplished – gratefully – by machine. The pulpy juice, known as 'must', is put into vats to ferment and sulphur dioxide is added to prevent contamination. The temperature is regulated, and if the sugar content is too low to bring about fermentation, sugar can be added.

For **vin rouge** (red wine), the grape skins are left in the must for about three weeks. The skins add colour and tannin, which imparts an astringent taste and is an important preservative, allowing red wines to mature for years. The must takes a couple of weeks to ferment, producing a new wine with an alcoholic content of about 15%. **Vin blanc** (white wine) takes longer and is fermented at a lower temperature. The earlier the fermentation of white wine is stopped, the sweeter the wine is due to a higher sugar content.

After fermenting, the wine is left to settle and is then poured into containers – usually wooden vats for the red or stainless-steel ones for the white. Red wine can be left for up to two years in the casks, and is filtered before bottling (see the boxed text opposite). Finally, the wine is either mixed from various vats to produce a blend or poured straight into the bottle.

SOMETHING FISHY IS GOING DOWN

Vegetarians might not be aware that egg whites or maybe even crustacean shells are going down along with their vin. Both are necessary to settle particles suspended in the wine. Traditionally, ox blood and ground crab shells were used. Nowadays, egg white is mainly used. Vegetarian wines use a chemical substitute or don't bother to clarify the wine at all.

Organic winemaking is one of the fastest-growing sectors of the industry. And, while many winemakers are converting their vineyards, they are not allowed to call their wine organic for three years; it takes that long for non-organic fertilisers and pesticides to be leeched from the soil. Organic wine bottles are produced from recycled glass, and labels might be made from renewable paper sources. Some organic winemakers eschew cork and use natural beeswax to seal their bottles.

There's no symbol used in France to designate vegetarian or organic wines. Look for descriptions attesting that the Écovert organic association has certified the wine, or ask the wine seller. Some fine kosher wines are made nowadays, and they certainly won't contain ox blood or crab shells.

Grape Varieties

Wine drinkers who are used to ordering bottles of Chardonnay or Cabernet Sauvignon can be forgiven for wondering why their favourites are not available in France. That's because here it's most often the region and the village that define wines, not the **cépage** (grape variety).

Chablis, dry and crisp, is made from the **Chardonnay** grape. There are about 80 AOC (see boxed text) white wines in Burgundy alone made from the Chardonnay grape, each one with its own character and price range. Even Champagne is made from Chardonnay. It just doesn't make sense here to simply ask for '**un verre de Chardonnay**' (a glass of Chardonnay).

Just as Chardonnay has become synonymous with white Burgundy, **Cabernet Sauvignon** and **Merlot** grapes are the base for the deep, rich red wines from Bordeaux. Most Bordeaux wines are blends of these two grapes, sometimes with the less robust **Cabernet Franc** thrown in.

Whether you spend 1800FF on a Mouton-Rothschild or 40FF on a Saint Émilion, the blend of the grapes used in the wine isn't mentioned on the label. Merlot tends to dominate wines from some parts of northern Bordeaux and can comprise up to 70% of all the vines planted. Both Merlot and Cabernet Sauvignon age well; the best Bordeaux can be stored for decades.

Syrah (known in Australia as Shiraz) is planted mainly in the Rhône Valley to make the heavy, red Hermitage wines. Syrah is also grown in the southeast, where it is used to boost or improve cheaper wines.

ASSURANCES OF WINE QUALITY

Like all food products in France, wine production is strictly supervised by the government. Under French law, wines are divided into four categories:

Appellation d'Origine Contrôlée (AOC)

AOC wines have met stringent regulations governing where, how and under what conditions they are grown, fermented and bottled. They can cover a wide region, a sub-region, or a commune or village. Some wine regions only have a single AOC, such as Alsace, while Burgundy is chopped into scores of individual AOCs. Wines with an AOC are almost always good and usually superb. AOC quality is assured because each year a producer must renew their status. In poor years, a grower may lower the AOC status or even settle to call it **vin de table** (table wine).

Individual wine regions then have power to splice and dice the quality of their own produce, and this is where things get really confusing. For instance, Bordeaux set standards for its best wines as long ago as 1855. Some regions, like the Loire, don't bother.

Pinot Noir is used in the more subtle red Burgundies. This grape variety produces wine best drunk under 10 years of age. It's also used to make Champagne (minus its skins) and a light Alsatian red, often served chilled.

Sauvignon Blanc produces the flowery, dry whites of Sancerre and Pouilly-Fumé. **Chenin Blanc**, mostly associated with the Loire's dry, white Vouvray, can be used to make dry, semi-dry or sweet wine. Chenin Blanc also goes in the sparkling wine called Crémant de Loire.

Sémillion is used in Sauternes from Bordeaux. It's particularly suited for *Botrytis cinerea*, the 'noble rot' fungus that increases the sugar content and produces a sweet dessert wine. **Cabernet Franc** is used to cut red Bordeaux wines made from the heavier Cabernet Sauvignon and Merlot grapes. It's also the base for Chinon, the Loire's heaviest wine.

Gamay is used to make light, fruity Beaujolais and the younger Beaujolais Nouveau. **Aligoté** makes a crisp, cheap and ordinary white Burgundy that's best drunk young. **Marsanne** and **Viognier** are two grapes used almost exclusively in making white Rhône wines, with Viognier the dominant variety.

Muscat is used to make sweet dessert wines in the south. In Alsace it's used for dry but aromatic wines. Interestingly, Alsace is the one region where wine is known by its grape varieties. **Riesling**, **Sylvaner** and **Pinot Blanc** are dry, crisp wines made from grapes of those names – quite different from their namesakes in other countries. **Gewürztraminer** is also dryer than similarly named wines abroad though it can be relatively fruity or spicy.

Vin Délimité de Qualité Superieure (VDQS)

These are good wines from a specific place or region that follow rigorous tests, though an AOC wine has stricter criteria both for wine production and tasting.

Vin de Pays (Country Wine)

Wines with this label are of reasonable quality and are generally drinkable because there are some standards that need to be met. You can recognise them from the word **pays** on the label in front of a region or department (such as Vin de Pay d'Oc).

Vin de Table (Table Wine)

These wines are also known as **vin ordinaire** and there's only two rules governing their production: only real, authorised grapes can be used and the alcoholic content must be between 8.5%-15%. You can buy litre bottles from supermarkets, but if you buy directly from the producer you'll pay next to nothing (bring a container). Spending an extra 10FF can often make a big difference in quality, drinkability and the severity of your hangover.

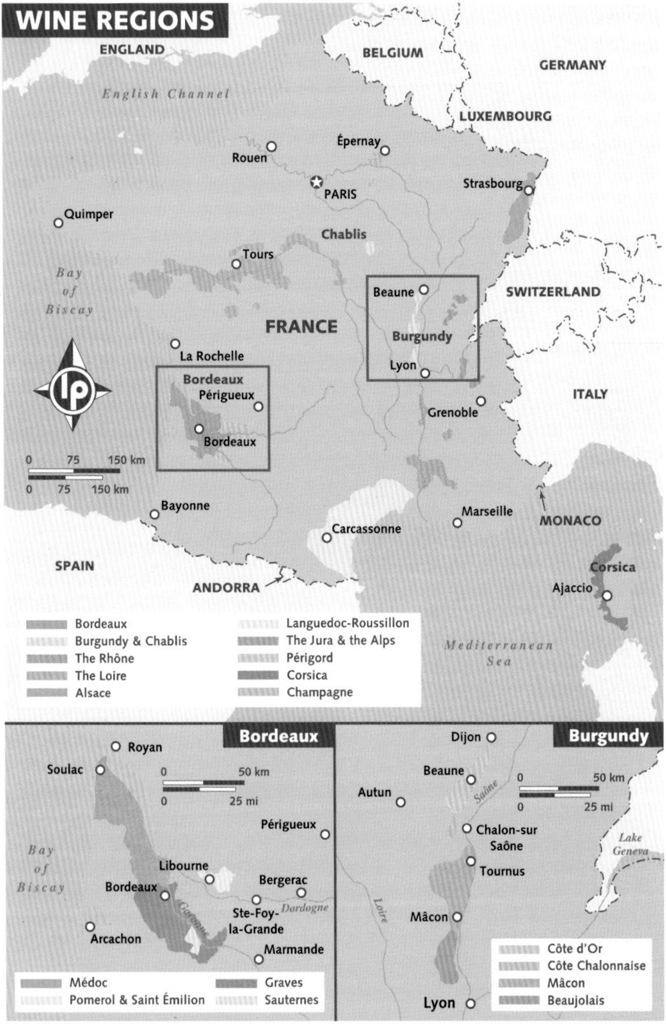
WINE REGIONS
ENGLAND
BELGIUM
GERMANY
English Channel
LUXEMBOURG
Rouen
Épernay
Strasbourg
PARIS
Quimper
Chablis
Tours
Bay of Biscay
Beaune
SWITZERLAND
FRANCE
Burgundy
La Rochelle
Lyon
Bordeaux
Périgueux
Bordeaux
ITALY
Grenoble
0 75 150 km
0 75 150 km
Bayonne
Marseille
MONACO
Carcassonne
SPAIN
Corsica
ANDORRA
Ajaccio
Bordeaux
Burgundy & Chablis
The Rhône
The Loire
Alsace
Languedoc-Roussillon
The Jura & the Alps
Périgord
Corsica
Champagne
Mediterranean Sea
Bordeaux
Royan
Soulac
0 50 km
0 25 mi
Périgueux
Bay of Biscay
Libourne
Bergerac
Bordeaux
Garonne
Ste-Foy-la-Grande
Dordogne
Arcachon
Marmande
Médoc
Graves
Pomerol & Saint Émilion
Sauternes
Burgundy
Dijon
Beaune
Autun
Saône
0 50 km
0 25 mi
Chalon-sur Saône
Lake Geneva
Tournus
Loire
Mâcon
Côte d'Or
Côte Chalonnaise
Mâcon
Beaujolais
Lyon

Wine-Producing Areas

Bordeaux

Bordeaux has been synonymous with full-bodied red wine since the time of the Romans. Britons, who call them clarets, have had a taste for Bordeaux reds since the mid-12th century. King Henry II, who controlled the region through marriage, tried to gain the favour of locals by granting them tax-free trade status with England. Thus began a roaring business in wine exporting that continues to this day.

Bordeaux has the perfect climate for producing wine, and its proximity to the Atlantic Ocean helps protect its grapes from both frost and excessive heat. As a result, Bordeaux produces more quality wine than any other region in the world. Bordeaux's wine status can be dated to 1855 when 60 of the region's 2000 vineyards were given quality rankings. That's when terms like **premier grand cru** (first of the great growths) came into use. Today no other part of France has the same position in the wine pecking order as Bordeaux. It took more than a century for Bordeaux winemakers to lobby successfully for another 100 wines to be included in the ranking. But they were not allowed to be called **grand cru**, so you'll see categories such as **cru grand bourgeois**, what are effectively third growths. Even so, some of the lower-ranked wines are considered better than their more senior peers.

THE BEST YEARS OF THEIR LIVES

Millésimes (vintages) are important for wines here because France's climate can be so damn fickle. This is especially true in Bordeaux, which is buffeted by winds coming off the Atlantic Ocean. There's only so much even the best winemaker can do to make up for heavy rain at harvest time. And then there are the microclimates; a good year for a red Graves might be terrible for a Sauternes produced just a few kilometres away.

Most wine guides and magazines list the best vintages for recent decades. In general it's not easy to find the best wines at your local wine shop and they're never very affordable. Although Bordeaux wines can keep for decades, don't think you're getting a great bottle from, say, 1977, which was considered a mediocre year. And by now the stuff could be off altogether. Red Burgundies don't keep as long as their heavier counterparts in Bordeaux – they're best drunk between five and 10 years old. As for white Burgundies, 1988 and 1989 were in such great demand you probably won't find any left. More recently, 1997 was a great year, as was 1996, 1995 and 1992. For Rhône wine drinkers, Châteauneuf-du-Pape from 1989 and from 1990 is considered perfect. The 1998 is also excellent. In Alsace, 1997 and 1990 are two recent years to look out for.

Because Bordeaux has relied so heavily on exports, the wine has traditionally been sold by owners of the **châteaux** (vineyards) at auctions to merchants. Sometimes, the wine is sold before it's been bottled, as merchants take bets on its quality by buying 'futures contracts'. You'll find some wine shops in the region where you can buy wine several years before it's available in shops. Although you can sometimes find a great bargain, don't forget that you might have to come back in a few years to pick up the actual bottles.

The upshot is that Bordeaux vineyards have never relied on individuals to buy their product, so the region isn't as geared up to receiving visitors as are Burgundy, Alsace or Champagne. In any case, when a vintage bottle of Château d'Yquem can command as much as 1800FF, there isn't much need to rely on passing trade.

The wines of the Atlantic Coast are not so well known and the reason is obvious at first sip: most are local 'sand' wines of little or no distinction and there's actually a Rosé des Dunes and a Blanc Marine.

Médoc

Médoc lies on the left bank of the Gironde River. This wide and sandy estuary ends to the south at Bordeaux, the bustling regional capital whose fortune (and fame) is based on the wide trade. The best known wines of the Médoc region are from Margaux, Pauillac, Saint Julien and Saint Estèphe. The town of Pauillac alone has three top-growth wines: Mouton-Rothschild, Latour and Lafite-Rothschild. It's possible to visit the Mouton-Rothschild Estate throughout most of the year, but don't expect the same welcome down the road at Château Lafite-Rothschild, where appointments must be made well in advance.

Pomerol & Saint Émilion

Northeast of Bordeaux above the Dordogne River lies Pomerol in the Libornais region, home to the most expensive wines in the world. Petrus, king of them all, produces a mere 160 casks a year on average. Wines here are made mostly from Merlot grapes, which impart a velvety taste.

More affordable are the wines of Saint Émilion, southeast of Pomerol, whose vineyards were first planted by the Romans. The town, which is still encircled by its medieval wall, later became an important church centre. This has given rise to a number of labels with ecclesiastical roots, such as Couvent des Jacobins. The quality, and price, of Saint Émilion wines is determined by terrain. Cheval Blanc, among the most expensive, grows closest to Pomerol, and shares its chalky, iron-rich soil. Around the plains that surround Saint Émilion, the soil becomes more sandy. Here the quality of the wine deteriorates – and the price drops.

Despite their different locations and geographies, all Saint Émilion wines share the same AOC. Top of the league is the **premier grand cru classé** wines, of which there are about 10, and the **grand cru classé** ones, numbering about 70, whose status is reviewed every decade. Vignerons can also pitch for a particular vintage to get a grand cru accolade, and hundreds of these appear year in and out. They might, however, be happy just to stick with the generic Saint Émilion name, which keeps the price of their wine competitively low.

Graves

It's the pebbly soil (**gravelleux** means 'gravelly') that gives wine from this large region a spicy, almost smoky character. Red wines make up about half of all production and, although there are many top-growth wines, Graves falls behind Médoc, Pomerol and Saint Émilion in prestige even though it's the oldest. This is because Bordeaux nobles moved their vineyards from the south to the north at the end of the Middle Ages. The Dutch, with their skill at building dikes, helped reclaim land in the Gironde estuary, and it's here that the landed gentry went to cultivate grapes for their top tipples. When the Médoc wines were classified in 1855, Graves was largely ignored and became even more of a backwater.

There are about 370 vineyards south of the Pessac-Léognan area. There's no cooperative structure in place to sell wines and a lot of the production there is still traditional, making for a wide range of lesser-known wines, especially whites. The popularity of whites from Graves comes in and goes out of fashion. These whites, mainly dry, have a slight almond taste, and many aren't expensive.

FOREIGN TASTE CHÂTEAU

Château Haut Brion, the oldest top wine estate in Bordeaux and one of the best known labels, proves just how reliant Bordeaux wines have been on foreign tastes. It has been owned by Americans since 1935, but long before it was purchased by banker Clarence Dillon the estate was popular in England. Sales of the garnet-coloured wine across the Channel go back 500 years, and Londoner Samuel Pepys praised it in his diary after a lunch in 1663. He soon spread the word, and the wine became the talk of the town. The Pontac family, which owned Haut Brion, opened a tavern in London called the Pontac's Head and, understandably enough, served wine produced at their estate. Even such luminaries as Jonathan Swift and Daniel Defoe frequented the joint.

Sauternes

Thanks to the Sémillion and Sauvignon Blanc grapes, which provide the perfect vehicle for the *Botrytis cinerea* mould, we have the sweet, sticky, luscious, golden nectar that is Sauternes. Under normal circumstances, *Botrytis cinerea* is a winemaker's nightmare, turning plump fruit into a mouldy mess. In the right conditions though – late autumn morning mists followed by sunshine – the blight causes grapes to shrivel almost to a raisin, concentrating the sugar content. Picking the grape at the perfect time is crucial. After all, this process is known as 'noble rot' and the idea is to select royal grapes, not common ones.

Sauternes' steep price has also been linked to nobility. The 19th-century Russian imperial court took a fancy to Château d'Yquem, ordering cases of the best known Sauternes. Discriminating fans were enjoying it long before, however, and the American statesman (and future president) Thomas Jefferson stopped by to pick some up during a stint in France in the 1770s.

The process involved in producing a good vintage of Sauternes, one that can easily last 40 years, is labour-intensive and the yields are low. New World wines make more affordable Sauterne (that's without the 's') by adding sugar, and critics charge that the result is a thinner wine with little bouquet. The real Sauternes isn't cheap. Château d'Yquem produces an estimated one glass of wine per vine and doesn't even bother to produce the nectar in bad years. That's why most mere mortals are unlikely to ever have the chance to sample this grand-mère of Sauternes.

There are five villages in the Sauternes region, including Barsac, where you'll find cheaper wines. The production process and standards are the same as in the village of Sauternes, but the different soil makes for a lighter wine. Barsac wine can still legally be called Sauternes, however. Sauternes wines were also classified back in the 19th century into one first great growth (which went to Château d'Yquem, naturally), first growths (11) and second growths (13). There are generic Sauternes but they aren't in the same wonderful dessert-wine league as their higher-classed cousins.

The vineyard of Château d'Yquem, Sauternes

Burgundy

Burgundy is a patchwork of tiny vineyards in villages strung along a narrow valley. At the northern tip is the Chablis area while the south is home to Beaujolais. But for true wine lovers, the best Burgundy wines are found along the Saône River from Dijon to Mâcon.

With myriad microclimates, the Burgundy area counts hundreds of different AOCs. Some holdings, however, are as small as a row or two, barely enough to produce two dozen cases, and others holdings are rarely larger than 10 hectares.

Pinot Noir and Chardonnay grapes are the predominant varieties here, but the whites don't have the same oaky taste of Australian or Californian Chardonnays. The Burgundy style is more delicate, and are among the best white wines France has to offer. The reds are lighter than those from Bordeaux and are drunk younger. Burgundy wines aren't cheap. In fact the typical Burgundy costs more than the average Bordeaux. This is because of the area's limited production.

TOP OF THE CLASS

The classification of Burgundy wines is a complicated process. The bulk of wine made in Burgundy (65%, in fact) simply has the Bourgogne AOC, or a sub-region that includes the word **Bourgogne** in its name. Next up the scale of quality are wines with **communal** or **village** appellations (23% of production). There are 53 villages and in each one the vineyards are divided into little plots called **climats**. The climats are then ranked, with the best gaining premier **cru** (growth or vineyard) status . There are over 500 of these. At the top of the heap are the grand cru, accounting for only 1% of production. It gets hugely confusing because the village or commune name is part of the label used for grand crus. The price tag can help sort things out for you, of course.

Chablis

Chablis is considered part of Burgundy even though it's isolated from the region. This quintessentially dry, white wine is made – like all quality Burgundy whites – exclusively from the Chardonnay grape. Chablis' soil is poor and the area under cultivation surprisingly small. The seven grand cru vineyards lie together on a single slope. There are a dozen or so premier crus and vignerons number about 250, most of whom just bottle wine with the Chablis AOC.

Côte d'Or

The town of Beaune, overflowing with wine merchants, **caves** (wine cellars) and restaurants, is in the middle of Burgundy's main wine-producing region, the Côte d'Or. The villages of this area are grouped into **communes**, an appropriate term as the grapes are often sold by individuals to a collective wine producer. These wines can be excellent, though they are rarely as delicious (and never as expensive) as those that carry the label of a great château.

The area north of Beaune is called the Côte de Nuit. South of Beaune are Pommard, Meursault and Puligny-Montrachet. Then there's Le Montrachet, a single eight-hectare vineyard with 15 owners that produces perhaps the best dry white wine in the world.

Many winemakers along the Côte d'Or open their doors for tastings. The best vintages aren't always available and you won't find many bargains. Still, it's not only fun, but chatting with winemakers, breathing in the mustiness of a cellar and seeing the very vines that produced a memorable vintage will make that wine special. You'll be more likely to remember a particular wine if you've sampled it on the spot.

Côte Chalonnaise & Mâcon

South of the Côte d'Or come the lesser known Côte Chalonnaise and the Mâcon regions. Mâcon vineyards use Chardonnay grapes, and here you'll find wines almost as good at their more aristocratic cousins on the Côte d'Or at a fraction of the price. Most wines here simply carry the Mâcon appellation but 36 villages have the right to call themselves Mâcon-Villages or to append the name of their village to the word 'Mâcon'. The most famous of all wines from Mâcon is the dry, soft Pouilly-Fuissé wine, which vies with the top white Burgundies in quality and price.

Beaujolais

The Gamay grape is the queen of Beaujolais. When grown in the sandy soil in this region, Gamay produces Beaujolais Nouveau, a light, unpretentious red wine. The new crop can't be sold legally until the third Thursday of November and promoters have successfully exported the idea that the first batch of an extremely ordinary wine is something to celebrate. Signs proclaiming '**le Beaujolais nouveau est arrivé!**' (the new Beaujolais has arrived!) can now be found from Perth to Prague.

The soil farther north contains more granite. Here the Gamay grape is used in the Beaujolais Villages, which produce wines that take themselves a bit more seriously. Fleurie, Brouilly and Morgan are villages with relatively cheap, light, drinkable wines.

The Rhône

The vineyards around the Rhône are second only in quality to Bordeaux. The region is divided into northern and southern areas by a 70km vineless 'no man's land' of fruit orchards. The difference between the two regions couldn't be greater, even though they are lumped together for classification. In the northern town of Vienne, the Rhône is a powerful river fed by the Alps. Here grape vines cling to steep, granite soil and the harvest is back-breaking, labour-intensive work. Wine production is limited to gutsy reds and steely whites. Syrah is the dominant grape for red wines here and has been so for a long time. The most notable red wines are Hermitage and Crozes-Hermitages. The two, despite their similar names and geographical proximity, are very different. Hermitage wines are heavier and age; Crozes-Hermitages, being lighter, are best drunk young. White wines from the northern Rhône are made mostly from Marsanne grapes grown in chalk, producing an aromatic and strong wine. The Viognier grape is used to a lesser extent. Wines include Condrieu, Saint Joseph and Château Grillet, which gets the superlative of being the smallest AOC in all of France.

The southern Rhône region sprawls away from the river as it approaches the Mediterranean. The bulk of the wine is sold to communal wine cooperatives. They either bottle the stuff (and it can be of poor quality) or it's shipped off by the lorry load to be sold to bigger wine concerns for mass production. Several villages are allowed to apply their own names on labels, and this wine is among the best of the region.

Châteauneuf-du-Pape is the best known of the Rhône wines. Bordeaux wines are France's best known blends, but they pale in comparison to Châteauneuf when it comes to mixing up grapes. Up to 13 different varieties can be thrown together to make the wine, though usually about a half-dozen are used. The wine is best drunk after about five years.

Sémillon grapes in a Bergerac vineyard, Périgord

The Loire

The sunny, fertile Loire region, with its magnificent vineyards, is a great place for wine lovers. Most vineyards here are small and winemakers are used to selling directly to Parisians who take day trips to buy their favourite wines. Keep an eye out for signs reading **dégustation** (tasting) or **vente directe** (direct sales) on the roads. Vineyards tend to be planted on slopes away from the water because this region can flood. Although sunny, the climate is moist and not all grape varieties thrive here. Still, the Loire produces the greatest variety of wines in the country.

The most common grapes are the Muscadet, Cabernet Franc and Chenin Blanc varieties. Wines tend to be light and delicate. There are no premier crus or grand crus within this region, however; the best wines simply get an AOC. The more specific a description the better the wine. Look for labels that mention a particular vineyard as well as the village and region. Wines from the Loire tend to be better priced than those from Bordeaux or Burgundy.

In the caves of the Loire region

The region is best known for its dry whites and rosés, though you can also find the sweet white Coteaux du Layon or Quarts de Chaume. Quality ranges from the Gros Plant du Pays Nantais, which has the dubious distinction as being the country's cheapest white, to Pouilly-Fumé and Sancerre, among the country's best.

Viticulture in the upper Loire is dominated by the Sauvignon Blanc grape. The soil here ranges from the chalky terrain around Sancerre (AOC) to the limestone slopes of Menetou-Salon (AOC) and the gravel-sand soils of Reuilly (AOC). Coteaux du Giennois is the fourth AOC appellation in this area. Sancerre is probably the best known, and it's here that you can find subtle rosés and cherry reds from small pockets of Pinot Noir vineyards.

The Touraine wine area stretches from Blois in the east to Saumur in the west. Vouvray is the area's best known dry white wine. It's made exclusively from the Chenin Blanc grape. Many producers here also produce a Champagne-like white or rosé called Crémant de Loire. The wine gets its bubbles from a second, year-long fermentation in the bottle. Troglodyte caves around Saumur are perfect for ageing this sparkling wine.

Full-bodied, ruby-red Chinon wines are made from the Cabernet Franc grape and vary considerably; wines grown on chalky soil are better suited to ageing than those cultivated on gravel terraces on the Vienne riverbanks. Bourgueil and Saint Nicolas de Bourgueil are among the Loire's most sought-after appellations. Bourgueil can be stored for five years or so, but Saint Nicolas matures at a younger age.

The Saumur vineyards sprawl across three départements from Tours to Anjou. This is rosé country, with Rosé de la Loire considered to be the best. Saumur-Champigny, a light and fruity wine, is arguably the best red from this region.

The Muscadet vineyards around Nantes are the valley's largest. Muscadet is one of the few grapes in France that is also a type of wine. The best wines – dry whites – come from south of Nantes and get the Muscadet Sèvre-et-Maine appellation. Gros Plant du Pays Nantais wine is produced from the Folle Blanche grape, a hardy native of southwest France which grows on almost any soil. It's been cultivated around Nantes for 500 years and is very cheap.

KNIGHTS IN CHINON

Since 1961, Chinon wine has been promoted by the Brotherhood of Rabelaisian Singers, a fraternity of 30,000 honorary brothers named after Rabelais, the hedonistic 16th-century writer born in Chinon and famed for his taste for the local vintage. The brotherhood's five annual chapters (solemn and ceremonial occasions) mark key dates in the viticulture calendar. For example, the Chapitre des Vendanges celebrates the annual harvest. Chapters are held in the painted caves at the foot of the Château de Chinon. In Rabelais' epic *Gargantua and Pantagruel*, Pantagruel drinks chilled wine at these caves. Indeed Rabelais' fictional **temple de la dive bouteille** (temple of the holy bottle), where Pantagruel ends his long quest for the sacred flask, is said to be based on these mysterious caves. The yellow vests and red caps that the brothers wear are a distinctive feature at Chinon's annual wine fair on the second weekend in March.

Alsace

For people not used to drinking the French grape varieties, Sylvaner, Riesling, Muscat, Gewürztraminer or Pinot Gris might seem like cloyingly sweet wines. They're not. Gewürztraminer, the fruitiest of the lot, is often cited as the only wine that complements spicy Thai food, but it cannot be described as a sweet wine. On the whole, Alsatian wines range from crisp to fruity and full-bodied. And Muscat, the grape variety used to make honey-like dessert wines in the south, is a dry aromatic wine served as an aperitif in Alsace.

Muscat grapes, Alsace

Alsace doesn't have old vineyards as Bordeaux does. Most wines just have the Alsace AOC appellation along with the name of the grape variety and producer. The best **terroirs** (plots of land for growing wine), which can have several owners or producers, were granted grand cru status in 1983. There are about 50 of them, and only Riesling, Muscat, Gewürztraminer and Pinot Gris grapes can be used. Regardless of the type of grape, Alsatian wine is always served in distinctive, slender green bottles.

The Haut Rhin villages of Riquewihr and Ribeauvillé are both packed with tourists and **winstubs** (traditional Alsatian wine bars). Ribeauvillé's claim to fame is its Riesling. The wineries around the Bas Rhin village of Barr produce this part of Alsace's best wines, while the top Sylvaners in Alsace come from Mittelbergheim. The northernmost village of Marlenheim produces light red wines – similar to rosé – from Pinot Noir grapes.

Languedoc-Roussillon

This region was long the centre for mass-produced, thin and cheap wine that was used to cut heavier imports. Following violent protests over Italian imports in the mid-1970s, farmers were subsidised to cut down their vines and replant with better quality AOC grapes, hence today's production of the fine Coteaux du Languedoc, Faugères, Corbières and Minervois wines. Banyuls, Muscat de Rivesaltes and Maury are three of Roussillon's delicious sweet white wines. For a drier tipple look for Côtes du Roussillon (reds, whites and rosés), Côtes du Roussillon Villages (reds) or Collioure (reds and rosés). The region still produces everyday **vin de table** (table wine). Many of the **vin de pays** (country wines) that are promoted as affordable table wines in shops around the world are from this region. Traditionally, the high-yielding Aramon grape was planted here. Recently, the sun-loving Syrah and Cabernet Sauvignon have gained acceptance.

One of the better known wine-growing areas is Corbières, which got AOC status only in 1985. This is divided into a coastal area, home of the red Fitou, and the mountains, which produce full-bodied wines that can age. Languedoc's best known region is Minervois, which produces reds and rosé wines. Wines made here with the Carignan grape produce a wine with a peppery taste and raspberry overtones.

One of the more unusual tipples produced in these parts is what the French call **vin doux naturel**, red or white wine made from Muscat grapes to which a neutral spirit has been added before fermentation begins. Banyuls, which comes from four towns around the Côte Rocheuse, produces a grand cru fortified wine.

The Pont du Gard, Languedoc-Roussillon

The Jura & the Alps

High in the Jura mountains, the town of Arbois is the centre for Côtes du Jura wines and is noted for its full-bodied dry rosés, which are drunk chilled. The unique **vins jaunes d'Arbois** (Arbois yellow wines) have a taste not unlike sherry and are drunk as an aperitif. The best vins jaunes, however, come from Château Chalon to the southwest of Arbois. They are made from grapes infected with 'noble rot'; the wines they produce are sweet and rich. Vin jaune goes well with Comté cheese. From the lower alpine slopes of the Savoy come the best of the Vins de Savoie: the whites of Chignin, Crépy, Roussette and Seyssel. The last can be both still and sparkling; try it with Beaufort cheese.

Périgord

Périgord's vineyards, mainly around Bergerac, make the best wine in central France, with equal harvests of reds and whites, both dry and sweet. The best known red wine is Côtes de Bergerac, while a decent Bergerac rosé is Château des Eyssards. An excellent sweet vintage is Monbazillac, usually drunk with dessert or fruit.

Merlot grapes in a Bergerac vineyard, Périgord

Corsica

Winemaking is now the Corsica's largest agricultural industry and counts seven AOC wines; nearly all are reds or rosés. Try Figari, a full-bodied red from the southern tip of the island, the rosé of Patrimonio grown near Bastia or the Cap Corse dry whites from the north.

Champagne

Champagne is a relative latecomer to the French wine scene, arriving in the 17th century thanks to Dom Pierre Pérignon. This innovative monk of the Benedictine Abbey at Hautvilliers perfected a technique for making sparkling wine of consistent quality. Earlier attempts had proved remarkably – even explosively – unpredictable. He put his product in strong, English-made bottles and capped them. He sealed in the bubbles with a new kind of bottle stopper – corks brought from Spain and forced into the mouth of the bottle under high pressure.

DOM PERIGNON
1638 - 1715
MOËT &

Statue of Dom Pérignon at the Moët & Chandon Champagne House, Épernay

Champagne is made from the red Pinot Noir grape, the black Pinot Meunier or the white Chardonnay, grown in a cluster of villages near the towns of Reims and Épernay. The Champagne region's vineyards are among the world's most northerly, and difficult growing conditions is one reason the stuff costs so much. Vines are vigorously pruned and trained to produce a small quantity of high-quality grapes. The grapes are pressed close to where they're grown and extra care is taken to make sure no skins from the Pinot grapes slip into the vats. The grapes may be pressed up to five times. The first couple of pressings produce the best must.

After the grapes have been pressed by local growers, the must is taken to one of the Champagne **maisons** (houses) where it's all thrown together to produce the taste a particular maker is known for. Combining grapes from different vineyards and even mixing vintages is known as **cuvée.**

Bottles of champagne stored in the Moët & Chandon cellars, Épernay

7 LES RICEYS
ROUTE
TOURISTIQUE DU
CHAMPAGNE

Tourist trail through Champagne

The process of producing Champagne is a long one. There are two fermentation processes, the first in casks, and the second after the wine has been bottled and sugar and yeast has been added. In years of an inferior vintage, older wines are blended to create what is known as 'nonvintage' Champagne.

For two months in early spring the wine is aged in cellars kept at 12°C. During this period the wine turns effervescent. The sediment that forms in the bottle is removed by **remuage**, traditionally a painstakingly slow process in which each bottle – stored horizontally on racks – is rotated slightly by hand every day for two to three months until the sludge works its way to the cork. Nowadays, the bigger maisons use computers and machines that do the trick in days, keeping a few traditional racks for tourists. Next comes **dégorgement**: the neck of the bottle is frozen, creating a blob of solidified Champagne and sediment, which is then removed.

At this stage, the Champagne's sweetness is determined by adding syrup dissolved in old Champagne. If the final product is labelled **brut**, it is extra dry. Champagne labelled **extra-sec** is very dry (but not as dry as brut), **sec** is dry and **demi-sec** is slightly sweet. The sweetest Champagne is labelled **doux**. There is also **rosé** (pink Champagne), a blend of red and white wine that has long been snubbed by connoisseurs. Champagne made only from the white Chardonnay grape is called **blanc de blancs**.

Finally, the bottles of young Champagne are laid in a cellar. Ageing lasts for between two and five years (and sometimes longer), depending on the vintage.

Some of the most famous Champagnes are Moët et Chandon, Veuve Cliquot, Mercier, Mumm, Krugg, Laurent-Perrier, Piper-Heidsieck, Dom Pérignon and Taittinger. Champagne of equal quality, sometimes at about half the price, can be found in the villages where many small producers welcome visitors to their cellars for tastings. Some villages, such as Bouzy, even make delicious red wine.

Other Alcoholic Drinks
Aperitifs

Meals are often preceded by an appetite-inducing aperitif. It's usually something sweet or slightly bitter, but a white Vouvray, a sweet **vin jaune** (yellow wine) from the Jura or a glass of Champagne make lovely aperitifs. Chambéry in Savoy makes a dry and herbal vermouth that is another good way to kick off a meal. Various kinds of **ratafia**, a drink obtained by infusing fruit or nuts in alcohol rather than by distillation, can also be sipped before a meal.

APERITIFS
Shop sign in Lyon

KIR FOR A DRINK?

Since the mid-17th century French titans have been flattered – or have flattered themselves – with having dishes named after them so they could live on in culinary perpetuity. Whatever would have become of the Marquis de Béchamel without his creamy sauce of a namesake? And had Antoine-Auguste Parmentier believed in, say, the rutabaga as the staple for the masses instead of the potato, would his name not have ended up on the compost heap of history instead of in menus?

A man who was able to bulldoze his way into the history books, the dictionary (in lower case, it must be said) and better cocktail bars everywhere was one Félix Kir (1876-1968), deputy mayor of Dijon for 28 years. While white wine mixed with blackcurrant liqueur had been a popular aperitif since at least the late 19th century, sales of the liqueur had flagged during and after WWII, apparently because saccharine had replaced the sugar used in its manufacture. Kir adopted what was called **vin blanc cassis** as Dijon's drink, rechristened it and served it at official functions to whomever and whenever the cameras were flashing. Crème de cassis sales boomed, and the world had a colourful and very tasty new aperitif.

Traditionally the ratio for mixing a kir is one part blackcurrant liqueur to two parts white Aligoté wine, which is the way you'll be served it in Burgundy. But elsewhere the blackcurrant liqueur is reduced to a quarter (or less) and any white wine will do. A **kir royal** is crème de cassis with Champagne. In Lyon they drink a version that substitutes white wine with red and call it a **Communard** in honour of the supporters of the socialist Paris Commune of 1871.

The classic French aperitif, however, is a **kir** (white wine with blackcurrant liqueur; see the boxed text Kir for a Drink earlier in this chapter). **Pineau des Charentes** (an AOC distillation of must and Cognac) and **porto** (port) are both drunk as aperitifs rather than after the meal. **Pastis**, popular all over the country but a particular favourite in the south, is an aniseed-flavoured aperitif often mixed with water. It's strong, refreshing and cheap. Popular brand names are Pernod and Ricard, both distilled in Marseille, but among the better distillers is Jean Boyer Pastis Arôme. If mixing pastis, pour the water in first, otherwise the two won't mix properly and may take on a slightly soapy taste. Among the bitterest of all aperitifs are Gentiane and Salers, both made from the bitter root of the wild gentian plant.

Pastis with water and ice

Digestives

Digestives are usually ordered after dessert along with coffee. France's most famous **marcs** (grape brandies) are the highly refined, double-distilled Cognac from Charente and the earthier Armagnac from the region of the same name in Gascony.

Marcs are a clever way of making use of an over-production of fruit. The grape skins and pulp left over after being pressed for wine are distilled and made into the celebrated **marc de Champagne**, **marc de Bourgogne** (from Pinot Noir) and **marc du Jura**. A distillation of **marc du Jura** with the addition of unfermented grape juice becomes **marcvin du Jura**.

Eaux-de-vie (literally, waters of life) are distilled, usually clear brandies made and flavoured with locally grown fruits, herbs or nuts. Of the many varieties, **kirsch**, a cherry concoction, is the most famous. **Mirabelles** (yellow plums), **quetsches** (dark red plums) and **framboises** (raspberries) are used in Alsace and Lorraine to make some of the best eaux-de-vie. **Calvados** is an apple brandy made in Normandy that ages beautifully; **poire William** is a pear-based eau-de-vie. The **eau-de-vie de noix** (walnut eau-de-vie) from Limousin is excellent.

Eaux-de-vie varieties made in the mountains range from the sublime – the **prunelle** (sloe), for example – to the ridiculous. Mouthe, a town known as the North Pole of France (record low, -38°C) is the mother of **liqueur de sapin** (fir tree liqueur).

Eaux-de-vie in the Fauchon wine cellar, Paris

VS I LOVE YOU

Cognac, which Victor Hugo called "the liqueur of the gods", is made of grape brandies of various vintages, aged in oak barrels and then blended by an experienced **maître de chai** (warehouse master). Each year, some 3% of the volume of the casks – the so-called 'angels' share' – evaporates through the pores in the wood, nourishing the tiny black mushrooms that thrive on the walls of the Cognac warehouses.

Since the mid-18th century – when the process for turning 9L of mediocre, low-alcohol wine into 1L of Cognac was invented – many of the key figures in the Cognac trade have been Anglophones: Jean Martell was born on Jersey, Richard Hennessey hailed from Ireland and Baron Otard was of Scottish descent. To this day, several of the most common Cognac classifications are in English: VS (very special; aged five to seven years); VSOP (very special old pale; aged eight to 12 years); Napoléon (aged 15 to 25 years); and XO (extra old; aged for about 40 years).

All but a tiny fraction of Cognac's Cognac is sold outside of France, especially in the UK, Japan and other markets where the major producers have spent centuries building brand loyalty. The label Grande Fine Champagne on some labels, by the way, refers to the wine produced in the region of that name and has nothing to do with *the* Champagne.

Liqueurs, produced all over the country, are sweeter and lighter than eaux-de-vie. Most are made from grapes, eau-de-vie, sugar and either fruit or the essences of aromatic herbs. Well-known brands include Cointreau from the Loire region, Bénédictine from Normandy and orange-spiced Grand Marnier made in the Île de France. Voiron in the Alps is where members of the Carthusian order have been making the world-famous digestive, Chartreuse, on and off since 1737. It is a sweet, sticky and very strong (55% proof) tipple made from dozens of herbs (some of them medicinal) and comes in a green and a yellow variety. It's definitely an acquired taste.

For the finest fruit liqueurs, look for the words 'crème de ...' as in **crème de cassis** (blackcurrant liqueur). Védrenne in Burgundy makes an excellent assortment, including its own cassis, **crème de pêche de vignes** (made from peaches growing wild in vineyards) and the unusual **crème de châtaignes** (chestnut liqueur). There's also no shortage of liqueurs made from mountain flowers. Génépy is made from Alpine wormwood, a flower that grows at 2500m, and Izarra is a Basque liqueur supposedly distilled from '100 flowers of the Pyrenees', which comes in two varieties: yellow and the more potent green.

Beer & Cider

The **bière** (beer) served in bars and cafés is usually one of the national brands like Kronenbourg, 33 or Pelforth and totally forgettable. You're almost better off – shudder – drinking American beer. Imported beers such as Leffe from Belgium are a popular alternative. But Alsace, with its close cultural ties to Germany, produces some excellent local beers, such as Bière de Scharrach, Schutz Jubilator and Fischer.

The north, close to Belgium and the Netherlands, has its own great beers, including Saint Sylvestre Trois Monts, Colvert and Terken Brune. Brewers around the city of Lille produce **bières de garde** (literally, keeping beers), which are strong and fruity. They are bottled in what look like Champagne bottles, corked and wired. Popular among young Bretons is the new crop of beers made by boutique breweries including Lancelot barley beer and Telenn Du buckwheat beer. Corsica has its own unique brews including La Pietra (a full-bodied beer made from chestnuts) and Colomba (a light, herby lager).

Cidre (apple cider) is made in many areas, including Savoy, Picardy and the Basque Country (where it is called *sagarnoa*). But cider's real home is Normandy and Brittany, where it's traditionally served in tea cups. It's the perfect accompaniment to crêpes. Ciders to look out for include Cornouaille (AOC) as well as those produced in the towns of Morlaix, Hennebont and the Val de Rance. You'll also find **poiré** (perry or pear cider) in Picardy and Normandy.

Apples used for producing cider, Normandy

Old cider barrels, Normandy

Non-alcoholic Drinks
Coffee
Café (coffee) took France by such storm in the mid-17th century that the establishments where it was served became the focal points for social life and lent their name to the lexicons of most languages. Few people in the world today would have trouble understanding the word 'café'.

Une tasse de café (a cup of coffee) can take various forms and names in a café, but the most ubiquitous is espresso, made by forcing steam through ground coffee beans. A small, black espresso is called **un café noir**, **un café nature**, **un express** or simply **un café**. You can also ask for a **grand** (large) version. Espresso here can often taste more sour than bitter as it should, and does, in Italy. **Un café crème** is an espresso with steamed milk or cream; **un petit crème** is a smaller size while **un grand crème** is a bigger one. **Un café au lait** is lots of hot milk with a little coffee served in a large cup or even a bowl. A **noisette** (literally, hazelnut), on the other hand, is an espresso with just a dash of milk.

The French consider American and British coffee undrinkably weak and tasteless; they sometimes jokingly call it '**jus de chaussettes**' (sock juice). They will serve it, or something similar, if you ask for **un café allongé** or **un café long**, so called because it has been 'lengthened' by adding extra hot water. A cup of decaffeinated coffee is **un café décaféiné** or **un déca**. **Café filtre** is filtred coffee.

Tea & Hot Chocolate
The French have never taken to **thé** (tea) the way Anglophones have, and there's a slightly prissy and even snobbish association attached to it here. Even worse, many people consider it somewhat medicinal and drink **thé noir** (black tea) only when they are feeling unwell. **Salons de thé** (tearooms) are trendy and somewhat pricey (see Salon de Thé in the Where to Eat & Drink chapter).

Tea is usually served **nature** (plain) or **au citron** (with lemon) and never with milk. If you do like it white just ask for '**un peu de lait frais**' (a little fresh milk). **Tisanes** or **infusions** (herbal teas) are widely available across France, and the most popular ones are **tisane de menthe** (mint tea), **tisane de camomille** (camomile tea) and **tisane de tilleul** (tea made with dried linden blossoms).

Chocolat chaud (hot chocolate), available at most cafés, varies greatly and can be excellent or verging on the undrinkable. Should you be lucky enough to find chocolat chaud made from Valhrona, the king of French chocolate, it will certainly be the former (see Confectionery in the Staples & Specialities chapter).

Hot chocolate and croissants

Water & Mineral Water

All tap water in France is safe to drink, so there is no real need to buy bottled water unless you've been overdoing it (see the boxed text).

THE TRUE WATERS OF LIFE

Anyone who has ever spent several weeks eating and drinking their way through France (yes, we have suffered) knows that the threat of the dreaded **crise de foie** (literally, liver crisis; a bilious attack, bad indigestion or just a genteel way of saying a hangover) hangs over you like that sword did Damocles. This is where **eau minérale** (mineral water) comes in. It douses, it flushes and it saves you from the 'crisis'. As they say, 50 million French people can't be wrong – they drink billions of litres each year. The following are the most popular mineral waters in France. Each one has its followers who swear their brand is the only way to go, but in a crisis any one of them will do.

Badoit	France's oldest bottled mineral water with the tiniest of bubbles and medium taste, from the Loire region
Évian	a light, still mineral water from the spa town Évian-les-Bains, the 'pearl of Lake Geneva'
Perrier	the famous, highly carbonated mineral water in a distinctive green bottle from Languedoc
Pierval	flat spring water from Normandy
Parot	medium-tasting sparkling water from the Auvergne
St-Yorré	a salty sparkling mineral water from a town near Vichy in the Massif Central
Thonon	still mineral water from Thonon-les-Bains, the main French town on Lake Geneva
Vals	light sparkling water from Vals-les-Bains in the Auvergne
Vichy Célestins	bitter, slightly saline mineral water from the once fashionable spa town in the Massif Central
Vittel	popular still mineral water from Lorraine sold in vending machines everywhere
Volvic	a very neutral still water from the Auvergne

If you prefer to have tap water with your meal rather than a soft drink or wine, don't be put off if the waiter scowls: law mandates that restaurants serve tap water to clients who so request it. In Paris, raise a smile by asking for **Château Tiberi** (Jean Tiberi is the current mayor of Paris).

Otherwise you can order **eau minérale** (mineral water), which comes **plate** (flat; no bubbles) or **gazeuse** (carbonated), or **eau de source** (spring water), which is usually flat. A **Perrier tranche** (a glass of carbonated Perrier with a slice of lemon) is a popular café drink for teetotallers and/or the plain thirsty.

BADOIT
BADOIT
S.Yorre
S.Yorre
VICHY
VICHY
VICHY
evian

Buying mineral water, Paris

Squashes & Soft Drinks

One popular and inexpensive café drink is **sirop** (fruit syrup or cordial) served mixed with water, soda or with a carbonated mineral water like Perrier. Popular syrup flavours include **cassis** (blackcurrant), **groseille** (red currant), **grenadine** (pomegranate), **menthe** (mint) and **citron** (lemon).

A **citron pressé** is a glass of iced water (either flat or carbonated) with freshly squeezed lemon juice and sugar added to taste – American-style lemonade, in fact. A glass of freshly squeezed orange juice is an **orange pressée**. The glass is only half-filled and is accompanied by sugar and water to sweeten and dilute as you choose. **Limonade** is lemon-lime soda (or British lemonade). A **panachée** or **bière panachée** is a shandy (a mixture of limonade and beer).

SOFT DRINKS

A soft-drinks trolley, Paris

All the international brands of **boissons non alcoolisées** (soft drinks) are available, as well as many overly sweet, fizzy local ones like Orangina, Fruji and Pschitt! The French are not particularly fond of drinking very cold things, though this is changing. If you would like your drink that way, ask for **des glaçons** (some ice cubes).

home cooking & traditions

The French are a very hospitable race – their agricultural wealth and culinary heritage might have disposed them to this – and they entertain at home frequently. If you show an enthusiasm for French food, it won't be long before someone invites you for dinner. This will give you the enviable opportunity to try **cuisine familiale** (home cooking) and a chance to have a long, hard look at a French kitchen.

The word **cuisine** denotes both cooking (**faire la cuisine** in French) and the room – the kitchen – in which it all takes place. It's difficult to generalise about kitchens in France; how each is set up and what it contains will depend on the owner's wealth, age and profession, and whether it's in a city flat or a country manse. Most kitchens will look pretty familiar, but in certain regions you may spot a few unfamiliar items: a traditional **galettière** (half-stove, half-griddle) or an electric **crêperie** for making galettes and crêpes in Brittany; something more unusual like a **tripière**, once an indispensable utensil for many tripe-loving Norman households; or a **raclettière** for melting Raclette cheese in Savoy. Even in big city kitchens you may spot traditional cookware. If the residents are North African, they're bound to own a **couscousier** for steaming couscous or a **tajine** (earthenware pot) used to make the eponymous stew of meat and dried fruits. And what self-respecting Asian family in France today doesn't have an overworked electric rice cooker?

All French kitchens have a few things in common, however. First of all they're always pretty crumby. That's not us making a judgement on their design, cookware or the size of the room at all. Just as Asian kitchens are plagued by rice grains that lodge in any hole or orifice that is open or unplugged, French kitchens are plagued by **miettes** (crumbs), the detritus of the oft-consumed baguettes that seek refuge on any available flat surface.

French kitchens always have cupboard space for kitchen equipment and other utensils, benches or counters for chopping and slicing, a sink, a refrigerator, a stove with an oven (usually gas) and – Dieu du ciel! – a **four à micro-onde** (microwave oven) generally used to warm up prepared dishes.

Generally a hostess or host – chefs have traditionally been men in France and there's no stigma attached to a man cooking here – will have things under control by the time guests arrive. At least one of the three courses served is likely to have been bought outside. It may be **pâté de campagne** (country pâté) for a starter, for example, or more likely a **tarte aux poires** (pear tart), say, for dessert. The French have never been averse to letting experts take care of complicated dishes and have used the services of **traiteurs** (caterers or delicatessens) and **pâtissiers** (pastry cooks) for centuries.

The kitchen table or counter will be laden with items from the market or shop – fresh loaves of bread, vegetables cut in strips to garnish the soup, a bottle of wine already opened. There will be little pots of herbs on the windowsill and a cookery book or two (such as the evergreen *Les Recettes faciles de Françoise Bernard*), which are often used more for inspiration than the recipes themselves. Perhaps there will be some surplus from the orchard or vegetable garden – wonderful **mirabelles** (yellow plums) if in Alsace or the tiniest of **artichauts** (artichokes) if in Provence – or something sent up from their family in the provinces: grand-mère's famous **confiture aux myrtilles** (bilberry jam) or **eau-de-vie de prune** (plum brandy) from Oncle Jacques.

Table set for an outdoor lunch, Périgord

A RABBIT, WINE & AN EMPTY FRIDGE

My father coined the phrase **la cuisine inspirée** (inspired cooking) to justify his empty fridge, which usually contained nothing more than coffee, butter and a carton of milk. He had never been able to shop weekly and finally accepted this as his fate, deciding that he could only cook when he was inspired. He lived spontaneously.

Occasionally this inspiration failed him but then fate would intervene, usually in the form of a dead animal. As rabbit hunting is common in the Fôret d'Orléans, my father would often find himself in possession of someone's surplus bunny. He had never been known to refuse a rabbit and so always figured highly in the list of worthy recipients. With it he would prepare the classic **lapin rôti** (roast rabbit).

On this occasion I arrived home to find him sitting in the kitchen, cigarette in hand, glass of wine on the table in front of him. He was deep in thought. The first thing he said was "I know it's disgusting to smoke in the kitchen. I've been given a rabbit – shall we eat it?". Thankfully his larder was better stocked than the fridge so the ingredients for a marinade were on hand – sage, mustard, sunflower oil, garlic, salt and pepper.

He removed the head and gutted the rabbit, being extra careful with the liver, which he would add to the dish later. He cut the rabbit into a few manageable pieces, prepared the marinade and methodically rubbed it into the meat. Satisfied with a job well done, he delivered the rabbit to the oven, and retired to the next room to watch the news. Moments later he yelped "**merde les légumes**!" (loosely, "oh golly, the vegetables") and sent me out into the rain to track down some carrots and new potatoes while he opened another bottle of wine.

This early in spring new potatoes were still a bit of a luxury; however, I knew of an épicerie that made a point of getting them first. The only problem was that it was 15 minutes' walk away and due to close at any moment. I sprinted, arriving to find the owner, a hunched old man, closing shop. He stared at me while I pummelled on his window and, for a moment, I thought all was lost. Finally he ambled towards me and opened the door. "You're lucky", he said. Gasping, I asked him whether he had any new potatoes. Without a word he disappeared into the back of the shop leaving me waiting awkwardly between rows of mustard and bottled herbs. After 10 minutes I began to wonder if he had forgotten me. I called out to him but was answered by an eerie silence. Approaching the back of the shop I could just make out rummaging noises accompanied by the occasional grunt or gasp. "Monsieur?" I called out. Still no answer but this time I could hear the sound of steps. Finally the little man popped out of somewhere carrying a large box. "You're really very lucky", he said again.

I arrived home soaking wet to find my father relaxing in the kitchen with another cigarette and glass of wine. He looked pleased with himself. In his social circle it was a matter of prestige to acquire a good wine cheaply, to come across bargains that had somehow been overlooked. For him, to buy an expensive wine no matter how good was laziness. Anyone could do it. Obviously this was a good drop because he was deep in analysis of its qualities.

"Try some of this", he said. I was cold, hungry and in no mood to share his wine appreciation. This didn't stop him from telling me he had picked up the wine in a small village near the border of Switzerland. His estimation that it could have been sitting in the shop for years impressed me little. I asked about the rabbit. "It's ruined", he mumbled as if it was my fault. "Dry." I passed him the vegetables with a sigh. He handled the tubers delicately. "They're beautiful this year. How about I sauté them?" Within seconds the sound of chopping filled the room and, by the time I refilled my father's glass with wine, he was standing over the stove. Frying the potatoes with his eyes closed, the aromatic steams soaked his senses. He looked over at me and smiled. "Ah ... la cuisine inspirée."

Olivier Breton

AïL
POMMES DE TERRE

Garlic and potatoes for sale, Normandy

DEFENSE DE FUMER

Utensils

The **batterie de cuisine** (kitchen equipment) and **utensiles** (utensils) you'll encounter here will not be unlike ones you use at home. They'll be all your basic steel, cast iron or copper pots and pans, a collection of **casseroles** (saucepans), **poêles** (frying pans), **poêlons** or **cocottes** (casseroles), **marmites** (pots), **bassines à ragoût** (large stew pots) and so on. The best copper pots are made in Villedieu-les-Poêles in Normandy. A **faitout** (or **fait-tout**) is a multipurpose pot or stew pot. Note that a **casserole** is not a casserole but a saucepan and that a **cassolette**, an earthenware dish used for baking, has nothing to do with **cassoulet**, the classic Langudoc dish of beans and preserved meat that is cooked in a **poêlon en terre cuite** (earthenware casserole).

Pots and pans like **plats à sauter** or **sauteuses** (sauté pans), **braisières** (braising pans), **poissonières** (fish kettles) and **bains-marie** (double boilers) are for those who spend a whole lot more time in the kitchen and prepare more elaborate dishes.

Hand-held utensils might include a **fouet** (whisk), **louche** (ladle), **presse-ail** (garlic press or crusher), **écumoire à friture** (skimmer or slotted spoon) and a collection of **couteaux** (knives), everything from a **couteau à éplucher** (peeling knife) to a scary-looking **couperet** (chopper or cleaver).

People who like to bake will have various **moules** and **plats** (tins) at their disposal, such as a **moule à soufflé** (soufflé pan), **moule à manqué** (deep sponge cake pan) or a **plat à four** (baking dish). A **tourtière ronde** is good for making quiche.

There are two trendy items that seem to have found their home in every kitchen in the land these days. The first is an **essoreuse à salade** (literally, a salad wringer). Put the salad in the covered colander and give the toggle a sharp pull and – voilà – dry lettuce. The second item has revolutionised the French kitchen: a **planche à pain** (bread board) with a difference. Essentially a shallow wooden tray into which a wooden lattice has been fitted, it catches all the crumbs as you slice, which can then be dumped into the waste bin (though we suspect gremlins come out at night and dump the tray on the floor).

A Really Serious Cook (RSC) will have kitted out his or her kitchen with gadgets seldom used but, well, horses for courses, even when it comes to utensils. These items might include a **coupe volaille** (poultry scissors), **turbotière** (turbot poacher), **poissonière à truite** (trout poacher) or a **poêlon escargots** (snail pan).

For the RSC who bakes there are **moules à tarte Tatin** (two-handled tins for flipping over the famous upside-down apple pie) as well as pans that look like they were made for a doll's house for preparing things like **petits fours** (small cakes or pastries). And where would such cooks be without their wide-mouthed **bassine à confiture** (preserving pan)?

Kitchenware for sale at E Dehillerin, Les Halles, Paris

French Fries

One item you are likely to see in a French kitchen is a **friteuse** (deep-fryer) used to make – what else? – **frites**, the famous French French fries

As chip fanciers, we know the secrets to make the perfect frites (and you read them here first). Slice the potatoes uniformly (2cm by 8cm). Put them in a bowl of cold salted water and let them soak for an hour, changing the water once or twice to remove some of the excess starch. Then dry them thoroughly on kitchen towels or a dish cloth.

Heat the oil and put the potatoes in a **grille** (deep-frying basket). When the oil reaches 180°C plunge the basket into the friteuse, which will cause the temperature to drop. After about 10 minutes, when the potatoes start to take on a slightly waxy look and glisten, remove the basket from the oil and let it rest for about five minutes and allow the oil to heat back up. Put the basket back in the deep-fryer and cook till the chips are golden brown (10 minutes).

Try to use a good variety of chipping potatoes – the Ratte du Touquet (or Bintje) from the north is excellent. The oil should be neutral-tasting and be able to reach a high temperature without burning (peanut or groundnut oil is best). The real secret to making award-winning frites, however, is to melt some **graisse de bœuf** (beef dripping) in with the oil.

Rummaging through someone's kitchen drawer – not a nice thing, we know, but very telling – may produce such useful items (gifts, probably) as **couteaux à huîtres** (knives for shucking oysters and clams) and **couteaux à foie gras**, serrated knives with holes in the blade and a two-pronged tip that produce a nice clean slice of foie gras every time – hey, we own a pineapple knife, Hawaii's greatest contribution to mankind after the ukulele.

But our favourite little kitchen item is a **fil à Roquefort**, a wire cutter like they use in **fromageries** (cheese shops) to slice cheese. But this one has a marble base so it's perfect for slicing such temperature-sensitive items as foie gras, mousses, terrines and pâtés, as well as that Roquefort cheese.

Val de Rance

celebrating with food

At the risk of sounding facile, food itself makes French people celebrate and, hey, any excuse for a party. Of course there are birthdays, engagements, weddings and christenings, and these are marked in ways seen throughout the modern industrialised world today. Like everywhere, though, there are special holidays where traditions – however watered down or secularised if religious – still endure.

One tradition that is very much alive is called the **jour des rois** (kings' day) and takes place in early January, marking the feast of the Epiphany. A **galette des rois** (kings' cake), a puff pastry with frangipane cream, a little dried **fève** bean (or plastic or silver figurine) and topped with a gold paper crown is placed on the table. The youngest person in the room goes below the table and calls out who should get each slice. The person who gets the slice with the bean is named king or queen, dons the crown and chooses his or her consort. This tradition is popular not just at home among families but also at offices and parties.

A PONTOISE PARTY

We'd arrived in Paris late and ate an uninspiring meal at a trendy restaurant while gossiping and catching up with our hostess. Having downed more than a few glasses of wine we were rolling by the time we got back to her place to throw ourselves into our pits, but looked forward to a bit of marketing the next day and a quiet Saturday night in.

We were on our third black coffee late the next morning and contemplating our shopping list when the telephone rang. "That was my sister", said our hostess. "I completely forgot. It's her boyfriend's surprise birthday party tonight. We're going to have to go to Pontoise."

Pontoise ... wasn't that deep in the north country? A land of igloos and Eskimos, snowshoes and the Klondike? It sounded a rather harsh place.

The party started off a bit, well, slowly. Picture the scene: a large sitting room with chairs against the walls and two groups – all the men in one corner, all the women in the other. What was this? A church dance in the Australian outback? The party-thrower, sister of our hostess, began to set the dishes out on the buffet tables – charcuterie and cheese, salads and a range of tartes and gâteaux not seen since Marie-Antoinette told us all to eat that cake. The room went still, the two groups eyed one another and slowly moved forward to begin that evergreen communal rite called **bouffer** (gobbling).

And like a groundswell the whispering began among the ranks. "Have you tried the **tomates glacées** (glazed tomatoes)?" asked a woman of her companion. "They're stuffed with green bean puree!" Another was quizzing the baker. "Now where did you get the cherries for the **clafoutis** (custard and cherry tart)? Are they **d'Auxerre** (from Auxerre in Burgundy, famous for its cherries)? So very sweet." Behind us an elderly gentleman regaled a younger one wearing a white coat (apparently the man responsible for the stunning tomates glacées) with tales of days and dishes of times past. "I just adore **les grands vins** ..." he said. We had reached Pontoise for sure, but we had arrived in la belle France.

Procession at the Gypsy Festival, Saintes-Maries-de-la-Mer, Camargue, Provence

At **Chandeleur** (Candlemas, marking the Feast of the Purification of the Virgin Mary) on 2 February, family and friends gather together in their kitchens to make **crêpes de la Chandeleur** (sweet pancakes). **Pâques** (Easter) is marked here as elsewhere with **œufs en chocolat** (chocolate eggs, often filled with candy fish and chickens) and there is always an egg hunt for the kids. The traditional meal at Easter lunch is **agneau** (lamb) or **jambon de Pâques** (Easter ham), which – like hot-cross buns in Britain – seems to be available throughout the year. In Lyon, the Easter treat is

LE NÖEL DE MAMIE

Nothing beats a grandmother's culinary touch, and Christmas provides the pinnacle of my **Mamie's** (grandmother) gastronomic dash. Each year she marshals a team of assorted relatives into her kitchen to cook for our infinitely extending family which, this year, was gathered under one roof for the first time in a decade.

I was met at the door by Jean-Paul, an old family friend, whose sole contribution to the festive tradition was excessive drinking. He led me to the huge loungeroom, already enveloped in a blue-grey fog of cigarette smoke. Two long dining tables were set up on opposite sides of the room in the interests of keeping children and adults apart; a blessing for both parties. Everyone had already helped themselves to an aperitif – home-made kir, whisky or beer from the fridge. As the adults smoked and drank, children ran amok, doors slammed and greetings were hurled at the constant stream of guests entering the room.

My father was already passing out samples of his latest batch of super-strong **poire William** (pear brandy) bottled with a whole pear inside, usually drunk as a digestive. Despite the breach of protocol, a number of enthusiasts were gathered around him wincing at its strength but complimenting nonetheless. The brandy's quality increased in direct proportion to the number of glasses consumed.

Escaping the smoke, I found Mamie and two uncles in the kitchen shucking oysters, the starter for many Christmas meals across France. The clicking of oyster knives accompanied an argument about genetically modified food, the topic of the moment. Mamie rushed to embrace me while my uncles, oblivious to my arrival, dodged each other's knives as they waved their arms expressively in the debate.

From the stove came the comforting smell of our main course, **pintade aux marrons** (guinea fowl with chestnuts). Our family always preferred this bird to turkey, our own tradition. Mamie asked me whether Yves, her youngest and most unpunctual son, had arrived yet. As it was only midday I told her it was unlikely and she cursed him, "**nom de dieu qu'il est chiant celui la**" (God he gives me the shits). She yelled across the lounge

bugnes (lemon-flavoured fritters) dusted with castor sugar, and in Burgundy they mark the day with **jambon de Pâques persillé** (cubed ham in a parsley aspic). On Whit Sunday, people in Marseille tuck into **columbiers** (or **biscuits de la Pentecôte**), special cookies made for this holiday.

After the **dinde aux marrons** (turkey stuffed with chestnuts) eaten at **Noël** (Christmas), a **bûche de Noël** (log of chocolate and cream or ice cream) is served. Our host (of Pontoise fame) still talks nostalgically of the meringue mushrooms topping the log that she and her sister would fight over.

as to his whereabouts and was encouraged, in chorus, to relax as there was no rush. She brushed off their nonchalance and stated that lunch would be served without the recalcitrant son.

After shouts of "bon appétit" everyone began gulping the oysters down, dousing them with a red wine vinaigrette containing finely chopped shallots. Yves – the tardy son – timed his arrival quite well. An alcoholic warmth had already enveloped the room and he entered sheepishly amidst good-natured yells of "alors!" and a glare from Mamie.

I sat next to Jean-Paul who, in a morose, slurred tone, began to tell me how hard life was, using accounts of his own failures as examples. I divided my attention between him and the oysters. The highlight of his life was seeing Brigitte Bardot sunbathing topless many decades ago. It was all downhill from there. He finished his monologue with a plea for me not to turn out an alcoholic like him. In the awkward silence which followed, we both reached for our drinks. He lit a filterless Gitane, the most putrid smelling cigarette ever, and blew the smoke over the last of my oysters.

Suddenly a piercing scream startled the room; a skirmish had broken out at the children's table. Two young sisters had been wrestling over half a baguette. One of them, presumably the loser, sat crying, her face full of crumbs. The winner had broken the baguette over her younger sister's head. The adults stifled their laughter as their mother rushed to the scene.

As soon as the smell of chestnuts and guinea fowl wafted across the room, the two little girls could have strangled each other for all anyone cared. All eyes turned to the food. The dish matched the mood perfectly; special enough to mark an occasion, yet hearty enough to avoid pretension. A true French celebration is one where you simply appreciate the food without analysis. As everyone began to eat, the din settled to a respectful murmur. Even the children calmed down for all of five minutes – the food had cast its spell. Jean-Paul said that no matter how hard things became you could at least rely on what he called **bonne bouffe** (good grub). He looked over at Mamie, yelled his appreciation and, between mouthfuls, began another rambling monologue.

Olivier Breton

A YEAR EN FÊTE

The following is just a sampling of the festivals celebrating food or wine throughout France each year. Check with any tourist office to verify the dates as they can change.

January **Saint Vincent Tournante** (named after the patron saint of vintners) is the largest wine festival in the world. It is held in a different village of Burgundy each year, on the last weekend of the month.

February Menton, the warmest spot on the Côte d'Azur, celebrates its most famous product, the lemon, with the **Fête des Citrons** on Mardi Gras.

March **Salon Internationale l'Agriculture**, France's largest agriculture show, brings raw materials (animals, produce, wines) to Paris.

Concours du Meilleur Boudin is a three-day festival and competition devoted to the noble blood sausage held at Mortagne-au-Perche in Normandy over the last weekend of the month.

Chinon's annual **wine fair** is held on the second weekend of the month (see the boxed text Knights In Chinon in the Drinks Chapter).

April Bayonne in the Basque Country honours its lovely ham with **Foire aux Jambons** (Ham Fair) just before Easter.

May The **Fête de Cuisine** takes place all along Brittany's Côtes d'Armor.

In the last week of May, the town of Saintes-Maries-de-la-mer in Camargue becomes a feast of colour and festivity for the **Gypsy Festival**. Gitans (Gypsies) converge on the village to celebrate the feast of Saint Sara, the patron Saint of the Gypsies. As well as dancing, music and eating, the pilgrims carry statues of Saint Sara, Mary Jacob and Mary Salome through the town and to the sea.

June	The **Fête des Cerises** (Cherry Festival) in early June is the main event of the year in the Basque Country town of Itxassou. The **Fête du Vin** (Wine Festival) takes place in Bordeaux in late June and early July.
July	The **Fête du Thon** (Tuna Festival), held on the first Saturday in July, is a time when sports organisations set up stands and sell tuna dishes around Saint Jean de Luz. In late July, Tours holds the **Foire à l'Ail et au Basilic** (Garlic and Basil Fair).
August	On the third weekend of the month, wine and food products from the Loire region are available at Chinon's **Marché à l'Ancienne**, a re-creation of a 19th-century farmers' market. Colmar in Alsace is at its liveliest during the first 10 days of the month, when the town holds its **Foire Régionale des Vins d'Alsace** (Regional Wine Fair of Alsace). The fair is also a good place to sample local food specialities. Other special events this month include a sardine festival in Concarneau in Brittany on the last Sunday, and a festival feting the **saucisse de Morteau** (Morteau pork sausage) in the Doub village of the same name in the Jura.
September	The **Foire aux Fromages** (Cheese Fair) at La Capelle in Picardy takes place over the first weekend of the month. In the northern town of Licques, a **festival** is held to honour the turkey.
October	This month brings the **Fête des Vendanges** (Harvest Festival) to Carcassonne in Languedoc. Primarily a drinking festival hosted by the Caveau des Vins in the castle district, the festival marks the region's grape harvest. The **Fête du Piment** (Chilli Festival) is held late in the month at Espelette in the Basque Country.
November	The **Foire Internationale Gastonomique**, Dijon's celebrated two-week food fair, is held at the city's Parc des Expositions in the first half of November, allowing visitors the chance to sample cuisines from Burgundy and other parts of France.
December	**Marchés de Noël** (Christmas markets) offering an array of delicacies are particularly popular in the north (at Lille from late November to 31 December) and in Alsace (at Strasbourg in Place Broglie, Place de la Cathédrale and Place de la Gare from early December until New Year's Eve).

At Christmas lunch, families throughout Provence eat **les treize desserts** (the 13 desserts) ranging from orange-flavoured bread and nougats to a variety of fresh and dried fruits that represent Christ and the 12 Apostles. **Fruits confits** (candied or glazed fruit), such as apricots, tangerines, plums, lemons and even melons, are popular gifts at Christmas and New Year in Provence. A traditional Christmas dish in Charente is fresh oysters accompanied by **saucisses au vin blanc**, sausages cooked with white wine.

Produits régionaux

regional
variations

There are many reasons for the amazing variety of regional cuisines in **l'Hexagone** (the Hexagon), as this six-sided nation is often called. Climate and geography have been especially important: the hot south favours olive oil, garlic and tomatoes, while the cooler, pastoral north prefers cream and butter. Coastal areas specialise in mussels, oysters and saltwater fish, while those near lakes and rivers make full use of the freshwater fish available.

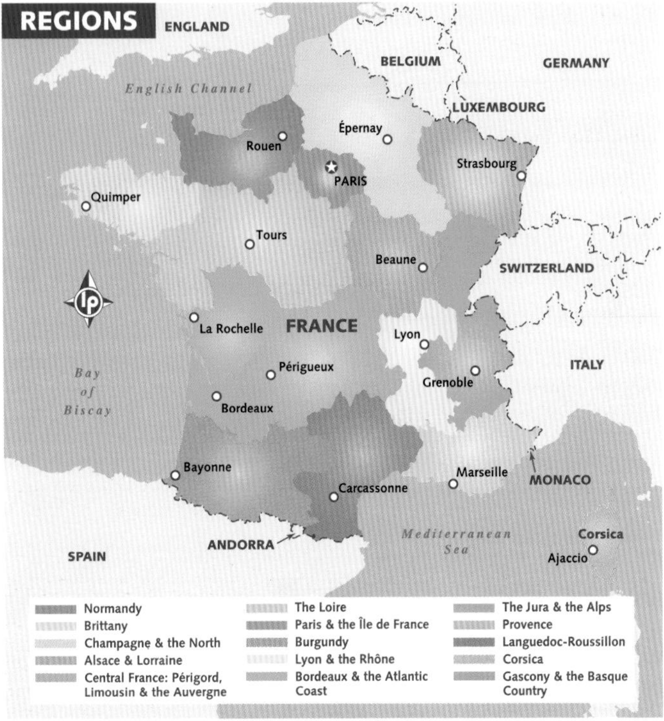
REGIONS
ENGLAND
BELGIUM
GERMANY
English Channel
LUXEMBOURG
Épernay
Rouen
Strasbourg
PARIS
Quimper
Tours
Beaune
SWITZERLAND
La Rochelle
FRANCE
Lyon
Périgueux
ITALY
Bay of Biscay
Grenoble
Bordeaux
Bayonne
Marseille
MONACO
Carcassonne
Mediterranean Sea
Corsica
ANDORRA
SPAIN
Ajaccio
Normandy
Brittany
Champagne & the North
Alsace & Lorraine
Central France: Périgord, Limousin & the Auvergne
The Loire
Paris & the Île de France
Burgundy
Lyon & the Rhône
Bordeaux & the Atlantic Coast
The Jura & the Alps
Provence
Languedoc-Roussillon
Corsica
Gascony & the Basque Country

In France, borders are not firmly drawn and there's much spill over; you'll encounter influences of Gascon cuisine in Provence, and it is sometimes difficult to distinguish Breton food from Loire region cuisine. And, as is the case everywhere, people eat dishes from outside their region – a **choucroute**, say, in a Marseille brasserie – but these dishes will never be as good as they are when they're eaten at home; the ingredients and the preparation just won't be there to give them their authentic tastes.

French cuisine is typified by certain regions, most notably Normandy, Burgundy, Périgord, Lyon and, to a lesser extent, Provence and Alsace. Still others such as the Loire region and Languedoc-Roussillon have made incalculable contributions to what can generically be called French cuisine.

Normandy

Normandy is a large fertile region that stretches along the English Channel from Brittany to Picardy. It is divided into Upper and Lower Normandy by the Seine River. The topography here is one of flat grasslands and **bocages**, farmland sub-divided by hedges and trees, interrupted by gentle hills. The climate is mild but damp, excellent for grazing and for most crops except grapes.

Vikings from Scandinavia first invaded this region in the 9th century. Many of these Norsemen established settlements and ultimately lent their name to the region. They introduced cattle and, through interbreeding, produced the brown and white Norman cow, whose milk and cream has shaped the development of local cuisine even greater than the other two in the Norman culinary 'trinity': apples and seafood.

Each Norman cow produces an average of 5000 litres (1100 gallons) of milk annually, which is why the region supplies roughly half of France's dairy products. Cream is an integral part of many of the region's rich, thick sauces (such as **sauce normande**), and Norman butters are particularly sought-after, especially those from Neufchâtel and Isigny. Among Normandy's cheeses, Camembert reigns supreme (see the boxed text Camembert: Celebrated, Not Royal later in this chapter). But there are a great many others, including heart-shaped **Neufchâtel**, salty **Pont l'Évêque** and strong-smelling **Livarot**.

Omelette de la Mère Poulard

Le Mont-Saint-Michel's celebrated omelette, the world's first, is at its fluffiest when cooked over a woodfire stove.

Ingredients

10	eggs
100g/31/2oz	butter
1 tablespoon	thick cream
	salt and pepper

Separate the eggs whites and yolks into two bowls. Beat the whites until they rise in peaks, then beat the yolks thoroughly. Place the butter on a hot pan. When it begins to bubble, add the egg yolks, pepper and salt to taste. When the eggs begin to set, mix in the thick cream and beaten egg whites. Shake the pan continuously over the fire. Fold the omelette and serve on a warm plate.

Serves 4

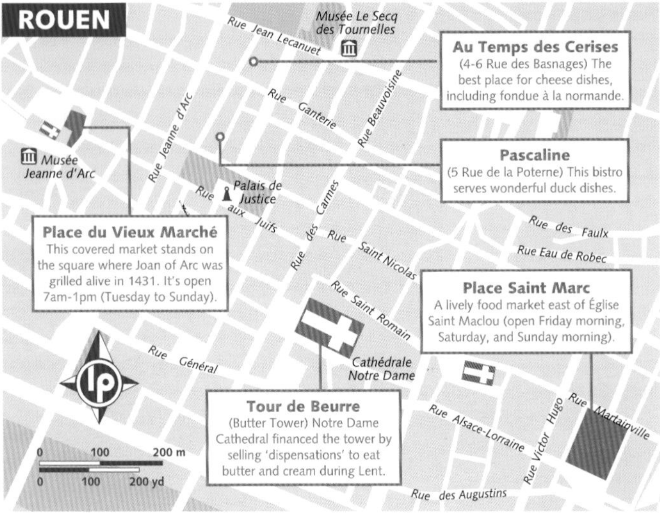
ROUEN
Musée Le Secq des Tournelles
Rue Jean Lecanuet
Au Temps des Cerises
(4-6 Rue des Basnages) The best place for cheese dishes, including fondue à la normande.
Rue Ganterie
Rue Beauvoisine
Rue Jeanne d'Arc
Musée Jeanne d'Arc
Pascaline
(5 Rue de la Poterne) This bistro serves wonderful duck dishes.
Palais de Justice
Rue aux Juifs
Rue des Carmes
Place du Vieux Marché
This covered market stands on the square where Joan of Arc was grilled alive in 1431. It's open 7am-1pm (Tuesday to Sunday).
Rue des Faulx
Rue Eau de Robec
Rue Saint Nicolas
Rue Saint Romain
Place Saint Marc
A lively food market east of Église Saint Maclou (open Friday morning, Saturday, and Sunday morning).
Rue Général
Cathédrale Notre Dame
Tour de Beurre
(Butter Tower) Notre Dame Cathedral financed the tower by selling 'dispensations' to eat butter and cream during Lent.
Rue Alsace-Lorraine
Rue Victor Hugo
Rue Martainville
Rue des Augustins
0 100 200 m
0 100 200 yd

Trouville, Honfleur and Cherbourg are the places to go for seafood; their markets are crammed with lobsters, crayfish, langoustines, prawns, tiny scallops, oysters, mussels and an endless variety of fish. Specialities include **matelote à la normande** (sometimes called **marmite**), a creamy fish **bouillabaisse** and **sole à la normande** (sole with shrimps).

Apples are the third essential of Norman cuisine, and **cidre** (cider) is used extensively in cooking. Of course they drink it too (see Beer & Cider in the Other Drinks chapter). Apples are also the base for the region's signature pastry, **tarte normande**.

Normandy's culinary offerings do not start and end with dairy products, apples and seafood. Pigs, traditionally fed on apples and the cast-offs from dairies, are raised here and charcuteries offering terrines, pâtés, **boudins** (blood sausages), **fromage de tête** (head cheese) and the famous **andouille de Vire** (Vire smoked sausage) abound. Also common are **galantines**, cold dishes of boned, stuffed, pressed meat (especially pork here) that is presented in its own jelly, often with truffles and pistachio nuts. One Norman dish that may not be to everyone's taste is **tripes à la mode de Caen**, tripe combined with ox or calf's trotters, cider or Calvados, carrots, leeks, onions and herbs, and slow-cooked in a clay pot sealed with a paste of flour and water.

Rouen, the gastronomic capital of Normandy, is celebrated for its duck dishes. The ducks are slaughtered by choking in order to retain the blood, which is then used to make the accompanying sauces. A typical duck dish is **canard à la rouennaise** (stuffed duck in red wine), but there are countless others, including duck cooked with cherries.

CAMEMBERT: CELEBRATED, NOT ROYAL

While Roquefort from Languedoc-Roussillon is said to be 'the king of cheeses', Camembert de Normandie (AOC) is arguably the country's most famous and is copied around France and the world. Although a woman named Marie Herel (1781-1855) is credited with inventing Camembert and is honoured with a statue in Vimoutiers, the cheese was made at least as early as the 17th century. Perhaps honour should really go to one Monsieur Ridel, the man who in 1890 invented the round little boxes in which it could be sent around the world.

A good Camembert (there are lots of tasteless, elastic ones around) should be covered in white bloom (or mould) and the centre should be creamy yellow – not runny. However, some people prefer it half-ripened with a white layer in the centre.

DON'T MISS – Normandy

- **Brioches** – both sweet and savoury ones from Gournay, which claims to have invented them
- **Bénédictine** – a potent digestive of saffron, myrrh, cinnamon and some two dozen other herbs and spices made in Fécamp since the 16th century
- **Route du Cidre** – a tour of cider producers in the Pays d'Auge, north of the area around Cambremer
- **Moules à la crème normande** – mussels in cream sauce with a dash of cider
- **Canard à la rouennaise** – duck stuffed with its liver and served with a red wine sauce

Route du Cidre

Brittany

Brittany occupies the westernmost tip of France and is surrounded by the open sea on three sides. Though there are some mountains in the region, low-lying plains and gentle uplands predominate. Brittany's spectacular coastline is washed by the Gulf Stream, a warm ocean current flowing from the Gulf of Mexico. As a result, the region enjoys a very mild, though wet climate, which helps to produce some of the nation's finest spring vegetables. As in Normandy, the grasslands support milch cows (the smaller black-and-white Breton variety) and sheep feed on the salt marshes. The pigs of Brittany produce some of the country's best smoked sausages, especially from Quimperlé. Some of the finest salt in the world is collected from the salt marshes of the Guérande Peninsula (see the boxed text Salt of the Sea in the Staples & Specialities chapter).

In the 5th century, the region's west was settled by descendants of Celts driven from the British Isles by Anglo-Saxon invaders. The Celtic influence seems to have had little or, depending on your viewpoint, a great effect on local food. Many gastronomes say Breton cuisine is mediocre or, worse, non-existent. It's true that little cheese is produced here (Saint Paulin being one of the few exceptions) and its only wine – a Muscadet – disappeared when

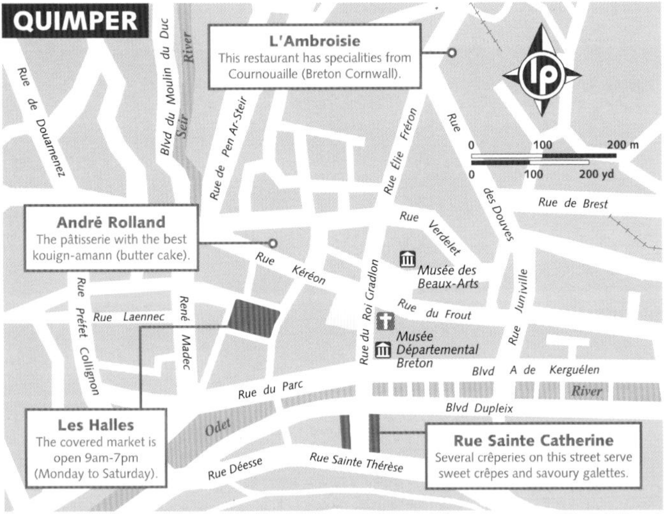
QUIMPER
L'Ambroisie
This restaurant has specialities from Cournouaille (Breton Cornwall).
André Rolland
The pâtisserie with the best kouign-amann (butter cake).
Les Halles
The covered market is open 9am-7pm (Monday to Saturday).
Rue Sainte Catherine
Several crêperies on this street serve sweet crêpes and savoury galettes.
Rue de Douarnenez
Blvd du Moulin du Duc
Seir River
Rue de Pen Ar-Steir
Rue Élie Fréron
Rue des Douves
Rue de Brest
Rue Verdelet
Rue Kéréon
Rue du Roi Gradlon
Musée des Beaux-Arts
Rue du Frout
Musée Départemental Breton
Rue Juniville
Rue Préfet Collignon
Rue Laennec
René Madec
Rue du Parc
Blvd A de Kerguélen
River
Blvd Dupleix
Odet
Rue Déesse
Rue Sainte Thérèse
0
100
200 m
0
100
200 yd

LES JOHNNIES

Before the arrival of large vehicular ferries, Roscoff farmers would load up their small boats with the celebrated pink onions grown locally, sail to Britain, where onions did not grow well, and sell them door to door by bicycle. The lads and young men on bikes, their handlebars loaded down with swaying onion braids, became such a familiar sight in Wales and England that they were affectionately called 'Onion Johnnies'. According to one report written in 1964: "The prices of Roscoff onions are so reasonable, and the accents of the boy salesmen so appealing, that many a South Kensington housewife has the walls of her kitchen festooned with the bulbs".

The tradition apparently began in 1828 when a 20-year-old grower name Henri Ollivier sailed to Plymouth to sell what he'd grown himself and returned several days later not only richer but carrying what to most Bretons, who ate buckwheat, was a luxury: white bread. Others followed his lead, and a century later some 1500 Roscoff Johnnies were crossing the Channel each year between September and March.

Rising at dawn, they spent the day transporting up to 100kg of onions from door to door and ringing doorbells (perhaps a bit too vigorously sometimes, which earned them their second nickname, 'the bell breakers'). The job was not only arduous but dangerous: when a boat called the *Hilda* sank in 1905, 28 Johnnies drowned.

The number of registered Johnnies dropped rapidly in the late 20th century and by the mid 1970s only about 150 remained. Today about 25 still sell their prized onions from door to door, but they're old boys now and times have changed – they go by car. To learn more about Onion Johnnies and their history, visit the Maison des Johnnies museum in the desanctified Chapelle de Sainte Anne in Roscoff.

the area around Nantes was 'moved' into the Loire-Atlantique département, but the gentle climate produces some of the country's best young cauliflower, carrots, artichokes, peas and pink onions.

Brittany is indeed a paradise for lovers of seafood, especially shellfish: oysters from Cancale and the Morbihan Gulf coast; scallops and sea urchins from Saint Brieuc; crabs from Saint Malo; and lobsters from Camaret, Concarneau and Quibéron. But even the most popular method of preparing lobster in local restaurants – **homard à l'armoricaine** (flamed in brandy and simmered in white wine) – isn't Breton at all, despite the allusion to the region's coastal areas called Armor ('Land of the Sea' in Breton). It is in fact a corruption of **homard à l'américaine**, a dish created in Paris in the 19th century by a Languedocien chef who had worked in Chicago.

Without a doubt the **crêpe** (wheat pancake) and **galette** (buckwheat-flour pancake) are the royalty of Breton cuisine. The main difference between the two lies in the composition of their batter. A crêpe is made from wheat flour and is usually sweet; the **crêpe beurre-sucre**, made with butter and sugar, is the classic variety but anything from fruit and jam to liqueurs can be added (see the recipe in the French Banquet chapter). The buckwheat flour used in a galette is a traditional staple of the region, and the fillings are always savoury. A **galette complète** comes with ham, egg and cheese but seafood ones – with crab, lobster, scallops – are also very popular.

Among the sweets you'll encounter here are **gâteau breton**, a rich pound (or Madeira) cake, often made with nuts and dried fruit, and **far breton** (*farz forn* in Breton), a golden flan often made with prunes.

DON'T MISS – Brittany

- **Wholesale fish markets** – especially the one in Concarneau with a guided tour available daily in the early morning
- **Huîtres de Belon** – among Brittany's best oysters
- **Cotriade d'Armor** – fishermen's stew that combines a number of local fish and mussels with onions, potatoes and herbs
- **Kouign-amann** – 'butter cake'; sweet Breton pastry rolled in butter and sugar
- **Musée Départemental Breton** in Quimper – exhibits on the history, furniture, costumes, crafts and archaeology of Brittany
- **Berlingots** – a hard (boiled) sweet from Morbihan
- **Maison des Johnnies** – a museum dedicated to the lives and times of the Onion Johnnies of Roscoffs

Champagne & the North

These two regions make up the country's historical flatlands, including the famous French Flanders, conjuring up poppy-strewn fields that are as flat as the popular **gaufres** (waffles) consumed here. Champagne is of course home to the sparkling wine that is the toast of, well, every toast. The name Champagne comes from the Latin *Campania* (Land of the Plains).

They say that the best cooking is found only in the areas that grow wine grapes, but there are two many exceptions to that rule. Normandy has little or no wine but produces an excellent cuisine. Champagne makes wine – in fact, the most famous wine in the world – but has little to show in the way of special dishes. There is much agricultural wealth here, however.

The north hugs the coast of the English Channel and Boulogne has been an important fishing port for over a millennium. The fields of Picardy provide much of the wheat for France's bakeries, and some of the cheeses – mild in Champagne, sharper or more strong-tasting in the north – are excellent. And if you shouldn't eat food with Champagne or commit the ultimate sacrilege and cook with it – why would you want to dissolve all those expensive bubbles? – there's always the north's beers (see Beer & Cider in the Drinks chapter).

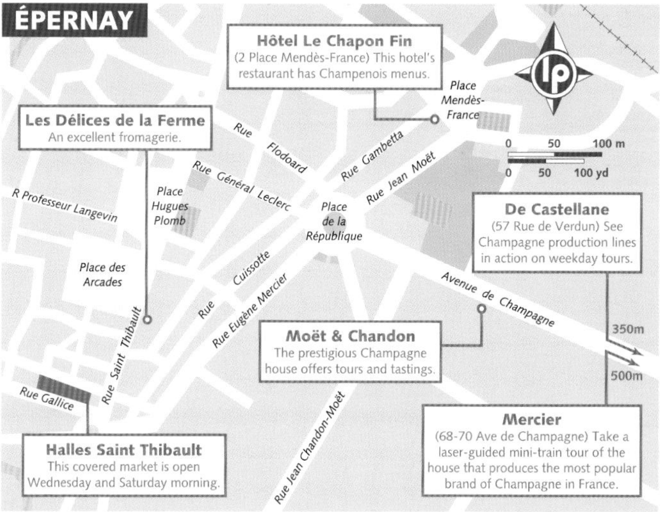
ÉPERNAY
Hôtel Le Chapon Fin
(2 Place Mendès-France) This hotel's restaurant has Champenois menus.
Les Délices de la Ferme
An excellent fromagerie.
De Castellane
(57 Rue de Verdun) See Champagne production lines in action on weekday tours.
Moët & Chandon
The prestigious Champagne house offers tours and tastings.
Mercier
(68-70 Ave de Champagne) Take a laser-guided mini-train tour of the house that produces the most popular brand of Champagne in France.
Halles Saint Thibault
This covered market is open Wednesday and Saturday morning.
Place Mendès-France
Rue Flodoard
Rue Gambetta
Rue Jean Moët
Rue Général Leclerc
R Professeur Langevin
Place Hugues Plomb
Place de la République
Place des Arcades
Rue Cuissotte
Rue Eugène Mercier
Avenue de Champagne
Rue Saint Thibault
Rue Gallice
Rue Jean Chandon-Moët
350m
500m
0 50 100 m
0 50 100 yd

Carbonnade de bœuf, the north's best known dish, is beef braised with onions and beer. **Hochepot**, from where the English 'hodgepodge' is derived, is a thick soup made from all sorts of meat (but especially oxtail) and vegetables that are stirred or shaken while cooking (**hocher** means 'to shake'). **Pot-au-feu** is essentially the same except that the meat isn't browned first.

The choice of fresh fish and shellfish here is extensive, from cod and Dover sole to Boulogne's mussels and Picardy cockles. Much of the fish finds its way into a northern stew of saltwater fish, potatoes and white wine called **chaudrée** (thus 'chowder' in English). A similar dish in Champagne is

Flamiche (Flemish leek pie)

Leeks cooked in a pastry crust is one of the most popular dishes in the north of France.

Ingredients

4	leeks
50g/2oz	butter
200ml/4/5 cup	fresh cream
300g/9oz	puff pastry
1	egg yolk
1	small bunch chives

Wash the leeks, removing the coarse outer layers and much of the green tops, and slice thinly. Warm the butter with one tablespoon of water in a saucepan, stir in the leeks, cover and cook over gentle heat for about five minutes to wilt them. Season with salt and pepper, stir in the fresh cream, and leave to cook for five minutes or so. Drain the leeks, reserving the cooking liquid. Cool and refrigerate.

Preheat the oven to 200°C (400°F). Roll the puff pastry out thinly and, using the loose base of a 25cm pie tin, cut two circles from it. Put one circle onto a baking sheet lined with non-stick baking paper. Beat the egg yolk with two tablespoons of cold water and brush around the rim of this pastry circle. Spread the leeks over the centre leaving a 2-3cm border uncovered. Put the other pastry circle across on top and press the edges together with your fingers. Brush the whole surface thoroughly with the remaining egg.

Allow to sit for 15 minutes, then bake for 20-25 minutes until the pastry is golden brown. In the meantime, transfer the cooking liquid from the leeks to a small pan and cook to reduce to a good, creamy consistency. Snip in the chives and correct the seasoning. Serve warm, cut into wedges at table, with the sauce on the side.

Serves 4 to 6

matelote champenoise. Salted or pickled herrings served with potatoes as a starter has now entered the league of 'generic French dishes' but also look for **hareng saur** (smoked herring) or **hareng bouffi** (salted and smoked herring).

Charcuterie and beer are a very compatible couple, and Lille is a major producer of both. But the damp weather doesn't lend itself to air-drying; instead terrines and pâtés are common; such as **pâté de canard** (duck pâté) from Amiens. The **jambon d'Ardennes** (Ardennes smoked ham) is excellent.

This region is rich in cooler climate vegetables such as cabbage, potatoes, beets, watercress, Belgian endive and leek. **Flamiche** is leek baked in a pastry shell (see recipe). The main fruit crops here are apples, pears and soft fruits, which are made into cider, perry (pear cider) and sweets.

Among Champagne's best cheeses are two AOC cow's milk cheeses: **Chaource**, a mild cheese that smells of mushrooms, and **Langres**, a cheese with a hollow top in which **marc** (grape brandy) is sometimes poured before eating. Favourite cheeses in the north include the pungent **Maroilles** that is washed in beer while ripening, and the Edam-like **Mimolette**.

Pastries and other sweets in the north can be pretty basic, with **pain d'épice** (gingerbread), **gaufres** (waffles eaten with sugar and cream) and a brioche-like concoction with currants called **gâteau battu** or **kokeboterom** heading up the list. In Champagne look out for **biscuits de Reims** (thin macaroons) as well as **massepain** (marzipan). In Langres, along with that fine cheese, you'll fine **nougat de miel** (honey nougat).

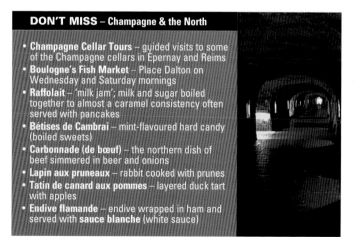

DON'T MISS – Champagne & the North

- **Champagne Cellar Tours** – guided visits to some of the Champagne cellars in Épernay and Reims
- **Boulogne's Fish Market** – Place Dalton on Wednesday and Saturday mornings
- **Raffolait** – 'milk jam'; milk and sugar boiled together to almost a caramel consistency often served with pancakes
- **Bétises de Cambrai** – mint-flavoured hard candy (boiled sweets)
- **Carbonnade (de bœuf)** – the northern dish of beef simmered in beer and onions
- **Lapin aux pruneaux** – rabbit cooked with prunes
- **Tatin de canard aux pommes** – layered duck tart with apples
- **Endive flamande** – endive wrapped in ham and served with **sauce blanche** (white sauce)

Alsace & Lorraine

Alsace and Lorraine have little more in common than that ampersand that joins them together. Though often spoken of as one unit, these two north-eastern regions are linked by little more than an accident of history. Alsace and part of Lorraine were annexed by Germany in 1871, and in the decades before WWI – after which they were returned – they became a focus of French nationalism. Alsace (*Illsass* in Alsatian) is heavily influenced by Germany and German culture; the local language is an early dialect of German akin to Yiddish. Lorraine is about three times the size of Alsace and very French; indeed, the ultimate French icon, Joan of Arc, was born here in 1412.

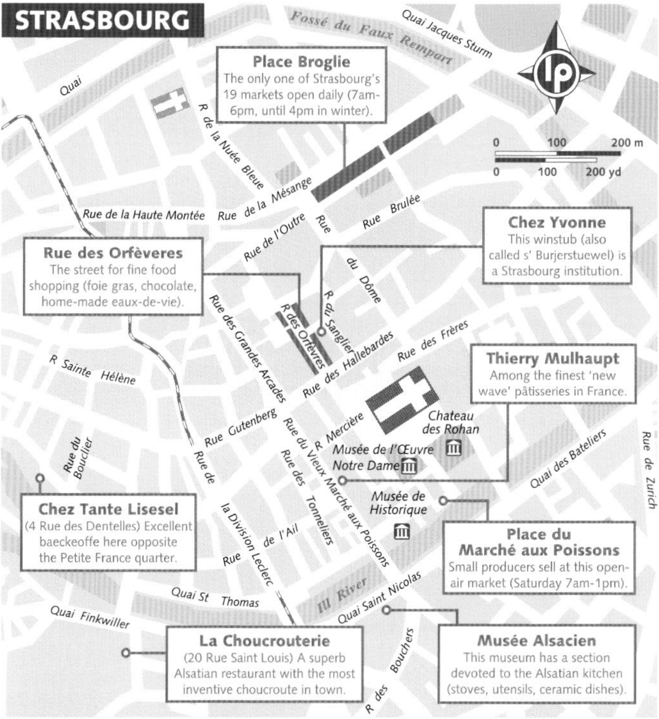
STRASBOURG
Place Broglie
The only one of Strasbourg's 19 markets open daily (7am-6pm, until 4pm in winter).
Chez Yvonne
This winstub (also called s' Burjerstuewel) is a Strasbourg institution.
Rue des Orfèveres
The street for fine food shopping (foie gras, chocolate, home-made eaux-de-vie).
Thierry Mulhaupt
Among the finest 'new wave' pâtisseries in France.
Chez Tante Lisesel
(4 Rue des Dentelles) Excellent baeckeoffe here opposite the Petite France quarter.
Place du Marché aux Poissons
Small producers sell at this open-air market (Saturday 7am-1pm).
La Choucrouterie
(20 Rue Saint Louis) A superb Alsatian restaurant with the most inventive choucroute in town.
Musée Alsacien
This museum has a section devoted to the Alsatian kitchen (stoves, utensils, ceramic dishes).
Fossé du Faux Rempart
Quai Jacques Sturm
Quai
R de la Nuée Bleue
Rue de la Mésange
Rue de la Haute Montée
Rue de l'Outre
Rue du Dôme
Rue Brulée
R du Sanglier
R des Orfèvres
Rue des Grandes Arcades
Rue des Hallebardes
Rue des Frères
R Sainte Hélène
Rue Gutenberg
R Mercière
Chateau des Rohan
Musée de l'Œuvre Notre Dame
Rue du Bouclier
Rue de la Division Leclerc
Rue du Vieux Marché aux Poissons
Rue des Tonneliers
Musée de Historique
Quai des Bateliers
Rue de Zurich
Rue de l'Ail
Quai St Thomas
Quai Finkwiller
Ill River
Quai Saint Nicolas
R des Bouchers
0 100 200 m
0 100 200 yd

Flammenkuche served with five types of wine, Alsace

What the two regions do share are the Vosges, a forested massif that separates the hilly Lorraine plateau from the fertile valleys and plain of Alsace. Winters can be rigorous, especially in Alsace, and summers long and hot, which supports the region's celebrated fruit orchards and vineyards (see Wine in the Drinks chapter).

Nowhere in France is food more 'foreign' than in Alsace, and most of the dishes on offer in **winstubs** (traditional Alsatian wine bars) are not found anywhere else, except in **brasseries**, whose cuisine still reflects that venerable institution's Alsatian origins (see the Where to Eat & Drink chapter).

On the savoury side, you're likely to find **baeckeoffe** (literally, baker's oven), a stew made of several kinds of meat and vegetables that have been marinated for two days. Traditionally it is assembled at home before being cooked in a nearby bakery oven. **Choucroute alsacienne** (or **choucroute garnie**) is pickled cabbage flavoured with juniper berries and served hot with sausages, bacon, pork and/or ham knuckle (see the recipe in the

THE NOBLE PIG

Charcuterie, products prepared from what is known in these parts as **le seigneur cochon** (the noble pig), are among the favourite foods of Alsatians. The first choice for most is the **saucisse de Strasbourg** (also called **knackwurst** or simply **knack**), a thick frankfurter, but the varieties, most of which you'll not find outside the region's border, can appear endless.

Blutwurst	pig's blood sausage made with onions and spices, and eaten hot with stewed apples and mashed potatoes
Cervelas	mild, all-pork sausage flavoured with garlic, boiled and eaten hot with mustard
Hiriwurst	a smoked sausage of pork and beef eaten with vegetables or in soup
Landjaeger	distinctive flat pork and beef sausages eaten on their own or in a potage
Presskopf	head cheese served in a sharp vinaigrette
Schieffala	salted and smoked pork shoulder that is eaten with horseradish, potatoes cooked with small onions and pickled turnips
Schwarzwurst	smoked black sausage sliced thin and eaten cold
Waedele	ham knuckle that is crucial (for some) in a choucroute or served hot with mustard

French Banquet chapter). It is usually accompanied by cold beer or a local wine – Riesling, the king of Alsatian wines, or a chilled Pinot Noir.

Alsatians enjoy savoury pies and tarts in many forms. A **ziewelküche** (or **tarte à l'oignon**) is an onion tart not dissimilar to a quiche, while a **tourte** is a raised pie with ham, bacon or ground pork, eggs and leeks sometimes flavoured with Riesling. But the most popular of this genre is **flammekuche** (**tarte flambée** in French), which you'll see for sale in every bakery in the region. It's a thin layer of pastry topped with cream, onion, bacon and sometimes cheese or mushrooms and cooked in a woodfire oven.

The Alsatian table is heavy with – but not uniquely composed of – meat. The Alsatian version of **matelote** (fish stew) uses river fish like pike, carp and especially eel, often cooked with Riesling. Trout, a local favourite, is often served smoked or poached in broth. The damp fields and the streams of Alsace are a perfect breeding ground for frogs, and **cuisses de grenouille** (frog's legs), which are now mostly imported, are served gratin or within a cream-based soup.

Among Alsace's range of fresh vegetables, the region's white asparagus are highly prized and only available for a couple of weeks in May. An unusual addition to soups here are **jets d'houblon** (hop shoots).

Due to the abundance of fine fruits and nuts in the region, Alsace's pâtisseries are well stocked with scrumptious cakes and pastries. The most ubiquitous is **kugelhopf**, a mildly sweet sultana and almond cake baked in a ring-shaped mould and easily identified by its ribbed shape. **Birewecke** is a rich, moist fruit cake that isn't ready until at least a week after cooking. **Tarte alsacienne** is a custard tart made with local fruits, including the wonderful **quetsches** (sweet purple plums). Fruits are also dried and made into wonderful confitures. Alsace also produces virtually every fruit eau-de-vie (called **schnaps**) imaginable – including one made from holly – but the finest is **framboise**, made from raspberries. Chocolate, introduced by Jewish settlers from Germany and Eastern Europe in the 17th century, is particularly fine in Strasbourg.

The favourite cheese in Alsace is **Munster** (see Cheese in the Staples & Specialities chapter). **Bibbelskas** is a cream cheese served with herbs and horseradish and eaten as a main course.

While of high quality, the dishes of Lorraine pale in comparison to those of Alsace. First and foremost is **quiche**, which can mean just about anything nowadays. But a real **quiche lorraine** is a simple, savoury custard of egg and cream thickly studded with bacon and baked in a pastry shell. Add marinated pork and veal and it becomes a **tourte à la lorraine**. Lorraine is as fond of charcuterie as Alsace is, especially its **boudin** (smooth sausage), and prepared pork of all types is the basis for Lorraine's second signature dish, **potée lorraine**, a soupy stew of pork and vegetables.

Lorraine has a decided sweet tooth. The province is credited with creating such stalwarts as the **madeleine** (small scallop-shaped cake flavoured with lemon) and **baba au rhum** (rum-soaked sponge cake); Bar-le-Duc is famed for its jams and jellies made from currants (traditionally pipped with a goose feather). Some of the best **macarons** (macaroons) in France are made in Nancy, as are the distinctive **bergamotes**, translucent squares flavoured with honey and bergamot pear. Verdun is celebrated for its **dragées** (sugared or Jordan almonds). There's also bonbons made from Vosges pine honey, good for a sore throat.

The orchards of Lorraine also yield the main ingredients for eaux-de-vie; among the best are made from quetsche, **kirsch** (cherry) and the wonderful **mirabelle** (a small yellow plum).

DON'T MISS – Alsace & Lorraine

- **Beignets** – sugared doughnuts filled with jam made from morello cherries, apricots, blackcurrant, raspberry and **églantine**, the fruit of the wild rose
- **Pâté en croûte** – a cocktail snack of pâté encased in pastry; served everywhere but Strasbourg is where it first appeared and it's still the best
- **Spritz** – dry little Alsatian biscuits flavoured with everything from lemon to anis.
- **Route du Vin d'Alsace** – the 170km Alsatian Wine Route that runs along the eastern foothills of the Vosges past colourful villages, hilltop castles and roadside cellars offering crisp white Riesling and spicy Gewürztraminer
- **Macarons de Nancy** – a relatively simple but rich blend of egg whites, sugar and almonds

The Loire

The borders of the region called the Loire are as fluid as its many rivers and tributaries. Some think of it only as the valley of the celebrated Loire River with its magnificent châteaux; others, including political map-makers, stretch it as far as the coast. But the culinary heartland of the Loire, from which most other areas take their cue, is the historical region of the Touraine.

The Loire region is France at its gentlest and most refined, palpable in its harmonious landscapes, languid rivers, elegant architecture and wonderful wines such as Sancerre and Saumur (see Wine in the Drinks chapter). When French people stop thinking of themselves as products of their respective provinces and look for their French common denominator, they end up at

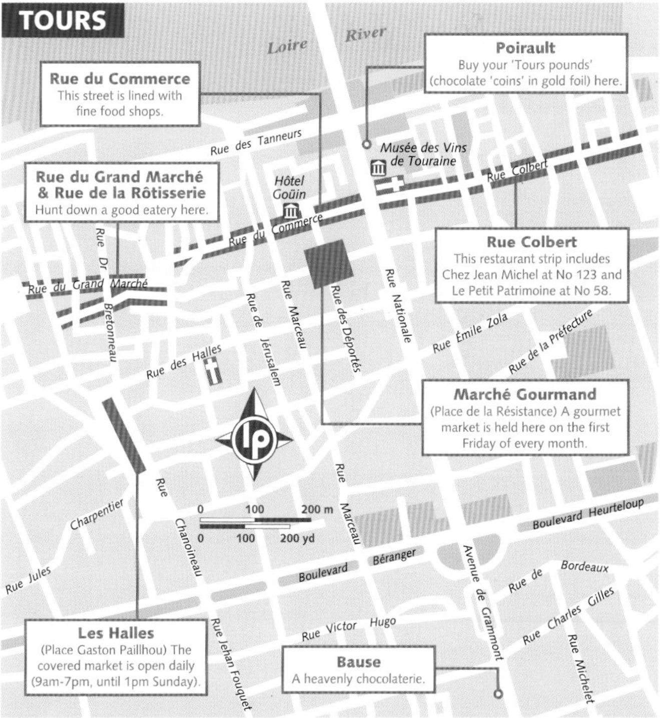
TOURS
Loire River
Rue du Commerce
This street is lined with fine food shops.
Poirault
Buy your 'Tours pounds' (chocolate 'coins' in gold foil) here.
Rue des Tanneurs
Musée des Vins de Touraine
Rue du Grand Marché & Rue de la Rôtisserie
Hunt down a good eatery here.
Hôtel Goüin
Rue Colbert
Rue du Commerce
Rue Colbert
This restaurant strip includes Chez Jean Michel at No 123 and Le Petit Patrimoine at No 58.
Rue Dr Bretonneau
Rue du Grand Marché
Rue de Jérusalem
Rue Marceau
Rue des Déportés
Rue Nationale
Rue Émile Zola
Rue de la Préfecture
Rue des Halles
Marché Gourmand
(Place de la Résistance) A gourmet market is held here on the first Friday of every month.
Rue Marceau
Rue Chanoineau
Rue Charpentier
Rue Jules
0 100 200 m
0 100 200 yd
Boulevard Heurteloup
Boulevard Béranger
Avenue de Grammont
Rue de Bordeaux
Rue Charles Gilles
Rue Victor Hugo
Rue Jehan Fouquet
Rue Michelet
Les Halles
(Place Gaston Paillhou) The covered market is open daily (9am-7pm, until 1pm Sunday).
Bause
A heavenly chocolaterie.

the Loire. This is also where they would arrive should they embark on a search for 'French cuisine'. The region's cuisine should be familiar to many people for it was the cooking refined in the kitchens of the region's châteaux in the 16th century that became the cuisine of France as a whole. This is the birthplace of rillettes, coq au vin and tarte Tatin (see the recipe in the Staples & Specialities chapter) – dishes known to French food aficionados the world over. It is also the place to try them as they should really be prepared.

Take **rillettes**, the shredded potted meat enjoyed throughout France. It has a tendency to be greasy elsewhere but in Tours, where it was first prepared, only the neck of the pig is used and the result is finer. Here you will also find rillettes prepared with duck, goose, rabbit and flavoured with Vouvray, the white wine produced east of Tours. Newfangled preparations include **rillettes de thon** (fresh tuna rillettes) and **rillettes de saumon** (salmon rillettes).

Don't miss the opportunity to try **rillons**, chunks of fatty pork or duck cooked until crisp and crunchy, and sometimes mixed with rillettes or foie gras; **jambon d'Amboise**, an especially fine ham; and **boudin blanc**, a smooth white sausage stuffed with chicken breast.

Freshwater fish abound in the Loire and its tributaries. Pike and shad are often served **au beurre blanc**, a slightly sharp white sauce that goes perfectly with freshwater fish. In spring, smaller fish such as gudgeon and smelt often appear in a fry-up called **friture**, and baby eels are cooked into omelettes.

THE LITTLE BUTTER

France's best known butter biscuit – **le petit beurre**, with its just-asking-to-be-nibbled tooth-combed edge – originates in Nantes. It is the timeless creation of the LU biscuit factory, born out of a cake shop run by Monsieur Lefèvre and Mademoiselle Utile (hence the name).

In 1886 the first petit beurre was baked, and by 1897 LU was baking 15 tonnes of 200 different cookie types per day. The factory's octagonal tower, with its ornate dome and sculpted angel, is a beautiful example of early 20th-century eclecticism. Its twin, which stood on the opposite side of Ave Carnot, was destroyed during WWII. In 1922 a warehouse, topped with two squat towers shaped like biscuit boxes, was built on the corner of Rue Crucy; the original, giant-sized petit beurre on its facade ensures it remains distinguishable today.

Since 1986, when the BSN group took control of LU (manufactured under the General Biscuits name today), the petit beurre has been baked in La Haie-Fouassière, south of Nantes.

Nicola Williams wrote Lonely Planet's The Loire *and* Provence *guides.*

The Loire region has been called the 'garden of France' and quality produce of all types is grown here – the asparagus of Candes and Vineuil; the new potatoes and hazelnuts of the Loiret; the beans from Anjou; **cardons** (an artichoke-like vegetable); and many apple varieties, including the renowned **Reinette d'Orléans** and **Reine des Reinettes**. But the region is particularly known for two things: mushrooms and prunes. **Champignons de Paris** are raised in 'caves' (actually quarries from where stones for the region's châteaux were mined); the 'Paris' extension refers to where these cultivated mushrooms – once considered a luxury – were going, not where they were grown. The **pruneaux de Tours** (prunes dried from luscious Damson plums) compete only with **pruneaux d'Agen** (Agen prunes) in quality. They are often cooked in poultry, pork or veal dishes, or end up as **pruneaux fourrés** (stuffed prunes).

Special cakes and pastries specific to this region include the celebrated **gâteau de pithiviers**, a round puff pastry case filled with frangipane cream. Tours is also proud of its **livres tournois** (Tours pounds), chocolates wrapped in gold foil to resemble what was the city's monetary unit in medieval times.

Much of the cheese produced in the valleys of the Loire region is made from goat's milk, including the log-shaped **Sainte Maure de Touraine** (see Cheese in the Staples & Specialities chapter). Another ash-covered goat's milk cheese is **Valençay**, shaped like a truncated pyramid. Local lore has it that the cheese's form was once a perfect pyramid until Napoleon, who spent the night at the castle of Valençay en route from his disastrous campaign in Egypt, cut off the top with his sword in fury when he saw it.

DON'T MISS – The Loire

- **Musée du Champignon** – the Mushroom Museum at Saint Hilaire Saint Florent near Saumur
- **Champigons farcis de rillettes de Tours** – mushroom caps stuffed with Tours rillettes
- **Rillettes de Tours** – the classic pork version of rillettes
- **Rillons** – chunks of crispy pork or duck
- **Musée du Vin** – the Museum of Wine in Tours
- **Tarte Tatin** – arguably the most famous dessert in France
- **Civet d'anguilles au vin de Loire** – eel stew flavoured with Loire wine
- **Salade tourangelle** – rillons, hazelnuts and Sainte Maure cheese on a bed of salad greens

Paris & the Île de France

When it comes to food, Paris has everything and nothing. As the culinary centre of the most aggressively gastronomic country in the world, it has more generic French, regional and ethnic restaurants, fine food shops and markets than any other place in France. But Parisian cuisine is a poor relation of that extended family known as provincial cuisine. That's because those greedy country cousins have consumed most of what was once on Paris' own plate. Today very few dishes are associated with the capital.

The celebrated American author Ernest Hemingway seemed to like the cuisine of Paris well enough. In *A Moveable Feast* he wrote, "If you are lucky to have lived in Paris as a young man, then wherever you go for the rest of your life, it stays with you, for Paris is a moveable feast". He wasn't necessarily referring to the comestibles of the capital, but he might as well have been. He thoroughly enjoyed (and described in detail) his **fines de claires** (oysters) and crisp Chablis wine at La Closerie des Lilas on the Boulevard du Montparnasse, and his **cervelas** (fat pork sausage) with mustard sauce at the Brasserie Lipp on Boulevard Saint Germain. And the characters in his novel *The Sun Also Rises* always relished the **soupe à l'oignon** (onion soup; see the recipe in the Staples & Specialities chapter) and **pieds de cochons** (pig's trotters) served at the Les Halles market in the wee hours after a night of getting 'tight'.

Paris is encircled by the Île de France, the 12,000 sq km 'Island of France' shaped by five rivers. The Île de France was the seed or kernel from which France the kingdom and republic grew, and has been celebrated for

LA RUELLE DE LA BACTÉRIE

One of Paris's largest areas for ethnic restaurants is squeezed into a labyrinth of narrow streets just across the Seine from Notre Dame. The Greek, North African and Middle Eastern restaurants between Rue Saint Jacques, Blvd Saint Germain and Blvd Saint Michel attract mainly foreign tourists, who are unaware that people refer to these nearby streets as 'bacteria alley'. To add insult to injury, many of the poor souls who eat here are under the impression that this little maze is the famous Latin Quarter. You'll be better off avoiding these establishments that ripen their meat and seafood in the front window and look elsewhere for ethnic food: Blvd de Belleville in the 20th arrondissement for Middle Eastern; nearby Rue de Belleville in the 19th for Thai and Vietnamese; and Chinatown in the 13th for Chinese, especially Ave de Choisy, Ave d'Ivry and Rue Baudricourt.

Crabs for sale at Rue Mouffetard market, Paris

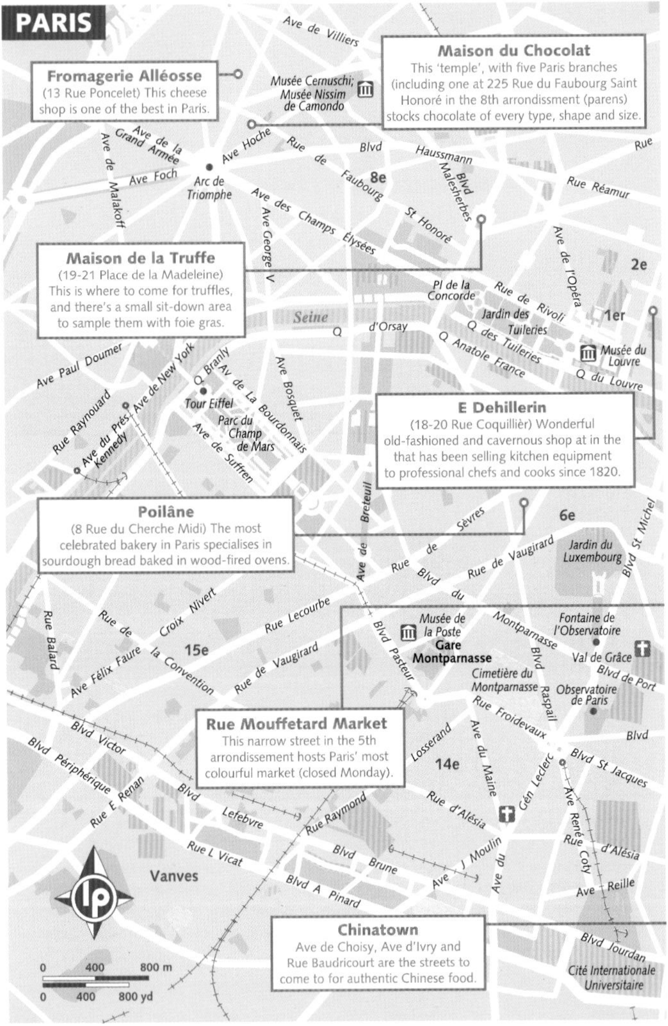
PARIS
Fromagerie Alléosse
(13 Rue Poncelet) This cheese shop is one of the best in Paris.
Maison du Chocolat
This 'temple', with five Paris branches (including one at 225 Rue du Faubourg Saint Honoré in the 8th arrondissment (parens) stocks chocolate of every type, shape and size.
Maison de la Truffe
(19-21 Place de la Madeleine) This is where to come for truffles, and there's a small sit-down area to sample them with foie gras.
E Dehillerin
(18-20 Rue Coquillièr) Wonderful old-fashioned and cavernous shop at in the that has been selling kitchen equipment to professional chefs and cooks since 1820.
Poilâne
(8 Rue du Cherche Midi) The most celebrated bakery in Paris specialises in sourdough bread baked in wood-fired ovens.
Rue Mouffetard Market
This narrow street in the 5th arrondissement hosts Paris' most colourful market (closed Monday).
Chinatown
Ave de Choisy, Ave d'Ivry and Rue Baudricourt are the streets to come to for authentic Chinese food.
Ave de Villiers
Musée Cernuschi; Musée Nissim de Camondo
Ave de la Grand Armée
Ave de Malakoff
Ave Foch
Arc de Triomphe
Ave Hoche
Rue de Faubourg St Honoré
Blvd Haussmann
Blvd Malesherbes
8e
Rue Réamur
Rue
Ave des Champs Elysées
Ave George V
Ave de l'Opéra
2e
Pl de la Concorde
Rue de Rivoli
Jardin des Tuileries
1er
Seine
Q d'Orsay
Q des Tuileries
Q Anatole France
Musée du Louvre
Q du Louvre
Ave Paul Doumer
Ave de New York
Q Branly
Av de La Bourdonnais
Ave Bosquet
Tour Eiffel
Parc du Champ de Mars
Ave de Suffren
Rue Raynouard
Ave du Prés Kennedy
Ave de Breteuil
Rue de Sèvres
6e
Blvd du Montparnasse
Rue de Vaugirard
Jardin du Luxembourg
Blvd St Michel
Rue Balard
Rue de la Convention
Croix Nivert
Rue Lecourbe
15e
Ave Félix Faure
Rue de Vaugirard
Blvd Pasteur
Musée de la Poste
Gare Montparnasse
Fontaine de l'Observatoire
Val de Grâce
Blvd de Port
Blvd Raspail
Cimetière du Montparnasse
Observatoire de Paris
Rue Froidevaux
Blvd
Blvd Victor
Blvd Périphérique
Losserand
14e
Ave du Maine
Gén Leclerc
Blvd St Jacques
Rue E Renan
Blvd Lefebvre
Rue Raymond
Rue d'Alésia
Ave René Coty
Rue d'Alésia
Rue L Vicat
Blvd Brune
Ave J Moulin
Ave du
Vanves
Blvd A Pinard
Ave Reille
Blvd Jourdan
Cité Internationale Universitaire
0 400 800 m
0 400 800 yd

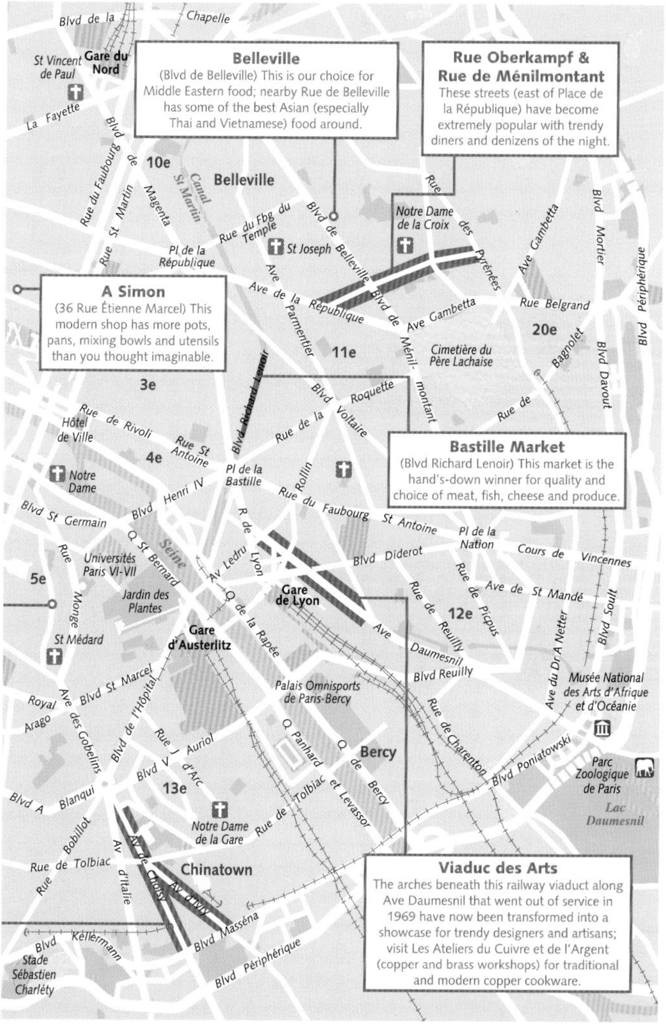
Belleville
(Blvd de Belleville) This is our choice for Middle Eastern food; nearby Rue de Belleville has some of the best Asian (especially Thai and Vietnamese) food around.
Rue Oberkampf & Rue de Ménilmontant
These streets (east of Place de la République) have become extremely popular with trendy diners and denizens of the night.
A Simon
(36 Rue Étienne Marcel) This modern shop has more pots, pans, mixing bowls and utensils than you thought imaginable.
Bastille Market
(Blvd Richard Lenoir) This market is the hand's-down winner for quality and choice of meat, fish, cheese and produce.
Viaduc des Arts
The arches beneath this railway viaduct along Ave Daumesnil that went out of service in 1969 have now been transformed into a showcase for trendy designers and artisans; visit Les Ateliers du Cuivre et de l'Argent (copper and brass workshops) for traditional and modern copper cookware.
Blvd de la Chapelle
St Vincent de Paul
Gare du Nord
La Fayette
Rue du Faubourg St Martin
Blvd de Magenta
10e
Canal St Martin
Belleville
Rue du Fbg du Temple
Blvd de Belleville
Pl de la République
St Joseph
Notre Dame de la Croix
Rue des Pyrénées
Ave Gambetta
Blvd Mortier
Blvd Périphérique
Ave de la République
Ave Parmentier
Blvd de Ménil-montant
Rue Belgrand
20e
11e
Cimetière du Père Lachaise
Rue de Bagnolet
Blvd Davout
Blvd Richard Lenoir
3e
Rue de la Roquette
Blvd Voltaire
Rue de Rivoli
Hôtel de Ville
Rue St Antoine
4e
Notre Dame
Pl de la Bastille
Rollin
Blvd Henri IV
Rue du Faubourg St Antoine
Blvd St Germain
Pl de la Nation
Cours de Vincennes
Seine
Q St Bernard
R de Lyon
Blvd Diderot
Universités Paris VI-VII
Rue Monge
5e
Av Ledru
Jardin des Plantes
Gare de Lyon
Rue de Reuilly
Rue de Picpus
Ave de St Mandé
12e
Ave du Dr A Netter
Blvd Soult
Q de la Rapée
Gare d'Austerlitz
St Médard
Ave Daumesnil
Blvd Reuilly
Musée National des Arts d'Afrique et d'Océanie
Palais Omnisports de Paris-Bercy
Blvd St Marcel
Royal
Arago
Ave des Gobelins
Blvd de l'Hôpital
Rue de Charenton
Blvd Poniatowski
Rue J d'Arc
Blvd V Auriol
Q Panhard et Levassor
Bercy
Q de Bercy
Parc Zoologique de Paris
Lac Daumesnil
13e
Blvd A Blanqui
Rue Bobillot
Notre Dame de la Gare
Rue de Tolbiac
Av de Choisy
Av d'Italie
Chinatown
Av d'Ivry
Blvd Kellermann
Blvd Masséna
Stade Sébastien Charléty
Blvd Périphérique

REGIONAL VARIATIONS

its food for centuries. The market gardeners of the Île de France traditionally supplied Paris with fresh produce. Today, while the region has become more urbanised, the green and gentle 'island' has clung to many of the products it knows best. A list of fruits and vegetables reads like a map of Paris' suburban transport network: Argenteuil asparagus, Crécy carrots, Montmorency cherries, Palaiseau strawberries, Provins rose petals (used to make jam), Montlhéry tomatoes, **champignons de Paris** ('Paris' mushrooms grown for – not in – the capital) and so on.

Dishes associated with Paris and the Île de France are few: **vol-au-vent** (literally, flight in the wind; a light pastry shell filled with chicken or fish in a creamy sauce); **potage Saint-Germain** (a thick green pea soup); **gâteau paris-brest** (a ring-shaped cake filled with butter cream and topped with flaked almonds and icing sugar); and the humble onion soup and pig's trotters relished by Hemingway's Lady Brett Ashley and Jakes Barnes. Deep-frying potatoes and other dishes has always been a speciality here as well (see the boxed text French Fries in the Home Cooking & Traditions chapter). A dish served **à la parisienne** is a combination of vegetables along with potato balls that have been sauteed in butter, glazed in meat drippings and sprinkled with parsley.

At the same time, a lot of dishes have been created here that seem to have flown the coop and settled elsewhere. Brittany's **homard à l'américaine**, lobster chunks simmered in white wine and tomatoes, was created in Paris. **Sole normande**, a dish of sole caught off the Norman coast cooked with shrimps in a white cream sauce, was first made in the Île de France. Even **crêpes Suzette**, those thin pancakes served with liberal doses of orange-flavoured brandy and usually associated with Brittany, were first served in Paris with Grand Marnier made at Neauphle-le-Château.

Like the Indian curry and Turkish kebabs of London, ethnic food has become as Parisian as onion soup; the **nems** (spring rolls) of Vietnam and China, the couscous dishes of North Africa, the **boudin antillais** (West Indian blood pudding) from the Caribbean and the **yassa** (meat or fish grilled in onion and lemon sauce) of Senegal are eaten with enthusiasm throughout the capital. Ethnic food is what Paris does better than any other city in France.

The Île de France excels at cheesemaking. First and foremost, this is the birthplace of the celebrated **Brie**, the soft, wheel-like cheese made in the region of the same name. Among the best are the refined **Brie de Meaux** and the saltier, earthier **Brie de Melun**. The town of Coulommiers gives its name to a smaller type of Brie sold nestling on a bed of straw, and **Feuille de Dreux**, a slightly fruity cheese from the town of Dreux, ripens under chestnut **feuilles** (leaves) to prevent the cheeses from sticking together.

DON'T MISS – Paris & the Île de France

- **Rue Mouffetard Market** – the narrow street in the 5th arrondissement hosts Paris' most colourful market
- **Maison de Truffe** – (19-21 Place de la Madeleine in the 8th arrondissement) the place for truffles
- **E Dehillerin** – (18-20 Rue Coquillière in the 1st arrondissement) a cavernous shop that has been selling kitchen equipment to professional chefs and cooks since 1820
- **Chinatown** – (Ave de Choisy, Ave d'Ivry and Rue Baudricourt in the 13th arrondissement) the streets to come to for authentic Chinese food
- **Belleville** – (Blvd de Belleville in the 20th arrondissement) our choice for Middle Eastern food; nearby Rue de Belleville in the 19th has some of the best Asian (especially Thai and Vietnamese) food in Europe
- **Bastille Market** – (Blvd Richard Lenoir in the 11th arrondissement) this is the winning market for quality and choice of meat, chacuterie, fish, cheese, fruit and vegetables
- **Rue Oberkampf & Ménilmontant** – the area in the northern part of the 11th arrondissement has become extremely popular with trendy diners and denizens of the night
- **Maison de Chocolat** – the temple of chocolate, with five Paris branches (including one at 225 Rue du Faubourg Saint Honoré) stocks chocolate of every type, shape and size
- **Poilâne** – the celebrated bakery at 8 Rue du Cherche Midi in the 6th arrondissement specialises in sourdough bread baked in woodfire ovens

10F
10 FRS
10F 10F 10
PARIS
PARIS
PARIS

Burgundy

Burgundy is a region of contrasts. The gentle rolling countryside around Chablis in the northwest gives way to the forested slopes of Morvan and the cattle country around Charolles. To the east, on the banks of the Saône River and its tributaries, are Burgundy's celebrated vineyards, producing arguably the best unblended wines in the world. Travelling through these towns and villages is like reading a wine list: Gevrey-Chambertin, Nuits-Saint-Georges, Beaune – many will be old friends or at least acquaintances.

When the Burgundians arrived from their homeland on the shores of the Baltic Sea in the 5th century, they found a land planted with vines, grain crops and mustard. This agricultural legacy of the Romans would in time determine what and how Burgundy would eat, and the region's pre-eminent position on the trade route between the Mediterranean and northern Europe would bring prosperity. Indeed, by the 14th century, what had become the

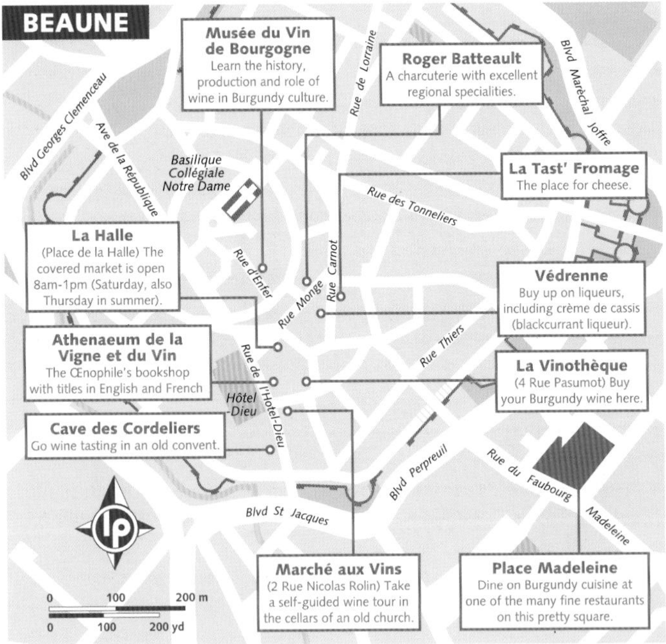
BEAUNE
Musée du Vin de Bourgogne
Learn the history, production and role of wine in Burgundy culture.
Roger Batteault
A charcuterie with excellent regional specialities.
La Tast' Fromage
The place for cheese.
La Halle
(Place de la Halle) The covered market is open 8am-1pm (Saturday, also Thursday in summer).
Védrenne
Buy up on liqueurs, including crème de cassis (blackcurrant liqueur).
Athenaeum de la Vigne et du Vin
The Œnophile's bookshop with titles in English and French
La Vinothèque
(4 Rue Pasumot) Buy your Burgundy wine here.
Cave des Cordeliers
Go wine tasting in an old convent.
Marché aux Vins
(2 Rue Nicolas Rolin) Take a self-guided wine tour in the cellars of an old church.
Place Madeleine
Dine on Burgundy cuisine at one of the many fine restaurants on this pretty square.
Blvd Georges Clemenceau
Ave de la République
Basilique Collégiale Notre Dame
Rue de Lorraine
Blvd Maréchal Joffre
Rue des Tonneliers
Rue d'Enfer
Rue Monge
Rue Carnot
Rue Thiers
Rue de l'Hotel-Dieu
Hôtel-Dieu
Blvd Perpreuil
Rue du Faubourg Madeleine
Blvd St Jacques
0 100 200 m
0 100 200 yd

Dukedom of Burgundy was richer and more powerful than the Kingdom of France itself. Burgundy's cooking can be described as cuisine bourgeoise at its finest – solid, substantial and served in generous portions. Given what the Romans left behind them, it's not surprising that the 'trinity' of the kitchen here is beef, wine and mustard.

The region's best known dish, **bœuf à la bourguignonne** (what the rest of France and the world calls **bœuf bourguignon**) is beef marinated and cooked in young red wine with mushrooms, onions, carrots and bacon. Any dish described as **à la bourguignonne** will be prepared with a similar sauce, which is called **meurette**.

DIJON CUTS THE MUSTARD

Dijon vous appelle gourmets	Dijon calls all you gourmets
Pour ce régal que nul ne tarde	Let no one tarry for this treat
De vour l'offrir, on nous permet:	It's now allowed to offer you:
Cassis, pain d'épice et moutarde!	Blackcurrants, gingerbread and mustard!

A traditional poem

Mustard, by far France's most popular condiment with 50,000 tonnes consumed annually, was introduced by the Romans, who used the seeds to flavour and preserve food and are said to have scattered them while tramping along the spice route from the south. Dijon and mustard have been an inseparable couple since at least the 13th century but, oddly, this is one famous French product that does not have an AOC – producers from Marseille to Lille can call their mustard 'Dijon' as long as it meets some very basic manufacturing rules.

Mustard is a condiment made from the seeds of a family of plants called Cruciferae. There are some 40 different species of this herb, but French manufacturers use brown or black mustard or a combination of the two. The mustard seeds are cleaned, soaked in must (unfermented grape juice; from which the word 'mustard' is derived), ground into flour, sifted and mixed with vinegar, water and sometimes wine and other flavourings before being bottled.

Mustard flour is virtually tasteless; it requires the addition of liquid to release the oils that give it its bite. The degree to which it is ground, the ratio of flour to liquid and the addition of other solids determines the strength, which can range from **douce** (mild) to **forte** (fiery). Mustard also comes in a variety of colours – from yellow and brown to green (such as **moutarde à l'estragon**) or even violet (such as **moutarde au cassis** which is mixed with blackcurrant). One of the most popular (and mildest) varieties is **moutarde en grains à l'ancienne**, made with coarsely ground and whole seeds.

Coq au vin (chicken stewed in wine with mushrooms, bacon, onion, herbs and garlic) is best made with fresh young wine from the Côtes de Nuit. Quite a few other Burgundian dishes are prepared with cream-based sauces, especially veal and ham ones, though **andouillette de Mâcon** (a small pork sausage) is served grilled with a mustard sauce as is **lapin rôti** (roast rabbit).

Charcuterie and ham – both raw and air-dried from the free-range pigs of Morvan – are of excellent quality. Burgundian pâtés and terrines are often flavoured with herbs and marc and bound with caul fat before being cooked.

As typical of Burgundy bœuf à la bourguignonne are those gastronomic gastropods, **escargots** (snails). But the snail here is not the **petit gris** (Helix aspersa), the 'little grey' eaten throughout France, but the large **escargot de Bourgogone** (Helix pomatia) raised on grape leaves and the tastiest available.

The region's most famous condiment is mustard (see the boxed text Dijon Cuts the Mustard earlier in this chapter). The Burgundian capital, synonymous with mustard for centuries, is the centre though it is also made elsewhere in Burgundy, including Beaune, and even in other parts of France such as Meaux in the Île de France.

Burgundy boasts an enviable choice of quality produce, including Auxonne asparagus and Auxerre cherries. Perhaps nothing is more typical of

Bœuf à la bourguignonne

This is the classic dish of Burgundy.

1½kg/3lb	braising or top round beef	60ml/¼ cup	hot water
	salt and pepper	50g/2oz	butter
500ml/2 cups	red Burgundy wine	3 tablespoons	flour
250g/8oz	bacon or salt pork	2	carrots
12	tiny onions	300g/9oz	mushrooms
	garlic		

Cut the beef into small chunks and brown it quickly in a small amount of bacon fat. Pour off the excess fat and replace it with the hot water. Salt lightly, pepper, cover tightly and let it simmer. Prepare the sauce by melting the butter, adding the flour and stirring constantly until golden yellow. Then add the wine, a little at a time, and let stand on a low flame for 45 minutes. Pour the sauce over the beef and simmer gently for 3½ hours. Cut the salt pork in little cubes, brown it in butter, add the onions, carrots and garlic, and let simmer for 1½ hours. Add to the meat one hour before serving and add the mushrooms in the last 10 minutes.

Serves 6

Burgundy than **cassis** (blackcurrants), which were grown instead of grapes after the disastrous *phylloxera* epidemic in the 19th century. Blackcurrants are used in jams, pastries and **crème de cassis** (blackcurrant liqueur).

Among the sweets with the strongest Burgundian brand is **pain d'épices** (gingerbread), brought to Burgundy from the Holy Land by the Crusaders, and which traditionally takes up to eight weeks to prepare. It comes in many forms, including **nature** (plain), **aux fruits glacées** (with pieces of candied fruit) and **aux amandes** (with almonds). For the fancier varieties, look for the name Mulot & Petitjean. **Nonnettes** (little nuns) are spiced buns that taste similar to gingerbread. On the other hand (or end, as the case may be), the imaginatively named **pets de nonne** (nun's farts) are very light, deep-fried fritters often served hot with sugar or fruit coulis. **Rochers de Morvan** are bizarre marzipan concoctions in the shape and colours of little stones. The oldest confectionery still manufactured in France is **Anis de l'Abbaye de Flavigny**, little oval bonbons with an aniseed centre produced in the village of Flavigny-sur-Ozerain northwest of Dijon since the 13th century.

Burgundy's best known cheese is **Époisses de Bourgogne**, a strong-smelling, fine-textured cheese washed in marc during ripening. Other favourites are: **Aisy Cendré**, a soft cheese (often Époisses) buried in ash for up to a month and good with a light red wine; **Abbaye de Cîteaux**, a mild, semi-hard cheese made by the Cistercians that goes well with Beaujolais; and **Clacbitou**, an oblong-shaped goat's milk cheese from the Charolles. Try it with Burgundy's Aligoté white wine.

DON'T MISS – Burgundy

- **Escargots bourguignons** – classic Burgundy snails baked with garlic butter
- **Anis de l'Abbaye de Flavigny** – tiny round bonbons with an aniseed centre
- **Route du Vin de Bourgogne** – the wine route through villages and towns from Dijon to Mâcon
- **Musée du Vin de Bourgogne** – Beaune's Museum of Burgundy Wines
- **Œufs en meurette** – eggs poached in a red wine sauce
- **Joue de bœuf bourguignonne** – beef cheek in red wine sauce
- **Potée bourguignonne** – hearty vegetable and meat stew, often made with ox tail

Lyon & the Rhône

Many people consider Lyon to be France's gastronomic temple, beating even Paris in terms of quality. They chant the litany of this temple's hallowed chefs and restaurateurs as evidence – names like Paul Bocuse, Alain Chapel, Roger Roucou, Jean-Paul Lacombe. Detractors, on the other hand, argue that Lyon has always treated top-class diners with grace and style, leaving the rest to fend for themselves. A decent *affordable* meal in Lyon is an elusive thing, they claim. Of course, if these folk had a taste for what Americans used to call 'variety meats', they'd be in hog heaven itself (see the boxed text).

Lying at the crossroads of some of France's richest agricultural areas, Lyon has always enjoyed an unequalled supply of quality foodstuffs. Anyone in doubt need only visit La Halle de Lyon, a stone's throw from the city's main train station; it is one of the best stocked food markets in France.

OFFAL TIME IN A LYON BOUCHON

There are those who can't live without their organs and those who can't live with them. We're non-committal at the top, enjoying the occasional dish of brains prepared in a browned butter or perhaps even veal sweetbreads on a dare. We have nice things to say about tongue (but only beef or ox tongue, braised or pickled) and will take a detour south for liver, especially if the creature honked or quacked. But all those other bits – the lungs, heart, kidneys and trotters? They don't have a leg to stand on, as far as we're concerned.

But it was a cold winter's night in Lyon, we were on a quest and friends we were visiting knew where they were going – to Chez Hugon, a popular **bouchon** on pedestrian Rue Pizay. A gourmand's got to do what a gourmand's got to do.

In the world of Lyonnais gastronomy, a bouchon is a small, friendly, unpretentious restaurant that serves traditional Lyonnais cuisine. Elsewhere in France the word conjures up more prosaic associations like 'bottle stopper', 'cork' or even 'traffic jam', but these have no connection. **Bouchon** is Old French for 'bush' and refers to the practice of hanging out branches in front of taverns in the Middle Ages.

We were welcomed by the owner, Madame Hugon – even in the very masculine world of French cuisine, it has always been women who have run these traditional-style restaurants – who may or may not have been impressed by our ordering a **pot** (a 46cL glass bottle in which wine is always served in a bouchon). It's a queer-looking thing really, with a solid, 3cm-thick glass bottom and an elastic band round its neck to prevent wine drips when pouring – which made us feel a bit like children. Could we have a couple of bibs, please? And mind your manners; in a

The most typical local charcuteries here are **saucisson de Lyon**, which confusingly can be both an air-dried sausage eaten as is and a boiling one for Lyon's trademark dish, **saucissons aux pommes** (sausages with potatoes). The local **boudin blanc** (veal sausage) is usually excellent, and **andouillettes** (smoked sausages), often made with veal in these parts, will tempt those who don't have an affinity for pork intestines.

Quenelles are poached dumplings made of pike or poultry that can be light and savoury or, if badly prepared, dense and glutinous. They are usually served with a **sauce Nantua**, a creamy crayfish sauce. Keep an eye out for **mousse de pigeon**, an exceptionally light pigeon terrine. Other specialities include **grillades de bœuf à la moëlle** (grilled steak with bone marrow) and **poularde demi-deuil** (literally, chicken in half-mourning; a fattened chicken with truffles).

bouchon you do *not* cross your knife and fork across the plate when you've finished a course as is usual in France. You keep your cutlery for the duration of the meal, wiping them clean with a piece of bread.

So under the watchful gaze of Madame Hugon, we studied the menu: **rosette de Lyon**, a large pork slicing sausage whose name may come from its pinkish colour or for the puckered sphincter appearing at the tied end; **tête roulée** (literally, rolled head), a kind of head cheese; **tablier de sapeur** (literally, fireman's apron), a beef tripe cut into pieces, breaded, grilled and served with mayonnaise or garlic butter; **sabodet**, a boiling sausage made from pig's head and shaped like a clog; and **lard tiède**, the fat of back bacon with little or no lean served warm.

One of our friends seemed somewhat disappointed with the fare on offer that evening. "Perhaps we should have gone to a **resto-boucherie**", he said. A resto-boucherie is just what it sounds like – a restaurant in the back of a butcher shop which is, needless to say, heavily carnivorous. We'd passed one earlier that afternoon. Through the window and across the butcher blocks speckled with blood we could see the tables set for the next day's meaty lunchtime.

But Chez Hugon did offer 'lighter fare' and the less initiated among us chose the path of least resistance: **gâteau de foie de volaille aux quenelles sauce Nantua** (chicken liver cake served in – not with or beside – pike dumplings in a tangerine-coloured fishy sauce) and **saucissons de Lyon aux lentilles** (sausages served with lentils). Here lentils are known as **caviare de Croix Rousse**, the 'caviar' of the neighbourhood once inhabited by silk workers and now the hippest part of Lyon.

Did we want dessert? Madame Hugon wanted to know. There was chocolate cake and prunes with fresh cream, and of course more pots. Pot-heads all, we chose the last.

Of the city's pastries and confectioneries, the best known are **bugnes** (lemon-flavoured fritters) traditionally eaten around Easter. The **marrons glacés** (candied chestnuts) from Ardèche, the manufacture of which many of Lyon's silk workers turned to when the industry floundered in the late 19th century, are superb; look for the Faugier or Sabotin brands. With Valhrona being made at Tain-l'Hermitage just downriver, it's no surprise that Lyon's proudest boast is its chocolates, particularly those made by the firm Bernachon (see Confectionery in the Staples & Specialities chapter). We like the **coussins de Lyon** (literally, Lyon cushions), thumb-sized pieces of chocolate cream flavoured with Curaçao and encased in luridly coloured marzipan.

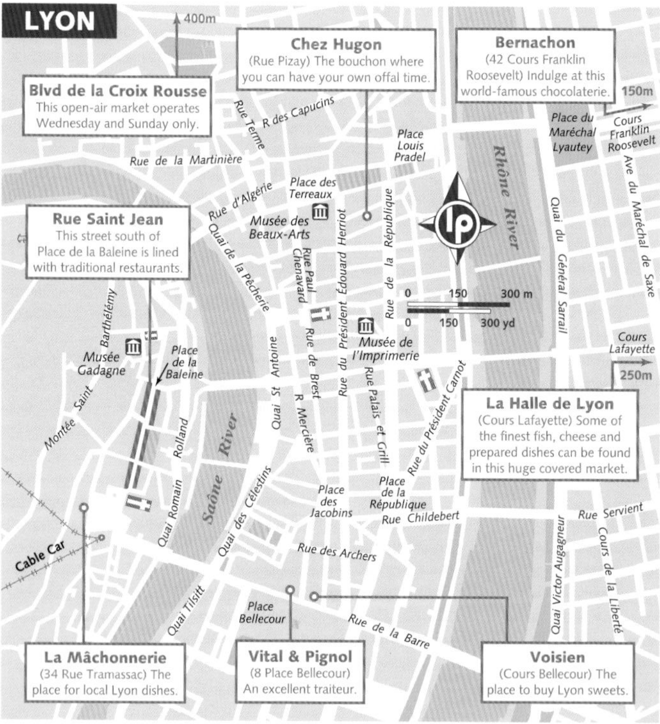
LYON
400m
Chez Hugon
(Rue Pizay) The bouchon where you can have your own offal time.
Bernachon
(42 Cours Franklin Roosevelt) Indulge at this world-famous chocolaterie.
150m
Blvd de la Croix Rousse
This open-air market operates Wednesday and Sunday only.
Rue Terme
R des Capucins
Place du Maréchal Lyautey
Cours Franklin Roosevelt
Place Louis Pradel
Rhône River
Rue de la Martinière
Place des Terreaux
Rue d'Algérie
Rue Saint Jean
This street south of Place de la Baleine is lined with traditional restaurants.
Musée des Beaux-Arts
Quai de la Pêcherie
Rue Paul Chenavard
Rue du Président Édouard Herriot
Rue de la République
Quai du Général Sarrail
Ave du Maréchal de Saxe
0 150 300 m
0 150 300 yd
Barthélémy
Musée Gadagne
Place de la Baleine
Quai St Antoine
Rue de Brest
Musée de l'Imprimerie
Cours Lafayette
250m
Montée Saint
Rolland
R Mercière
Rue Palais et Grill
Rue du Président Carnot
La Halle de Lyon
(Cours Lafayette) Some of the finest fish, cheese and prepared dishes can be found in this huge covered market.
Saône River
Quai des Célestins
Place des Jacobins
Place de la République
Rue Childebert
Rue Servient
Quai Romain
Cable Car
Rue des Archers
Quai Victor Augagneur
Cours de la Liberté
Quai Tilsitt
Place Bellecour
Rue de la Barre
La Mâchonnerie
(34 Rue Tramassac) The place for local Lyon dishes.
Vital & Pignol
(8 Place Bellecour) An excellent traiteur.
Voisien
(Cours Bellecour) The place to buy Lyon sweets.

Lyon's favourite cheese is **Saint Marcellin**, a soft white cheese made from goat's (or sometimes cow's) milk; try it with the greatest of all Rhône wines, Châteauneuf-du-Pape (see Wine in the Drinks chapter). When Saint Marcellin is cured in marc for at least a month it becomes **Arômes au Gène de Marc** and is perfect with a glass of Marc de Côtes de Rhône. The same cheese cured in white wine is **Arômes de Lyon. Bresse Bleu** is a pasteurised cow's milk blue cheese from Rhône-Alpes with a soft rind of white mould and creamier than most bleus.

DON'T MISS – Lyon & the Rhône

- **Quenelles de brochet au sauce Nantua** – pike dumplings in a creamy crayfish sauce
- **Cervelle de Canut** – literally, silkworker's brains; herbed fresh cheese eaten as a dip or as a cheese course at the end of a meal (also called **claqueret lyonnais**)
- **Nougat blanc de Montélimar** – the best white nougat of roasted almonds, egg whites and honey
- **Bernachon chocolates** – especially the **palets d'or**, 'gold disks' of chocolate cream dipped in bitter chocolate
- **Cervelas pistaché et truffé** – fat boiled sausages studded with pistachios and truffles
- **Saucisson chaud au Mâcon** – pork sausage cooked in red wine

The Jura & the Alps

Mountains form a natural border on France's eastern frontier, and the Jura and the Alps have little in common beyond this task of separation and their rigorous climates. The Jura mountains are younger, lower and are heavily forested; below them are the lowlands and valleys of Franche-Comté. The Alps region (composed of Savoie – or Savoy – and the Dauphiné) peaks at snow-capped Mont Blanc (4807m), Europe's highest mountain.

Like most mountainous areas, both regions generally have poor soil for crops but good pasturage, with abundant waterways. Although there are culinary borrowings and exchanges up and down the region – the cuisine of Burgundy, for example, has influenced dishes of Franche-Comté and vice versa, while the food of Savoy has had its effects on Rhône Valley cuisine – the shared trinity in kitchens here is freshwater fish, cheese and potatoes.

The Jura is not celebrated for its gastronomy; the traditional staple here was a gruel of cornmeal called **gaude**. And while historical Franche-Comté has its flavourful **écrevisses de Nantua** (Nantua crayfish) and **poulet de Bresse** (Bresse chicken), better things are done with these creatures elsewhere (see the boxed text Bresse of Chicken in the Staples & Specialities chapter). Nonetheless, there are a number of tasty treats awaiting you. **Jésus**, for

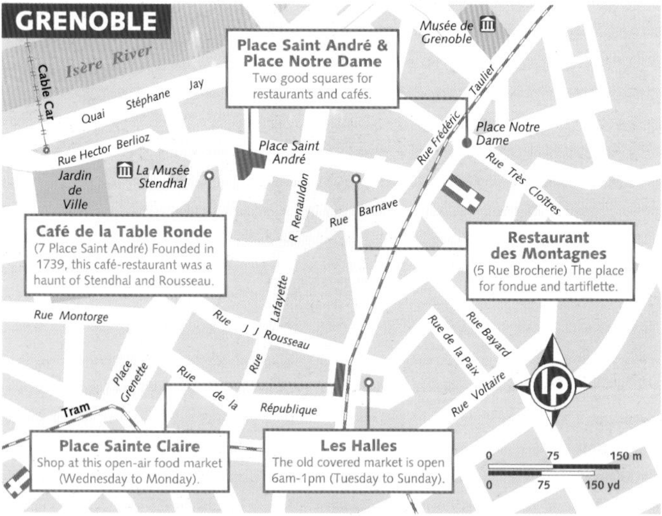
GRENOBLE
Isère River
Cable Car
Quai Stéphane Jay
Rue Hector Berlioz
Jardin de Ville
La Musée Stendhal
Place Saint André & Place Notre Dame
Two good squares for restaurants and cafés.
Musée de Grenoble
Taulier
Rue Frédéric
Place Notre Dame
Rue Très Cloîtres
Place Saint André
R Renauldon
Rue Barnave
Café de la Table Ronde
(7 Place Saint André) Founded in 1739, this café-restaurant was a haunt of Stendhal and Rousseau.
Restaurant des Montagnes
(5 Rue Brocherie) The place for fondue and tartiflette.
Rue Montorge
Rue J J Rousseau
Rue Lafayette
Rue de la Paix
Rue Bayard
Rue Voltaire
Place Grenette
Rue de la République
Tram
Place Sainte Claire
Shop at this open-air food market (Wednesday to Monday).
Les Halles
The old covered market is open 6am-1pm (Tuesday to Sunday).
0
75
150 m
0
75
150 yd

example, is a fat little version of **saucisse de Morteau** (Morteau pork sausage) and is easily identifiable by the wooden peg on its back end, attached after being smoked over a pine and juniper fire in a traditional mountain hut. Its name probably comes from the tradition of serving it on Christmas Eve. **Brési** is thinly sliced, air-dried beef. The smoked hams of the Savoy are excellent, as are the region's **œufs** (eggs).

The favourite way to cook fish here is in a **pochouse**, a kind of fish stew that is also enjoyed in and around Burgundy. It usually includes pike, perch, carp, eel, tench and grayling (and whatever else happens to be biting in the lakes and streams), cooked with onion, garlic, white wine and perhaps a dash or two of **marc de Jura**, the region's celebrated grape brandy.

But the region's greatest contribution to the country's kitchens and tables are its cow's milk cheeses, especially **Comté**, an AOC cooked pressed cheese not unlike Swiss Gruyère (but with few or no holes) and today the most popular cheese in France. Other favourites include **Morbier**, similar to Comté but milder with a distinctive (and harmless) streak of black ash running through the centre; **Bleu du Haut Jura**, a mild AOC blue-veined cheese; and the incomparable **Vacherin du Haut-Doubs**, better known as **Mont d'Or** (see the boxed text Hot Box of the Highlands later in this chapter).

Fondue Savoyarde

This is the classic fondue eaten at the table and ideally accompanied by a chilled Savoy wine like Chignin or Crépy.

Ingredients

2	garlic cloves
500ml/2 cups	dry white wine
500g/1lb	Comté or Gruyère cheese, cubed
120ml/½ cup	kirsch
	pepper to taste
	croûtons

Rub an enamelled saucepan or chafing dish with cut garlic cloves then discard them. Pour the white wine into the pan and add the cubed cheese. Melt over a low flame, stirring constantly with a wooden spoon, until a smooth creamy paste is obtained. Just before serving, blend in the kirsch and add pepper to taste. Traditionally each guest spears a croûton with a long-handled fork, dips it into the fondue and lifts it out, twisting the fork at the same time.

Serves 4

HOT BOX OF THE HIGHLANDS

It's hot, it's soft and it comes in a box. **Vacherin du Haut Doubs** (also called **Mont d'Or**) is the only French cheese to be eaten with a spoon. Made between mid-August and March with unpasteurised cow's milk from red cows grazing above an altitude of 800m, it derives its unique nutty taste from the spruce bark in which it's wrapped. Louis XV adored it. In the 18th century it was called fat cheese, wood cheese or box cheese. Today, Mont d'Or is named after the mountain village from which it originates. Connoisseurs cut a small hole in the top of the soft-crusted cheese and fill it with white wine (sometimes adding chopped onions and garlic), then wrap it in aluminium foil and cook it in the oven for 25 minutes to create a **boîte chaude** (hot box).

Just 11 factories in the Jura are licensed to produce Vacherin Mont d'Or, which ironically has sold like hot cakes since 1987 when 10 people in Switzerland died from listeriosis after consuming the Swiss version, made just across the border (see the Fit & Healthy chapter). French cheese buffs are quite frank about the Swiss scandal's popularisation of their own centuries-old cheese. They believe the bacterial tragedy only happened because the Swiss copycats pasteurised their milk.

Nicola Williams wrote Lonely Planet's The Loire *and* Provence *guides.*

Comté is the prime ingredient in **fondue**, the Jura's trademark dish. Fondue means 'melted' in French and that's essentially what it is – melted cheese with the important additives of white wine, pepper and a little **kirsch** (cherry brandy). It is kept hot and liquid under flame at the table, and eaten with small pieces of bread speared on a fork.

Cooking in the Alps is not dissimilar to that in the Jura: heavy and hearty. While the wheat grown in Savoy valleys is used to make **ravioles** (ravioli-like pasta filled with spinach or cheese) it's the potato that comes to the fore here; any dish described as **à la dauphinoise** or **à la savoyarde** will be (or have) potatoes. **Pommes de terre dauphinoises**, for example, are sliced potatoes baked with milk, cream, eggs, seasoning (especially nutmeg) and cheese.

Contrary to what most people think, a **gratin** does not always include cheese but bread crumbs, which are sprinkled on the top of a dish before it is baked. A **gratin dauphinois** then is **pommes de terre dauphinoises** (with or without the cheese) and a crust, while a **gratin savoyard** is almost the same dish but with stock substituted for the milk or cream. **Cardons**, an artichoke-like vegetable popular in the Loire, are also made into gratins as are **cèpes**, for the mountains are mushroom country in the autumn. The **morilles** of Jura, collected in springtime, are also prized.

The big, wheel-shaped cheeses of Savoy are among the most popular varieties in France, and Beaufort (AOC) a grainy, fruity member of the **Gruyère** family, stands head and shoulders above the rest. **Raclette** is as popular here as it is across the border in Switzerland. It is seldom eaten on its own but heated over a spit shaped like half a wheel and then scraped off with a knife. The traditional way to eat this gluey substance is with boiled potatoes and pickles.

Sweet specialities of this region include the **pogne savoyard**, a brioche flavoured with orange water and filled with fruit, and the liqueur-filled chocolate truffles from Chambéry. In Grenoble you'll find **noix de Grenoble** (a sweet walnut candy) and **gâteau aux noix** (walnut cake).

DON'T MISS – The Jura & the Alps

- **Fondue savoyarde** – the quintessential fondue eaten at the table
- **Glace de sapin** – fir tree ice cream, the first (and probably last) time you'll lick cold turpentine
- **Saline Royale** – the semicircular Royal Salt Works and a showpiece of early Industrial Age town planning, 30km south-west of Besançon
- **Grande Chartreuse Distillery** – the distillery at Voiron, 26km north of Grenoble, where the Chartreuse liqueur is made
- **Jésus de Morteau au vin blanc** – smoked pork sausages cooked in white wine
- **Gratin de crozets** – Savoy-style pasta with cheese

Bordeaux & the Atlantic Coast

The pristine beaches, sand dunes, pine forests and salt marshes of the Atlantic coast stretch from the English Channel all the way to the Spanish frontier. Some 100km from the Atlantic lies Bordeaux, founded by the Romans in the 3rd century BC. From 1154 to 1453, it prospered under the rule of the English, whose fondness for the region's red wine gave impetus to the local wine industry. Even today, the city's most important economic activity is the marketing and export of Bordeaux wines.

On the Atlantic you'll want to eat as much fish – particularly shellfish – as you can. In La Rochelle, France's second-largest fishing port after Boulogne and *the* gastronomic capital of this coast, you'll find cultivated

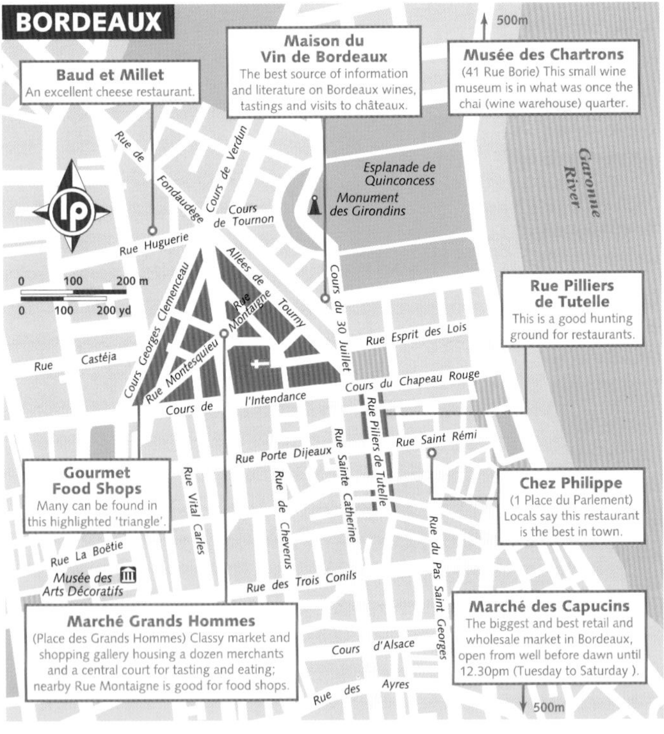
BORDEAUX
Baud et Millet
An excellent cheese restaurant.
Maison du Vin de Bordeaux
The best source of information and literature on Bordeaux wines, tastings and visits to châteaux.
Musée des Chartrons
(41 Rue Borie) This small wine museum is in what was once the chai (wine warehouse) quarter.
500m
Garonne River
Esplanade de Quinconcess
Monument des Girondins
Rue de Fondaudège
Cours de Verdun
Cours de Tournon
Rue Huguerie
Allées de Tourny
Cours Georges Clemenceau
Rue Montaigne
Rue Montesquieu
Cours du 30 Juillet
0 100 200 m
0 100 200 yd
Rue Castéja
Rue Esprit des Lois
Cours du Chapeau Rouge
Cours de l'Intendance
Rue Pilliers de Tutelle
This is a good hunting ground for restaurants.
Rue Saint Rémi
Rue Porte Dijeaux
Rue Sainte Catherine
Rue Vital Carles
Rue de Cheverus
Gourmet Food Shops
Many can be found in this highlighted 'triangle'.
Chez Philippe
(1 Place du Parlement) Locals say this restaurant is the best in town.
Rue du Pas Saint Georges
Rue La Boëtie
Musée des Arts Décoratifs
Rue des Trois Conils
Marché Grands Hommes
(Place des Grands Hommes) Classy market and shopping gallery housing a dozen merchants and a central court for tasting and eating; nearby Rue Montaigne is good for food shops.
Marché des Capucins
The biggest and best retail and wholesale market in Bordeaux, open from well before dawn until 12.30pm (Tuesday to Saturday).
Cours d'Alsace
Rue des Ayres
500m

mussels, oysters (try the fat ones of Arcachon), small shrimps, evil-looking spider crabs, cockles, whelks, clams, queen scallops and so on. A favourite way to eat mussels – a kind of French clambake called an **éclade** – is to roast them on a wooden board covered with pine needles on the beach. At La Rochelle's market and in its restaurants the choice of fish is endless; you'll find ray, hake, and even hake roe and cheeks, which are the best part of any fish, as any self-respecting ichthyophile would tell you. An especially fine fish is the **solette**, a small sole that also goes by the name **langue d'avocat** (literally, lawyer's tongue).

Though you'll find lots of fish dishes on offer in Bordeaux, this is essentially carnivore country; the **bœuf bazadais** (beef raised near Bazas) is France's best – and most expensive. Very few menus omit the city's signature dish: **entrecôte à la bordelaise** (also called **entrecôte marchand de vin**; a rib steak in a rich brown sauce of Bordeaux wine, shallots, butter, herbs and bone marrow). The excellent **agneau de Pauillac** (meat from lambs that feed on salt marshes) is often served with truffles. Savoury pies – **tourtières** or **tourtes** – made with chicken are a speciality of Angoulême.

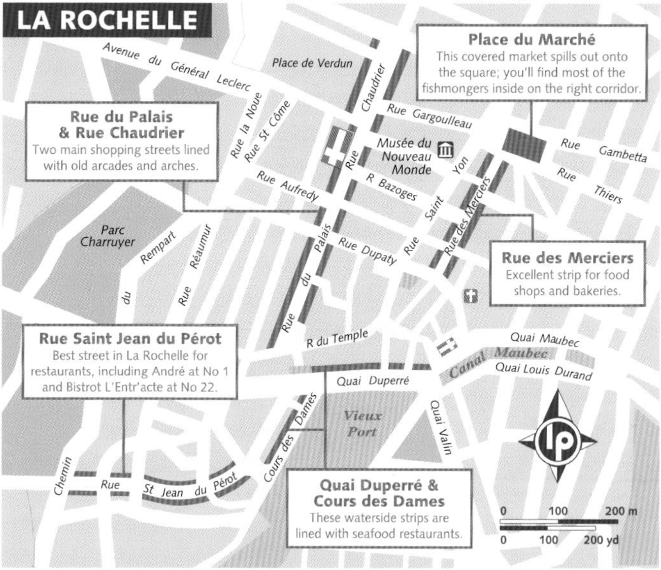
LA ROCHELLE
Place du Marché
This covered market spills out onto the square; you'll find most of the fishmongers inside on the right corridor.
Rue du Palais & Rue Chaudrier
Two main shopping streets lined with old arcades and arches.
Rue des Merciers
Excellent strip for food shops and bakeries.
Rue Saint Jean du Pérot
Best street in La Rochelle for restaurants, including André at No 1 and Bistrot L'Entr'acte at No 22.
Quai Duperré & Cours des Dames
These waterside strips are lined with seafood restaurants.
Avenue du Général Leclerc
Place de Verdun
Chaudrier
Rue Gargoulleau
Rue la Noue
Rue St Côme
Musée du Nouveau Monde
Rue Gambetta
Rue Thiers
Rue Aufredy
R Bazoges
Rue Saint Yon
Rue des Merciers
Parc Charruyer
Rempart du
Rue Réaumur
Rue du Palais
Rue Dupaty
R du Temple
Quai Maubec
Canal Maubec
Quai Louis Durand
Quai Duperré
Vieux Port
Quai Valin
Cours des Dames
Chemin
Rue St Jean du Pérot
0 100 200 m
0 100 200 yd

The wonderful hams of Poitou are cured with herbs, spices and Cognac, ingredients often used in the region's pâtés and terrines. Look for the rough-cut **terrine charentaise au cognac** and the **terrine landaise à l'armagnac**, which uses Armagnac, Cognac's rival brandy. **Farci poitevin** is a pâté special to Poitou that is flavoured with herbs and baked in cabbage leaves.

Snails, which are called **lumas** in Poitou and **cagouilles** in Charente, are often prepared in a tarte or a casserole with wine, Cognac and tomato. Tiny **pibales** (baby eels), only available early in the year, are fried in garlic and oil.

Among the fruits and vegetables of the region, the large Marmande tomatoes, Rochelle leeks and Landes asparagus are worth looking for. **Mojettes** are white beans that are cooked with lamb or ham. The excellent

DON'T MISS – Bordeaux & the Atlantic Coast

- **Plateau de fruits de mer** (or **Panaché de coquillages**) – a tray or plate of mixed cold seafood or shellfish and the best way to try what's on offer from the Atlantic
- **Wine Tastings** – available in many Bordeaux towns and villages, including Saint Émilion
- **Pâté de lapin au cognac** – rabbit pâté flavoured with Cognac
- **Tarte charentaise** – flat tart filled with fruit preserves
- **Merrine** – fanciful name combining **terrine** and **mer** (sea); a 'mousse' of lobster, cod or scallop
- **Musée du Cognac** – the museum at 48 Blvd Denfert-Rochereau in the town of Cognac
- **Mouclade de moules** (also called **mouclade rochelaise** and **mouclade charentaise**) – a cream-based mussel stew flavoured with garlic, saffron and Cognac or pineau des Charentes
- **Mijoté d'agneau aux mojettes** – lamb cooked with kidney-shaped white beans from Vendée
- **Jonché niortaise au coulis de framboise** – mild, slightly grainy fresh goat's milk cheese with raspberry coulis
- **Gâteau landais** – thin layers of pastry soaked with Cognac and baked with butter, sugar and orange-flower water (**croustade** is gâteau landais with a prune filling)
- **Macarons de Saint Émilion** – Light and airy macaroons
- **Salade de pètoncles et artichauts** – Salad of queen scallops and baby artichokes

cantaloupes of Charente, often made in **confiture de melon**, are available till as late as mid-October.

Cheese in the region is predominantly the goat's milk variety, though **Caillebotte** is an unsalted fresh cow's milk cheese. **Jonché** is a mild, slightly grainy fresh goat's milk cheese made near Niort in Poitou and often served with jam or fruit as a dessert. The quintessential Bordeaux cake or pastry are the sweet and chewy **cannelés** (caramelised brioche-like pastries). **Millas de Bordeaux** (or **millard de Bordeaux**) is a custard flavoured with cherries and baked in a pastry shell. Confectionery delights include **bouchons de Bordeaux** (chewy caramels), **noisettines du Médoc** (cooked hazelnuts rolled in sugar) and **marrons glacés** (candied chestnuts).

Plateau de fruits de mer

58

Central France: Périgord, Limousin & the Auvergne

Although all three upland regions of central France share similar histories and are firmly steeped in rural life, each has its own distinctive landscape, ambience and cuisine. Périgord, better known to many English speakers as the Dordogne (the name of the most important of the region's rivers), is a land of valleys, fields and forests, prehistoric painted caves, châteaux and, in the south, vineyards. It is one of France's main gastronomic centres and especially renowned for rich dishes made with locally grown products.

The tranquil hills of Limousin, the fine china of Limoges and the tapestries of Aubusson present the quintessential image of France. The abundance of water nourishes the grasslands that make Limousin a major producer of beef as it does the many fruit and nut orchards. Farther east are the higher plateaus and mountains of the Massif Central, which encompass the region of the Auvergne. The terrain, the climate and even the Auvergnats themselves are often described in French as **rude** (rugged, harsh and tough). In a word this too is its cuisine: **potée auvergnate** (a hearty soup-stew of cabbage, bacon, pork sausages and potatoes) and lots of **cochonailles** (pork products), including the popular **salaisons d'Auvergne** (Auvergne salt-cured meats).

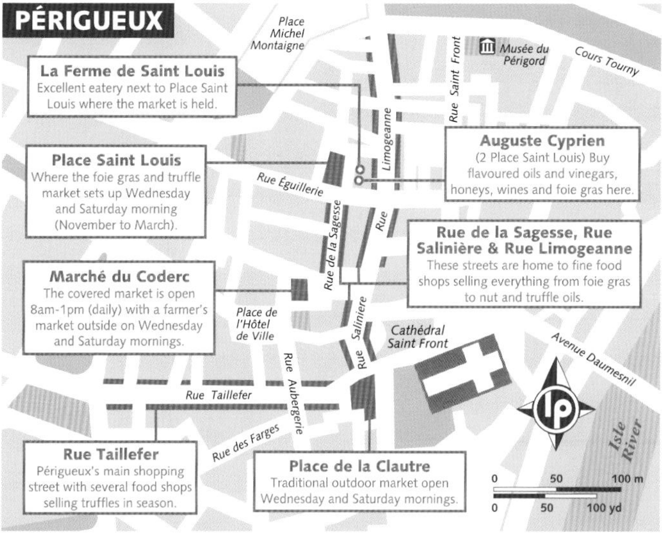
PÉRIGUEUX
Place Michel Montaigne
Musée du Périgord
Cours Tourny
Rue Saint Front
Limogeanne
Rue Éguillerie
Rue de la Sagesse
Rue
Rue Salinière
Place de l'Hôtel de Ville
Cathédral Saint Front
Avenue Daumesnil
Rue Taillefer
Rue Aubergerie
Rue des Farges
Isle River
0 50 100 m
0 50 100 yd
La Ferme de Saint Louis
Excellent eatery next to Place Saint Louis where the market is held.
Place Saint Louis
Where the foie gras and truffle market sets up Wednesday and Saturday morning (November to March).
Auguste Cyprien
(2 Place Saint Louis) Buy flavoured oils and vinegars, honeys, wines and foie gras here.
Rue de la Sagesse, Rue Salinière & Rue Limogeanne
These streets are home to fine food shops selling everything from foie gras to nut and truffle oils.
Marché du Coderc
The covered market is open 8am-1pm (daily) with a farmer's market outside on Wednesday and Saturday mornings.
Rue Taillefer
Périgueux's main shopping street with several food shops selling truffles in season.
Place de la Clautre
Traditional outdoor market open Wednesday and Saturday mornings.

A Salers cow near Cantal, Auvergne

Périgord is famous for truffles and poultry. Most prized among the latter are the ducks and geese whose livers are turned into **pâté de foie gras** (duck or goose liver pâté), which is sometimes flavoured with Cognac and truffles. Regional dishes described as **à la périgourdine** – duck, goose, chicken or beef – usually come with a rich brown sauce made with foie gras and truffles.

Confit de canard and **confit d'oie** are duck or goose joints cooked very slowly in their own fat. The preserved fowl is left to stand for some months before being eaten. Also common are **galantines** (cold dishes of boned, stuffed, pressed poultry) and **ballotines** (their warm equivalents). Another speciality is **cou d'oie farci** (goose neck stuffed with pork and veal mince). **Graisse d'oie** (goose fat) is the most important fat in the region's traditional cuisine, and **huile de noix** (walnut oil) is used as a seasoning and in salads.

TREASURES OF THE EARTH & SKY

Every Wednesday and Saturday morning between November and March, Périgueux is alive with the sound of honking: geese, ducks, automobiles, vendors and buyers flock to the celebrated foie gras and truffle market on Place Saint Louis to surrender, sell and purchase fatted livers.

The market opens about 9am, and merchants set their goods out on tables under tarpaulins. These makeshift tents are pungent with the smells of fat and smoked poultry, damp earth and truffles. Unplucked ducks and geese go on sale, their necks hanging long off the table like a thick white fringe. On tables farther down the line what looks like an anserine anatomy lesson is in progress, with every part of the cranky creature on offer: giblets; breast meat; wings; pinions; carcasses for making soup stocks and sauces; those wringable necks with or without skin; fat either whole or rendered; breast; skin; and of course **foies** (livers) – huge and a pale pinkish if offered by the pricey Madame Oie (350-500FF a kilo), smaller and redder from Madame Canard (200-250FF a kilo).

For those who can't handle a butcher's knife, there are ready-made items: **cous d'oie farcis avec foie** (goose necks stuffed with liver); disk-like **sanguettes** (flattened sausages made from duck or goose blood); **jambon de canard** (salted or cured duck breast meat); and **grillons** (chunks or fatty duck or goose cooked until crisp).

Sparkling amid all the blood and guts are the 'black diamonds' of Périgord, the odourific fresh truffles. These golf ball-sized tumours bear heart-stopping price tags (1800-3500FF a kilo for the best ones from Sorges). But if you are in the market for truffles, buy them here; they go for at least 580FF per 100g in the chichi markets of nearby Bordeaux. And plan to come to Périgueux on Saturday. While a number of vendors put their prized jewels on offer at the midweek market, the Saturday market invariably has a better selection.

Châtaignes (chestnuts), once a staple food in Périgord, are now used as a flavouring; they can be stuffed in a goose before roasting or bound into sausages and blood puddings. Chestnuts are also used in cakes and pastries; one of the region's best desserts is **gâteau aux châtaignes** (chestnut cake).

Limousin has become the virtual meat factory of France, with pork, lamb and beef in abundance. A **gigot brayaude** is a leg of lamb studded with cloves of garlic and served – **à la limousine** – with red cabbage braised with chestnuts. Meat **tourtes** (pies) are also popular, especially veal and chicken ones. And all that water means freshwater fish are a popular staple, often ending up in a **friture** (fry-up). Lush Limousin is also noted for its fruits: the plums and greengages of Corrèze and the cherries that go into its trademark dessert, **clafoutis aux cerises** (cherries covered with a thick batter and baked).

When it comes to vegetables, Auvergne is able to turn the lowly to the exalted. Its **lentilles du Puy** (Puy lentils) have an AOC, and the world's best cooks have their fingers on that pulse. Of all things, the carrot makes its bed here and Vichy is as closely associated with it as it is with mineral water. Anytime you see the word 'Vichy', there will be sweet orange root vegetables – unless it's on the label of a bottle of that water. The area of Cantal is to pork what Bresse is to chicken. While in Auvergne, keep charcuterie in your mind and mouth; the air-dried sausages and hams are among the best. The region's high grasslands provide ideal grazing, and Auvergne's cheeses are another of its strengths. The most popular are **Cantal**, a cow's milk cheese, and **Saint Nectaire**, a pressed cheese. **Bleu d'Auvergne** and the mild **Fourme d'Ambert** are the region's best blues. An Auvergne speciality is **truffade**, a sticky blend of potatoes, cheese and garlic eaten with sausages.

DON'T MISS – Central France: Périgord, Limousin & the Auvergne

- **Foie Gras & Truffle Market** – at Place Saint Louis in Périgueux
- **Clafoutis aux cerises** – Limousin's trademark dessert; cherries covered with a thick batter and baked
- **Gâteau de miel aux noisettes** – honey cake with hazelnuts, from Aubusson in Limousin
- **Huile de noix** and **huile de noisettes** – walnut and hazelnut oil on sale everywhere in Périgord
- **Écomusée de la Truffe** – the truffle Museum at Sorges in Périgord
- **Musée du Foie Gras** – foie gras Museum at Thiviers in Périgord
- **Lentilles vertes du Puy aux saucisses fumées** – smoked pork sausages with green lentils

Provence

Ah, Provence – few places evoke the azure sea, sunny skies, fresh produce and good life like this region. Provence is large, stretching from the Italian border in the east to the Camargue delta and Languedoc in the west. To the north, the terrain rises, with Mont Ventoux reaching 1909m – once you've exchanged olive trees for firs, you know you've left Provence. And to the south is the ever present Mediterranean, which has surrendered its briny treasures since time immemorial.

No other region of France looks to its terrain, the seasons and its past for culinary inspiration. The Roman legacy of olives, wheat and wine remain the trinity of Provence's cuisine, and many dishes are prepared with

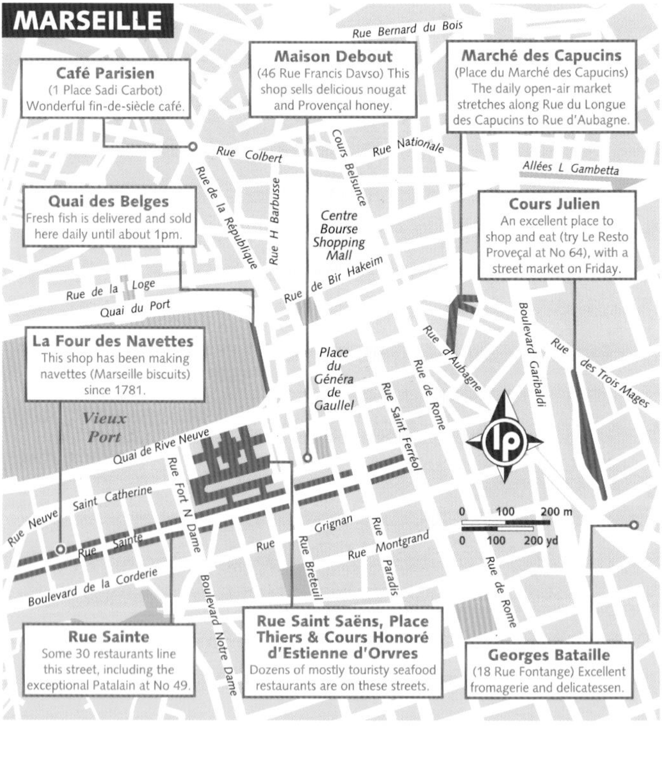
MARSEILLE
Café Parisien
(1 Place Sadi Carbot) Wonderful fin-de-siècle café.
Maison Debout
(46 Rue Francis Davso) This shop sells delicious nougat and Provençal honey.
Marché des Capucins
(Place du Marché des Capucins) The daily open-air market stretches along Rue du Longue des Capucins to Rue d'Aubagne.
Quai des Belges
Fresh fish is delivered and sold here daily until about 1pm.
Cours Julien
An excellent place to shop and eat (try Le Resto Proveçal at No 64), with a street market on Friday.
La Four des Navettes
This shop has been making navettes (Marseille biscuits) since 1781.
Rue Sainte
Some 30 restaurants line this street, including the exceptional Patalain at No 49.
Rue Saint Saëns, Place Thiers & Cours Honoré d'Estienne d'Orvres
Dozens of mostly touristy seafood restaurants are on these streets.
Georges Bataille
(18 Rue Fontange) Excellent fromagerie and delicatessen.
Rue Bernard du Bois
Rue Colbert
Cours Belsunce
Rue Nationale
Allées L Gambetta
Rue de la République
Rue H Barbusse
Centre Bourse Shopping Mall
Rue de Bir Hakeim
Rue de la Loge
Quai du Port
Rue d'Aubagne
Boulevard Garibaldi
Rue des Trois Mages
Place du Généra de Gaullel
Rue de Rome
Rue Saint Ferréol
Vieux Port
Quai de Rive Neuve
Rue Fort N Dame
Rue Neuve Saint Catherine
Rue Sainte
Rue Grignan
Rue Breteuil
Rue Montgrand
Rue Paradis
Boulevard de la Corderie
Boulevard Notre Dame
0 100 200 m
0 100 200 yd

LE MENU RAPIDE

We'd dined on bouillabaisse the night before at Fonfon, the best place in Marseille for Provence's trademark dish according to friends, the hotel staff, our taxi driver and anyone else who had an opinion. Bowl after bowl of saffron-scented creamy broth, crisp toast spread with **rouille**, heaps of scorpion fish, John Dory, monkfish and conger eel – we could hardly lift ourselves off our chairs at the end.

In the morning we went marketing, with the first stop being the fish market at the Vieux Port. Wide-eyed customers grappled and haggled over of squid, octopus, sole, turbot, eel and rockfish as colourful as parrot fish along a coral reef. Then we walked and gawked and nibbled our way through the Marché des Capucins, with everything from Jerusalem artichokes and bitter Seville oranges to herbs and lavender on offer.

We had a train to catch, but wanted to check out a renowned cheese shop near the Place Notre Dame du Mont to sniff and sample some **brousse**, a fresh ewe's or goat's milk cheese indigenous to Provence. We had an hour or so to spare and made our way up the hill to Georges Bataille. It was something more than a cheese shop. Though there was a vast array of cheeses on sale – including brousse in all its incarnations – an equally large area was given over to a delicatessen of exquisite Provençal treats, including a small eating area. With our noses flattened on the glass display cases, the shop assistant asked if she could be of any help. When we inquired as to why the **alouette sans têtes** looked more like meatballs than 'headless larks' she smiled. "Are you from Boston?" she asked.

Now for a French person to pick out a regional American accent when hearing English is impressive, but for her to be able to do it in French – well. We got to talking, she told us about her visits to 'Bean Town' and, well, we got hungry. We stayed for lunch.

But it had to be a **menu rapide** and we – and she – wasted no time. A selection of three **tians**, delightful little Provençal gratins of aubergines, vegetables and goat's milk cheese, were followed by those 'decapitated birds' – not larks at all but slices of meat wrapped around a stuffing – and a **daube provençale** in which the beef was substituted for duck and served with **panisses** (little patties of fried chickpea flour). The wine flowed – but we had to fly.

This being Provence, laid-back and sultry, we were told not to rush, that there were more important things to do (like eat dessert), that there would always be another train. But we were men on a mission; we'd accomplished our cheesy task (and had tried the **Banon à la Feuille**, brousse dipped in eau-de-vie and wrapped in chestnut leaves) and, in spite of ourselves, we'd even managed another Provençal meal. The charcuterie of Lyon and the wines of Burgundy awaited.

olive oil and generous amounts of garlic. Tomatoes are another common ingredient, and you can safely assume that any dish described as **à la provençale** will be prepared with garlic-seasoned tomatoes. Other produce frequently appearing on local menus are aubergines, courgettes (zucchini), onions and little artichokes. Tomatoes, aubergines and courgettes, stewed together along with green pepper, garlic, various aromatic herbs and olive oil, produce that perennial Provençal favourite, **ratatouille**, served hot or cold.

Aïoli is a sauce prepared by mixing a freshly made mayonnaise (olive oil, egg yolks and a bit of lemon) with lots of freshly crushed garlic. It is spread generously on hot or cold vegetables and especially on poached codfish.

Provence's most famous soup is **bouillabaisse**, from the French **bouillir** (to boil) and **baisser** (to lower, as in the flame). It is made with at least three kinds of fresh fish, always including **rascasse** (scorpion fish), cooked for 10 minutes in broth with onions, tomatoes, saffron, bay leaves, sage and thyme. Bouillabaisse, which is eaten as a main course, is usually served with toast and **rouille** (spicy mayonnaise of olive oil, garlic, chilli peppers and fish broth) that some people mix into the soup but most spread on the toast. The best bouillabaisse is made in Marseille, though the English poet William Makepeace Thackeray (1811-63) wrote a ballad praising one he'd had in Paris. Touriste! **Bourride** is another fish stew made with firm-fleshed white fish in a stock of onions, tomatoes, garlic, herbs and olive oil thickened by egg yolk and often served with aïoli.

Provence is sometimes called 'the garden of France' because of its superb herbs, fruits and vegetables. The region is also famous for its honey, which comes in a multiple of varieties, and locally pressed olive oil, especially that from Les Beaux-de-Provence and Nyons (see Oils & Fats in the Staples & Specialities chapter). Olive oil, fennel, bay leaf and lemon are the most authentic flavourings for fish in Provence. Truffles are harvested from November to April, especially around Vaison-la-Romaine. Depending on the season, all these delicacies are available fresh at local food markets.

A favourite way to eat raw vegetables is with **anchoïade**, a dipping sauce or paste of olive oil, garlic and anchovies. **Tapenade** is a savoury spread of black olives, olive oil, capers, lemon and anchovies. **Mesclun** is a popular mixture of salad greens including rocket, lamb's lettuce and endive.

The provençaux have never been big meat eaters – the terrain was not well disposed for large grazing animals – and traditionally they turned to game and birds like blackbirds, thrushes and larks for a source of protein. A popular dish, eaten especially in winter, however, is **bœuf en daube** (beef stewed with red wine, onions, garlic, vegetables and herbs) and often served with fresh pasta, while the **agneau d'Alpilles** (lamb from the 'little Alps' around Les Baux) figures on many menus. Charcuterie makes only an occasional appearance at the table, though **saucisson d'Arles** (air-dried

Socca with beer, Nice, Provence

pork and beef sausage) is excellent. **Pieds et paquets** (literally, feet and packages; sheep's feet wrapped in tripe and cooked with wine and tomatoes) is a favourite dish in Marseille.

Of course there's always been the Mediterranean and its bounty of fishy delights. Along with the usual red and grey mullet, bream, sea bass, mussels and spiny lobster are wonderful things like **oursins** (sea urchins), the orange roe of which is scooped out with a spoon like a soft-boiled egg, and the clam-like **violets** (sea squirts), whose iodine-infused yellow flesh tastes of the very sea itself. **Brandade de morue** is a delightful purée of salt cod, oil (or milk) and mashed potatoes.

Provence cheeses are mostly variations of **brousse**, an unsalted ewe's or goat's milk cheese that is rather bland; **Brousse du Rove** is a commercial version produced near Marseille that goes well with a Côtes de Provence

DON'T MISS – Provence

- **Navettes** – canoe-shaped biscuits flavoured with anis, chocolate, cinnamon, but most authentically with orange blossom or rose water
- **Fougasse** – lattice-shaped flat bread with many variations: slit and flavoured with orange or brandy; brushed with olive oil and sprinkled with herbs; or studded with bacon bits or black olives
- **Tian** – mousse-like gratin of vegetables or cheese cooked in a small earthenware dish
- **Socca** – crêpe-like snack popular in Nice made from chickpea flour and olive oil
- **Pissaladière** – Provençal 'pizza'; a thick crust covered with puréed onions and garlic and flavoured with anchovies and black olives
- **Pan bagnat** – a large round bread roll brushed with olive oil and filled with tomatoes, green peppers, olives, onions and anchovies
- **Barre marseillaise** – rich bar of soft chocolate flavoured with, among other things, lemon and thyme
- **Limande poêlée à la crème d'ail, brandade de morue** – pan-fried lemon sole with garlic cream, seasoned salt and cod purée
- **Rougets au pistou** – mullet in basil sauce
- **Poivrons grillés à l'anchoïade** – green peppers grilled with anchoïade
- **Seiches au basilic** – squid cooked with basil
- **Pigeon aux gousses d'ail** – pigeon cooked with garlic cloves

rosé. **Banon à la Feuille** is an aged version of brousse dipped in eau-de-vie and wrapped in chestnut leaves.

With so much honey, spices and herbs (including lavender, Provence's quintessential aroma), pastries and cakes are made, and consumed, in abundance. **Navettes**, canoe-shaped biscuits flavoured with – among other things – anis and orange blossom, are a speciality of Marseille, and **nougat noir** (black nougat of honey, caramelised sugar and toasted almonds) is made everywhere; try Nougat Fouque from Signes. The **Calissons d'Aix** (ground almonds and glazed fruits in a hard shell) are consumed with relish throughout France. Nice and Apt excel at making **fruits confits** (glazed fruits), and you'll see small, irregularly shaped loaves of bread called **mouna** studded with the stuff. **Tarte tropézienne** is a tooth-achingly sweet pie that comes from from Saint Tropez.

FROMENTERIE
navettes
5.80f

Gascony & the Basque Country

Gascony and the Basque Country (*Euzkadi* in Basque) occupy France's southwestern corner. It is an area of varied topographies, cultures and cuisines, but Gascony and the Basque Country have one thing in common: the Pyrenees, which forms a natural boundary between France and Spain. The Pyrenees are not as high as the Alps, but their passes and valleys have always been more difficult to penetrate.

The food of Gascony is deceivingly simple and always very hearty, high in protein, fat and salt. Perhaps no dish is more evocative of Gascony than **garbure**, a thick soup or stew of cabbage, beans, potatoes, vegetables, herbs, spices and preserved meats, such as duck, goose or pork or a combination of the three; the pot should be so full of 'treats' that a ladle pushed into it will stand straight. It is a dish that requires meticulous attention – the type of pot used (always earthenware), the order of ingredients, when it should

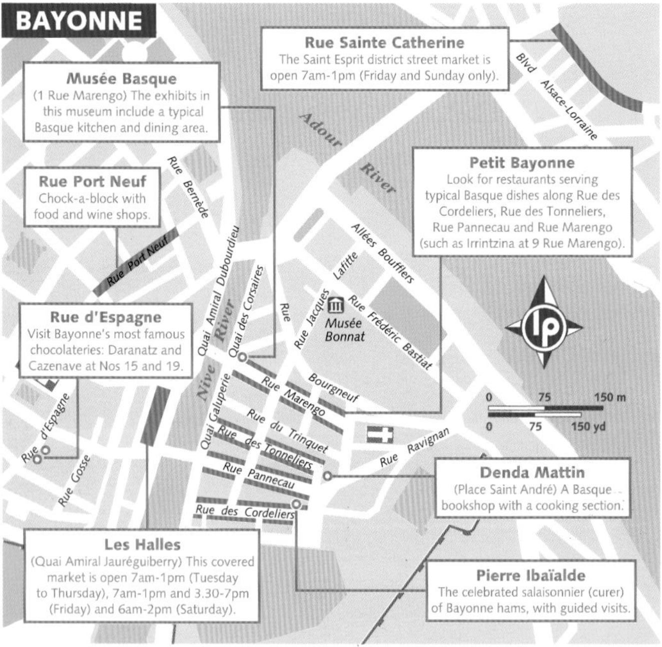
BAYONNE
Musée Basque
(1 Rue Marengo) The exhibits in this museum include a typical Basque kitchen and dining area.
Rue Sainte Catherine
The Saint Esprit district street market is open 7am-1pm (Friday and Sunday only).
Rue Port Neuf
Chock-a-block with food and wine shops.
Petit Bayonne
Look for restaurants serving typical Basque dishes along Rue des Cordeliers, Rue des Tonneliers, Rue Pannecau and Rue Marengo (such as Irrintzina at 9 Rue Marengo).
Rue d'Espagne
Visit Bayonne's most famous chocolateries: Daranatz and Cazenave at Nos 15 and 19.
Denda Mattin
(Place Saint André) A Basque bookshop with a cooking section.
Les Halles
(Quai Amiral Jauréguiberry) This covered market is open 7am-1pm (Tuesday to Thursday), 7am-1pm and 3.30-7pm (Friday) and 6am-2pm (Saturday).
Pierre Ibaïalde
The celebrated salaisonnier (curer) of Bayonne hams, with guided visits.
Adour River
Nive River
Blvd Alsace-Lorraine
Rue Bernède
Rue Port Neuf
Quai Amiral Dubourdieu
Quai des Corsaires
Allées Boufflers
Lafitte
Rue Jacques
Rue Frédéric Bastiat
Musée Bonnat
Rue Bourgneuf
Rue Marengo
Rue du Trinquet
Rue des Tonneliers
Rue Pannecau
Rue des Cordeliers
Quai Galuperie
Rue Ravignan
Rue d'Espagne
Rue Gosse
0 75 150 m
0 75 150 yd

be brought to the boil and the temperature lowered are all important elements. Another speciality is **salmis de palombe**, wood pigeon partially roasted then simmered in a rich sauce of wine, shallots and onions.

People in both regions prefer salted and prepared meats to pâtés and terrines. While **saucisse de Toulouse**, a fat, mild-tasting pork sausage, is enjoyed here, the staple prepared meat is **jambon de Bayonne**, the locally prepared Bayonne ham. It is usually eaten sliced as is, but is also prepared in **jambon à la bayonniase** (ham braised in Madeira wine). In the home, goose fat is used to cook everything from garbure to eggs.

Fish dishes, especially those made with hake, abound on the coast. Try **joues de merlu** (hake cheeks), the choicest part of that and any finned creature. Fresh tuna, sardines and anchovies are the specialities around Saint Jean de Luz. Also popular is baby squid, served in a variety of ways including **à l'encre** (in its own ink) or **en persillade** (in a blend of chopped parsley and garlic). A Basque fish stew called **ttoro** may include hake, eel and monkfish as well as tomatoes, white wine and that most Basque of flavourings: red chilli peppers (see the boxed text). Skip it if it contains shellfish as it will be cooked to a frazzle.

Basques love cakes and pastries but the most popular of all is **gâteau basque**, a relatively simple layer-cake that is filled with cream or cherry jam. Also be on the lookout for the **toutière de Gascogne** (or **croustade**), a pastry with a large sweep away 'veil' top filled with apples or prunes and sprinkled with Armagnac.

THE RED GOLD OF ESPELETTE

Among the essential ingredients of Basque cooking are **piments rouges** (deep-red chillies) that you'll see hanging out to dry, brightening up houses and adding that extra bite to many of the region's dishes. The best chillies come from the village of Espelette, near the Spanish border.

According to the Basques: it requires a powerful throat formed by the Midi sun to eat Espelette chillies. In truth they are relatively mild, three times weaker than Cayenne pepper. Even so, Espelette chillies are flavourful. After the chillies have dried sufficiently (usually about two months) they are ground and sifted into a red powder. This powder is used in cooking and is also rubbed into Bayonne ham to preserve it and add flavour.

A cooperative called Biperra (Basque for chilli pepper) safeguards and promotes the 'red gold' of the Basque Country and awards annual prizes to the best varieties. A **Fête du Piment** (Chilli Festival) is held every year at Espelette in late October.

Bayonne is a major chocolate centre – indeed up to the 17th century it was the only region where chocolate was made – and the names Cazenave and Daranatz are celebrated nationwide for their quality. A local speciality are the **tourons de Bayonne** (also known as **ttourons**; marzipan sweets with pistachios and/or candied fruit).

The range of cheese in this part of France is not enormous, the preferred variety being what is simply called **ardi gasna** (ewe's milk cheese) and served with **confiture d'Itxassou** (fruit preserves from the town of Itxassou). One of the best varieties widely available is the AOC **Ossau-Iraty**; try it with Herrika-Arnoa, a dry white Basque wine, or Irouléguy, an AOC wine that is available in both red and white varieties from St Étienne de Baïgorry. Another favourite cheese here is **Cabécou de Rocamadour**, an AOC goat's milk cheese from Midi-Pyrenées served warm with salads or stored in oil and rosemary.

Armagnac, second only to Cognac in the panoply of world brandies, is made from the grapes that grow on the slopes of that Gascon area near Auch (see Digestives in the Drinks chapter).

Poulet Basque

This is the signature dish of the Basque Country

Ingredients

1-1½kg/2-3lb	chicken, cut into large pieces
	salt and pepper
50ml/¼ cup	cooking oil
4	large tomatoes, peeled and seeded
6	green peppers, seeded and cut in julienne strips
6	mild red peppers, seeded and cut in julienne strips
60g/2oz	mushrooms, sliced
180g/6oz	ham, diced
250ml/1 cup	white wine
1 tablespoon	chopped parsley

Season the chicken with salt and pepper and brown in oil in a heavy saucepan. Add the tomatoes, peppers, mushrooms and ham, then pour in the white wine. Cover and cook over a moderate flame for 30 minutes. Arrange the chicken pieces on a heated platter and keep warm. Reduce the sauce, add additional seasoning if necessary and pour over the chicken. Sprinkle with one tablespoon of chopped parsley.

Serves 4

DON'T MISS – Gascony & the Basque Country

- **Marmitako** – tuna cooked in a ragoût of tomatoes, onions, peppers and white wine and served with potatoes
- **Macarons de Bayonne** – Basque macaroons (*muxux* in Basque) that are heavier and chewier than the usual
- **Ardi gasna** – generic Basque name for nutty-flavoured 'ewe's milk cheese'
- **Écomusée de la Tradition Basque** (Saint Jean de Luz Nord) and the **Musée du Chocolat** in Biarritz
- **Garbure béarnaise** – the classic version of the trademark Gascon meat and vegetable stew
- **Haxoa d' Espelette** – veal ragout with red chilli
- **Poulet basque** – chicken cooked with tomatoes, onions, peppers and white wine
- **Piperade** – peppers, onions and tomatoes cooked with scrambled eggs and ham; Basque comfort food
- **Merlu à la koskera** – hake with a sauce of peas, potatoes and asparagus

Languedoc-Roussillon

Lying in the extreme southeast of the country, **Languedoc-Roussillon** is linked – like Alsace & Lorraine – by little more than a punctuation mark. Until the 1960s Languedoc and Roussillon were two historic provinces united only by the Mediterranean and their sun-baked climates.

As every student of French 101 knows, Languedoc's name is derived from *langue d'oc*, the name of the Catalan-related language that was displaced by the northern *langue d'oïl*, the forerunner of modern French. Roussillon, whose name comes from the **rousse** (russet) colour of its soil, is often called French Catalunya and with good reason: it was part of the kingdom of Catalunya-Aragon from the 12th century until the Treaty of the Pyrenees (1659). Catalan is still widely spoken.

Distinct cooking styles separate Languedoc and Roussillon. Most basic is their use of different fats. While Roussillon uses olive oil in its dishes as liberally as its cousins to the south in Spain do, Languedoc makes greater use of goose fat – though they do use olive oil in the area near Provence.

No dish is more evocative of Languedoc than **cassoulet** (a casserole or stew with beans and meat). This dish is classic **cuisine campagnarde** (peasant cooking) and uses the best local ingredients and most refined techniques.

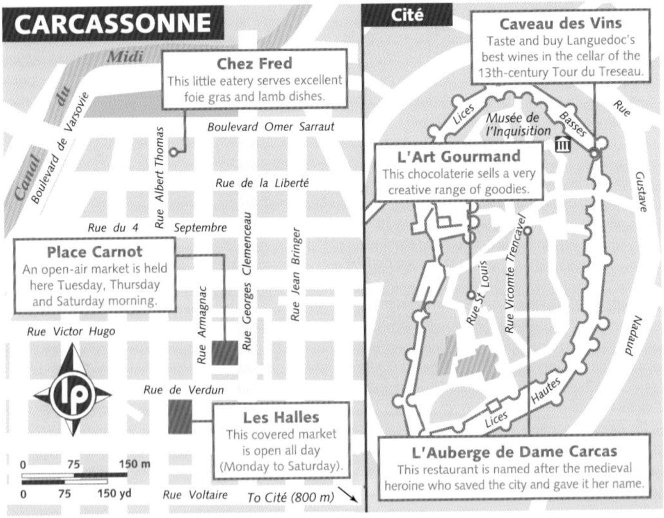
CARCASSONNE
Canal du Midi
Boulevard de Varsovie
Chez Fred
This little eatery serves excellent foie gras and lamb dishes.
Boulevard Omer Sarraut
Rue Albert Thomas
Rue de la Liberté
Rue du 4 Septembre
Place Carnot
An open-air market is held here Tuesday, Thursday and Saturday morning.
Rue Armagnac
Rue Georges Clemenceau
Rue Jean Bringer
Rue Victor Hugo
Rue de Verdun
Les Halles
This covered market is open all day (Monday to Saturday).
0 75 150 m
0 75 150 yd
Rue Voltaire
To Cité (800 m)
Cité
Caveau des Vins
Taste and buy Languedoc's best wines in the cellar of the 13th-century Tour du Treseau.
Lices
Musée de l'Inquisition
Basses
Rue Gustave Nadaud
L'Art Gourmand
This chocolaterie sells a very creative range of goodies.
Rue St Louis
Rue Vicomte Trencavel
Hautes
Lices
L'Auberge de Dame Carcas
This restaurant is named after the medieval heroine who saved the city and gave it her name.

Cassoulet is labour-intensive – the beans must be well soaked to allow the germination that sweetens them, and the cooking must be long and slow to meld the flavours.

Of course like so many trademark dishes, cassoulet changes in its make-up from area to area and even from town to town. For while the **cassoulet de Castelenaudary**, perhaps the most celebrated version of the dish, cooks only pork (in all its guises) with its beans, the Carcassonne version adds mutton, and the cassoulet from Toulouse, the centre of Languedoc until the 1960s, contains all of the above plus its most celebrated contribution to gastronomy, **saucisse de Toulouse** (fat, mild-tasting pork sausage). All cassoulets, however, share several key ingredients: goose fat, herbs, onion and garlic, and a sprinkling of bread crumbs before it is put in the oven.

Saucisse de Toulouse, the region's best known charcuterie, often comes **à la languedocienne**, sauteed in goose fat and served with tomato, parsley and capers. But 'in the Languedoc style' isn't an immutable recipe; it can be a garlicky garnish of tomatoes, aubergines and **cèpes** (boletus mushrooms).

What has been baptised 'the divine Occitan gastropod' – the snail – is immensely popular here; **cargolade** (or **gargoulade** in Roussillon) is a complicated dish in which the snails are cooked slowly in broth seasoned with herbs, and served with a sauce of bacon, onion, anchovies and sausage.

The Mediterranean Sea provides a wealth of seafood, especially lobster, tuna, sardines, anchovies and mussels. Notable Languedoc fish dishes include **langouste à la sétoise** (spiny lobster stew) and **brandade de morue**, a salt cod purée popular in Provence, but sometimes eaten here with truffles.

In Roussillon, Spanish and Catalan influences are immediately obvious, with **tapas** (Spanish hors d'œuvre) served everywhere in wine bars. But

REGIONAL VARIATIONS

THE KING OF CHEESES

The mouldy blue-green veins running through Roquefort are, in fact, the seeds of microscopic mushrooms, picked in the caves at Roquefort then cultivated on leavened bread. During the cheese's ripening process – which takes place in the same natural caves cut into the mountainside – delicate draughts of air stream through the cave, encouraging the blue *penicillium roqueforti* to eat its way through the white cheese curds.

Roquefort ranks as one of France's priciest and most noble cheeses. In 1407 Charles VI granted exclusive cheesemaking rights to the villagers of Roquefort. In the 17th century, the Sovereign Court of the Parliament of Toulouse imposed severe penalties against fraudulent cheesemakers trading under the Roquefort name.

Roussillon can also claim its own specialities, especially its signature dish **ouillade** (or **ollada**), a beef and bean stew cooked separately in a heavy pot called an **ouille**. Among other Roussillon dishes are: **bouillinade** (a local bouillabaisse combining fish, potatoes and pimentos); **fricandeau** (fresh tuna braised in a fish stock with olives or anchovies); **civet de langoustes au Banyuls** (stew of spiny lobster, tomatoes, shallots, garlic and ham cooked in wine); and **esqueixade de bacallà** (cod salad).

Roussillon is very rich in stone fruits, notably apricots and peaches. **Cerises de Céret** are celebrated for being the first cherries to ripen in France (late April).

Among the favourite pastries and sweets in the region are the **croquettes au miel** (honey tarts) from Narbonne, the **gâteau sec au poivre** (pepper biscuits) from Limoux and the **fruits confits** (candied fruit) from Carcassonne. One particular gastronomic oddity in these parts are **petits pâtés de Pézenas** (also called **diabolos**), which are savoury-sweet mincemeat (as in mutton) pies said to have been inspired by the Indian servants of Clive of India, who stayed near Pézenas in 1766.

DON'T MISS – Languedoc-Roussillon

- **Canard sauté au Fitou** – duck sauteed in Fitou wine
- **Moules de Bouzigues** – Bouzigues mussels eaten on the half-shell
- **Nougat noir de Perpignan** – sweet black nougat from the capital of Roussillon
- **Jambon cru de la Montagne Noir** – superb raw ham from the 'Black Mountain' near Carcassonne
- **Boles de Picolat** (or **boules de Picoulat**) – spicy pork meatballs in a bean casserole
- **Salade catalane** – salad greens with peppers, tomatoes and anchovies
- **Aligot de Lozère** – potato, cheese and garlic purée
- **Petits pâtés de Pézanas** – sweet and savoury mincemeat pies

Corsica

Corsica is the most geographically diverse of all the Mediterranean islands. The hundreds of kilometres of clear-water beaches that turn the island into a circus of holiday-makers in summer give way to granite mountains of up to 2000m, which cover almost two-thirds of the terrain.

Despite a brief period of self-rule in the mid-18th century, Corsica has been dominated by a patchwork of outsiders since earliest times, including Etruscans, Phoenician Greeks, Romans, Pisans and Genoans (who bequeathed them their language, Corsu, a Tuscan dialect of Italian). The island has been an integral part of France since 1769, the very year in which Corsica's favoured son, Napoleon Bonaparte, was born.

Both Corsica's geography and history have played important roles in forming its cuisine, a simple but hearty style of cooking that some French mainlanders are apt to look down upon as coarse. Due to a very real fear

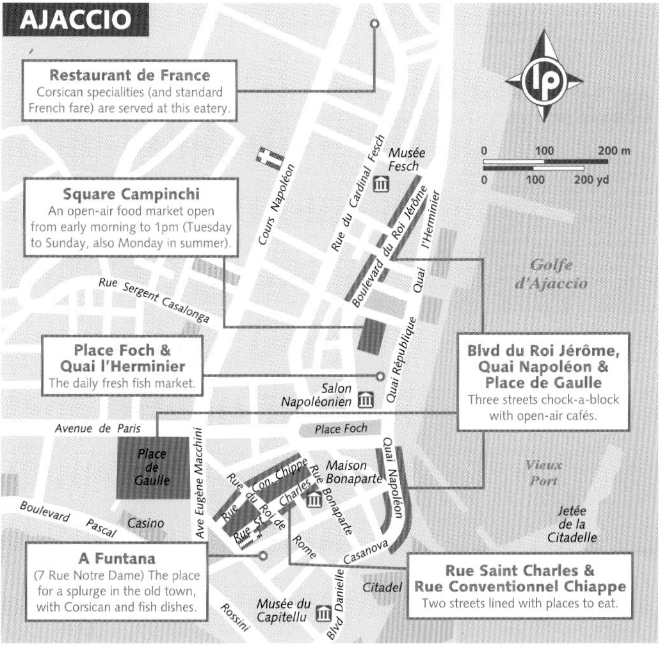
AJACCIO
Restaurant de France
Corsican specialities (and standard French fare) are served at this eatery.
Square Campinchi
An open-air food market open from early morning to 1pm (Tuesday to Sunday, also Monday in summer).
Place Foch & Quai l'Herminier
The daily fresh fish market.
Blvd du Roi Jérôme, Quai Napoléon & Place de Gaulle
Three streets chock-a-block with open-air cafés.
A Funtana
(7 Rue Notre Dame) The place for a splurge in the old town, with Corsican and fish dishes.
Rue Saint Charles & Rue Conventionnel Chiappe
Two streets lined with places to eat.
0 100 200 m
0 100 200 yd
Musée Fesch
Rue du Cardinal Fesch
Cours Napoléon
Boulevard du Roi Jérôme
Quai l'Herminier
Golfe d'Ajaccio
Rue Sergent Casalonga
Quai République
Salon Napoléonien
Avenue de Paris
Place Foch
Place de Gaulle
Ave Eugène Macchini
Maison Bonaparte
Quai Napoléon
Vieux Port
Boulevard Pascal
Casino
Rue Con. Chippe
Rue du Roi de Rome
Rue St Charles
Rue Bonaparte
Casanova
Jetée de la Citadelle
Citadel
Blvd Danielle
Musée du Capitellu
Rossini

of invasion, Corsicans tended to avoid the coastal areas, settling in the more protected mountains. This cut them off from exterior influence and trading, with the result that their cuisine is traditionally based solely on what the land – and not the sea – could produce.

The hills and mountains were ideal for raising goats, sheep, cows and pigs; the inland streams yielded trout and eels. Small kitchen gardens raised a bounty of produce, especially courgettes, artichokes, asparagus and aubergines; in leaner times they could rely on the fruit of the ubiquitous chestnut trees. The maquis, made up of shrubs mixed with rosemary, laurel, lavender and thyme, would flavour most dishes, along with olive oil, wild mint, fennel, tomatoes, honey, oranges and **cédrat**, a sweeter variety of lemon. These raw materials have come together to create such trademark Corsican foods as **stufatu** (mutton stew); **premonata** (beef braised with juniper berries); **cabri** (kid) roasted with rosemary and garlic); smoked and air-dried sausages; polenta made with cornmeal or chestnut flour; and goat's and sheep's milk cheeses. Recipes for blackbird and other wild birds, roasted with sage or cooked as a **salmis** (partially roasted, then simmered in wine, shallots and onions) further attest to the ingenuity of an isolated people.

Lonzo aux Haricots Blancs

This delicious, colorful dish takes its flavour from the lonzo sausage, which can be substituted by a spicy coppa or prosciutto.

2 cups	white beans, cooked
1 tablespoon	olive oil
1	medium onion
2	cloves garlic
4	slices lonzo
2	tomatoes
2 tablespoons	thyme
	pepper
125ml/½cup	white wine

Heat the olive oil in a frying pan and add the lonzo, garlic and onion, stirring constantly to prevent burning. Cook on a low heat for three minutes. Blanche the tomatoes in boiling water for a few minutes then peel off the skins when they are cool enough to touch. Chop and add to pan with thyme and pepper. Let simmer at a higher heat with lid off for 5 minutes. Pour in the wine and beans and stir. Raise the heat and simmer until the liquid is nearly gone. Add salt and pepper to taste.

Serves 2

THE FRUIT OF THE BREAD TREE

The Corsicans were relying on the ubiquitous chestnut trees as early as the 16th century, when the Genoese rulers started requisitioning Corsica's grain crop for use back home. The tree became known as **l'arbre à pain** (the bread tree) because of the many uses the Corsicans found for **farine de châtaigne** (chestnut flour). These days the flour is primarily used to make pastries and other sweets.

Chestnutty delights include **falculelli** (pressed and frittered Corsican brocciu cheese served on a chestnut leaf), **délice à la châtaigne** (Corsican chestnut cake), **castagnacci** (chestnut flour pudding) and, last but not least, **bière à la châtaigne** (chestnut beer).

The Corsicans' taste for spice and strong flavours is most evident in their sausages and hams, whose particular flavour is derived from free-range pigs who traditionally feed on chestnuts, acorns, and plants imbued with the fragrance of the maquis. From these herb-saturated porcines come the prosciutto-like **coppa** and **lonzo**, both of which are also names for cuts of pork, as well as the thinner **figatelli**. Both domestic pigs and **sangliers** (boars) are often cooked **en daube** (stewed with red wine, onions, garlic, vegetables and herbs).

Once the risk of invasion had disappeared and people left the mountainous hinterland to live by the sea, fish became an integral part of the Corsican diet. Spiny lobster, cuttlefish, red mullet, tuna, cod, sea bream and small rockfish are prepared in a variety of ways: steamed with garlic, olive oil and tomatoes; baked with maquis herbs; and stuffed with **brocciu**, a type of Corsican cheese. The rockfish are usually reserved for a local spicy version of bouillabaisse called **ziminu**. **Cigale de mer**, literally 'sea cricket' or 'sea cicada', is a flat, spiny lobster with sweet succulent flesh. As in Provence, the roe of sea urchins is a popular, brine-infused starter.

Corsicans exploited their herds of sheep and goats, and developed a number of cheeses. The island's most popular cheese and the only one with an AOC is **brocciu**, a chameleon-like cheese that can be eaten fresh, when it is almost like ricotta, or as a rather mild and creamy, crumbly cheese when drained, salted and aged. Made from the **petit-lait** (whey) of either goat's or ewe's milk, brocciu can be stuffed in calamari, artichokes or ravioli; melted in cannelloni and flat Corsican omelettes; baked in pastries; spread on polenta; eaten with jam for breakfast; fried in doughnuts; or made into **canistrone** (cheese tarts). **Tomme Corse** is a semi-hard, granular raw ewe's milk cheese.

DON'T MISS – Corsica

- **Corsican Cheeses – Fleur du Maquis** and **Brin d'Amour**, two semi-soft ewe's milk cheeses that have a strong herby scent, with rinds covered in savory, rosemary and juniper berries
- **Corsica's flavoured beers** – La Pietra (made from chestnuts) and Colomba (made with the flavours of the maquis)
- **Beignets au brocciu à la farine de châtaigne** – brocciu cheese frittered in chestnut flour
- **Saucisson sec d'âne** – air-dried sausage made from donkey meat (worth a dare)
- **Ziminu à la calvaise** – seafood soup Calvi style, the most authentic (and spiciest) version of this 'Corsican bouillabaisse'
- **Stufatu** – a delicious stew of mutton cooked with ham, tomatoes and white wine
- **Rogets à la bonifacienne** – mullet cooked with anchovies, tomatoes and garlic

Though many sweets are prepared with chestnut flour (see the boxed text The Fruit of the Bread Tree earlier in this chapter), Corsica does not rely entirely on this staple. Other delights include **fiadone** (lemon-flavoured sponge cake filled with soft brocciu), **fougazi** (big, flat, aniseed-flavoured biscuits), **canistrelli** (sugar-crusted biscuits, often flavoured with lemon, almonds or even white wine), **moustachole** (bread with big sugar crystals on top) and **gayshelli** (sugared biscuits). A speciality found only in Bonifacio is **paides morts**, a nut and raisin bread that translates rather ominously as 'bread of the dead'.

shopping

& markets

France is renowned for its extraordinary chefs and restaurants, bu another of the country's premier culinary delights is to stock up or delicious fresh breads, pastries, cheese, fruit, vegetables and preparec dishes. Shopping here is as an enjoyable experience as sitting dowr for a gourmet **pique-nique** or cooking a meal with friends.

Specialist Shops

Most people in France buy a good part of their food from a series of small neighbourhood shops, each with its own speciality, though like everywhere more and more people are relying on supermarkets and hypermarkets. At first, having to go to four shops and stand in four queues to fill the fridge (or assemble a picnic) may seem a waste of time, but the whole ritual is an important part of the way many French people live their daily lives.

Boulangerie
Pâtisserie
Île St Louis, Paris

Since each **commerçant** (shopkeeper) specialises in only one type of food, he or she can provide all sorts of useful tips: which round of Camembert is ripe, which wine will complement certain foods and so on. In any case, most products for sale at charcuteries, pâtisseries and traiteurs are clearly labelled. We often ask ourselves why that is so since the French are such experts in things gastronomic. Perhaps they just need a reminder of the abundance available to them.

As the whole set up is geared to people buying small quantities of fresh food each day, it is perfectly acceptable to purchase just enough for single meals: a few **tranches** (slices) of meat to make yourself a sandwich, perhaps, or a **petit bout** (small hunk) of sausage. You can also request enough **pour une/deux personne(s)** (for one/two persons). Even small villages have a selection of food shops, and remote hamlets are usually served by mobile grocers, butchers and bakers. Note that many specialist food shops are closed on Sunday afternoon and Monday.

MEETING & GREETING

The easiest way to improve your relations with French merchants is always to say '**bonjour, monsieur/madame/mademoiselle**' when you walk into a shop, and '**merci, monsieur** ... **au revoir**' when you leave. **Monsieur** means 'sir' and can be used with any male person who isn't a child. **Madame** is used where 'Mrs' or 'ma'am' would apply in English, whereas **mademoiselle** (Miss) is used when talking to unmarried women. When in doubt, use madame.

When buying fruit, vegetables or flowers anywhere except at supermarkets, do not touch the produce or blossoms unless invited to do so. Show the shopkeepers what you want and they will choose for you.

Boucherie

A **boucherie** (butcher) sells fresh meats including beef, lamb, pork and chicken, but for a wider range of poultry products you have to go to a specialist (see Marchand de Volaille later in this chapter).

Boucherie Chevaline

This is a butcher's shop that specialises in **viande de cheval** (horsemeat), though they might also be able to sell you some nice **côtes de chèvre** (goat ribs). A boucherie chevaline is identifiable by the gilded horse's head above the entrance. Some people prefer horsemeat to other meat, in part because it is less likely to have been produced using artificial hormones and has less fat (see the boxed text Horse d'Œuvre in the Staples & Specialities chapter).

Boulangerie

Fresh bread is baked and sold at France's 36,000 **boulangeries** (bakeries), which supply three-quarters of the country's bread. Bread is baked at various times during the day, so it's available fresh as early as 6am and also in the afternoon. Most boulangeries close for one day a week, but the days are staggered so that a town or neighbourhood is never left without a place to buy a loaf – except, perhaps, on Sunday afternoon. Places that sell bread but don't bake it on the premises are known as **dépôts de pain**. You can ask for your loaf of bread to be **coupé en deux** (cut in two) or, for a small fee, sliced.

Charcuterie

A **charcuterie** is a delicatessen offering sliced meats, pâtés, terrines, rillettes etc though they sometimes sell other things like seafood salads and even casseroles. But such pre-prepared meals are bought at a **traiteur** (see Traiteur later in this chapter). Most supermarkets have a charcuterie counter.

Chocolaterie

This is a shop selling only chocolate; most chocolateries specialise in their own products made right on the premises.

Confiserie

Sweets including chocolate made with the finest ingredients can be found at confiseries, which are sometimes found within boulangeries and pâtisseries.

Épicerie

An **épicerie** (literally, spice shop) is a small grocery store with a little bit of everything, including fruit and vegetables. It is also sometimes known as an **alimentation générale**. Most épiceries are considerably more expensive than supermarkets, especially in the cities, though some – such as branches of the Casino and Stoc chains – are more like minimarkets. Some épiceries are open on days when other food shops are closed, and many family-run épiceries stay open until late at night.

Fromagerie

If you buy your cheese in a supermarket, you're likely to end up with unripe and relatively tasteless products unless you know how to select each variety. Here's where a **fromagerie**, sometimes also called a **crémerie**, comes in. The owner, a true expert on matters dairy, can supply you with cheese that is appropriately ripe and will almost always let you taste before you decide what to buy. Just ask and they will cut you a little piece from under the rind so as not to damage the cheese's appearance. Most fromageries sell both whole and half-rounds of Camembert, so you don't have to buy more than you're likely to eat in a day or two. Most fromageries group their cheeses in the same way we've described in the Staples & Specialities chapter: goat's milk cheeses, blue or veined cheeses, soft cheeses, semi-hard cheeses and hard cheeses.

Appenzell
Murols
Munster
NOUVION

Cheese in a fromagerie, Paris

Marchand de Légumes et de Fruits

Fruit and vegetables are sold by a **marchand de légumes et de fruits** (greengrocer) and at food markets and supermarkets. You can buy whatever quantity of produce suits you, even if it's just three carrots and a peach. The kind of produce on offer varies greatly from region to region, from season to season, and some things are available in only one small region for a limited time of the year. Many **primeurs** (the first fruits and vegetables of the season) come from Brittany and Provence. **Biologique** (or **bio**) means grown organically, without chemicals (see the boxed text Letters & Labels in the Staples & Specialities chapter).

Marchand de Vin

Wine is sold by **marchands de vin** (or a **caviste**), such as the shops of the Nicolas chain, which – in its favour – often displays local wines on sale in its windows. Wine shops in close proximity to the vineyards of Burgundy, Bordeaux, the Loire region and other wine-growing areas are often called **vinothèques** and offer tastings.

Marchand de Volaille

A **marchand de volaille** is a butcher's shop specialising in poultry, and is sometimes called a **volailler**. Here you can buy such varieties as **poulet fermier** (free-range chicken) and **poulet de grain** (corn-fed chicken), which will cost much more than a regular bird.

Marché

A **marché** (food market) – covered or open, in a country town or the big city – is the best place to buy your meat, fish, cheese and produce for a number of reasons: quality, choice, price and sheer entertainment value (see At the Market later in this chapter).

Pâtisserie

Mouth-watering pastries are available at a pâtisserie. Some of the most common pastries include **tarte aux fruits** (fruit tarts), **pain aux raisins** (a flat, spiral pastry made with custard and sultanas) and **religieuses** (eclairs that resemble a nun's habit – vaguely). Pâtisseries often sell ice creams and sorbets as well (see Pâtisserie in the Staples & Specialities chapter).

HELMSTETTER
1776
Pâtisserie sign, Colmar, Alsace

Poissonerie

DEGUSTATION SUR PLACE
PORTER
Poissonnerie

Fresh fish and shellfish are available from a **poissonnerie** (fishmonger). People have such a taste for fish that poissonneries in inland cities and towns often have as a big a selection as the ones closer to the coast.

Supermarché & Hypermarché

Both town and city centres usually have at least one department store with a large **supermarché** (supermarket) section in the basement or on the first floor. Stores to look for include Monoprix, Prisunic and Nouvelles Galeries. In Paris, the cheapest edibles are sold at the no-frills supermarkets of Ed, l'Épicier. Most larger supermarkets have charcuterie and cheese counters, and many also have in-house boulangeries.

The cheapest place to buy food is at a **hypermarché** (hypermarket), such as those of the Auchan, Carrefour, Intermarché, E Leclerc and Rallye chains, where you'll pay up to 40% less for staples than at an épicerie. Unfortunately, they're nearly always on the outskirts of town, often in an area accessible only by car.

Traiteur

If the word **traiteur** (caterer) is written on a shop sign, it means that the establishment sells ready-to-eat dishes: casseroles, salads of all shades and hues, and many more elaborate dishes. Traiteurs are a picnicker's delight and a godsend to people who want something better than takeaway but can't be bothered cooking. French people have never hesitated about buying prepared food to take home from a traiteur.

Triperie

A **triperie** is a butcher's shop specialising in fresh tripe, dressed tripe, as well as ready-to-eat tripe dishes.

Viennoiserie

Croissants, brioches and pains au chocolat (a flat 'croissant' filled with chocolate) and the like are called **viennoiseries** and are usually bought at boulangeries. You can tell if a croissant has been made with margarine or butter by the shape: margarine croissants have their tips almost touching, while those made with butter have them pointing away from each other.

At the Market

In most towns and cities, many of the products mentioned in Specialist Shops are available one or more days a week at **marchés en plein air** (open-air markets; also known as **marchés découverts**), and up to six days a week at **marchés couverts** (covered markets; often known as **les halles**). Markets are usually cheaper than food shops and supermarkets, and the merchandise, especially fruit and vegetables, is fresher and of better quality.

In smaller towns and villages, markets have a vital social function. Like cafés, they are important meeting places, especially for small-scale farmers who have their weekly chat while selling their wares. There is no bargaining, and weighing is sometimes still done with hand scales.

What you'll find depends on the region and the season. In spring and summer, the markets of Provence – the open-air ones in Aix-en-Prevence and Carpentras spring to mind – are awash with olives, goat's cheese, garlic, lavender, honey, peaches, melons and a whole host of other sun-kissed products. Nothing comes close to La Rochelle's covered market for fresh Atlantic fish and shellfish, and the foie gras and truffle market in Périgord is an epicure's delight (see the boxed text Treasures of the Earth & Sky in the Regional Variations chapter). But no other place has the sheer variety of markets like Paris does (see the boxed text To Market later in this chapter).

Avoid the temptation to take a shopping list and just allow your five senses to take over. In the words of Glynn Christian, author of *Edible France*, "lists for shopping pinch the imagination and close the eyes to what is on display".

AUX BEAUX

Les Halles covered market, Bayonne, Basque Country

BASTILLE MARKET

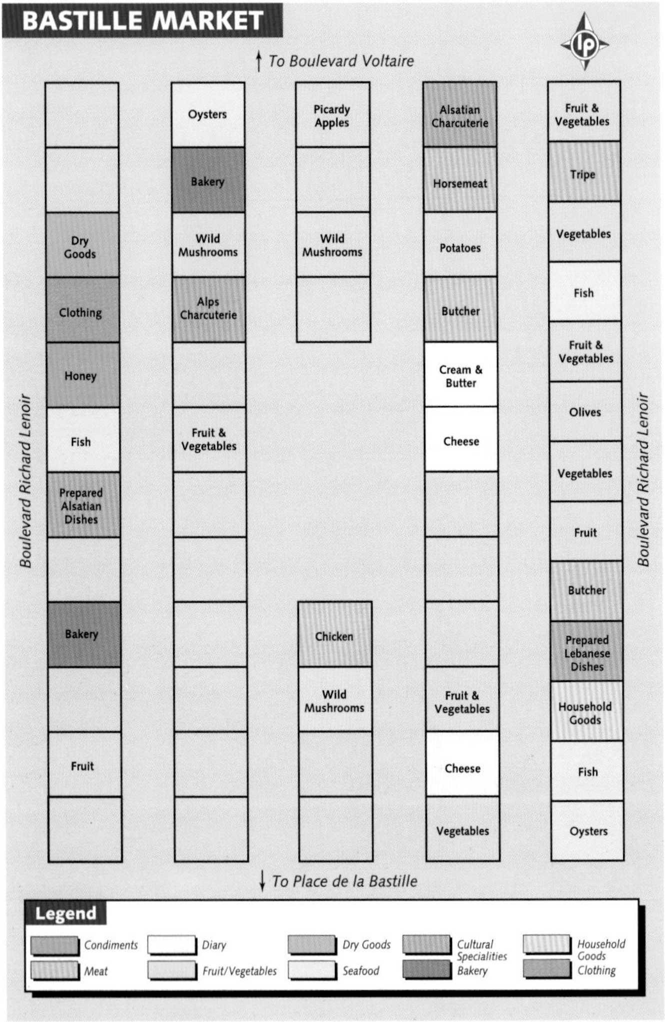
To Boulevard Voltaire
Oysters
Bakery
Wild Mushrooms
Alps Charcuterie
Fruit & Vegetables
Picardy Apples
Wild Mushrooms
Chicken
Wild Mushrooms
Alsatian Charcuterie
Horsemeat
Potatoes
Butcher
Cream & Butter
Cheese
Fruit & Vegetables
Cheese
Vegetables
Fruit & Vegetables
Tripe
Vegetables
Fish
Fruit & Vegetables
Olives
Vegetables
Fruit
Butcher
Prepared Lebanese Dishes
Household Goods
Fish
Oysters
Dry Goods
Clothing
Honey
Fish
Prepared Alsatian Dishes
Bakery
Fruit
Boulevard Richard Lenoir
Boulevard Richard Lenoir
To Place de la Bastille
Legend
Condiments
Meat
Diary
Fruit/Vegetables
Dry Goods
Seafood
Cultural Specialities
Bakery
Household Goods
Clothing

TO MARKET, TO MARKET

If, while strolling through Paris on a Saturday morning, you notice throngs of basket-toting people passing you by with great determination, and others, laden down with bags, going the opposite direction at a more relaxed pace, you have stumbled upon the most Parisian of weekend pastimes: shopping at the street food market. There is no better way to be mistaken for a native; forsake that day at the Louvre, grab a **panier** (basket) and load up on fresh provisions.

Paris counts 57 **marchés découverts** (open markets, usually open 9am-2.30pm twice a week), and 18 **marchés couverts** (covered markets; usually open 9am-1pm and 4-7pm six days a week). Completing the picture are a slew of independent **rues commerçantes**, pedestrian streets where the shops spread onto the cobblestones and set up outdoor stalls.

To foreigners, food markets in the capital are the most delightful of all Parisian stereotypes. They offer the usual French standbys and more – fresh vegetables and fruit, meat, bread, pâtisseries, dozens of cheeses, charcuterie, prepared dishes, foie gras, nuts, fish and flowers – all painstakingly displayed beneath chalkboards with the prices marked in that characteristic French scrawl. Tradespeople and peddlers ply basket-repair services, Oriental carpets, sewing machines and kitchen utensils. In spring, children sell bunches of heady, purple lilacs. A Paris market fulfils every fantasy we have entertained about the City of Light.

But markets are far more than a cute picture postcard, a remembrance of a France past. They are very much a symbol of Paris present and an integral part of modern life. Touring them gives you a look at a cross section of the peoples that make up Paris today. Some people think that modernisation is taking its toll on the city's markets. While immense shopping centres or hypermarkets are banned from within city limits, moderately sized **supermarchés** abound, menacing the market with convenient one-stop shopping and longer opening hours. Are they making markets irrelevant?

Probably not, for markets still offer many seductive advantages. Dependable quality is ensured through the relationship of the vendors and their repeat customers. Truck-garden culture brings in fresh produce that reflects the seasons in a way the mass-produced produce of supermarkets cannot. The sometimes daunting number of competing stands allows you to pick and choose for quality and price. The flourishing immigrant populations are bringing new blood to the old tradition with booming ethnic markets. Markets can be a lifesaver on a Sunday, when large supermarkets close their doors. And the very Gallic desire to cling to **l'art de la gastronomie** for the sake of tradition (if not practicality) cannot be discounted.

The following is a list of 10 Paris markets based on the variety of their produce, ethnicity and the neighbourhood. They are **la crème de la crème**.

Rue Montorgueil, *between Rue de Turbigo and Rue Réaumur, 2nd arrondissement (metro Les Halles)*

A plaque on colourful Rue Montorgueil calls it 'a bastion of gastronomy and the food trade since the 13th century'. Even after Paris' 700-year-old wholesale market, Les Halles, was moved from this area to the southern suburb of Rungis in 1969, food remains the party line here – witness the shops offering everything from live crayfish to vintage wines and wholesale foie gras to kitchenware. Don't miss the stunning pâtisserie Stohrer at No 51 and the historic restaurant Au Rocher de Cancale at No 78, where the characters in Balzac's *La Comédie Humaine* hung out. The market is open all day Tuesday to Sunday.

Maubert, *Place Maubert, 5th arrondissement (metro Maubert-Mutualité)*

A hop from the Seine, Place Maubert reigns over Saint Germain des Prés, the most upscale part of the bohemian 5th arrondissement. A small, cheerfully cramped group of merchants spread over the pavements of this little triangle of intersecting streets. Pleasant cafés lining one side of the market provide a nice break from shopping. Tourists will appreciate Maubert's close proximity to the Île de la Cité, Notre Dame and the Jardin du Luxembourg. The market is open in the morning on Tuesday, Thursday and Saturday.

Rue Mouffetard, *5th arrondissement (metro Monge or Censier-Daubenton)*

The endearingly rumpled Rue Mouffetard is home to Paris' university students, whose lively bars rub shoulders with food stores on the narrow, hilly street beloved by Hemingway. This is the city's most picturesque market street. Pyramids of fruit, suspended rabbits and chickens, and wonderful strong-smelling cheese shops make it a true moveable feast. Dine at a bargain bistro (try Rue du Pot de Fer), and finish with a drink where the local students do, at a café on the dreamy little Place de la Contrescarpe. The Rue Mouffetard market is open all day Tuesday to Sunday.

Rue Mouffetard

Rue Cler, *7th arrondissement (metro École Militaire)*
Rue Cler is a breath of fresh air in a sometimes stuffy neighbourhood (most of the city's governmental buildings are nearby). A short sunny market street near the Eiffel Tower, the Rue Cler market feels like a party on weekends when the whole neighbourhood – from yuppies to ageing madames – turn out en masse. Have a **café crème** (espresso with cream or milk) at the popular Café du Marché at No 38 and watch the dignified grands-mères, poodles in their push carts, meeting friends and evaluating the produce. The market is open all day Tuesday to Sunday.

Saint Quentin, *85 Blvd de Magenta, 10th arrondissement (metro Gare de l'Est)*
The wholesale market, Les Halles in the 1st arrondissement, is long gone, but a handful of other iron-and-glass covered markets remain from this architectural style so popular in the late 19th century. A welcome respite from the cold in winter, covered markets are a classier precursor of our modern shopping malls. Built in 1866, Saint Quentin is a maze of corridors lined with gourmet food stalls. A café counter where vendors stand for an afternoon brew and a fountain in the middle of the market complete the illusion of a town within a city. Saint Quentin is open 9am-1pm and 4-7pm Tuesday to Sunday.

Bastille, *Blvd Richard Lenoir, 11th arrondissement (metro Bastille)*
A subterranean canal runs under Blvd Richard Lenoir, forming a wide, open space above, perfect for what many consider to be Paris' quintessential neighborhood market. It is also one of the biggest, with over a dozen stalls for every type of food. Here you can observe locals exchanging **bises** (kisses on the cheek) and pleasantries with vendors over great piles of endives, courgettes, peppers and leeks. Buy a rich hunk of Gruyère cheese and a crusty baguette for a picnic at the exquisite Place des Vosges. The Bastille market is open Tuesday and Sunday morning only.

Aligre, *Place d'Aligre, 12th arrondissement (metro Ledru-Rollin)*
Although gentrification has brought rising rents and hip bars to neighbouring areas, Place d'Aligre remains a solid Arab and North African enclave. Exotically garbed mothers carry babies on their backs as they bargain down the price of plantains. Competing vendors call out their prices in several different languages. Muslim butchers display whole sheep with their prices marked in Arabic. Browse the adjoining covered Marché Beauvau and the large flea market, then take mint tea and a honey pastry at the North African La Ruche à Miel, a tearoom at 19 Rue d'Aligre. Beauvau is open all day Tuesday to Sunday.

Grenelle, *Blvd de Grenelle, between Rue de Lourmel and Rue du Commerce, 15th arrondissement (metro La Motte Piquet-Grenelle)*

The Grenelle market runs below an elevated train line and is surrounded by stately Haussmann boulevards and elaborate Art Nouveau apartment blocks. On market days all of Paris prepares for the week's dinner parties by picking up such goodies as nuts and dates, stuffed snails, buckets of paella and Alsatian choucroute. Grenelle is open Wednesday and Sunday morning only.

Batignolles-Clichy, *Blvd des Batignolles, between Rue des Batignolles and Rue Puteaux, 17th arrondissement (metro Rome)*

Spread out under the filtering light of plane trees, Batignolles-Clichy is one of two **marchés bio** (organic markets) in Paris. The trade of organic produce is government-regulated (though still regarded with suspicion by traditionalists). Feast your eyes on **galettes de blé** (wheaten galettes), hearty whole-wheat breads and pâtisseries, rough and simple cheeses, yoghurt and healthy looking vegetables. The market is open on Saturday morning only.

Market sales, Paris

Belleville, *Blvd de Belleville, 11th-20th arrondissements (metro Belleville)*

Like the Beauvau market at Place d'Aligre, Belleville provides a fascinating entry into the large, vibrant ethnic communities of the eastern neighbourhoods, home to African, Middle Eastern and Asian immigrants as well as artists and students. The market is a joy to behold, with what seems like kilometres of tables groaning with colourful vegetables, miniature pineapples, lychees and fresh dates on their branches. Cheerful vendors, offering slices of mangoes and playfully sparring with their competitors across the aisles, turn this market into a real show. The Belleville market is open Tuesday and Friday morning only.

Emma Bland is a New York-based freelance writer and magazine editor who loves exploring the markets of Paris.

A French Picnic

If you can't afford to eat in expensive restaurants and want to avoid the standard fare of tourist menus such as steak-frites, crème caramel and so on, you can still enjoy France's epicurean delights by buying food at markets or speciality shops. It's the best way to sample the local delicacies of a particular region.

French people love the great outdoors almost as much as they love eating, so the popularity of the **pique-nique** – in parks, forests, by the sea or lakeshore – is no surprise. Besides fruit from the markets they will go to a charcuterie, a fromagerie and a traiteur to stock up on provisions. Pique-nique favourites that travel well include **saucisson sec** (air-dried sausage); cheese of all types; **museauu de bœuf en vinaigrette** (a kind of beef brawn in vinaigrette); **filets de harengs à l'huile** (herring fillets in oil); **anchois marinées** (marinated anchovies), **macédoine de fruits de mer** (mixed seafood salad); and **macédoine de légumes** (mixed vegetable salad).

Most long-distance trains have a **voiture-buffet** (buffet car). Though the bill of fare can sound fairly appetising when read out by the conductor, it's not – and over-priced to boot. Pack your own refreshments before boarding and enjoy a picnic **à roues** (on wheels).

Picnic in the Loire

Things to Take Home

There are many items that will catch your eye while perusing markets and shops – flavoured oils and foie gras from Périgord or smoked garlic from Boulogne – and you'll probably want to take some of them home. One of the best buys in France is goose or duck **confit** (preserved meat) and foie gras. Confit is best bought in sealed jars; it will keep for four years if unopened. Foie gras is best bought **mi-cuit** (half-cooked or preserved) or shrink-wrapped. Admittedly they're part of chains, but the Comtesse du Barry and the Ducs de Gasconie shops have a decent selection of preserved foods.

Other good buys include **purée de marrons** (chestnut purée); pâtés in jars; **fruits glacés** (glazed or candied fruit), **pruneaux fourrés** (prunes stuffed with sweet cream or other filling); jams; flavoured oils and vinegars; and of course booze. Look for alcohol that is impossible to get at home: any of the eaux-de-vie from Alsace and Lorraine; the delightful crèmes from Burgundy; pineau des Charentes; and marc de Champagne (see the Drinks chapter).

QUARANTINE RULES

Australia and New Zealand have strict quarantine rules to protect their unique wildlife, and every single item of food or plant matter must be declared, even holy water. Declaring them doesn't mean they're banned, but items that won't be allowed in include: milk products; raw and unroasted nuts; egg products; fresh fruit and vegetables; salmon and trout products (conditions apply); live plants (although many seeds are acceptable); and most pork and pig products. You won't have trouble with dried foods if they are dirt-free, so a bag of dried **cèpes** (boletus mushrooms) or **marrons glacés** (candied chestnuts) should definitely find its way into your bag. North America can pose some of the same difficulties as Australasia. Some fruit, vegetables and plants may be acceptable but must be declared and be free of pests. Most meat products are banned, while fresh mushrooms and truffles are OK if free of dirt. Baked goods are also allowed in, so too most confectionery, and dried foods such as tea and roasted coffee. Some seeds and plant matter require permits.

But think twice before buying. There are no restrictions on the import or export of foodstuffs within EU borders and the limitations on duty-paid alcohol are generous. Taking foodstuffs back to Australia, New Zealand and the USA, however, poses a different problem (see the boxed text). In that case switch over to hand-painted porcelain dishes and crystal stemware.

CAFE DE FLORE

Bar des 13 Coins
BAR

INDIANA

where to eat & drink

f Britain is a nation of shopkeepers, as Napoleon once famously aid, than France is a nation of restaurateurs. The French eat out requently, and the owner of the **restaurant du quartier** (neighbourhood restaurant) is generally held in great esteem as a source of nowledge (and not just about food and drink).

There is no problem dining alone in France for either males or females, and it is rare to share a table. Those who feel uncomfortable eating solo in a formal setting, however, should choose the much more relaxed **brasseries** or **bistros** (see Places to Eat & Drink later in this chapter).

When you enter most types of eateries, you should always greet the staff member at the front with a cheery '**bonjour**' (good day) or '**bonsoir**' (good evening), as the case may be (see the boxed text Meeting & Greeting in the Shopping chapter). It is considered rude to just walk in and cast your eyes around for a table. If you haven't booked, you'll be taken more seriously if you ask for the number of **couverts** (covers) you need rather than just stating the number of **personnes** (people). Never, ever, summon the waiter by shouting '**garçon!**', which they always seem to do in old movies. Garçon means 'boy' and saying '**s'il vous plaît**' (please) is the way it's done now.

PAYING UP

With the exception of cafétérias and self-service restaurants, most eateries take credit cards. Visa (known here as **Carte Bleue**) is the most widely accepted, followed by MasterCard (Access or Eurocard). American Express cards are not very useful except at upscale restaurants. The machine used for payment, known as a **machine Carte Bleue** or a **sabot** (clog; for its shape), is usually hand-held and brought to the table.

French law requires that restaurants and cafés include the **service** (service charge; usually 12-15%). A word of warning: **service compris** (service included; often abbreviated as 's.c.' at the bottom of the bill) means that the service charge is included in the price of each dish. **Service non-compris** (service not included) or **service en sus** (service in addition) means that the service charge is calculated *after* the food and drink you've ordered is added up. In either case you pay the total of the bill only, and a **pourboire** (tip) is not necessary nor expected. However, most people leave a few francs in restaurants, unless the service was bad. They rarely tip in cafés and bars when they've just had a coffee or other drink.

Traditionally, 'going Dutch' (ie, splitting the bill) at restaurants was regarded an uncivilised custom, and the person who did the inviting would usually pay. Nowadays close friends and colleagues will usually split the cost equally. However, they will never calculate it down to the last franc and centime.

Places to Eat & Drink

There's a vast number of eateries in France where you can get a full lunch or dinner, a snack or even breakfast, such as it is (see Breakfast in The Culture of French Cuisine chapter). Most have defined roles though some definitions are becoming a bit blurred.

Auberge

An **auberge** (inn), which may also appear as an **auberge de campagne** or an **auberge du terroir** (country inn), is just that: a relaxed restaurant serving traditional country fare attached to a rural inn or small hotel. If you see the word attached to an eatery in the city, they're just being cute.

An auberge in Périgord

Bar

A **bar**, **bar américain** (cocktail bar) or **bar à vins** is an establishment dedicated to elbow-bending and rarely serves food beyond pre-made sandwiches. A **bar à huîtres** is an 'oyster bar'.

Bistro

A **bistro** (often spelled **bistrot**) can really be anything, a pub with inexpensive, forgettable snacks and light meals, or a bar with a fully fledged restaurant menu.

Brasserie

Unlike the vast majority of restaurants, **brasseries** – which can look very much like cafés – serve full meals, drinks and coffee from morning until late at night. The inexpensive dishes served almost always include **choucroute** (sauerkraut) and sausages because the brasserie (literally, brewery) originated in Alsace. Most people don't go to a brasserie for the food, however, but for the lively atmosphere and, of course, the convenience.

Buffet

A **buffet** (or **buvette**) is a kiosk usually found at train stations and airports selling drinks, filled baguettes and snacks. It's very basic fare and not always as cheap as you would think.

Café

Cafés are an important focal point for social life here, and sitting in a café to read, write, talk with friends or just daydream is integral to the day-to-day existence of many. Frequenting a café, like shopping at outdoor markets, is a way of keeping in touch with the neighbourhood and maximising the chance of running into friends. Only basic food is available in most cafés. Common options include a baguette filled with Camembert or pâté, a **croque-monsieur** (grilled ham and cheese sandwich) or a **croque-madame** (a croque-monsieur topped with a fried egg). But the main focus here, of course, is **café** (coffee; see Coffee in the Drinks chapter).

Outdoor dining, Paris

Croque-monsier with blue cheese

Pan Bagnat

Pissaladière, a tart with onions and anchovies

Three factors determine how much you'll pay in a café: where the café is situated; where you are sitting within the café; and what time of day it is. A café on a grand boulevard (such as Blvd du Montparnasse or the Champs-Élysées in Paris) will charge considerably more than a place that fronts a quiet side street. Once inside, progressively more expensive tariffs apply at the **zinc** or **comptoir** (counter), in the **salle** (inside seating area) and on the **terrasse** (pavement terrace), the best vantage point from which to see and be seen. Some of the cheapest soft drinks may be available only at the bar. The price of drinks goes up at night (usually after 8pm). It really comes down to this: you are not paying for your espresso or mineral water as much as for the right to occupy an attractive and visible bit of ground. Ordering a cup of coffee (or anything else) earns you the right to sit there for as long as you like. Rarely, if ever, will you feel pressured to order something else. You usually run a tab at a café and pay the **addition** (bill) just before you leave. If your waiter is going off duty, you may be asked to pay up at the end of his or her shift, however.

Chefs enjoying lunch, Lyon

Cafétéria

Many cities have **cafétérias** offering a good selection of cheap dishes you can see before ordering, a factor that can make life easier if you're travelling with children. Cafétéria chains include Flunch, Mélodine and Casino.

Crêperie

A **crêperie** (sometimes called a **galetterie**) specialises in **crêpes** (thin pancakes), cooked on a flat surface and then folded or rolled over a filling. In some regions, the word crêpe refers only to sweet crêpes made with regular wheat flour, whereas a savoury crêpe – more accurately a **galette** – is made with buckwheat flour and filled with cheese, mushrooms and the like. You'll find a preponderance of crêperies in Brittany, birthplace of both the crêpe and galette, but they are also popular throughout the country.

Cooking crêpes at Crêperie Val de Rance, Saint Malo, Brittany

Ferme-Auberge

A **ferme-auberge** (literally, farm inn) is a working farm that serves diners traditional regional dishes made from ingredients produced on the farm itself. The food is usually served **table d'hôte** (literally, host's table), meaning in set courses with little or no choice.

Relais Routier

A **relais routier** (or just **routier**) is a café or truck stop usually found on the outskirts of towns and along major roads that cater to truck drivers. These places provide a quick, hearty break from cross-country driving and are not as rough-and-ready as similar places in the USA or UK.

Restaurant

The **restaurant**, the French word for 'restorative', comes in many guises and price ranges – from ultra-budget **restaurants universitaires** (university canteens) to upmarket **restaurants gastronomiques** (gourmet restaurants).

French restaurants almost always specialise in a particular variety of food (such as French regional or traditional, North African, Vietnamese or Senegalese). There are lots of restaurants where you can get an excellent French meal for 150-200FF – Michelin's *Guide Rouge* is filled with them – and they usually offer what the French call a **bon rapport qualité-prix** (good value for money). Some of the best French restaurants in the country are attached to hotels, and those on the ground floor of budget hotels often have some of the best deals in town. Almost all are open to non-guests. Chain restaurants with standard menus are a definite step up from fast-food places and usually offer good-value though uninspired menus. Among the most common are Hippopotamus; the bistro-like Batifol; Bistrot Romain; and Léon de Bruxelles, which specialises in **moules et frites** (mussels with French fries).

An important distinction between a brasserie and a restaurant is that while a brasserie serves food throughout the day, a restaurant is usually open only for lunch (12.30-2.30pm) and dinner (7-10.30pm). Almost all restaurants close for 1½ days (a full day and either one lunch or one dinner period) each week and this schedule is sometimes posted on the front door. Chain restaurants are usually open throughout the day (and sometimes the night in Paris), seven days a week.

Waiter taking mussels and fries to a table, Honfleur, Basse-Normandy

Restaurants also always have a **carte** (menu) posted outside so you can decide before going in whether the selection and prices are to your liking. It is considered extremely rude to walk out after you have sat down and received your menu. (For information on the various types of menus offered at French restaurants, see the Understanding the Menu chapter.)

Restaurant meals in France are almost always served with bread, which may or may not be accompanied by butter. If you run out of bread in your basket, don't be afraid to ask the waiter for more.

Restaurant Libre-Service

A **restaurant libre-service** is a 'self-service restaurant' similar to a cafétéria. Prices are low and the atmosphere generally sterile.

Restaurant Rapide

This is a 'fast-food restaurant' be it imported (McDonald's, Pizza Hut and KFC, with branches all over France) or home-grown like Quick.

Restaurant Universitaire

All French universities have several **restaurants universitaires** (university canteens) subsidised by the Ministry of Education and operated by the Centre Régional des Œuvres Universitaires et Scolaires (CROUS). They serve very cheap (typically under 30FF) and filling meals, and are sometimes open to visitors.

Saladerie

This is a casual restaurant serving a long list of **salades composées** (mixed salads). A saladerie is rare to find, though.

Salon de Thé

A **salon de thé** (tearoom) is a trendy and somewhat pricey establishment that usually offers quiches, salads, cakes, tarts, pies and pastries in addition to black and herbals teas and coffee. It is almost always non-smoking.

Winstub

Unique to the Alsace region, a **winstub** – reminiscent of an Alsatian home with its hand-painted plates, chequered tablecloths and old photos – was originally a wine-tasting room run by a wine producer. Today winstubs serve wine as well as hearty Alsatian dishes, many of which are made with wine. They always sport impossibly long names such as s' Burjerstuewel and s' Munsterstuewel. Nowadays many are touristy or cater to a well-heeled crowd. The places to drink beer in Alsace were once known as a **bierstub** but these days they exist more in memory than in reality.

Ethnic Food

France has a considerable population of immigrants from its former colonies and protectorates in North and West Africa, Indochina, the Middle East, India, the Caribbean and the South Pacific, as well as refugees from every corner of the globe, so an exceptional variety of reasonably priced ethnic food is available both in big cities and smaller towns.

North African

If curry has become an integral part of Britain's cuisine, the same can be said about couscous in France. One of the most delicious and easy-to-find North African dishes, couscous is steamed semolina served with vegetables and a spicy, meat-based sauce. It is usually eaten with lamb shish kebab, **merguez** (small, spicy sausages), **méchoui** (barbecued lamb on the bone) or chicken. The Moroccan, Algerian and Tunisian versions all differ slightly. Another Moroccan favourite is **tajine** (a delicious slow-cooked stew of meat, lemons, prunes or other dried fruits) and is usually eaten by dipping small pieces of bread into it.

Merguez and méchoui

At the end of a meal, North African restaurants always offer **thé de menthe** (mint tea), which is poured from a great height from brass teapot to tiny cup by the waiter. Also available is an array of luridly coloured, ultra-sweet desserts that are displayed in the window. A popular choice is **zlabia**, a bright-orange, pretzel-shaped, honey-smothered delicacy that you see everywhere.

African

Sub-Saharan African food is popular in many cities but especially Paris and Marseille. Among Senegalese favourites, things to try are **tiéboudienne** (the national dish of rice baked in a thick sauce of fish and vegetables); **yassa** (chicken or fish grilled in onion and lime sauce); **mafé** (beef or chicken stew or curry served with peanut sauce); and **bassissalte** (millet couscous). Specialities from Togo include **lélé** (flat, steamed cakes made from white beans and shrimp and served with tomato sauce); **gbekui** (a sort of goulash made with spinach, onions, beef, fish and shrimp); and **djenkommé** (grilled chicken with semolina noodles).

MARCHE D'AFRIQUE
PRODUITS
EXOTIQUE

Store displaying its Afro-Caribbean food, Paris

Asian

France's many immigrants from Asia, especially Vietnam and Cambodia, have brought their food to every corner of the country. Vietnamese restaurants, many of them run by ethnic Chinese who fled Vietnam, generally offer good value, but little authentic food. In the major cities, you can also sample the cuisines of Cambodia, Japan, Korea, Tibet and Thailand.

Most dishes will be familiar to you – only the names have been changed: **nem** (fried small Vietnamese spring or egg roll eaten rolled up in a lettuce leaf with mint and fish sauce); **rouleau de printemps** or **pâté imperial** (uncooked Vietnamese spring roll of moistened rice paper with salad, mint and prawns); **pâté aux légumes au poulet/aux crevettes** (Chinese vegetable/chicken/shrimp spring or egg roll); **bouchée aux crevettes/au porc** (varieties of Chinese dim sum called **siu mai** and **har gau**); and **raviolis pékinois** (fried crescent-shaped pork dumplings called **guo tie**).

Vegetarians & Vegans

Vegetarians make up a small minority in a country where **viande** (meat) once also meant 'food', and are not very well catered for, as specialised vegetarian restaurants are few and far between. Only the cities are likely to have vegetarian establishments, and these may look more like laid-back cafés than restaurants. Still, their fare is usually better than the omelettes and cheese sandwiches available from ordinary cafés.

Other options include saladeries, though you should carefully scan the menu as many of the dishes also include meat. Some restaurants have at least one vegetarian dish on the menu, though it may be one of the **entrées** (starters or first courses). Unfortunately, very few set menus include vegetarian options. The best (perhaps only) way for vegetarians to assemble a real meal is by ordering one or more entrées.

Strict vegetarians should note that most cheeses in France are made with **lactosérum** (rennet), an enzyme derived from the stomach of a calf or young goat, and that some red wines (including all Bordeaux) are clarified with the albumin of egg whites. But there are alternatives (see Cheese in the Staples & Specialities chapter and the boxed text Something Fishy Is Going Down in the Wine & Champagne chapter).

Vegetables for sale at a greengrocer, Paris

Kosher

There has been a Jewish community in France for most of the time since the Roman period and French Jews were the first in Europe to be granted full citizenship (1790). Today the Jewish population, which grew substantially during the 1960s as a result of immigration from Algeria, Tunisia and Morocco, numbers about 650,000.

But from the look of things most don't keep **kascher** (kosher) or don't eat out very often; the only places where you'll find kosher restaurants of any number are in Paris, Strasbourg and Marseille, all traditional Jewish centres. In the capital, kosher (mostly Ashkenazic) restaurants are clustered in the Marais (4rd arrondissement) either on or near Rue des Rosiers. For Sephardic kosher food head for the North African-Jewish restaurants on Rue Richer, Rue Cadet and Rue Geoffroy Marie just south of the Cadet metro stop in the 9th arrondissement or the ones lining Blvd de Belleville in the 20th arrondissement.

Children

It is sometimes said in France that the nation treats its children as adults until they reach puberty – at which time they revert to being children again. You'll see a few **petits hommes** (little men) and **petites dames** (little ladies) dining decorously on the town with their parents, but only restaurants offer a **menu enfant** (children's set menu), usually available for children under 12. Some restaurants have high chairs and baby seats and offer features of interest for parents with children, including an enclosed area or terrace allowing games. Cafétérias are a good place to bring kids if you just want to feed them fast and cheaply (see Cafétérias earlier in this chapter).

Alimentation pour bébés (baby food) is readily available in grocery shops and supermarkets, but the vast majority of goods in jars are produced by Nestlé. Typically French, some of the products sound, well, good enough to eat: **petits légumes au bœuf**, **coquillettes jambon à la tomate**, **jardinière de légumes**. Nestlé also produces **Le P'tit Menu**, with the meat and vegetable 'courses' in separate trays. A company called Guigoz makes a range of dry, flavoured baby cereals. For **lait maternisé biologigique** (organic formula or baby milk) choose Babybio with a green label.

Crêpes
Fruits de Mer
Dégustation à Toute Heure

understanding the menu

If you can't tell the **entrée** (starter or first course) from the **entremet** (dessert) or, for that matter, from the **entrée** if you're American (who oddly still call main courses by that name), it won't take you too long to figure out that people here usually order three courses when they eat out. Still, the order and arrangement of dishes

Types of Menus

Virtually all eateries – from restaurants and brasseries to university canteens – post their **carte** (menu) on the window, or write the **plats du jour** (daily specials) on a chalkboard and place it on the pavement. That way you can choose your eatery before entering.

When ordering **à la carte** (choosing each dish separately from the menu) one option worth considering is the **plat du jour** (dish of the day), a speciality that changes daily. Restaurants in France rarely have minimum charges, so it's possible for people who are not particularly hungry to order a main dish without the other accompanying courses. Ordering two entrées instead of an entrée and a main course is not as common in France as it is in some other countries.

Cochon A L'Oreille Restaurant, Paris

The vast majority of French restaurants offer at least one fixed-price, multicourse meal known as a **menu**, **menu à prix fixe** or **menu du jour**. A **menu** (not to be confused with a **carte** – throughout this book we put **menu** in bold to distinguish it from the English word 'menu') almost always costs much less than ordering à la carte. When you order a three-course **menu**, you usually get to choose an entrée, such as salad, pâté or soup; a main dish (meat, poultry or fish dishes, including the plat du jour, are generally on offer); and one or more final courses (usually cheese or dessert). **Carte** is the word for the menu itself; a **carte des vins** is a wine list.

In some places, you may be able to order a **formule** or **menu touristique**, which usually has fewer choices but allows you to pick two of three courses (such as an entrée and main course, or a main course and dessert). In many restaurants, the cheapest lunch **menu** is a much better deal than the equivalent one available at dinner.

Many upscale restaurants offer a **menu dégustation**, which allows you to sample small portions of up to six courses, and/or a multicourse **menu gastronomique** (gourmet menu). **Table d'hôte**, more often seen in country inns or farmhouses that accept diners, means set meals are served with little or no choice.

Zucchini flower beignets, Nice, Provence

Reading the Menu

We can thank Isabeau of Bavaria, consort to Charles VI (ruled 1368-1422), for the first written menu. Apparently until that time people attending banquets frequently had to guess which dish they were being served or eating until Isabeau came up with the idea of writing it all down and called it an *escriteau*. It wasn't a true menu in the sense that people chose from it, but rather akin to a 'bill of fare'.

Carte
Spécialités à la carte
Le Castelbin
SAINT-JULIEN

Menu display in a restaurant window, Paris

These days, actually reading a French menu might be a difficult task for some people – even for those who speak the language. The main cards, often works of art, will usually be clear, but those blackboards of daily specials written in the peculiar (and often illegible) French style of handwriting and posted on a faraway wall may drive you apoplectic. Gratefully many restaurants print their specials on a separate sheet inserted in the main menu, and waiters are more than willing to recite the offerings of the day.

Drinks

The first thing a waiter will ask you when you've sat down is what you would like as a **boisson** (drink or beverage). Some people have an aperitif such as a **kir** (white wine with blackcurrant liqueur) or a glass of Champagne, while others may decide to wait for the **vin** (wine). Wine is almost always drunk with meals in French restaurants, and many people also order a bottle of mineral water at the same time. At the end of a meal, after dessert and with coffee, some drink a digestif (Cognac, eau-de-vie, liqueur). Drinks cost extra unless the menu states **boisson comprise** (drink included), in which case you may get a beer or a glass of mineral water. If the menu says **vin compris** (wine included), you'll probably be served a 250ml **pichet** (jug) of wine. The rarely seen **vin à volonté** suggests a bottomless glass. The waiter will always ask if you would like coffee to end the meal, but this will almost always cost extra.

Leffe
Leffe

Draught beer, Paris

A wine bottle display, Paris

The Courses

While a traditional French meal at home can comprise up to six distinct **plats** (courses), this isn't the case in restaurants. A restaurant meal rarely consists of more than three or four courses: the **entrée** (starter), **plat principal** (main course) and **dessert** (dessert). Some people choose a **fromage** (cheese) course instead of dessert while others have both. Cream-based desserts might be listed under entremets (see entrements later in this chapter).

The following does not reflect a typical French menu; they haven't been this comprehensive since the fastest way home was by horse and carriage. But many modern restaurant cards will include three, four or even more of the headings.

Hors d'Œuvre

It's unlikely that you'll see **hors d'œuvre** (cold and/or warm snacks eaten before the start of the meal) on a restaurant menu; they are usually what are served at home with drinks. Still, many restaurants offer a couple of little **amuse-gueules** or **amuse-bouches** (literally, throat or mouth ticklers) to diners while they peruse the menu.

Entrées

The **entrée** (starter or first course) can include any number of items, including an **assiette de charcuterie** (plate of cold meats), pâtés, terrines, rillettes, various **salades composées** (mixed salads, which usually include poultry, fish or shellfish when offered as an entrée) and at least a couple of soups. More elaborate preparations you'll encounter include such things as **foie gras poêlée aux pommes et au Calvados** (goose liver cooked with apples and Calvados) or **escargots bourguignons** (snails baked with garlic butter).

Salad Lyonnaise, Lyon

Soupes & Potages

Soups will sometimes come under their own heading, but more often they will be combined with the list of entrées.

Salades

Salads offered as a first course are more substantial – including meat, poultry or shellfish – than just a plain **salade** (green salad), **salade de tomates** (tomato salad) or a **mesclun** (a popular mixture of a half-dozen salad greens including rocket, lamb's lettuce and endive), and often rate a separate menu listing.

Plats Principaux

The **plats principaux** (main courses) offered at a restaurant will typically include several meat dishes prepared with **veau** (veal), **bœuf** (beef), **agneau** (lamb) and **porc** (porc); a couple of poultry dishes like **canard** (duck), **poulet** (chicken) and **poularde** (pullet) or game birds such as **caille** (quail) and **pintade** (guinea fowl); and a few **poisson** or **fruits de mer** (fish or shellfish) dishes. The cooking styles, ingredients and accompaniments of these dishes will depend on what region you're dining in (see the Regional Variations chapter).

Jarret de Porc at Cochon A L'Oreille, Paris

Viandes, Volailles, Poissons

A list of **viandes** (meats) often appears separately on menus, and includes all dishes prepared with beef, veal, pork, lamb, mutton, offal and sometimes poultry. **Volailles** (poultry; chicken, duck, goose, game birds) can also have a separate listing. When there is a separate **viandes** section on a restaurant menu, there's bound to be one for **poissons** or **fruits de mer** (fish or shellfish) as well.

Fromages

Cheese, which can sometimes be chosen over dessert as the third course, may be served as an individual **plateau de fromages** (cheeseboard) with a selection chosen for you, or a much larger tray carried (or wheeled) to the table from which you make your own selection. The 'accepted' limit is three or four but one of us – no names – has been known to go for more and lived to tell the tale. For cheese recommendations in five major categories, see Cheese in the Staples & Specialities chapter.

Desserts

Sweets run the gamut in France from various ice creams and fruit sorbets to mousses of every flavour and hue, to the nation's favourite baked dessert: **tarte Tatin** (see the boxed text A Tarte Is Born in the Staples & Specialities chapter).

Entremets

Entremets translates as 'between dishes', as that was when they were eaten in medieval times. These days entremets means sweets, usually cream-based ones, and the word sometimes appears on menus instead of **dessert**. Some people enjoy a boozy entremet – in the original sense of the word – called a Norman hole (see the boxed text).

THE NORMAN HOLE

Calvados is to the apple what Cognac is to the grape. Like its grape-based counterpart, this strong apple brandy is aged in oak casks for up to six years, and improves remarkably with age. Though Calvados is generally drunk as a digestif at the end of a meal, it is sometimes strengthened by adding cider must (or wort) to make **Pommeau**, which is sipped as an aperitif. But you might also be offered Calvados at a more unusual time as a **trou norman** (Norman hole). Normans are renowned for their hearty appetites – they are originally Scandinavians after all – and enjoy gargantuan repasts worthy of Rabelais on a special occasion. A glass of appley brandy in the middle of the meal is said to 'dig a hole' to allow room for more courses. In some restaurants, a trou normand now comes as Calvados-flavoured sorbet.

Fruit

At a French restaurant, you are as likely to get a peanut butter sandwich as a piece of **fruit nature** (plain fruit). You will, however, get fruit prepared in all sort of ways – from **macédoine** (mixed fruit salad) to **marmelade** (a thick purée of stewed fruits).

a french banquet

Cooking an authentic French meal– be it for a **copain** (boyfriend) **copine** (girlfriend) or a group of **amis** (friends) – should be a majo goal for when you get home, both to show off your newly founc culinary knowledge, and to use all the ingredients, seasonings anc

Choucroute à l'Alsacienne with sausage and bacon

The kind of atmosphere you create at your very own **dîner à la française** (French-style dinner party) depends on your purpose. You wanna party? Festoon the place tackily with flowers and/or balloons in the French **tricolore** (red, white and blue), put on some of France's best music – **sono mondial** (world music) like Algerian *raï* (Cheb Khaled, Jamel, Cheb Mami), Senegalese *mbalax* (Youssou N'Dour) or West Indian *zouk* (Kassav, Zouk Machine) – and, well, start to *guincher* (boogie). If you're into conversation, with some interesting sounds in the background, go for Jacques Brel, Georges Brassens, Léo Ferré and Barbara.

If it's the mating game you're playing, put flowers about – anthuriums with their deep-red heart-shaped leaves and slim white tips placed in a shallow vase and tied towards the top with **cordon bleu** (blue ribbon) are a suggestive choice. As for music, go for corny but romantic **chansons francaises** (French cabaret songs) as performed by Édith Piaf, Charles Trenet, Charles Aznavour and Juliette Gréco. And don't forget to light the candles.

Welcome your guests with an aperitif – a glass of white wine, a **kir** (white wine sweetened with blackcurrant liqueur) or glass of Champagne if you're feeling festive. French people continue to drink after dinner – be it more wine or digestives – but if you really want to get rid of your guests, you can try the age-old French method of serving them orange juice. They won't get the message as French guests would, though, and probably just think you're crazy.

When considering the menu, eschew anything too fussy or that requires a lot of work just before serving, such as **bouillabaisse**; you don't want to miss out on all the fun, the conversation and, well, who knows? Choose main courses you can prepare in advance such as **choucroute** and keep the starters and desserts simple.

The menus we've provided are for an intimate **dîner en tête-à-tête** (literally, dining head to head) and for a group dinner party. You can dispense with the cheese course and add to or subtract from the wine recommendations. Just don't forget to chill the bubbly and the whites, and to open the reds a good hour in advance.

Sunflowers at a florist, Paris

MENU À DEUX

Apéritif	Champagne
Entrée	Six oysters accompanied by a warm **saucisse au vin blanc** (small sausage cooked in white wine), a favourite dish of Charente on the Atlantic coast
Plat Principal	**Choucroute à l'alsacienne**, the quintessential Alsatian dish of sauerkraut cooked in white wine and served with **charcuterie** (see recipe)
Fromage	**Neufchâtel**, heart-shaped cow's milk from Normandy
Dessert	**Compote de figues fraîches** (fresh figs poached in syrup) or **fruits rouges à la crème Chantilly** (red or berry fruits with sweetened whipped cream), depending on the season
Vins	Alsatian Pinot Noir (red wine served chilled)/Riesling (white wine)/Sauternes (sweet, white dessert wine)

Choucroute à l'Alsacienne

This is Alsace's signature dish – sauerkraut cooked in wine with all of the trimmings.

Ingredients

30g/1oz	goose fat or lard	1	medium onion, diced
500g/1lb	unwashed sauerkraut	1	raw potato, diced
500g/1lb	salt pork	2	tablespoons kirsch
750g/11/2lb	spare ribs		
300ml/1¼ cups	Alsatian white wine		
12	juniper berries in a cheesecloth bag		
4	potatoes, baked in their skins		
	bouillon to cover the sauerkraut		

Melt the goose fat or lard in an earthenware cooking pot, Add the onions and cook until brown. Add the sauerkraut and cook for five minutes, stirring with a fork. Pour in the white wine and add the potatoes as well as the bag of juniper berries. Pour in the bouillon. Cover the pot and place over a low flame. When the sauerkraut has simmered for two hours, add the salt pork. Half an hour before serving, add the kirsch and spare ribs. Place the sauerkraut on a hot round platter and serve with the baked potatoes.

Serves 6

DINNER PARTY

Apéritif	**Kir**
Entrée	**Salade niçoise**, a fresh salad of tomatoes, lettuce, anchovies, green peppers, olives, hard-boiled eggs, basil and tuna (see recipe)
Plat Principal	**Cassoulet**, the classic Languedoc 'stew' of meat beans and vegetables
Fromage	A selection of any from the five main cheese types (eg, **Sainte Maure de Touraine**, **Roquefort**, **Brie**, **Cantal** and/or **Beaufort**)
Dessert	**Mont Blanc**, canned chestnut purée with or without a meringue base, and topped with crème Chantilly
Vins	Vouvray (white wine)/Côtes du Rhône Hermitage (red wine)/Banyuls (sweet, white fortified wine)

Salade Niçoise

This simple salad, a speciality of Nice, is a meal in itself.

Ingredients

6	ripe, firm tomatoes	salt
1 tin	anchovy fillets	lettuce
2	green peppers	ripe olives
3	hard-boiled eggs	olive oil
	vinegar	a few basil leaves

Cut the tomatoes in thin slices and remove the seeds. Salt lightly. Line a large round platter with lettuce leaves. Place the tomato slices on the bed of lettuce leaves, separated with strips of anchovy fillets. Scatter on thin rounds of pepper, ripe olives and sliced hard boiled eggs. Serve with an oil and vinegar dressing to which a touch of chopped basil may be added.

Serves 4 to 6

Fresh tomatoes at a roadside stall, Provence

Crêpes Beurre-Sucre

This is the classic recipe for making traditional Breton butter and sugar crêpes.

Ingredients

250g/1¾ cups	wheat flour
4	eggs
175g/¾ cup	sugar
3 sachets	vanilla sugar
750ml/3 cups	fresh full cream milk
	pinch of salt
	oil
250g/8oz	lightly salted butter for cooking

Put the flour into a large bowl, make a well in the centre and break an egg into it. Stir with a wooden spoon, gradually drawing in the flour. Add the three remaining eggs one at a time. Add the sugar, vanilla sugar and salt, and thin the mixture gradually with the milk, pouring it slowly into the centre of the batter. Cover the bowl with a cloth and leave the batter to rest for at least an hour

To cook the crêpes, melt the butter in a frying pan and tip in a small ladle of batter. Tip the pan in all directions to create the desired thinness of the crêpe. Cook the crêpe for one minute until the edges begin to colour. Take hold of the crêpe between thumb and index finger and with one swift movement lift and turn it over to finish the cooking. Continue until the batter is finished.

Makes 24 crêpes

Cidre

Sweet crêpes with an apple filling, Crêperie Val de Rance, Saint Malo, Brittany

fit & healthy

France is a healthy place. Your main risks are likely to be sunburn, foot blisters and insect bites. The following information will help you keep healthy while dining in France, but as French cuisine relies on fresh, quality ingredients, there should be no problems except perhaps the danger of an upset stomach from eating and

Water

Tap water all over France is safe to drink. However, the water in most French decorative fountains is not drinkable and – like the washbasin or sink taps in some public toilets and on some trains – may have a sign reading **eau non potable** (undrinkable water). It's very easy not to drink enough liquids, especially on hot days or at high altitudes – don't rely on feeling thirsty to indicate when you should drink. Not needing to urinate or very dark-yellow urine is a danger sign. France suffers from a lack of drinking fountains, so it's a good idea to carry a bottle of water, on sale everywhere.

Overindulging in Food & Drink

You might at first experience mild stomach problems or **mal au cœur** (nausea) if you're not used to copious amounts of rich dairy products and fat-based sauces. Many people find olive oil difficult to digest, and the first few days in the south of France may have you excusing yourself to the toilet more often than usual. Don't worry; both problems will sort themselves out quick enough. However, lots of heavy dishes and too much liquid indulgence can lead to the dreaded **crise de foie**, a bilious attack, bad indigestion or just a nice word for a hangover. Take Alka-Selzer or France's miracle over-the-counter lemon-flavoured fixer-upper, Citrate de Béthaïne, or flush your system out with any of the many brands of mineral water available (see the boxed text The True Waters of Life in the Drinks chapter).

LA VISITE

Workers taking cheese at a café, Paris

Allergies

If you are sensitive to seafood, never eat anything **cru** (raw) and avoid molluscs, especially **coquilles Saint-Jacques** (scallops) and **pétoncles** (queen or bay scallops). Fish and crustaceans also appear in dishes where you might not expect to find them: **sauce Nantua** is based on freshwater crayfish and **tapenade** (a spread of black olives, olive oil, capers and lemon) often contains anchovies. Watch out for nuts 'hidden' in sweets and chocolates, and pastries made from chestnuts and chestnut flour in Gascony and Corsica.

Migraine sufferers often find that such foods as mushrooms, cheese and red wine bring on attacks. A lot of French sauces contain red wine and within pâtés lurk bits of truffles, certain to bring on an attack.

Listeriosis

Listeriosis, an often fatal bacterial infection caused by eating tainted meat or dairy products, especially pork and cheese made from **lait cru** (raw or unpasteurised milk), is a serious problem in France. In early 2000, seven people died and more than two dozen more were made ill after eating commercially prepared **langue de porc en gelée** (pig's tongue in aspic); a short time later two people suspected of having eaten a certain type of **Époisses de Bourgogne**, a raw cow's milk cheese, died near Grenoble. These were hardly isolated cases: in the 1990s alone, some 371 people died in five different listeriosis outbreaks ascribed to tainted Brie cheese and pork rillettes.

Healthy people rarely contract listeriosis, though it can threaten the elderly, pregnant women and those with weak immune systems. Symptoms include high fever, severe headaches and nausea. It's highly unlikely that you'll get listeriosis from products bought at reputable shops or bearing an AOC, but if you are concerned, avoid those foodstuffs.

Diabetics

France has always used a tremendous amount of fat in its cuisine and much of it is sight unseen. Sauces based on saturated fats such as cream and animal fats can be extremely rich, and a vast number of cheeses, especially those made from raw milk, contain a high percentage of fat.

The French like fruit almost as much as their **sucreries** (sweet or sugary things) and you'll find an abundance available all year at greengrocers, markets and supermarkets. Be aware that lots of fruit juice in France is 'fruit drink' with lots of added sugar.

Recommended Reading

The following books were used in the research of *World Food France* and are highly recommended.

Albin Michel/CNAC, *L'Inventaire du patrimoine culinaire de la France: Languedoc-Roussillon.* One in a series of tomes that takes a comprehensive look at products and traditional recipes region by region.

Bernard, Françoise, *Les Recettes faciles de Françoise Bernard.* Some 250 classic recipes by France's best-selling cookbook writer.

Christian, Glynn, *Edible France: A Traveller's Guide.* A riveting region-by-region guide to French food, wine, shops, markets and specialities, but the book is so filled with typos, literals and misspellings that you will, in fact, just have to put it down.

Davidson, Alan & Jane, trans, *Dumas on Food.* Selections in English from Alexandre Dumas' ground-breaking *Le Grand dictionnaire de cuisine*, published in 1873.

Éditions Atlas, *Le Grand atlas des cuisines de nos terroirs.* Beautifully illustrated atlas of regional cooking with emphasis on **cuisine campagnarde** (country cooking).

Éditions Réalités, *La Belle France.* Excellent large-format anthology of French food published in 1964, but may be available at some second-hand bookshops.

Fielden, Christopher, *A Traveller's Wine Guide to France.* Lightweight guide with addresses; not a bad introduction for those new to the game though.

Lichine, Alexis, *Alexis Lichine's Guide to the Wines and Vineyards of France.* One of the most complete references to French wines around, though now somewhat outdated.

Masui, Kazuko & Tomoko Yamada, *French Cheeses.* The best reference on the subject in English and beautifully photographed like most Dorling Kindersley books.

Michelin *Guide Rouge.* The annual guide is filled with restaurant recommendations, which offer what the French call **bon rapport qualité-prix** (good value for money).

Montagné, Prosper, *Larousse Gastronomique.* The sourcebook everyone with a culinary query or a problem eventually reaches for, and still as fresh and fragrant as when it was first published in 1938.

Root, Waverley, *The Food of France.* A seminal work, with much focus on historical development, by an American correspondent based in France.

Strang, Jeanne, *Goose Fat & Garlic.* A classic collection of well-chosen country recipes from southwest France: Limousin, Gascony, the Basque Country and Languedoc.

Tannahill, Reay, *Food in History.* The spellbinding story of food around the world, from the daily diet in prehistoric caves to genetically modified food.

Wells, Patricia, *The Food Lover's Guide to France* & *The Food Lover's Guide to Paris.* Essential reading for those looking for specific restaurants and food shops from *la doyenne de la cuisine française* in English.

Worthington, Julian, *Exploring the Vineyards of France*

eat your words
language guide

302
311
372
BRASSERIE

Pronunciation

As transliterations give only an approximate guide to pronunciation, we've included this guide for those who want to try their hand at pronouncing French more like a native speaker. Transliterations are given in the far right column.

Vowels

a	as the 'u' in cup	**a**
e	as the 'e' in 'open'	**er**
é	as the 'e' in 'lemon'	**e**
è	as the 'e' in 'merry' but slightly longer	**eh**
i	as the 'i' in 'hit'	**ee**
o	as the 'o' in 'glorious'	**o**
u	as the 'u' in 'clue'	**ü**

Diphthongs

A combination of two vowel sounds that glide from one to another.

ai	as the 'e' in 'bet' but a bit longer	**eh**
eu	as the 'er' in the British 'berth' but shorter	**er**
oi	sounds like 'wa'	**wa**
ui	sounds like 'wi'	**wee**
au/eau	as the 'o' in 'or'	**oh**
ou	as the 'oo' in 'book'	**oo**

Nasal Vowels

an, am, en, em	as the the 'en' in 'encore'	**ã**
on, om	as the 'on' in 'bonjour'	**õ**
in, im, ain, aim, ein, eim, un	between the 'a' in 'ant' and the 'ai' in 'ain't'	**ũ**

Consonants

Unless shown below, French consonants are pronounced in a similar way to their English counterparts.

c	hard, like 'k' before **a**, **o**, and, **u**	**k**
	soft like 's' before **e**, **i**, and **y**	**s**
ç	always soft like 's'	**s**
g	hard like the 'g' in 'get' before **a**, **o**, and **u**	**g**
	soft like the 's' in 'pleasure' before **e** and **i**	**zh**
h	silent	
j	as the 's' in 'pleasure'	**zh**
l	as the 'l' in 'la' but the tip of the tongue sits higher than for an English 'l'	**l**
ll	as the 'y' in 'yellow'	**y**
q	as 'k'	**k**
s	between two vowels pronounced as 'z'	**z**
	elsewhere as the 's' in 'sit'	**s**
r	a scraping sound from the back of the throat, try gargling without any liquid	**r**

Legend

/	separator when no more than two options (not necessarily two words) in list, eg, *qu'elle/que lui* – eg, *Tu es/vous êtes un excellent cuisinier/une excellente cuisinière* OR when separating gender, eg, *sec/sèche.*
;	separator when more than two options in a list, eg, *rassis; sec/sèche; avarié(e); pas frais/fraîche*
( )	encloses gender, eg, (m), (f) OR article and gender, eg, (l, f), (les, m) OR female gender ending, eg, *froid(e)* OR subject marking, eg, *(drink), (vegetable)*
[ ]	encloses something that can be substituted, eg, Can I have a [beer], please? OR something optional, eg, I'll have [a] ...

Useful Phrases

General

Are you hungry?
ave-voo fũ? — *Avez-vous faim?*

I'm hungry.
zheh fũ — *J'ai faim.*

Do you like ...?
e-me-voo ...? — *Aimez-vous ...?*

I like it.
zhehm sa — *J'aime ça.*

I don't like it.
zher nehm pa sa — *Je n'aime pas ça.*

Where's the toilet?
oo sõ leh twah-leht/leh ve-se? — *Où sont les toilettes/les wc?*

Eating Out

restaurant	**rehs-toh-rã**	*restaurant*
cheap restaurant	**rehs-toh-rã bõ mar-she**	*restaurant bon marché*

Do you speak English?
par-le voo ã-gleh? — *Parlez-vous anglais?*

Table for ..., please.
ün tabl poor ... seel voo pleh — *Une table pour ..., s'il vous plaît.*

Do you accept credit cards?
prer-ne voo le kart der kre-dee? — *Prenez-vous les cartes de crédit?*

Do you have a highchair for the baby?
a-veh voo ün shehz oht poor ler bebe? — *Avez-vous une chaise haute pour le bébé?*

Can I smoke here?
es ker zher per fü-meh ee-see? — *Est-ce que je peux fumer ici?*

Just Try It!

What's that?
kes ker seh? *Qu'est-ce que c'est?*

What's the specialty of this region?
kehl eh la spes-ya-lee-teh der la rezh-yõ? *Quelle est la spécialité de la région?*

What's the speciality here?
kehl eh la spes-ya-lee-teh ee-see? *Quelle est la spécialité ici?*

What do you recommend?
kes ker voo mer kõ-se-ye? *Qu'est-ce que vous me conseillez?*

What are they eating?
ker mãzh teel? *Que mangent-ils?*

I'll try what s/he's having.
zher veh prã-dr la mehm shohz kehl/ker lwü-ee *Je vais prendre la même chose que qu'elle/lui.*

The Menu

Can I see the menu, please?
pwee-zhav-war la kart seel voo pleh? *Puis-je avoir la carte, s'il vous plaît?*

Do you have a menu in English?
a-ve voo ün kart ã-nã-gleh? *Avez-vous une carte en anglais?*

What is today's special?
kehl eh ler pla dü zhoor? *Quel est le plat du jour?*

I'd like ...
zher voo-dreh ... *Je voudrais ...*

I'd like the set menu, please.
zher veh prãdr ler mer-nü/la for-mül seel voo pleh *Je vais prendre le menu/la formule s'il vous plaît.*

What does it include?
khes ker ser-la kõ-prã? *Qu'est-ce que cela comprend?*

Is service included in the bill?
ler sehr-vees eht teel kõm-preeh dã la-dee-syõ? *Le service est-il compris dans l'addition?*

Does it come with salad?
ehs sehr-vee a-vehk der la sa-lad? Est-ce servi avec de la salade?

What's the soup of the day?
kehl eh la soop dü zhjoor? *Quelle est la soupe du jour?*

Throughout the Meal

What's in this dish?
kyee a teel dã ser pla? *Qu'y a-t-il dans ce plat?*

Not too spicy, please.
pa tro pee-kã/e-pee-se seel voo pleh *Pas trop piquant/épicé, s'il vous plaît.*

Is that dish spicy?
ser pla eht-teel pee-kã/e-pee-se? *Ce plat est-il piquant/épicé?*

I like it hot and spicy.
zher preh-fehr ser pla pee-kã/e-pee-se *Je préfère ce plat piquant/épicé.*

It's not hot. (temperature)
ser neh pa shoh *Ce n'est pas chaud.*

I didn't order this.
ser neh pa sa ker zhe ko-mã-de *Ce n'est pas ça que j'ai commandé.*

I'd like something to drink.
zher voo-dreh kehl-ker shohz a bwar *Je voudrais quelque chose à boire.*

Can I have a [beer], please?
pwee-zhav-war [ün bee-yehr] seel voo pleh? *Puis-je avoir [une bière], s'il vous plaît?*

Please bring me ...	**seel voo pleh pwee-zhav-war ...**	*S'il vous plaît, puis-je avoir...*
an ashtray	**ũ sãn-dree-ye**	*un cendrier*
some bread	**dü pũ**	*du pain*
a cup	**ün tas**	*une tasse*
a fork	**ün foor-sheht**	*une fourchette*
a glass	**ũ vehr**	*un verre*
a knife	**ũ koo-toh**	*un couteau*
a napkin	**ün sehr-vyeht**	*une serviette*
some pepper	**dü pwavr**	*du poivre*
a plate	**ün as-yeht**	*une assiette*
some salt	**dü sehl**	*du sel*
a spoon	**ün kwee-yehr**	*une cuillère*
a teaspoon	**ün per-teet kwee-yehr**	*une petite cuillère*
a toothpick	**ũ kür-dã**	*un cure-dent(s)*
some water	**der loh**	*de l'eau*
some wine	**dü vũ**	*du vin*

This food is ...	**ser pla/seht noo-ree-tür eh**	*Ce plat/cette nourriture est...*
cold	**frwa(d)**	*froid(e)*
delicious	**de-lee-syer/ de-lee-syerz**	*délicieux/ délicieuse*
burnt	**brü-le**	*brûlé(e)*
spoiled	**a-va-ree-ye/poo-ree**	*avarié(e)/pourri(e)*
stale	**ra-see; sek/sehsh; a-var-ree-ye; pa freh/frehsh**	*rassis; sec/sèche; avarié(e); pas frais/fraîche*
undercooked	**neh paz-zaseh kweeh(t)**	*n'est pas assez cuit(e)*

"Waiter, there's a fly in my soup."
gar-sõ eel-i-a eel-ee-a ün moosh dã ma soop
Garçon, il y a une mouche dans ma soupe.

Thank you, that was delicious.
mehr-see se-teh de-lee-syer
Merci, c'était délicieux.

Please pass on our compliments to the chef.
seel voo pleh fe-lee-see-teh le shehf poor noo
S'il vous plaît, félicitez le chef pour nous.

The bill/check, please.
la-dee-syõ seel voo pleh
L'addition, s'il vous plaît.

You May Hear

Would you like anything else?
de-zee-re voo ohtr shoz?
Desirez-vous autre chose?

We have no ... today.
noo na-võ pa der ... oh-zhoor-dwee
Nous n'avons pas de ... aujourd'hui.

Family Meals

You're a great cook!
tü eh/vooz-zeht ũ nehk-se-lã kwee-zeen-ye/ün ehks-se-lãt kwee-zeen-yehr!
Tu es/vous êtes un excellent cuisinier/une excellente cuisinière.

This is excellent!
seht tehk-se-lã/de-lee-syer!
C'est excellent/délicieux!

Do you have the recipe?
a-ve voo/a tü la rerh-seht?
Avez-vous/As-tu la recette?

Is this a family recipe?
es-ün rerh-seht de fa-mee-y?
Est-ce une recette de famille?

Are the ingredients local?
ser sõ deh prod-dwee der la rezh-yõ/dü tehr-war?
Ce sont des produits de la région/du terroir?

I've never had a meal like this before.
zher neh zha-meh mã-zhe ũ rer-pa kohm sa
Je n'ai jamais mangé un repas comme ça.

If you ever come to [Australia) I'll cook you a local dish.
see ũ zhoor voo ver-neh/tü vee-yũ ã [nohs-tra-lee] zher voo/ter preh-pa-rer-reh ün spes-ya-lee-teh
Si un jour vous venez/tu viens en [Australie], je vous/te préparerai une spécialité.

Could you pass the [salt], please?
poor-ree-ye voo mer pa-seh ler [sehl] seel voo pleh? — *Pourriez-vous me passer le [sel], s'il vous plaît?.*

Thanks very much for the meal.
mehr-see boo-kooh poor ler rer-pa — *Merci beaucoup pour le repas.*

I really appreciate it.
zha-pre-see vreh-mã — *J'apprécie vraiment.*

Special Needs

I'm a vegetarian.
zher swee ve-zhe-ta-ry-ũ/ ve-zhe-ta-ry-ehn — *Je suis végétarien/ végétarienne.*

I'm a vegan, I don't eat meat or dairy products.
zher swee ve-zhe-ta-ly-ũ/ ve-zhe-ta-ly-ehn zher ner mãzh nee vyãd nee proh-dweeih leh-tye — *Je suis végétalien/ végétalienne, je ne mange ni viande, ni produits laitiers.*

I don't eat ...	**zher ner mãzh pa der ...**	*Je ne mange pas de ...*
meat	**vyãd**	*viande*
chicken	**poo-leh**	*poulet*
poultry	**vo-lay**	*volaille*
fish	**pwa-sõ**	*poisson*
seafood	**frwee der mehr**	*fruits de mer*
pork	**por**	*porc*
cured/processed meats	**shar-kü-tree**	*charcuterie*

Do you have any vegetarian dishes?
a-veh voo deh pla ve-zhe-ta-ry-ũ? — *Avez-vous des plats végétariens?*

Can you recommend a vegetarian dish, please?
poo-veh voo mer kõ-se-ye ũ pla ve-zhe-ta-ry-ũ seel voo pleh? — *Pouvez-vous me conseiller un plat végétarien, s'il vous plaît?*

Does this dish have meat?
ehs-ker ser pla kõ-tyũ der la vyãd? — *Est-ce que ce plat contient de la viande?*

Can I order this without the meat?
pweezh ko-mã-de ser pla sã vyãnd? — *Puis-je commander-avoir ce plat sans viande?*

Is the sauce meat-based?
eks ker la sohs eht ta baz der vyãnd? — *Est-ce que la sauce est à base de viande?*

Does it contain eggs/dairy products?
ehs ker ser pla kõ-tyũ deh-zer oo deh prod-dwee leh-tyeh? — *Est-ce que ce plat contient des œufs ou des produits laitiers?*

Does this dish have gelatin?
ser pla kõ-tyũ-teel der la zhe-la-teen? — *Ce plat contient-il de la gélatine?*

I'm allergic to ...
zher swee-zal-ehr-zheek a ... — *Je suis allergique à ...*

Is it ...?	**es ...?**	*Est-ce ...?*
gluten-free	**sã glü-tehn**	*sans gluten*
lactose-free	**sã leh**	*sans lait*
wheat-free	**sã bleh**	*sans blé*
salt-free	**sã sehl**	*sans sel*
sugar-free	**sã sükr**	*sans sucre*
yeast-free	**sã ler-vür**	*sans levure*

I'd like this meal kosher.
zher voo-dreh ser pla ka-shehr — *Je voudrais ce plat kascher.*

Is this kosher?
es ker seh ka-shehr? — *Est-ce que c'est kascher?*

Is this organic?
es ker ser pla eh byoh? — *Est-ce que ce plat est bio?*

Self-Catering

Where is the nearest [market]?
oo ser troohv ler [mar-sheh] ler plü prosh? — *Où se trouve le [marché] le plus proche?*

Where can I find the [sugar]?
oo pweezh troo-veh dü [sükr]? — *Où puis-je trouver du [sucre]?*

Can I have a ...?	**pwee-zhav-war ...?**	*Puis-je avoir ...?*
bottle	**ün boo-teh-y**	*une bouteille*
box	**ün bwat**	*une boîte*
can	**ün kaneht**	*une boîte/canette*
packet	**ũ pa-keh**	*un paquet*
bag	**ũ sak**	*un sac*
tin of ...	**dü; de; des; de la ... ã kõ-sehrv**	*du; de; des; de la ... en conserve*

How much?
kõ-byũ? — *Combien?*

How much is [a kilo of cheese]?
kõ-byũ kooht [ũ kee-loh der fro-mazh]? — *Combien coûte [un kilo de fromage]?*

Do you have anything cheaper?
a-veh voo kehl-ker-shohz der mwũ shehr? — *Avez-vous quelque chose de moins cher?*

I would like [half] a kilo, please.
zher voo-dreh ũ [der-mee] kee-loh seel voo pleh — *Je voudrais un [demi] kilo s'il vous plaît.*

I'd like [six] slices of [ham].
zher voo-dreh [see] trãsh de [zhã-bõ] — *Je voudrais [six] tranches de [jambon].*

I don't want to buy anything.
zher ner ver ryũ nash-te — *Je ne veux rien acheter.*

I'm just looking.
zher rer-gahrd serl-mã — *Je regarde seulement.*

No!
nõ! — *Non!*

I'd like some ...	**zher voo-dreh ...**	*Je voudrais ...*
bread	**dü pũ**	*du pain*
butter	**dü berr**	*du beurre*
cheese	**dü fro-mazh**	*du fromage*
chocolate	**dü sho-ko-la**	*du chocolat*
eggs	**deh-zer**	*des œufs*
flour	**der la fa-reen**	*de la farine*
frozen foods	**deh sür-zher-le**	*des surgelés*
fruit & vegetables	**de frwee e deh le-güm**	*des fruits et des légumes*
ham	**dü zhã-bõ**	*du jambon*
honey	**dü myehl**	*du miel*
jam	**der la kõ-fee-tür**	*de la confiture*
margarine	**der la mar-ga-reen**	*de la margarine*
marmalade	**der la mar-mer-lad**	*de la marmelade*
milk	**dü leh**	*du lait*
olive/sunflower oil	**der lweel do-leev/der lweel der toor-ner-sol**	*de l'huile d'olive/de l'huile de tournesol*
pasta	**deh pat**	*des pâtes*
pepper	**dü pwavr**	*du poivre*
rice	**dü ree**	*du riz*
salt	**dü sehl**	*du sel*
sugar	**dü sükr**	*du sucre*
yoghurt	**ũ ya-yoort**	*un yaourt*

... 1olives	**deh-zo-leev ...**	*des olives ...*
black	**nwar**	*noires*
green	**vehrt**	*vertes*
stuffed	**far-see**	*farcies*

Can I taste it?
pwee-zh ler/la goo-te? *Puis-je le/la goûter?*

Will this keep in the fridge?
ser-la ser kõ-sehr-v-teel o freego/re-free-zhee-ra-terr? *Cela se conserve-t-il au frigo/réfrigérateur?*

Is this the best you have?
es ler myer/la meh-yerr ker voo-za-veh? *Est-ce le mieux/la meilleure que vous avez?*

What's the local speciality?
kehl eh la spe-see-ya-lee-te lo-kal/der la rezh-yõ? *Quelle est la spécialité locale/de la region?*

At the Bar

Let's have a drink.
õ bwa ũ koo (ũ vehr) *On boit un coup (un verre).*

Shall we go for a drink?
õ vah bwar ũ vehr? *On va boire un verre?*

I'll buy you a drink.
zher voo-zofr/tofr ũ vher *Je vous offre/t'offre un verre.*

Thanks, but I don't feel like it.
nõ mehr-see *Non, merci.*

I don't drink [alcohol].
zher ner bwa pah [dal-kol] *Je ne bois pas [d'alcool].*

What would you like?
kehs ker voo voo-le/tü ver bwar? *Qu'est-ce que vous voulez/tu veux boire?*

You can get the next one.
la pro-shehn toor-ne ser-rah poor twa *La prochaine tournée sera pour toi.*

I'll have ...
zher veh prãdr ... *Je vais prendre ...*

It's on me.
seh poor mwa *C'est pour moi.*

It's my round.
seh mah toor-ne *C'est ma tournée.*

Okay.
da-kor *D'accord.*

I'm next.
zher swee ler pro-shũ/la pro-shehn *Je suis le prochain/la prochaine*

Excuse me.
eks-küu-ze mwa *Excusez-moi.*

I was here before this lady/gentleman.
zhe-teh la a-vã ser mer-syer/seht madahm — *J'étais là avant ce monsieur/cette madame.*

I'll have [a] ...	**zher veh prãdr ...**	*Je vais prendre ...*
beer	**ün byehr**	*une bière*
brandy	**dü kon-yak**	*du cognac*
Champagne	**dü shã-pan-y**	*du Champagne*
cider	**dü seedr**	*du cidre*
cocktail	**ũ kok-tehl**	*un cocktail*
liqueur	**ün lee-kerr**	*une liqueur*
rum	**dü rom**	*du rhum*
whisky	**dü wees-kee**	*du whisky*

Cheers!
sã-te! — *Santé!*

No ice.
sã glas/glas-õ — *Sans glace/glaçons.*

Can I have ice, please?
pwee-zhav-war der la glas, seel voo pleh — *Puis-je avoir de la glace, s'il vous plaît?*

Same again, please.
la mehm shohz, seel voo pleh — *La même chose, s'il vous plaît.*

Is food available here?
eh-teel pos-seebl der mã-zhe ee-see? — *Est-il possible de manger ici?*

This is hitting the spot.
seht tehg-zak-ter-mã ser ker zher ver/noo voo-lõ — *C'est exactement ce que je veux/nous voulons.*

Where's the toilet?
oo sõ leh twah-leht/leh ve-se? — *Où sont les toilettes/les wc?*

I'm a bit tired, I'd better get home.
zher swee zũ per fa-tee-ge zher pre-fehr rã-tre — *Je suis un peu fatigué(e), je préfère rentrer.*

I'm feeling drunk.
zhe ũ koo dã lehl — *J'ai un coup dans l'aile.*

I'm pissed.
zher swee soo(l); eevr; boo-re — *Je suis soûl(e); ivre; bourré(e).*

I want to throw up.
zhe ã-vee der voh-meer — *J'ai envie de vomir.*

S/he's passed out.
eel/ehl eh-teevr mor(t) — *Il/elle est ivre mort(e).*

I'm hung over.
zhe la gerl der bwah — *J'ai la gueule de bois.*

Do you come here often?
ehs ker voo ver-ne/tü vyũ soo-vã ee-see? *Est-ce que vous venez/tu viens souvent ici?*

I really love you.
zher tehm vreh-mã bo-koo *Je t'aime vraiment beaucoup.*

What did I do last night?
kehs ker zhe feh la nwee dehr-nyehr? *Qu'est-ce que j'ai fait la nuit dernière?*

I'll have a vodka and lemonade
zher veh prãdr ũ vodka lee-moõ-nahd *Je vais prendre un vodka-limonade.*

Wine

May I see the wine list, please?
pwee-zhav-war la kart deh vũ seel voo pleh? *Puis-je avoir voir la carte des vins, s'il vous plaît?*

What is a good year?
kehl eh-tün bon a-ne poor ser vũ? *Quelle est une bonne année pour ce vin?*

Can you recommend a good local wine?
poo-veh voo mer kõ-se-ye ũ bõ vũ der la rezh-yõ? *Pouvez-vous me conseillez un bon vin de la région?*

May I taste it?
pweezh ler goo-te? *Puis-je le goûter?*

Which wine would you recommend with this dish?
kehl vũ mer kõ-se-ye voo a-vehk ser pla? *Quel vin me conseillez vous avec ce plat?*

I'd like a glass/bottle of ... wine.	**zher voo-dreh ũ vehr/ ün boo-teh-y der vũ ...**	*Je voudrais un verre/ une bouteille de vin ...*
red	**roozh**	*rouge*
rose	**roh-ze**	*rosé*
sparkling	**moo-ser**	*mousseux*
white	**blã**	*blanc*

This is excellent!
seht ehk-se-lã! *C'est excellent!*

This wine is good/bad.
ser vũ eh bõ/moh-veh *Ce vin est bon/mauvais.*

This wine has a nice/bad colour.
ser vũ a/na pah ün behl rohb *Ce vin a/n'a pas une belle robe.*

This wine is corked (off).
ser vũ eh boo-shon-e *Ce vin est bouchonné.*

English – French Glossary

In French, nouns always have a feminine or masculine form. In this glossary, the definite article has been included, **la** for feminine and **le** for masculine. Where the gender of a word is not obvious from the article (eg, **l'anis**), we have used the abbreviations (m) or (f) to indicate this. If a word can be both a noun and a verb, or if there is doubt as to what category the word is, we have used 'to' in front of the verb.

A

abalone	*or-moh*	**l'ormeau (m)**
advocaat	*a-dvo-kat*	**l'Advocaat (m)**
ale	*byehr [ā-glehz]*	**la bière [anglaise]**
[to be] allergic to	*[ehtr] a-lehr-zheek a*	**[être] allergique à**
allergy	*a-lehr-zhee*	**l'allergie (f)**
allspice	*pee-mā/katr-e-pees*	**le piment/quatre-épices**
almond	*a-mād*	**l'amande (f)**
anchovy	*ā-shwa*	**l'anchois (m)**
angelica	*ā-zhe-leek*	**l'angélique (f)**
anise/aniseed	*a-nees (vehr)*	**l'anis (vert) (m)**
aperitif	*a-pe-ree-teef*	**l'apéritif (m)**
appetiser	*amüz-gerl; amüz boosh; or-dervr*	**l'amuse-gueule (m); l'amuse-bouche (m); le hors-d'œuvre**
apple	*pom*	**la pomme**
apricot	*ab-ree-koh*	**l'abricot (m)**
artichoke	*ar-tee-shoh*	**l'artichaut (m)**
ashtray	*sā-dree-ye*	**le cendrier**
asparagus	*as-pehrzh*	**l'asperge (f)**
aspic	*zher-le*	**la gelée**
aubergine	*oh-behr-zheen*	**l'aubergine (f)**
avocado	*a-vo-ka*	**l'avocat (m)**
awful	*treh moh-veh(z)*	**très mauvais(e)**

B

bacon	*lar/beh-kon*	**le lard/bacon**
bad	*moh-veh(z)*	**mauvais(e)**
bake	*kweer oh foor/fehr der la pa-tees-ree*	**cuire au four/faire de la pâtisserie**
bakery	*boo-lāzh-ree*	**la boulangerie**
baking soda	*bee-kar-bo-nat der sood*	**le bicarbonate de soude**
banana	*ba-nan*	**la banane**
barbecue	*bar-ber-kyoo/(kü); fehr gree-yeh oh bar-ber-kyoo/(kü); fehr de gree-yad*	**le barbecue; faire griller au barbecue; faire des grillades**
barbecue grill	*gree-yad*	**la grillade**
barley	*orzh*	**l'orge (f)**

basil	*ba-zee-leek*	le basilic
bass	*bar/loo der mehr*	le bar/loup de mer
batter	*pat*	la pâte
bay leaf	*lor-ye*	le laurier
bean	*a-ree-koh*	le haricot
broad bean	*fehv*	la fève
butter bean	*a-ree-koh der lee-ma/ a-ree-koh der swa-sõ*	le haricot de Lima/ le haricot de Soissons
flageolet bean	*fla-zho-leh*	le flageolet
French/string bean	*a-ree-koh vehr*	le haricot vert
haricot bean	*a-ree-koh blã*	le haricot blanc
mung bean	*a-ree-koh mõ-go*	le haricot mungo
pinto bean	*a-ree-koh peen-toh*	le haricot pinto
red kidney bean	*a-ree-koh roozh*	le haricot rouge
runner bean	*a-ree-koh deh-spany*	le haricot d'Espagne
beef	*berf*	le bœuf
beef jerky (dried beef)	*berf se-she*	le bœuf séché
beefsteak tomato	*to-mat a far-seer*	la tomate à farcir
beer	*byehr*	la bière
beetroot	*beh-trav*	la betterave
berry	*beh*	la baie
bilberry (European blueberry)	*meer-tee-y/eh-rehl*	la myrtille/l' airelle (f)
bill/check (restaurant)	*a-dees-yõ*	l'addition (f)
bird	*wa-zoh*	l'oiseau (m)
birthday	*a-nee-vehr-sehr*	l'anniversaire (m)
bitter lemon	*shwehps*	le Schweppes
bitter	*a-mehr*	amer/amère
bitters	*a-mehr/bee-terr*	l'amer (m)/le bitter
black olive	*o-leev nwar*	l'olive noire (f)
black pudding	*boo-dũ nwar*	le boudin noir
black truffle	*trüf nwar*	la truffe noire
blackberry	*mür*	la mûre
blackcurrant	*ka-sees*	le cassis
blender	*meek-serr*	le mixeur
blood	*sã*	le sang
blue cheese	*blerr/fro-mazh a pat pehr-see-ye*	le bleu/le fromage à pâte persillée
blueberry (European)	*meer-tee-y/eh-rehl*	la myrtille/l'airelle (f)
boar (wild)	*sã-glee-ye*	le sanglier
boil	*(fehr) boo-yeer/ kweer a loh*	(faire) bouillir/ cuire à l'eau
book (booked)	*re-zehr-ve*	réserver (réservé(e))
bottle	*boo-teh-y*	la bouteille
bottle opener	*oov-rer-boo-teh-y*	l'ouvre-bouteille (m)
bourbon	*boor-bõ*	le bourbon
bowl	*bol; sa-la-dye; koop*	le bol; le saladier; la coupe

brains	*sehr-vehl*	la cervelle
braise	*breh-ze*	braiser
bran	*sõ*	le son
brandy	*brãn-dee; kon-yak; oh der vee*	le brandy; le cognac; l'eau-de-vie (f)
bratwurst	*broht-vohrsht*	le bratwurst
brazil nut	*nwa dü bre-zeel*	la noix du Brésil
bread	*pũ*	le pain
breakfast	*per-tee de-zher-ne*	le petit déjeuner
bream	*brehm*	la brème
breast	*blã; tã-drõ; pwa-treen*	le blanc (poultry); le tendron (veal, beef); la poitrine (lamb, beef)
brill	*bar-bü*	la barbue
brisket (beef)	*pwa-treen*	la poitrine
broad bean	*fehv*	la fève
broccoli	*bro-ko-lee*	le brocoli
broth	*boo-yõ*	le bouillon
brown lentil	*lã-tee-y blõd*	la lentille blonde
brussels sprout	*shoo der brü-sehl*	le chou de Bruxelles
to bubble	*pe-tee-ye/boo-yo-ne*	pétiller/bouillonner
buckwheat	*sara-zũ/ble nwar*	le sarrasin/le blé noir
bulghur (wheat)	*bool-goor*	le boulghour
to burn	*brü-le*	brûler
butcher	*boo-she*	le boucher
butcher's/butcher's shop	*boosh-ree*	la boucherie
butter	*berr*	le beurre
butter bean	*a-ree-koh der lee-ma/ a-ree-koh der swa-sõ*	le haricot de Lima/ le haricot de Soissons
buttermilk	*ba-berr*	le babeurre
butterscotch	*ka-ra-mehl*	le caramel
button mushroom	*shã-peen-yõ der pa-ree*	le champignon de Paris

C

cabbage (red/white)	*shoo (roozh/blã)*	le chou (rouge/blanc)
café	*ka-fe; bees-troh; troh-keh*	le café; le bistro(t); le troquet
café owner/manager	*pa-trõ/pa-tron der ka-fe*	le patron/la patronne de café
cake	*ga-toh*	le gâteau
cake/pastry shop	*pa-tees-ree*	la pâtisserie
camomile tea	*ka-mo-mee-y*	la camomille
can	*bwat*	la boîte
can opener	*oo-vrer-bwat*	l'ouvre-boîte (m)
candy	*bõ-bõ*	le bonbon
candy shop	*kõ-fee-zree*	la confiserie

cannellini bean	*a-ree-koh ka-ne-lee-nee*	le haricot cannellini
cantaloupe	*[mer-lõ] kã-ta-loo*	le [melon] cantaloup
caper	*kapr*	le câpre
capsicum (green/red/yellow)	*pwav-rõ (vehr/roozh/zhohn)*	le poivron (vert/rouge/jaune)
caramel	*ka-ra-mehl*	le caramel
caraway	*kü-mũ*	le cumin
caraway seed	*kü-mũ/grehn der kar-vee*	le cumin/la graine de carvi
cardoon	*kar-dõ*	le cardon
carrot	*ka-rot*	la carotte
cash	*ar-zhã*	l'argent (m)
cashew	*nwa der ka-zhoo*	la noix de cajou
cashier	*kes-ye/kes-yehr*	le caissier/la caissière
cauliflower	*shoo-flerr*	le chou-fleur
caviar	*kav-yar*	le caviar
cayenne pepper	*pwavr der ka-yehn*	le poivre de Cayenne
celebration	*feht*	la fête
celeriac	*sehl-ree rav*	le céleri-rave
celery	*sehl-ree*	le céleri
celery seed	*grehn der sehl-ree*	la graine de céleri
cereal	*se-re-al (grũ)/ se-re-al*	la céréale (grain)/les céréales (breakfast, f)
Champagne	*shã-pan-y*	le Champagne
chanterelle mushroom	*shã-ter-rehl*	la chanterelle
cheese	*fro-mazh*	le fromage
blue cheese	*blerr/fro-mazh a pat pehr-see-ye*	le bleu/le fromage à pâte persillée
cheese board	*pla-toh der fro-mazh*	le plâteau de fromages
cottage cheese	*fro-mazh freh*	le fromage frais
cream cheese	*fro-mazh blã*	le fromage blanc
goat's milk cheese	*fro-mazh der shehvr*	le fromage de chèvre
hard cheese	*fro-mazh a pat dür*	le fromage à pâte dure
sharp	*for*	fort
sheep's milk cheese	*fro-mazh der brer-bee*	le fromage de brebis
semi-hard cheese	*fro-mazh a pat der-mee-fehrm*	le fromage à pâte demi-ferme
soft cheese	*fro-mazh a pat mol*	le fromage à pâte molle
cheese shop	*fro-mazh-ree/ krehm-ree*	la fromagerie/ la crémerie
chef	*shehf kwee-zeen-ye/ shehf der kwee-zeen*	le chef cuisinier/ le chef de cuisine
cherry	*ser-reez*	la cerise
cherry tomato	*to-mat ser-reez*	la tomate cerise
chervil	*sehr-fer-y*	le cerfeuil
chestnut	*sha-tehn-y/ma-rõ*	la châtaigne/le marron
chicken	*poo-leh*	le poulet
chickpea	*pwa sheesh*	le pois chiche

chicory	*ã-deev/ shee-ko-re*	l'endive (vegetable, f)/ la chicorée (in coffee)
chilli	*pee-mã (roozh)/ shee-lee*	le piment (rouge)/ le chili
chips	*freet*	les frites (f)
chives	*see-boo-leht*	la ciboulette
chocolate	*sho-ko-la*	le chocolat
chocolate shop	*sho-ko-la-tree*	la chocolaterie
chop	*koht-leht*	la côtelette
chopping board	*plãsh a de-koo-pe*	la planche à découper
chopsticks	*ba-geht*	les baguettes (f)
chowder	*ver-loo-te der frwee der mehr/beesk*	le velouté de fruits de mer/la bisque
cider	*seedr*	le cidre
cinnamon	*ka-nehl*	la cannelle
citrus fruit	*a-grüm*	l'agrume (m)
clam	*pa-loord*	la palourde
clotted cream	*krehm frehsh/ e-pehs*	la crème fraîche/ épaisse
clove	*kloo der zhee-rofl*	le clou de girofle
clove (of garlic)	*goos [day]*	la gousse [d'ail]
cockle	*kok*	la coque
cocktail	*kok-tehl*	le cocktail
cocoa	*ka-ka-oh*	le cacao
coconut	*nwa der kokoh*	la noix de coco
cod	*ka-bee-yoh/mo-rü*	le cabillaud/la morue
coffee	*ka-fe*	le café
black coffee	*ka-fe nwar/per-tee nwar*	-noir/le petit noir
coffee grinder	*moo-lũ a ka-fe*	le moulin à café
coffee machine	*kaf-tyehr [e-lehk-treek]*	la cafetière [électrique]
coffee with hot milk	*ka-fe oh leh*	-au lait
coffee with ice cream	*ka-fe lyezh-wa*	-liégeois
coffee with steam milk or cream	*ka-fe krehm*	-crème
decaffeinated coffee	*ka-fe de-ka-fe-ee-ne/de-ka*	-décaféiné/le déca
expresso	*[ka-fe] ehks-prehs/ ehks-preh-soh*	le [café] express/ l'expresso (m)
cold	*frwa(d)*	froid(e)
condiment	*kõ-dee-mã*	le condiment
consomme	*kõ-so-me*	le consommé
cook	*kwee-zeen-ye/kwee-zeen-yehr*	le cuisinier/la cuisinière
to cook	*kweer; kwee-zee-ne; fehr la kwee-zeen*	cuire; cuisiner; faire la cuisine
cookie	*ga-toh sehk; per-tee ga-toh; bees-kwee*	le gâteau sec; le petit gâteau; le biscuit
cool	*freh/frehsh*	frais/fraîche
coriander	*kor-yãndr*	le coriandre

corn	*ma-ees*	le maïs
cornmeal	*fa-reen der ma-ees*	la farine de maïs
to cost	*koo-te*	coûter
cottage cheese	*fro-mazh freh*	le fromage frais
counter (at bar)	*kõ-twar/zũk*	le comptoir/le zinc
courgette/zucchini	*koor-zheht*	la courgette
couscous	*koos-koos*	le couscous
crab	*krab/toor-toh*	le crabe/le tourteau
cracked wheat	*ble kõ-ka-se*	le blé concassé
cranberry	*kan-behrzh*	la canneberge
cranberry sauce	*sohs oh kan-behrzh*	la sauce aux canneberges
crayfish	*e-krer-vees/ lã-goost*	l'écrevisse (freshwater, f)/la langouste (saltwater)
cream	*krehm*	la crème
clotted cream	*frehsh/epehs*	-fraîche/épaisse
sour cream	*ehgr*	-aigre
whipping cream	*a fweh-te/fler-reht*	-à fouetter/fleurette
cream cheese	*fro-mazh blã*	le fromage blanc
cress/watercress	*kreh-sõ*	le cresson
croissant	*krwa-sã*	le croissant
croquette	*kro-keht*	la croquette
cucumber	*kõ-kõbr*	le concombre
cumin	*kü-mũ*	le cumin
cup	*tas*	la tasse
to cure	*sa-le; se-she; fü-me*	saler (salt); sécher (dry); fumer (smoke)
currant	*gro-zehy*	la groseille
currant (dried)	*reh-zũ der ko-rũt*	le raisin de Corinthe
curry (powder)	*kü-ree*	le curry
cutlery	*koo-vehr*	les couverts (m)
cutlet	*koht-leht; koht; darn/trãsh*	la côtelette (beef, lamb, mutton); la côte (veal); la darne/tranche (fish)

D

dab (lemon sole)	*lee-mãd*	la limande
date	*dat*	la datte
deep-fry	*[fehr] freer*	[faire] frire
delicatessen	*shar-kü-tree/ treh-terr*	la charcuterie/ le traiteur
dessert	*de-sehr*	le dessert
dessert spoon	*kwee-yehr a de-sehr*	la cuillère à dessert
diabetic	*dya-be-teek*	diabétique

diarrhoea	*dya-re*	la diarrhée
dill	*a-neht*	l'aneth (m)
dinner	*dee-ne*	le dîner
donkey	*an*	l'âne (m)
dried fruit	*frwee sehk*	le fruit sec
drink (alcoholic)	*koo/vehr*	le coup/le verre
drink/beverage	*bwa-sõ*	la boisson
to drink	*bwar*	boire
drunk (to be)	*eevr/soo(l)*	ivre/soûl(e)
dry	*sehk/sehsh*	sec/sèche
duck	*ka-nar*	le canard
dumpling	*boo-leht/ree-sol*	la boulette/la rissole

E

each	*shak*	chaque
ear	*o-reh-y*	l'oreille (f)
Easter	*pak*	Pâques
to eat	*mã-zhe*	manger
eel	*ã-geey*	l'anguille (f)
eggplant	*oh-behr-zheen*	l'aubergine (f)
egg	*erf*	l'œuf (m)
fried	*sür ler pla*	sur le plat
hard-boiled	*dür*	dur
poached	*po-she*	poché
soft-boiled	*a la kok*	à la coque
scrambled	*broo-ye*	brouillé
endive	*ã-deev; free-ze/shee-kore*	l'endive (chicory, f); la frisée/la chicorée
entrée/starter	*ã-tre*	l'entrée (f)
expensive	*shehr*	cher/chère

F

farm	*fehrm*	la ferme
farm cheese	*fro-mazh fehr-mye*	le fromage fermier
farmhouse pâté	*pate der kã-pan-y*	le pâté de campagne
farmer	*a-gree-kül-terr/ a-gree-kül-trees*	l'agriculteur (m)/ l'agricultrice (f)
to fast (not to eat)	*zher-ne*	jeûner
fat	*grehs; gra/gras*	la graisse; gras/grasse
feed	*noo-reer*	nourrir
fennel	*fer-noo-y*	le fenouil
fennel seed	*grehn der fer-noo-y*	la graine de fenouil
fenugreek	*fer-nü-grehk*	le fenugrec
festival	*feht*	la fête
fig	*feeg*	la figue

fillet	*fee-leh; lõzh/ehs-ka-lop; foh-fee-leh/lõ-gleh*	le filet (meat, fish); la longe/l'escalope (veal, f); le faux-filet, l'onglet (beef, m)
to fillet	*de-zo-se/ de-koo-pe ã fee-leh*	désosser (meat)/ découper en filets (fish)
first course (starter)	*ã-tre*	l'entrée (f)
fish	*pwa-sõ*	le poisson
fishmonger (shop)	*pwa-son-ree*	la poissonnerie
fizzy	*ga-zer/ga-zerz*	gazeux/gazeuse
flageolet bean	*fla-zho-leh*	le flageolet
flank	*flã-sheh*	le flanchet
flavour	*sa-verr/par-fũ*	la saveur/le parfum (ice cream, yoghurt)
flounder	*fleh*	le flet
flour	*fa-reen*	la farine
food	*noo-ree-tür*	la nourriture
food processor	*ro-boh me-na-zhe*	le robot ménager
fork	*foor-sheht*	la fourchette
free-range	*eler-ve ã pleh-nehr*	élevé en plein air
French fries	*[pom] freet/*	les [pommes] frites (f)/
French/string bean	*a-ree-koh vehr*	le haricot vert
fresh	*freh/frehsh*	frais/fraîche
fresh juice	*zhü der frwee pre-se*	le jus de fruit pressé
fridge	*free-go/re-free-zhe-ra-terr*	le frigo/le réfrigérateur
frog	*grer-nooy*	la grenouille
frog's leg	*kwees der grer-nooy*	la cuisse de grenouille
frozen	*zher-le*	gelé(e)
fruit	*frwee*	le fruit
fruit cake	*kehk*	le cake
fruit juice	*zhü der frwee*	le jus de fruit
fruit and vegetable shop	*ma-ga-zũ der frwee e le-güm*	le magasin de fruits et légumes
to fry	*[fehr] freer*	[faire] frire
frying pan	*pwal [a freer]*	la poêle [à frire]

G

game	*zheeb-ye*	le gibier
game bird	*zheeb-ye a plüm*	le gibier à plume
garden pea	*per-tee pwa*	le petit pois
garlic	*ay*	l'ail (m)
gelatin	*zhe-la-teen*	la gélatine
gherkin	*kor-nee-shõ*	le cornichon
giblets	*a-ba*	les abats (m)
gin	*dzheen*	le gin
ginger	*zhũ-zhãbr*	le gingembre

glass	*vehr*	le verre
glass of water	*vehr doh*	le verre d'eau
glutinous rice	*ree glü-ã*	le riz gluant
goat	*shehvr*	la chèvre
goat's milk cheese	*fro-mazh der shehvr*	le fromage de chèvre
goose	*wa*	l'oie (f)
goose liver pâté	*pa-te der fwa gra*	le pâté de foie gras
gooseberry	*groh-zeh-y a ma-kroh*	la groseille à maquereau
grape	*reh-zũ*	le raisin
grapefruit	*pã-pler-moos*	le pamplemousse
grapefruit juice	*zhü der pã-pler-moos*	le jus de pamplemousse
to grate	*ra-pe*	râper
grater	*rap*	la râpe
gravy	*sohs oh [zhü der vyãd]*	la sauce [au jus de viande]
grayling	*õmbr [der reev-yehr]*	l'ombre [de rivière] (m)
grease	*weel/grehs*	l'huile (vegetable, f)/ la graisse (animal)
green (vegetable)	*le-güm vehr*	le légume vert
green lentil	*lã-tee-y vehrt*	la lentille verte
green olive	*o-leev vehrt*	l'olive verte (f)
green split pea	*pwa ka-se vehr*	le pois cassé vert
greengrocer	*mar-shã der frwee e der le-güm*	le marchand de fruits et de légumes
grill	*gree-yad; greel; greel*	la grillade (dish); le gril (on cooker); le grill (restaurant)
to grill	*[fehr] gree-ye*	[faire] griller
grocery	*e-pees-ree*	l'épicerie (f)
groundnut/peanut	*ka-ka-weht/ a-ra-sheed*	la cacahuète/ l'arachide (f)
to grow	*[ehr] poo-se*	[faire] pousser
guava	*go-yav*	la goyave

H

haddock	*ehg-ler-fũ/ ehg-ler-fũ; a-dok*	l'églefin (m)/ l'aiglefin (m); le haddock
hake	*ko-lũ; mehr-lü; mehr-lüsh*	le colin; le merlu; la merluche
half	*mwa-tye; der-mee*	la moitié; le/la demi(e)
halibut	*fle-tã*	le flétan
ham	*zhã-bõ*	le jambon
hamburger	*ã-boor-gerr*	le hamburger
hard	*dür*	dur(e)
hare	*lyehvr*	le lièvre
haricot bean (dried)	*a-ree-koh blã*	le haricot blanc

hazelnut	*nwa-zeht*	la noisette
head	*teht*	la tête
heart	*kerr*	le cœur
hen	*pool/poo-lard*	la poule/poularde
herbs	*ehrb*	les herbes (f)
herring	*a-rã*	le hareng
hominy	*grü-oh der ma-ees*	le gruau de maïs
honey	*myehl*	le miel
horse	*sher-val*	le cheval
horseradish	*reh-for*	le raifort
hospitality	*os-pee-ta-lee-te*	l'hospitalité (f)
hot	*shoh(d)*	chaud(e)
hot chocolate	*sho-ko-la shoh*	le chocolat chaud
hotel	*oh-tehl*	l'hôtel (m)
hungry [to be]	*[av-war] fũ*	[avoir] faim

I

ice	*glas*	la glace
ice cream	*glas*	la glace
ice cube	*glasõ*	le glaçon
icing sugar	*sükr glas*	le sucre glace
ingredient	*ũ-gre-dyã*	l'ingrédient (m)

J

Jalapeño pepper	*pee-mã zha-la-pe-nyo*	le piment jalapeño
jam	*kõ-fee-tür*	la confiture
jar	*poh/bo-kal*	le pot/le bocal
jelly	*zher-le*	la gelée
Jerusalem artichoke	*to-pee-nã-boor*	le topinambour
John Dory	*sũ-pyehr*	le Saint Pierre
jug (for water)	*ka-raf*	la carafe
jug (for wine)	*pee-sheh*	le pichet
juice	*zhü*	le jus
juicer	*sã-tree-fü-zherz*	la centrifugeuse
juniper	*zher-nyehvr*	le genièvre

K

kettle	*booy-war*	la bouilloire
kidney	*ron-yõ*	le rognon
kilo	*kee-loh*	le kilo
king prawns	*gã-ba*	les gambas (f)
kipper	*a-rã fü-me/ a-rãfü-me e sa-le*	le hareng fumé/le hareng fumé et salé
kitchen	*kwee-zeen*	la cuisine
knife	*koo-toh*	le couteau
boning knife	*koo-toh a de-zo-se*	le couteau à désosser

bread knife	*koo-toh a pũ*	le couteau à pain
butter knife	*koo-toh a berr*	le couteau à beurre
carving knife	*koo-toh a de-koo-pe*	le couteau à découper
paring knife	*koo-toh a e-plü-she*	le couteau à éplucher
serrated knife	*koo-toh dã-ter-le*	le couteau dentelé
knuckle	*zha-reh; zhã-bo-noh; mãsh der zhee-goh*	le jarret (pork, veal); le jambonneau (ham); le manche de gigot (lamb, mutton)
kosher	*ka-shehr*	kascher

L

ladle	*loosh/sehr-veer a la loosh*	la louche/servir à la louche
lager	*byehr blõd*	la bière blonde
lamb	*a-nyoh*	l'agneau (m)
lard	*sũ-doo; grehss (der por); lar-de*	le saindoux; la graisse (de porc); larder
leek	*pwa-roh*	le poireau
leg	*kwees; zhee-goh; zheet; kwee-soh/ nwa; kwee-soh; zhã-bõ*	la cuisse (poultry, frog); le gigot (lamb); le gîte (beef); le cuisseau/la noix (veal); le cuissot (venison); le jambon (pork)
legume	*le-gü-mee-nerz*	la légumineuse
lemon	*see-trõ*	le citron
lemon balm	*me-lees*	la mélisse
lemonade	*lee-mo-nad; see-tro-nad; see-trõ pre-se*	la limonade (fizzy); la citronnade (still); le citron pressé (pressed juice)
lemon sole (dab)	*lee-mãd*	la limande
lentil (brown)	*lã-tee-y*	la lentille
lettuce	*leh-tü/sa-lad*	la laitue/la salade
to like	*e-me*	aimer
Lima bean	*a-ree-koh der lee-ma/ a-ree-koh der swa-sõ*	le haricot de Lima/le haricot de Soissons
lime	*see-trõ vehr*	le citron vert
liqueur	*lee-kerr*	la liqueur
liquorice	*re-glees*	la réglisse
liver (pâté)	*(pa-te der) fwa*	le (pâté de) foie
lobster	*o-mar/ lã-goos-teen*	le homard (Atlantic)/ la langoustine (Mediterranean)
local	*lo-kal; re-zhyo-nal; dü pe-ee; dü tehr-war*	local; régional; du pays; du terroir

loin	*fee-leh; koht prer-myehr; lõzh; al-wa-yoh*	le filet; la côte première; la longe (veal); l'aloyau (beef, m)
lunch	*de-zher-ne*	le déjeuner

M

macadamia	*nwa der ma-ka-da-mya*	la noix de macadamia
mace	*ma-see*	le macis
mackerel	*ma-kroh*	le maquereau
Madeira wine	*vũ der ma-dehr*	le vin de Madère
main course	*pla prũ-see-pal*	le plat principal
mandarin	*mã-da-reen*	la mandarine
mange-tout pea	*mãzh-too/ pwa goor-mã*	le mange-tout/ le pois gourmand
mango	*mãg*	la mangue
marinade	*ma-ree-nad*	la marinade
marinate	*[fehr] ma-ree-ne*	[faire] mariner
marjoram	*mar-zho-lehn*	la marjolaine
market	*mar-she*	le marché
marmalade	*kõ-fee-tür/ mar-mer-lad do-rãzh*	la confiture/la marmelade d'oranges
marrow	*mwal/koorzh*	la moelle (bone)/la courge (vegetable)
Martini	*mar-tee-nee*	le Martini
marzipan	*pat da-mãd/ mas-pũ*	la pâte d'amandes/ le massepain
mayonnaise	*ma-yo-nehz*	la mayonnaise
meal	*rer-pa*	le repas
meat	*vyãd*	la viande
medium (cooked)	*a pwũ*	à point
melon	*mer-lõ*	le melon
menu	*kart*	la carte
meringue	*mer-rũg*	la meringue
mild	*doo/doos*	doux/douce
milk	*leh*	le lait
skimmed milk	*leh e-kre-me*	le lait écrémé
millet	*mee-yeh*	le millet
mince	*a-shee der vyãd; beef-tehk a-she; a-she*	le hachis de viande; le bifteck haché; hacher
mincer	*a-shwar*	le hachoir
mineral water	*oh mee-ne-ral*	l'eau minérale (f)
mint	*mãt/bõ-bõ a la mãt*	la menthe/le bonbon à la menthe (sweet, candy)
mixed salad	*salad kõ-poh-ze*	la salade composée
mixing bowl	*sala-dye*	le saladier

monkfish	*lot*	la lotte
morel mushroom	*mo-reey*	la morille
mortar	*mor-tye*	le mortier
muesli	*mwehs-lee*	le muesli
mulberry	*mür*	la mûre
mung bean	*a-ree-koh mõ-go*	le haricot mungo
mushroom	*shã-pee-nyõ*	le champignon
mussel	*mool*	la moule
mustard	*moo-tard*	la moutarde
mutton	*moo-tõ*	le mouton

N

napkin	*sehr-vyeht*	la serviette
neck	*ko-leh/ kol-ye*	le collet (lamb, mutton)/le collier (veal, beef, mutton)
noisy	*brwee-yã(t)*	bruyant(e)
non-smoking	*nõ-fü-merr*	non-fumeur
noodles	*noo-y*	les nouilles (f)
nougat	*noo-ga*	le nougat
nutcracker	*kas-nwa-zeht*	le casse-noisettes
nutmeg	*nwa der müs-kad*	la noix de muscade

O

oatmeal	*fa-reen dav-wan*	la farine d'avoine
oats	*av-wan*	l'avoine (f)
octopus	*poolp*	le poulpe
offal	*aba [de boosh-ree]*	les abats [de boucherie] (m)
oil	*weel*	l'huile (f)
to oil	*wee-le*	huiler
okra	*gõ-bo*	le gombo
olive	*o-leev*	l'olive (f)
olive oil	*weel do-leev*	l'huile d'olive (f)
omelette	*om-leht*	l'omelette (f)
onion	*on-yõ*	l'oignon (m)
red onion	*on-yõ roozh*	l'oignon rouge (m)
shallot onion	*e-sha-lot*	l'échalote (f)
spanish onion	*on-yõ deh-spany*	l'oignon d'Espagne (m)
orange	*o-rãzh*	l'orange (f)
orange juice; (freshly squeezed)	*zhü do-rãzh; o-rãzh pre-se*	le jus d'orange; l'orange pressée (f)
oregano	*o-ree-gã*	l'origan (m)
organic	*byo-lo-zheek; byoh; e-ler-ve byo-lo-zheek-mã*	biologique; bio (food, product); élevé biologiquement (poultry)

oven	*foor*	le four
oxtail	*ker der berf*	la queue de bœuf
oyster	*weetr*	l'huître (f)

P

paprika	*pa-pree-ka*	le paprika
Parma ham	*zhã-bõ der parm*	le jambon de Parme
parsley	*pehr-seel*	le persil
parsnip	*pa-neh*	le panais
passion fruit	*frwee der la pa-syõ*	le fruit de la passion
pasta (fresh)	*pat [frehsh]*	les pâtes [fraîches] (f)
pastrami	*pas-tra-mee*	le pastrami
pastry	*pat/pa-tees-ree*	la pâte (crust)/la pâtisserie (cake)
to pay for	*pe-ye*	payer
pea	*per-tee pwa*	le petit pois
snap pea	*pwa shoo-gerr snap*	le pois sugar snap
split pea	*pwa ka-se*	le pois cassé
peach	*pehsh*	la pêche
peanut	*ka-ka-weht/ a-ra-sheed*	la cacahuète/ l'arachide (f)
pear	*pwar*	la poire
pecan	*nwa der pe-kã; pa-kan; pe-kã*	la noix de pécan; la pacane; le pécan
peel (skin)	*poh*	peau
to peel	*e-plü-she*	éplucher
peeler	*e-plü-sherr*	l'éplucheur (m)
pepper (capsicum)	*pwav-rõ*	le poivron
pepper (white/black)	*pwavr*	le poivre (blanc/noir)
pepper mill	*pwav-ree-yehr*	la poivrière
peppermint	*mãt pwa-vre/ pas-teey der mãt*	la menthe poivrée (plant)/la pastille de menthe (sweet)
pepperoni	*pe-pe-ro-nee*	le pepperoni
perch	*pehrsh*	la perche
persimmon	*ka-kee*	le kaki
pestle	*pee-lõ*	le pilon
pheasant	*fer-zã*	le faisan
pickle	*ma-ree-nad; kõ-sehrv oh vee-nehgr; soh-mür*	la marinade; la conserve au vinaigre; la saumure (brine)
to pickle	*ma-ree-ne; kõ-sehrve oh vee-nehgr; soh-mü-re*	mariner; conserver au vinaigre; saumurer
pickled	*ma-ree-ne; kõ-sehr-ve oh vee-nehgr; soh-mü-re*	mariné; conservé au vinaigre; saumuré
pickling onion	*per-tee ton-yõ/ on-yõ grer-loh*	le petit oignon/ l'oignon grelot (m)

picnic	*peek-neek*	**le pique-nique**
pig	*ko-shõ*	**le cochon**
pigeon	*pee-zhõ*	**le pigeon**
pike	*bro-sheh*	**le brochet**
pine nut/kernel	*pee-nyõ (der pũ)*	**le pignon (de pin)**
pineapple	*a-na-nas*	**l'ananas (m)**
pinto bean	*a-ree-koh peen-toh*	**le haricot pinto**
pistachio	*pees-tash*	**la pistache**
plaice	*plee/kar-leh*	**la plie/le carrelet**
plate	*as-yeht/pla*	**l'assiette (f)/le plat**
plenty	*bo-koo*	**beaucoup**
plum	*prün*	**la prune**
plum tomato	*o-lee-veht*	**l'olivette (f)**
to poach	*po-she*	**pocher**
pomegranate	*grer-nad*	**la grenade**
poppy	*pa-voh*	**le pavot**
pork	*por*	**le porc**
pork sausage	*soh-sees/soh-see-sõ*	**la saucisse/le saucisson**
port	*por-toh*	**le porto**
a portion of ...	*par der ...*	**la part de ...**
pot	*poh/kas-rol*	**le pot (jam)/la casserole (saucepan)**
potato	*pom der tehr*	**la pomme de terre**
potato masher	*prehs-pü-re*	**le presse-purée**
poultry	*vo-lay*	**la volaille**
prawn	*krer-veht rohz/ boo-keh*	**la crevette rose/le bouquet (very rare)**
preservative	*a-zhã der kõ-sehr-va-syõ/ kõ-sehr-va-terr*	**l'agent de conservation (m)/ le conservateur**
preserves/jam	*kõ-fee-tür*	**la confiture**
pressure cooker	*oh-toh-kwee-zerr/ ko-kot-mee-nüt*	**l'autocuiseur (m)/la cocotte-minute**
provisions/food supplies	*pro-vee-zyõ*	**les provisions (f)**
prune	*prü-noh*	**le pruneau**
pub/bar	*bar*	**le bar**
puffball	*vehs-der-loo*	**la vesse-de-loup**
pulse	*le-güm sehk*	**le légume sec**
pumpkin	*see-trooy/po-tee-rõ*	**la citrouille/le potiron**
Puy lentil	*lã-teey [vehrt] dü pwee*	**la lentille [verte] du Puy**

Q

quail	*kay*	**la caille**
quality	*ka-lee-te*	**la qualité**
quantity	*kã-tee-te*	**la quantité**
quince	*kwũ*	**le coing**

R

rabbit	*la-pũ*	le lapin
radicchio	*tre-veez*	la trévise
radish	*ra-dee*	le radis
raisin	*reh-zũ sehk*	le raisin sec
rare (cooked)	*seh-nyã(t)*	saignant(e)
raspberry	*frã-bwaz*	la framboise
ray	*reh*	la raie
receipt	*rer-sü*	le reçu
red cabbage	*shoo roozh*	le chou rouge
red wine	*vũ- oozh*	vin rouge
red kidney bean	*a-ree-koh roozh*	le haricot rouge
red lentil	*lã-teey roozh*	la lentille rouge
red onion	*on-yõ roozh*	l'oignon rouge (m)
reservation	*re-zehr-va-syõ*	la réservation
restaurant	*reh-sto-rã; bees-tro; brass-er-ree*	le restaurant; le bistro(t); la brasserie
rhubarb	*rü-barb*	la rhubarbe
rib	*koht*	la côte
rice	*ree*	le riz
arborio	*ar-bor-yoh*	-arborio
basmati	*bas-ma-tee*	-basmati
brown	*brũ*	-brun
Camargue red	*roozh der ka-marg*	-rouge de Camargue
glutinous	*glü-ã*	-gluant
short-grain	*a grũ rõ*	-à grains ronds
wild	*soh-vazh*	-sauvage
ripe	*mür/feh*	mûr(e) (fruit)/fait (cheese)
roast	*roh-tee*	le rôti
to roast	*roh-teer/gree-ye*	rôtir (meat)/griller (peanuts)
rocket (vegetable)	*ro-keht/ roo-keht*	la roquette/la rouquette
rolled oats	*flo-kõ dav-wan*	le flocon d'avoine
rolling pin	*roo-loh a pa-tees-ree*	le rouleau à pâtisserie
rooster	*kok*	le coq
rosemary	*ro-ma-rũ*	le romarin
rum	*rom*	le rhum
rump	*kü-lot/ kroo-pyõ*	la culotte (beef)/le croupion (bird)
runner bean	*a-ree-koh deh-spany*	le haricot d'Espagne
rutabaga	*rü-ta-ba-ga*	le rutabaga
rye whisky	*wees-kee a baz der sehgl*	le whisky à base de seigle

S

saddle of lamb	*sehl da-nyoh*	la selle d'agneau
saffron	*saf-rã*	le safran
sage	*sohzh*	la sauge
sago	*sa-goo*	le sagou
sake	*sa-ke*	le saké
salad	*sa-lad*	la salade
salad bowl	*sa-la-dye*	le saladier
salami	*sa-la-mee/ soh-see-sõ sehk*	le salami/ le saucisson sec
salmon	*soh-mõ*	le saumon
salt mill	*sal-yehr*	la salière
salt	*sehl*	le sel
salt pork	*por sa-le/per-tee sa-le*	le porc salé/le petit salé
sardine	*sar-deen*	la sardine
sauce	*sohs*	la sauce
saucepan	*kas-rol*	la casserole
sauté	*soh-te*	sauter
savoury	*sar-yeht*	la sarriette
scales (for weighing)	*ba-lãs*	la balance
scallop	*ko-keey sũ zhak*	la coquille Saint-Jacques
scampi	*lã-goo-stin/ skã-pee*	la langoustine/ le scampi
scissors	*see-zoh*	les ciseaux (m)
sea bass	*loo der mehr*	le loup de mer
seafood	*frwee der mehr*	le fruit de mer
season	*seh-zõ*	la saison
seaweed	*alg*	l'algue (f)
self-service	*leebr-sehr-vees*	libre-service
semolina	*ser-mool*	la semoule
semi-hard cheese	*fro-mazh a pat der-mee-dür*	le fromage à pâte demi-dure
service charge	*sehr-vees*	le service
sesame seed	*grehn der se-zam*	la graine de sésame
shallot onion	*e-sha-lot*	l'échalote (f)
shallow-fry	*freer le-zhehr-mã*	frire légèrement
shandy	*pa-na-she*	le panaché
shank	*zha-reh*	le jarret
sharpening stone	*pyehr a eh-gee-ze*	la pierre à aiguiser
sheep's milk cheese	*fro-mazh der brer-bee*	le fromage de brebis
shellfish	*frwee der mehr*	le fruit de mer
sherry	*gze-rehs*	le Xérès
shin	*zha-reh*	le jarret
shop	*ma-ga-zũ/boo-teek*	le magasin/la boutique
short-grain rice	*ree a grũ rõ*	le riz à grains ronds
shoulder	*e-pohl*	l'épaule (f)
shrimp	*krer-veht greez*	la crevette grise

sieve	*ta-mee; pas-war*	le tamis (for sifting); la passoire (for draining)
to sieve	*ta-mee-ze*	tamiser
sifter	*ta-mee/soh-pood-rerz*	le tamis/la saupoudreuse (sugar)
silverside	*zhit a la nwa*	le gîte à la noix (beef)
simmer	*kweer a fer doo; mee-zho-te; mee-to-ne; fre-meer*	cuire à feu doux; mijoter; mitonner; frémir (water)
sirloin	*al-wa-yoh*	l'aloyau (m)
skewer	*bro-sheht; mehtr ā bro-sheht*	la brochette; mettre en brochette
skirt	*flā-sheh/āp*	le flanchet/la hampe
slice of	*trāsh der ...*	la tranche de ...
to smoke	*fü-me*	fumer
snack	*kas-kroot; rer-pa le-zhe; a-müz-gerl; a-müz boosh*	le casse-croûte; le repas léger; l'amuse-gueule (m); l'amuse-bouche (m)
snap pea	*pwa shoo-gerr snap*	le pois sugar snap
snapper	*roo-zheh*	rouget
soda water	*oh der sehlts/oh ga-zerz*	l'eau de Seltz (f)/ l'eau gazeuse (f)
soft cheese	*fro-mazh a pat mol*	le fromage à pâte molle
soft drink	*bwa-sō nō al-ko-lee-ze*	la boisson non alcoolisée
sole	*sol*	la sole
sorrel	*oh-zehy*	l'oseille (f)
soup	*soop/po-tazh*	la soupe/le potage
soup spoon	*kwee-yehr a soop*	la cuillère à soupe
soy [sauce]	*[sos] oh so-zha*	[sauce] au soja
soya bean	*so-zha; grehn der so-zha*	le soja; la graine de soja
soya milk	*leh der so-zha*	le lait de soja
Spanish onion	*on-yō deh-spany*	l'oignon d'Espagne (m)
sparerib	*tra-vehr der por*	le travers de porc
sparkling wine	*vū moo-ser*	le vin mousseux
spicy	*e-pee-se/pee-kā(t)*	épicé(e)/piquant(e)
spinach	*e-pee-nar*	l'épinard (m)
spirits	*spee-ree-tü-er/ al-kol*	le spiritueux/ l'alcool (m)
spoon	*kwee-yehr*	la cuillère
spring	*prū-tā*	le printemps
spring onion	*see-bool*	la ciboule
squash	*koorzh/ see-roh*	la courge (vegetable)/ le sirop (drink)
squid	*kal-mar/ ā-kor-neh*	le calmar/ l'encornet (m)

stale	*pa freh/frehsh*	pas frais/fraîche
star anise	*a-nees e-twa-le*	l'anis étoilé (m)
starter	*ã-tre*	l'entrée (f)
steak	*beef-tehk/stehk*	le bifteck/le steak
rib steak	*ã-trer-koht*	l'entrecôte (f)
sirloin steak	*foh-fee-leh*	le faux-filet
to steam	*kweer a la va-perr*	cuire à la vapeur
steamer	*koos-koos-ye*	le couscoussier
to steep	*ma-se-re/ ũ-fü-ze*	macérer (pickle)/ infuser (herb)
stew	*ra-goo; see-veh; blã-keht*	le ragoût; le civet (game); la blanquette (veal, chicken)
to stew	*kweer a le-too-fe/ ã ragoo*	cuire à l'étouffée/ en ragoût
still water	*oh plat*	l'eau plate (f)
stock	*fõ*	le fond
stout	*byehr brün*	la bière brune
straw (for drinking)	*pay*	la paille
strawberry	*frehz*	la fraise
streaky bacon	*lar/beh-kon mehgr*	le lard/bacon maigre
string bean	*a-ree-koh vehr*	le haricot vert
stuffing	*fars*	la farce
sturgeon	*eh-stür-zhõ*	l'esturgeon (m)
sugar	*sükr*	le sucre
summer	*e-te*	l'été (m)
sun-dried tomato	*to-mat se-she oh so-lehy*	la tomate séchée au soleil
supermarket	*sü-pehr-mar-she/ ee-pehr-mar-she*	le supermarché/ l'hypermarché (m)
swede	*rü-ta-ba-ga*	le rutabaga
sweet	*sükre*	sucré(e)
sweet (candy)	*bõ-bõ*	le bonbon
sweet basil	*ba-zee-leek*	le basilic
sweet potato	*patat doos*	la patate douce
sweet shop	*kõ-fee-zree*	la confiserie
sweetcorn	*ma-ees*	le maïs

T

table	*tabl*	la table
tablecloth	*nap*	la nappe
tangerine/mandarin	*mã-da-reen*	la mandarine
tap water	*oh dü ro-bee-neh*	l'eau du robinet (f)
tarragon	*ehs-tra-gõ*	l'estragon (m)
tartar sauce	*sohs tar-tar*	la sauce tartare
taste	*goo; sa-verr; par-fũ*	le goût; la saveur; le parfum (ice cream, yoghurt)

teaspoon	*per-teet kwee-yehr*	la petite cuillère
tea	*te*	le thé
camomile tea	*ka-mo-mee-y*	la camomille
decaffeinated tea	*te de-te-ee-ne*	-déthéiné
green tea	*te vehr*	-vert
herbal tea	*tee-zan/ũ-fü-zyõ*	la tisane/l'infusion (f)
mint tea	*te a la mãt*	-à la menthe
rosehip tea	*tee-zan oh see-no-ro-dõ*	la tisane au cynorhodon
tea with lemon	*te oh see-trõ*	-au citron
tea with milk	*te oh leh*	-au lait
tonic water	*shwehps*	le Schweppes
teller	*kes-ye/kes-yehr*	le caissier/la caissière
temperature	*tã-pe-ra-tür*	la température
tequila	*te-kee-la*	la tequila
thirsty [to be]	*[av-war] swaf*	[avoir] soif
thyme	*tũ*	le thym
tip	*poor-bwar/*	le pourboire
to tip	*do-ne ũ poor-bwar*	donner un pourboire
toast (tribute)	*tohst*	le toast
to toast	*por-te ũ tohst a*	porter un toast à
toast (bread)	*pũ gree-ye; tohst*	le pain grillé; le toast
to toast	*fehr gree-ye*	faire griller
toaster	*greey-pũ*	le grille-pain
tofu	*to-foo*	le tofu
toilet	*twa-leht/ ve-se*	les toilettes (f)/ les WC (m)
tomato	*to-mat*	la tomate
tongs (for salad)	*pũs (a sa-lad)*	la pince (à salade)
tongue	*lãg*	la langue
toothpick	*kür-dã*	le cure-dent(s)
topping	*na-pazh*	le nappage
topside	*zhit a la nwa*	le gîte à la noix (beef)
tripe	*treep*	la tripe
trout	*trweet*	la truite
truffle	*trüf*	la truffe
tuna	*tõ*	le thon
turbot	*tür-boh*	le turbot
turkey	*dũd; dũ-dõ; dũ-do-noh*	la dinde; le dindon; le dindonneau
turmeric	*kür-kü-ma/sa-frã de zũnd*	le curcuma/le safran des Indes
turnip	*na-veh*	le navet

V

vanilla	*va-neey*	la vanille
veal	*voh*	le veau
vegetable	*le-güm*	le légume

vegetable marrow	*koorzh*	la courge
vegetable oil	*weel ve-zhe-tal*	l'huile végétale (f)
vegetarian	*ve-zhe-ta-ryũ/ve-zhe-ta-ryehn*	végétarien/végétarienne
venison	*sher-vrer-y; zhee-bye; ver-neh-zõ*	le chevreuil; le gibier; la venaison
vinegar	*vee-nehgr*	le vinaigre
balsamic	*bal-za-meek*	-balsamique
cider	*der seedr*	-de cidre
malt	*der malt*	-de malt
rice	*der ree*	-de riz
wine	*der vũ*	-de vin
vodka	*vod-ka*	la vodka

W

waiter	*sehr-verr/sehr-verz*	le serveur/la serveuse
walnut	*nwa*	la noix
water	*oh*	l'eau (f)
mineral water	*oh mee-ne-ral/ oh der soors*	-minérale (f)/ -de source (f)
tap water	*oh dü ro-bee-neh*	-du robinet (f)
watercress	*kreh-sõ [der fõ-tehn]*	le cresson [de fontaine]
watermelon	*pa-stehk*	la pastèque
well-done (cooked)	*byũ kwee(t)*	bien cuit(e)
wheat	*ble/fro-mã*	le blé/le froment
wheat germ	*zhehrm der ble*	le germe de blé
whisk	*fweh/ ba-terr [e-lehk-treek]*	le fouet (manual)/ le batteur [electric]
to whisk	*fwete/batr*	fouetter/battre
whisky	*wees-kee*	le whisky
white cabbage	*shoo blã*	le chou blanc
white poppy seed	*grehn der pa-voh blã*	la graine de pavot blanc
white blood pudding	*boo-dũ blã*	le boudin blanc
white truffle	*trüf blãsh*	la truffe blanche
whitebait	*blã-shay/ per-teet free-tür*	la blanchaille (raw)/la petite friture (fried)
whiting	*mehr-lã*	le merlan
wholewheat	*kõ-pleh(t)*	complet/complète
wholewheat flour	*fa-reen kõ-pleht*	la farine complète
wild boar	*sã-glee-ye*	le sanglier
wild greens	*ehrb*	les herbes (f)
wild rabbit	*la-pũ der ga-ren*	le lapin de garenne
wild rice	*ree soh-vazh*	le riz sauvage
with/without ice	*a-vehk/sã glas/gla-sõ*	avec/sans glace/glaçons
wild greens	*sehrb*	les herbes (f)
wild rabbit	*lapũ*	le lapin de garenne
wild rice	*ree sohvazh*	le riz sauvage

wine	*vũ*	le vin
body	*kor*	le corps
bouquet	*bookeh*	le bouquet
colour	*rob*	la robe
corked wine	*vũ booshone*	vin bouchonné
dry	*sehk*	sec
full-bodied	*kee a dü kor; kor-se*	qui a du corps; corsé
grape	*rehzũ*	le raisin
harvest	*vãdãzh*	la vendange
light	*lezhe*	léger
new wine	*vũ noo-voh*	vin nouveau
oak barrel	*fü ã shehn*	le fût en chêne
red	*roozh*	rouge
sparkling	*mooser*	le mousseux
sweet	*dermee-sehk; doo*	demi-sec; doux
table wine	*vũ der tabl/ or-dee-nehr*	le vin de table/ ordinaire
very dry	*brüt*	brut
very sweet	*doo*	doux
vineyard	*veenyobl*	le vignoble
vintage	*re-kolt; mee-le-zeem*	la récolte (harvesting); le millésime (year)
white	*blã*	blanc
wine cellar	*kav a vũ*	la cave à vin
wine grower	*veenyerrõ/ veeteekülterr*	le vigneron/ le viticulteur
wine tasting	*degüstasyõ*	la dégustation
year	*ane*	l'année (f)
winter	*eevehr*	l'hiver (m)
with/without ice	*avehk/sã glas/sla-sõ*	avec/sans glace/glaçons
wooden spatula	*spa-tül ã bwa*	la spatule en bois

Y

year	*a-ne/ã*	l'année (f)/l'an (m)
yellow split pea	*pwa ka-se blã*	le pois cassé blanc
yoghurt	*ya-oort/yo-goort*	le yaourt/le yoghourt

Z

zucchini	*koor-zheht*	la courgette

French Culinary Dictionary

In French, nouns always have a feminine or masculine form. In this dictionary, the definite article has been included after the word, (**la**) for feminine and (**le**) for masculine, as well the plural article (**les**). When a word starts with a vowel and the gender is not obvious from the article, we have included the abbreviations (**m**) or (**f**) in the article explanation, eg, **ail** (**l', m**). Cross references are marked in bold, and regional information is in brackets after the definition eg, (Massif Central). Subgroups of a word are preceded by a dash eg, **–blanc** for **beurre blanc**.

A

abats (**les, m**) *a-ba* giblets
–de boucherie *der boosh-ree* offal
abattis (**l', m**) *a-ba-tee* giblets
Abbaye de Cîteaux (**l' m**) *abe-ee der seetoh* quite mild semi-hard cheese (Burgundy)
abricot (**l', m**) *ab-ree-koh* apricot
acra (**l', m**) *a-kra* small fried ball of spicy cod purée served as an appetiser, a speciality of Creole cooking
addition (**l', f**) *a-dees-syõ* bill/check (restaurant)
agneau (**l', m**) *a-nyoh* lamb
–de lait (**l', m**) *der leh* baby lamb, spring lamb
aiglefin (**l', m**) *ehg-ler-fũ* haddock
aigre-doux (**l', m**) *ehg-rer-doo* sweet & sour
aiguillette (**l', f**) *e-gwee-yeht* long & thin slice of meat, usually poultry breast, especially duck
ail (**l', m**) *ay* garlic
aile (**l', f**) *ehl* wing (bird or poultry)
aileron (**l', m**) *ehl-rõ* wing tip or pinion (poultry); fin (shark)
aïoli (**l', m**) *ay-o-lee* garlic flavoured mayonnaise sauce, served cold. Eggs & olive oil are emulsified, with garlic added. Often served with **bourride**. **Rouille** is one of its variations. (Provence)
airelle (**l', f**) *eh-rehl* bilberry or European blueberry similar to **myrtille**
–de marais *der ma-reh* cranberry (*see also* **canneberge**)
à la; à l'; au; aux *a la; a l'; oh; oh* served with; served in the manner of; served as in; in the style of
alcool (**l', m**) *al-kol* alcohol
aligot (**l', m**) *a-lee-goh* mashed potatoes, garlic & melted cheese, served hot as an **entrée** (Auvergne)
alose (**l', f**) *a-lohz* shad (fish)
alouette (**l', f**) *al-weht* lark
–sans tête (**l', f**) *sã teht* 'headless lark', thin piece of veal or beef rolled around a stuffing of minced meat, bacon or ham & braised
aloyau (**l', m**) *al-wa-yoh* sirloin
Alsace (**l', f**) *al-zass* situated on the River Rhine, the region produces mainly white wine & Pinot Noir red wine. It's the only region where wines are differentiated on the base of grape variety & not on geographical origin.
alsacienne, à l' *al-zas-yehn* 'Alsatian style', dish usually garnished with sauerkraut, pork, sausages or simmered with wine & mushrooms
amande (**l', f**) *a-mãd* almond
amande de mer (**l' f**) *a-mãd der mehr* queen or bay scallop
Amer Picon (**l', m**) *a-mehr pee-kõ* an **apéritif** with a wine & brandy base & quinine flavouring
amer/amère *a-mehr* bitter
américaine, à l' *a-me-ree-kehn* 'American style', generally a dish of fish or shellfish, particularly lobster, flamed in brandy & simmered in white wine & tomatoes

amuse-gueule (**l', m**) *a-müz-gerl* cocktail snack or appetiser; also **amuse-bouche**
ananas (**l', m**) *a-na-nas* pineapple
anchoïade (**l', f**) *ā-sho-yad* dip of puréed anchovies mixed with garlic & olive oil, served on hot bread or with raw vegetables (Provence)
anchois (**l', m**) *ā-shwa* anchovies
anchois marinés (**les, m**) *ā-shwa ma-ree-neh* marinated anchovies
ancienne, à l' (**f**) *ā-syehn* 'old style', there are many ways of preparing these dishes depending on the meat or fish served. Often served in a cream sauce with mushrooms, vegetables, onions or shallots, &/or with wine, & herbs. *(see also* **chocolat chaud à l'ancienne**)
andalouse à l' (**f**) *ā-da-looz* 'Andalusian style', usually a dish with green & red peppers, eggplant, tomatoes & garlic
andouille (**l', f**) *ā-dooy* smoked sausage made of pork tripe usually eaten cold
andouillette (**l', f**) *ā-doo-yeht* smaller version of **andouille** sausage, made of pork or sometimes of veal tripe
aneth (**l', m**) *a-neht* dill
angélique (**l', f**) *ā-zhe-leek* angelica; a herb usually candied, although an artificial substitute may be used
anglaise, à l' (**f**) *ā-glehz* 'English style', usually boiled meat or vegetables, especially potatoes; also breaded & fried vegetables, meat, fish or poultry
anguille (**l', f**) *ā-geey* eel
 –**au vert** (**l', f**) *oh vehr* dish of eel simmered in white wine, spinach, sorrel & herbs, served hot or cold with a lemon-flavoured white sauce
anis (**l', m**) *a-nees* anis, aniseed
anisette (**l', f**) *a-nee-zeht* anise-flavoured liqueur
Anjou (**l', m**) *ā-zhoo* region of the Loire producing mainly white wine
apéritif (**l', m**) *a-pe-ree-teef* alcoholic drink served before a meal to stimulate the appetite. Some have a wine or brandy base with herbs or bitters (**Amer Picon**, **Byrrh**), some a vegetable base, or some an aniseed base (**pastis**). Port, vermouth or liqueurs mixed with wine (eg **kir**) may also be served as an **apéritif**.
appellation d'origine contrôlée (**AOC**) (**l', f**) *a-peh-las-yō do-ree-zheen kō-troh-le* refers to officially recognised wines with a guarantee of origin. These wines are almost always good, at the very least, & may be superb.
araignée de mer (**l', f**) *a-ray-nye der mehr* spider crab
Armagnac (**l', m**) *ar-man-yak* wine-distilled brandy (Armagnac, Gascony)
armoricaine, à l' *ar-mo-ree-kehn* 'Armor (coastal Brittany) style', *(see* **américaine, à l'**)
artichaut (**l', m**) *ar-tee-shoh* artichoke
fond d'artichaut *fō d'ar-tee-shoh* artichoke heart
asperge (**l', f**) *as-pehrzh* asparagus
 –**d'Argenteuil** *dar-zhā-ter-y* green asparagus reputedly the best quality (Argenteuil, Île de France)
assiette (**l', f**) *as-yeht* plate
 –**anglaise** *ā-glehz* assorted cold meats with gherkins, served as an entrée or a light meal
 –**de charcuterie** *der shar-kü-tree* assorted pork & other meats products, including sausages, hams, **pâtés** & **rillettes**
 –**variée** *va-rye* assorted vegetables &/or meat or fish products
assorti(e) *a-sor-tee* assorted
aubergine (**l', f**) *oh-behr-zheen* eggplant/aubergine
avec *a-vhek* with
avec glace *a-vehk glas* with ice
avocat (**l', m**) *a-vo-ka* avocado

B

baba au rhum (le) *ba-ba oh rom* rum baba; small sponge cake, often with raisins, soaked in a rum-flavoured syrup after baking. Baba dough is also used to make the larger **savarin** cake.

bacon (le) *beh-kon/lar* bacon

–**fumé** *fü-me* smoked bacon

–**maigre** *mehgr* streaky bacon

baguette (la) *ba-geht* standard long & crispy loaf of bread; also chopstick

bain-marie (le) *bū-ma-ree* water bath consisting of a container of food immersed in a large, shallow pan of warm water placed in an oven or on top of a range. Food is cooked by gentle heat. The technique is designed to cook delicate dishes such as custards, sauces & savoury mousses without curdling or 'breaking' them. Also used to keep foods warm.

ballottine (la) *ba-lo-teen* boned meat, stuffed & poached

–**de volaille** *der vo-lay* poultry **ballottine** stuffed with forcemeat, served hot or cold in slices

banane (la) *ba-nan* banana

–**flambée** *flā-be* sliced banana, sautéed in syrup & usually flamed in rum

bar (le) *bar* bass

barbue (la) *bar-bü* brill or barbel, a carp-like fish

baron d'agneau (le) *ba-rō da-nyoh* spectacular roast; the two legs & the saddle of lamb roasted together

barquette (la) *bar-keht* small boat-shaped shell made of shortcrust pastry (sometimes puff pastry) with sweet or savoury fillings

–**aux marrons** *oh ma-rō* boat-shaped pastry shell filled with chestnut purée

basilic (le) *ba-zee-leek* basil

basquaise, à l' *bas-kehz* 'Basque style', usually prepared with tomatoes & sweet or red peppers; can also mean **cèpes**, potatoes & chopped Bayonne ham baked & served with roast meats

bassine à ragoût *ba-seen a ra-goo* large stew pot

bavarois (le) *ba-var-wa* Bavarian; a cold moulded dessert of cream &/or fruit purée set with gelatine or mousse

bavaroise (la) *ba-var-waz* syrupy tea that can be set into ice cream

bavette (la) *ba-veht* 'bib apron', flank steak

béarnaise (la) *be-ar-nehz* white sauce made of a wine or vinegar reduction beaten with egg yolks, & flavoured with tarragon, shallots & chervil, usually served hot with grilled beef or fish

Beaufort (le) *boh-for* hard, pressed & cooked cow's milk, without holes, but sometimes with thin horizontal cracks (Savoy)

Beaujolais (le) *boh-zho-leh* Burgundy's most southerly & extensive vineyards, producing mainly red wines

–**nouveau** *noo-voh* 'new **Beaujolais**' wine produced in the southern region

–**Villages** *vee-lazh* popular renowned **Beaujolais** from the north of the region

bécasse (la) *be-kas* woodcock, a game bird

Béchamel (la) *be-sha-mehl* milk-based sauce thickened with a **roux**

–**beignet** (le) *behn-yeh* vegetable, fish or even fruit fritter or doughnut. Commonly, a deep-fried dough dusted with sugar, often filled with jam or custard. Traditionally a speciality of carnival.

–**de pomme** *der pom* apple fritter

belon (la) *ber-lō* round pinkish oyster

Bénédictine (la) *be-ne-deek-teen* green liqueur (Normandy)

Bercy, à l' *behr-see* 'Bercy style', butter, white wine & shallot sauce

Bergamote (la) *behr-ga-mot* bergamot; citrus fruit

Berry (le) *be-ree* district of the Loire producing red, white & rosé wines

bette (la) *beht* Swiss chard
betterave (la) *beh-trav* beetroot
beurre (le) *berr* butter
–**d'ail** *day* garlic butter with shallots & chives
–**d'anchois** *dā-shwa* butter mixed with anchovies or anchovy paste
–**blanc** *blā* very popular emulsified white sauce made of a vinegar & white wine reduction blended with softened butter & shallots. This is a tricky sauce that can be stabilised by a touch of cream, & flavoured in many ways for fish, vegetable & poultry dishes.
–**de Charente** *der sha-rāt* the finest French butter (Poitou-Charentes)
–**de Deux-Sèvres** *der sehvr (see* **beurre de Charente**)
–**d'Échireé** *de-shee-re (see* **beurre de Charente**)
–**maître d'hôtel** *mehtr doh-tehl* butter flavoured with chopped parsley & lemon juice
–**noir** *nwar* 'black butter', butter browned until nearly burned, sometimes flavoured with capers & parsley
–**ravigote** *ra-vee-got* butter with herbs
bien cuit(e) *byū kwee* well-done
bière (la) *byehr* beer
–**blonde** *blōd* light-coloured or pale beer, lager
–**en bouteille** *ā boo-teh-y* bottled beer
–**brune** *brün* dark beer or stout
–**lager** *la-gerr* lager beer
–**de gingembre** *der zhūzhābr* ginger beer
–**pression** *preh-syō* draught/draft beer; beer on tap
bifteck (le) *beef-tehk* beefsteak
–**à la tartare** *a la tar-tar (see* **steak tartare**)
bigorneau (le) *bee-gor-noh* periwinkle, winkle
biologique/bio *byo-loh-zheek/byoh* organic
biscotte (la) *bees-kot* hard, dry biscuit; rusk; zwieback
biscuit (le) *bees-kwee* biscuit, cookie
bisque (la) *beesk* spicy shellfish soup or chowder, enriched with cream & **Cognac**
–**d'écrevisses** *de-krer-vees* spiced freshwater crayfish soup
–**de homard** *der o-mar* spiced lobster soup
blanc de blanc *blā der blā* white wine made of white grapes with white juice
blanc de volaille (le) *blā der vo-lay* boned breast of fowl, cooked without browning
blanchaille (la) *blā-shay* whitebait
blanquette de veau (la) *blā-keht der voh* veal stew in white sauce enriched with cream, vegetables & often mushrooms
Blaye *blehy* a region of Bordeaux producing mainly red & white wine
blé (le) *ble* wheat
–**noir** *nwar* buckwheat
blette (la) *bleht* Swiss chard
bleu (le) *bler* blue-veined cheese, often used to flavour dishes or sauces. They are long in maturing with a strong flavour & are at their best in summer & autumn. (Languedoc, Auvergne, Savoy & Jura)
–**d'Auvergne** *doh-vehrn-y* blue-veined cheese from Auvergne, an imitation **Roquefort** made with cow's milk. It appears firm, creamy, nicely blue & has a piquant flavour. The penicillium (blue mould) that gives the cheese its marbled character is implanted with long needles.
–**des Causses** *de kohs* creamy blue cheese from cow's milk inspired by **Roquefort** cheese & matured in ventilated caves just like its model (Massif Central)
–**du Haut-Jura** *dü oh-zhü-ra* blue-veined cheese (Jura)
–**de Laqueuille** *der la-ker-y* blue-veined cheese (Auvergne)
–**de Théziac** *der te-zyak* blue-veined cheese (Auvergne)

–**Termignon** *tehr-meen-yõ* excellent blue made in very limited quantities in the Alps
bleu (le) *bler* nearly raw beef; fish (usually trout) boiled in vinegar bouillon
bluet (le) *blü-eh* blueberry (Vosges)
bœuf (le) *berf* beef
–**bourguignon** *boor-geen-yõ* chunks of beef marinated in red wine, spices & herbs, stewed with mushrooms, onions, & bacon; also (& more properly) called **bœuf à la bourguignonne** (Burgundy)
–**en daube** *ã dohb* chunks of beef & chopped ham flamed in **Armagnac** brandy & stewed with red wine, onions, garlic, vegetables & herbs in a special hermetically sealed saucepan
–**miroton** *mee-ro-tõ* pre-cooked boiled beef slices, usually left over from **pot-au-feu**, gently stewed with onions
–**à la mode** *a la mod* larded chunks of beef, braised (& often marinated) in wine, either served hot with carrots & onions, or cold in aspic
–**salé** *sa-le* corned beef
boisson (la) *bwa-sõ* drink, beverage
–**non alcoolisée** *non al-kol-ee-ze* soft drink
bolet (le) *boleh* boletus mushroom, a family of wild mushroom with more than 60 different varieties (**cèpe** is the most renowned of these), known for their rich taste & meaty texture
bombe glacée (la) *bõb gla-se* ice cream dessert. Two different ice creams moulded together in a cone shape, decorated with candied fruits, candied (glazed) chestnuts & **Chantilly** cream.
bonbon (le) *bõ-bõ* sweet, candy
Bordeaux (le) *bor-doh* the part of France producing the most **AOC** wines is divided into several regions including Blaye, Bourg, Entre-deux-Mers, Fronsac, Graves, Médoc, Pomerol, Saint Émilion & Sauternes. **Bordeaux** red wine is often called claret in Britain.
bordelaise (la) *bor-der-lehz* red wine sauce with shallots, beef juices, thyme, & sometimes boletus mushrooms, usually served with rib steak
bouchée (la) *boo-she* various types of cocktail snacks or small puffs with a variety of fillings, served hot or cold.
–**au chocolat** *sho-ko-la* chocolate **bouchée**
–**à la reine** *a la rehn* round puff filled with poultry, sweetbread or veal dumplings & mushrooms, in white cream sauce
boucherie (la) *boosh-ree* butcher's shop
–**chevaline** *sher-va-leen* horsemeat butcher's shop
boudin (le) *boo-dũ* smooth sausage, may be grilled or pan-fried.
–**blanc** *blã* white veal, pork or chicken sausage
–**noir** *nwar* black pork blood sausage (*see also* **sanguette**)
–**aux pommes** *pom* black pudding served with apples
bouillabaisse (la) *boo-ya-behs* soup traditionally made of assorted fish stewed in a broth with garlic, orange peel, fennel, tomatoes & saffron. Modern versions include lobster & shrimps. The broth & the fish may be served separately, with croutons & **rouille**. (Marseilles)
bouilli(e) *boo-yee* boiled
bouillon (le) *boo-yõ* bouillon, broth, stock
boulangerie (la) *boo-lãzh-ree* bakery
Boule de Lille (la) *bool der leel* Edam-like bright orange hard cheese that can be aged up to 36 months
boulette (la) *boo-leht* small meatball or **croquette** (often leftovers) sautéed, browned, or poached in a broth
boulghour (le) *bool-goor* bulghur wheat
boulot (le) *boo-loh* whelk
bouquet garni (le) *boo-keh gar-nee* mix of herbs tied together, basically parsley, bay leaf & thyme. Variations may include peppercorns, rosemary, sage, celery leaves, marjoram, fennel or leek.

Bourge (le) *boorzh* region of Bordeaux, producing red & white table wine
Bourgogne (le) *boor-gon-y* Burgundy; divided into five main regions: **Beaujolais, Chablis, Côte d'Or, Côte Chalonnaise**, & **Mâconnais.** It produces the largest number of officially recognised wines of France's wine-growing districts.
bourguignonne, à la *boor-geen-yon* 'Burgundy style', dishes may include button mushrooms, bacon, & pearl onions or shallots, braised in red wine
bourride (la) *boo-reed* fish soup or stew using firm whitefish like monkfish. The broth thickened with **aïoli** & the fish are served together or separately with bread or croutons. (Provence)
Boursin (le) *boor-sũ* soft commercially made cheese spread flavoured with garlic & herbs
bouteille (la) *boo-teh-y* bottle
braisé(e) *breh-ze* braised
brandade de morue (la) *brã-dad der mo-*rü salt cod soaked & then puréed mixed with milk, olive oil, garlic & sometimes mashed potatoes. Can be served with croutons, covered with **Gruyère** cheese & browned in the oven, or in small pastry shells as an entrée. (Provence)
brebis (la) *brer-bee* ewe (female sheep)
Brebis des Pyrénées (la) *brer-bee de pee-re-ne* cheese made with ewe's milk (Basque Country)
brème (la) *brehm* bream
Bresse bleu (le) *brehs bler* rich, soft blue-veined cheese (Franche-Comté)
Brie (le) *bree* white, runny, soft cheese with honeycomb texture
–**de Coulommiers** *der koo-lom-ye* **Brie** cheese variety (Île de France)
–**de Meaux** *der moh* **Brie** cheese variety with a bloomy rind (Île de France)
–**de Melun** *der mer-lũ* **Brie** cheese variety (Île de France)
brioche (la) *bree-yosh* small roll or cake made of yeast, flour, eggs & butter, sometimes flavoured with nuts, currants or candied fruits, baked in many shapes & usually served at breakfast
broche (la) *brosh* spit roast
brochet (le) *bro-sheh* pike
brochette (la) *bro-sheht* kebab; grilled skewer of meat, fish or vegetables
brocoli (le) *bro-ko-lee* broccoli
brouillé(e) *broo-ye* scrambled (eggs)
brûlant *brü-lã* boiling
brûlot (le) *brü-loh* sugar flamed in brandy & added to coffee
brunoise (la) *brün-waz* finely diced vegetables simmered until tender in butter & stock, used to flavour soups, stuffing, sauces, fish or seafood dishes
brut (le) *brüt* extra dry (Champagne)
bruyant(e) *brwee-yã(t)* noisy
buccin (le) *bü-ksũ* whelk
bûche de Noël (la) *büsh der no-ehl* traditionally served for Christmas, a rolled sponge cake filled & covered with butter cream (usually chocolate, vanilla or coffee flavoured) or ice cream, decorated with meringue mushrooms & marzipan holly leaves
budget (le) *bü-dzheh* budget
buffet (le) *bü-feh* array of hot & cold foods. Generally includes **canapés, petits fours**, small puffs & tarts, cold fish & meats, sauces, salads & fruit.
bugne (la) *bü-ny* doughnut traditionally prepared for Shrove Tuesday. At their best hot & covered with sugar. (Lyon)
bulot (le) *bü-loh* whelk
Byrrh (la) *beer* a wine-based **apéritif** with quinine, fortified with brandy

C

Cabécou de Rocamadour *kab-e-koo der ro-ka-ma-door* goat's milk cheese (Midi-Pyrenées)
cabillaud (le) *ka-bee-yoh* cod
cacahuète (la) *ka-ka-weht* peanut
cacao (le) *ka-ka-oh* cocoa

café (**le**) *ka-fe* coffee
- **–allongé** *alõ-zhe* coffee 'lengthened' with extra water
- **–américain; à l'americaine** *a-me-ree-kũ; a la-me-ree-kehn* same as **café allongé**
- **–décaféiné** *de-ka-fay-ee-ne* decaffeinated coffee
- **–crème** *krehm* espresso coffee with steamed milk or (rarely) cream
- **–express** *ehks-prehs* espresso coffee
- **–filtre** *feeltr* filtered coffee
- **–frappé** *fra-pe* coffee ice cream mixed with whipped cream, sprinkled with cold coffee & **Cointreau** liqueur; also coffee syrup poured over crushed ice
- **–glacé** *gla-se* iced coffee*;* a coffee-flavoured ice cream dessert sprinkled with cold coffee & **Cointreau** liqueur
- **–en grains** *ã grũ* coffee beans
- **–instantané** *u\stã-ta-ne* instant coffee
- **–au lait** *oh leh* coffee with hot milk
- **–liégeois** *lyezh-wa* coffee with ice cream & topped with whipped cream
- **–long** *lõ* same as **café allongé**
- **–lyophilisé** *leeo-fee-lee-ze* freeze-dried instant coffee
- **–noir/nature** *nwar/na-tür* black coffee
- **–noisette** *nwa-zeht* 'hazelnut coffee', coffee with a dash of milk
- **–soluble** *sol-übl* instant coffee

caille (**la**) *kay* quail

caillette (**la**) *kay-eht* rissole or meatball

calmar (**le**) *kal-mar* squid

Calvados (**le**) *kal-va-dohs* apple brandy (Normandy)

camembert (**le**) *ka-mã-behr* pasteurised cow's milk cheese, soft & runny, with bloomy rind & pungent flavour. Probably the best known of French cheeses, originally produced in Normandy. Now they may be made anywhere or from any kind of milk, but the best varieties come from the Pays d'Auge.

canapé (**le**) *ka-na-pe* small, elaborately garnished open-faced sandwich, served cold or hot, as a snack or for lunch

canard (**le**) *ka-nar* duck
- **–nantais** *nã-teh* the most common breed of table duck
- **–à l'orange** *a lor-ãzh* duck braised with **Cognac** & **Cointreau**, served with oranges & an orange-based sauce
- **–à la rouennaise** *a la roo-eh-nez* stuffed duck in a red wine sauce
- **–sauvage** *soh-vazh* wild duck

caneton/canette (**le/la**) *kan-tõ/ka-neht* duckling

canistrelli (**le**) *ka-nee-stre-lee* sugar-crusted biscuits, often flavoured with lemon, almonds or even white wine (Corsica)

canistrone (**la**) *ka-nee-strohn* cheese tarts (Corsica)

canneberge (**la**) *kan-behrzh* cranberry; *(see also* **airelle de marais**)

cannelé (**le**) *ka-ner-le* brioche-like pastry made with corn flour, often spelled **canallé** (Bordeaux)

cannelle (**la**) *ka-nehl* cinnamon

Cantal (**le**) *kã-tal* smooth pressed & uncooked cheese at its best when well-aged & dry (Auvergne)

câpre (**le**) *kapr* caper

carafe (**la**) *ka-raf* carafe, decanter

carbonnade (**la**) *kar-bo-nad* selection of char-grilled meats (often pork). Sometimes refers to **bœuf en daube**.
- **–de bœuf** *der berf* stew of beef slices, onions & herbs, simmered in beer (Northern France)

cardon (**le**) *kar-dõ* artichoke-like vegetable

carotte (**la**) *ka-rot* carrot

carpe (**la**) *karp* carp
- **–à la juive** *a la zhweev* 'Jewish-style' carp, poached & served in aspic (Strasbourg)

carré (**le**) *ka-re* loin or rib
- **–d'agneau** *da-nyoh* rack of lamb
- **–de porc** (**au chou**) *der por (oh shoo)* loin of pork (with cabbage)
- **–de l'Est** *der l'ehst* square-shaped cheese made from cow's milk, mild flavoured (Vosges)

carrelet (le) *kar-leh* plaice
carte (la) *kart (la)* menu
à la- *a la* dishes chosen from the menu with a separate price applied to each of them *(see* **menu**)
–des vins *de vũ* wine list
carvi (le) *kar-vee* caraway seed
cassate (la) *ka-sat* ice cream combining different flavours, often studded with candied fruits
casse-croûte (le) *kas-kroot* snack
casserole (la) *kas-rol* saucepan
cassis (le) *ka-sees* blackcurrant (liqueur)
cassolette (la) *kas-o-leht* casserole dish; a small earthenware dish. Also dishes cooked in this container.
cassonade (la) *kas-o-nad* soft brown sugar
cassoulet (le) *kas-oo-leh* casserole or stew with beans & meat (South-West France)
–de Casteinaudary *der kas-te-noh-da-ree* pork **cassoulet** (in all its guises)
–de Carcassonne *der kar-ka-son* **cassoulet** made with mutton
–toulousain *too-loo-zũ* **cassoulet** made with meats such as goose or duck **confit**, mutton, pork, & **saucisse de Toulouse**, with duck fat & baked until the top is brown & crispy
céleri (le) *sehl-ree* celery
–rave *-rav* celeriac, celery root
cendre (sous la) *sãdr* baked in the embers
cépage (le) *seh-pazh* grape or vine variety
cèpe (le) *sehp* wild mushroom of the boletus family known for it's full flavour & meaty texture
céréale (la) *se-re-al* cereal or grain
cerf (le) *sehr* venison, hart, stag deer
cerfeuil (le) *sehr-fer-y* chervil
cerises (les, f) *ser-reez* cherries
–au kirsh *oh keersh* cherries marinated in cherry brandy
–noires *nwar* black cherries
cervelas (le) *sehr-ver-la* fat pork sausage cured with garlic & eaten hot
cervelle (la) *sehr-vehl* brains
Chablis (le) *shab-lee* region of Burgundy renowned for its white wine
chair (la) *shehr* flesh, meat
–à farce *a fars* forcemeat
–à pâté *a pa-te* meat for **paté**
–à saucisse *a soh-sees* sausage meat
chambrer *shã-bre* to bring wine gently to room temperature
Champagne (le) *shã-pany* generally the renowned sparkling white wine from this region, although ordinary red, white & rosé wines are also produced. It's sold according to the amount of sugar added, & can be **brut** (extra dry), **extra-sec** (very dry), **sec** (dry), **demi-sec** (slightly sweet), or **doux** (sweet).
champignon (le) *shã-peen-yõ* mushroom
–de Paris *der pa-ree* button mushroom
chanterelle (la) *shã-trehl* boletus mushroom; same as **girolle**
Chantilly (la) *shã-tee-yee* sweetened whipped cream flavoured with vanilla; also sweet or savoury sauces that have had whipped cream folded into them
chapelure (la) *sha-plür* breadcrumbs
chapon (le) *sha-põ* capon, castrated cock
charbonnade (la) *shar-bo-nad* charcoal-grilled meat
charcuterie (la) *shar-kü-tree* variety of pork products that are cured, smoked or processed, including sausages, hams, **pâtés** & **rillettes**; also the shop where these products are sold
charlotte (la) *shar-lot* dessert of bread slices or sponge fingers, lining a deep, round mould, then filled with fruits, whipped cream or a fruit mousse, & baked, or stiffened in fridge. Sometimes also savoury dishes of vegetables or fish cooked in a bain-marie.
Chartreuse (la) *shar-trerz* liqueur of herbs & spices served as a digestive or used to flavoured pastries. Green **chartreuse** is stronger than the yellow.
chasselas (le) *sha-sla* type of white table grape

chasseur (le) *sha-serr* 'hunter', sauce of white wine with mushrooms, shallots & bacon cubes
châtaigne (la) *sha-tehn-y* chestnut
château (le) *sha-toh* castle, vineyard
chateaubriand (le) *sha-toh-bree-yã* thick fillet or rump steak
chaud(e) *shoh(d)* hot, warm
chaud-froid (le) *shoh-frwa* 'hot-cold', a piece of poached or roasted meat, poultry, fish or game that, while cooling, is coated with a white creamy sauce that solidifies. The dish is decorated with tarragon, truffle or tomatoes & served cold, sometimes glazed with aspic.
chaudrée (la) *shoh-dre* Atlantic fish stew
chef de cuisine (le) *shehf der kwee-zeen* chef
cheval (le) *sher-val* horse/horsemeat
cheval, à *sher-val* 'mounted', steak served topped with a fried egg
chèvre (la) *shehvr* goat; the term generally refers to goat's milk cheese. These are various types of soft cheese with bloomy or natural rind. Their texture can be tender, hard, semi-hard or brittle, depending on maturing. Usually at their best in summer.
chevreuil (le) *sherv-rer-y* venison; roe deer
chicorée (la) *shee-ko-re* chicory, endive
chiffonnade (la) *shee-fo-nad* very fine julienne of green vegetables or leafy herbs used as a garnish
chipolata (la) *shee-po-la-ta* chipolata, a small sausage
chocolat *sho-ko-la* chocolate
  –chaud *sho* hot chocolate drink
  –chaud à l'ancienne *sho a lã-syehn* hot chocolate drink
chou (le) *shoo* cabbage
  –de Bruxelles *der brü-sehl* Brussels sprout
  –farci *far-see* stuffed cabbage
  –rouge *roozh* red cabbage
chou-fleur *shoo-flerr* cauliflower
choucroute (la) *shoo-kroot* sauerkraut; also refers to **choucroute garnie**
  –garnie *gar-nee* sauerkraut with assorted fresh & smoked meats & sausages or fish, simmered in white wine seasoned with garlic & juniper berries, & served on a huge platter; also called **choucroute alsacienne** (Alsace)
choux (le) *shoo* dessert made with **pâte à choux** pastry, eaten cold, plain, with sugar, or stuffed.
  –à la crème *a la krehm* cream puff
ciboule (la) *see-bool* spring onion; shallot
ciboulette (la) *see-boo-leht* chives
cidre (le) *seedr* cider
cigale de mer (la) *see-gal der mehr* 'sea cricket', a flat spiny lobster
citron (le) *see-trõ* lemon
citron pressé (le) *see-trõ preh-se* freshly squeezed lemon juice
citronnade (la) *see-tro-nad* lemon squash; lemonade
citronnelle (la) *see-tro-nehl* citronella/lemon grass
citrouille (la) *see-trooy* pumpkin
civelle (la) *see-vehl* small eel or alevin, generally served fried
civet (le) *see-veh* stew usually containing game marinated in red wine then stewed with onions, garlic, cloves, herbs, pepper & bacon. Traditionally thickened with the animal's blood. Fish can also be prepared as a **civet**.
  –de lapin/lièvre *der la-pũ/lyehvr* jugged rabbit/hare
Clacbitou (le) *clak-bee-too* oblong-shaped goat's cheese (Charolais)
clafoutis (le) *kla-foo-tee* dessert, not unlike a tart fruit covered with a thick custardy batter & baked until puffy, served hot or cold
  –aux cerises *oh ser-reez* black cherries baked in a thick batter, sometimes with cherry brandy added
claires (le) *klehr* marsh enclosures used in oyster farming
clam (le) *klam* clam

clémentine (la) *kle-mã-teen* type of tangerine
clos (le) *kloh* small vineyard; generally indicating a wine of exceptional quality
cochon (le) *ko-shõ* pig
–**de lait** *der leh* suckling pig
cochonnaille (la) *koh-sho-nay* product made from pork
cocktail (le) *kok-tehl* cold starter of shellfish & raw vegetables or fruits
coco (le) *ko-ko* type of haricot bean
cocotte (la) *ko-kot* heavy pot made in a material that stores heat well (cast iron or earthenware), used for simmering
cœur (le) *kerr* heart
–**d'artichaut** *dar-tee-shoh* artichoke heart
–**de filet** *der fee-leh* tenderloin steak
–**de palmier** *der palm-ye* heart of palm
Cognac (le) *kon-yak* the most renowned French grape-based distilled brandy (Charente)
coing (le) *kwũ* quince
Cointreau (le) *kwũ-troh* orange liqueur
colin (le) *ko-lũ* hake
colinot (le) *ko-lee-noh* small hake
colombo *ko-lõ-bo* spice mixture similar to curry powder, containing coriander, garlic, chilli, saffron, cinnamon & nutmeg, originally from the West Indies; also a stew of chicken, pork, crab or fish, seasoned with this powder; also called **columbo**
commande (la) *ko-mãd* order
–**sur** *sür* special order
commander *ko-mã-de* to order
compote (la) *kõ-pot* stewed fruit; dried or fresh fruits briefly stewed with sugar. Can be flavoured with vanilla, cinnamon, or citrus zest.
–**de pommes** *der pom* stewed apples
compris *kõ-pree* included
Comté (le) *kõ-te* yellowish, pressed & cooked cow's milk cheese with a tough, natural & brushed rind, golden yellow or brownish in colour (Franche-Comté)
concombre (le) *kõ-kõbr* cucumber
confiserie (la) *kõ-fee-zree* confectionery (sweets in general); also sweet shop or candy store
confit (le) *kõ-fee* a process to preserve meat, usually duck, goose or pork, for long periods of time. The meat is first salted to remove moisture, then cooked at the lowest of simmers & submerged in fat until it is tender, then stored in crocks & covered with the fat to prevent exposure to air.
–**de canard** *der ka-nar* duck **confit**
–**de fruits** *der frwee* glazed or candied fruit
–**d'oie** *dwa* goose **confit**
confiture (la) *kõ-fee-tür* jam
–**d'oranges** *do-rãzh* marmalade
congolais (le) *kõ-go-leh* a small coconut meringue cake
congre (le) *kõ-gr* conger eel
consommation (la) *kõ-so-ma-syõ* consumption; the general term for food & drink ordered in a café
consommé (le) *kõ-so-me* clarified meat, poultry or fish-based broth used as a base for sauces & soups; also the clear soup made with this broth, served hot or cold, sometimes garnished with chopped meat, vermicelli or eggs
–**célestin** *se-leh-stũ* chicken **consommé** with thin noodles
–**cheveux d'ange** *sher-ver dãzh* **consommé** with vermicelli noodles
–**en gelée** *ã zher-le* jellied **consommé**
–**julienne** *zhü-lyehn* **consommé** with shredded or thinly sliced vegetables
–**madrilène** *ma-dree-lehn* tomatoes & sweet peppers **consommé**
–**princesse** *prũ-sehs* **consommé** with diced chicken & asparagus tips
–**à la printanière** *a la prũ-tan-yehr* **consommé** with spring vegetables
–**de volaille** *der vo-lay* poultry **consommé**
contre-filet (le) *kõtr-fee-leh* beef sirloin roast

coq (le) *kok* cockerel/rooster
–**au vin** (le) *oh vũ* chicken stewed in wine with mushrooms & bacon. May be flamed with brandy.
–**de bruyère** *der brwee-yehr* grouse
coque (la) *kok* cockle
coquelet (le) *ko-kleh* young cockerel
coquillage (le) *ko-kee-yazh* shellfish
coquille Saint-Jacques *(la) ko-keey sũ-zhak* scallop, often served cooked, with **américaine** or **beurre blanc** sauce, or **gratinéed** in the shell
corbeille de fruits (la) *kor-behy der frwee* basket of assorted fruits
coriandre (la) *kor-yãdr* coriander
corne d'abondance (la) *korn da-bõ-dãs* 'horn of plenty' *(see* **trompette de la mort**)
cornichon (le) *kor-nee-shõ* gherkin
Corse (la) *kors* Corsica; Mediterranean island producing fine wine characterised by a rich, full-bodied taste
côte (la) *koht* chop containing eye fillet
–**d'agneau** *da-nyoh* lamb chop
–**de veau** *der voh* veal chop
Côte d'Or (la) *koht dor* region of Burgundy that comprises **Côte de Beaune** & **Côte de Nuits**, noted for its red & white wine
Côte de Beaune (la) *koht der bohn* the southern half of Burgundy's **Côte d'Or** producing mainly red wines
Côte de Nuits (la) *koht der nwee* region of Burgundy noted for its red wine
côtelette (la) *koht-leht* cutlet, chop
–**d'agneau** *da-nyoh* lamb cutlet
–**de veau** *der voh* veal cutlet
Côtes du Rhône (**les, f**) *koht dü rohn* this region extends from Vienne to Avignon along the banks of River Rhone, between the Burgundy & Provence wine districts. The region offers a great diversity of white, red & rosé wine of varying character.
coulis (le) *koo-lee* fruit or vegetable purée, usually used as a sauce, or sometimes as a flavouring agent in other sauces, soups or desserts
Coulommiers (le) *koo-lom-ye* soft, creamy cheese of the **brie** family (Île de France)
coupe (**la**) *koop* metal or glass dish usually for individual desserts; or the dessert served in such a dish
–**glacée** *gla-se* cold dessert with ice cream or flavoured-cream base, decorated with fruits, nuts, chocolate cream or **Chantilly** cream
–**aux marrons** *oh ma-rõ* **coupe** with sweet chestnut purée
courge (la) *koorzh* gourd or marrow
courgette (la) *koor-zheht* zucchini; courgette; baby marrow
court-bouillon (le) *koor-boo-yõ* well-seasoned cooking liquid or broth, used to poach fish or shellfish. Mainly wine or sometimes vinegar, water, herbs, & onions *(see also* **truite au bleu**)
couscous (le) *koos-koos* semolina (coarsely-ground wheat flour); also a North African dish of steamed semolina garnished with chunks of meat (usually chicken, lamb & mutton), sausages, various vegetables, chickpeas & raisins, & may be served with **harissa**, a spicy red chilli sauce
coûter *koo-te* to cost
couvert (le) *koo-vehr* number of people in a group at a restaurant; cover charge
–**gratuit** *grat-wee* no cover charge
–**vin et service compris** *vũ e sehr-vees kõ-pree* price includes wine, service & cover charges
crabe (le) *krab* crab
crème (la) *krehm* cream; also a dessert with cream; also a cream-based soup
–**anglaise** *ã-glehz* custard used as a cold sauce for desserts, or as a base for mousses or ice creams
–**brûlée** *brü-le* chilled caramelised custard cups, sprinkled with sugar
–**caramel** *ka-ra-mehl* baked custard flavoured with caramel
–**Chantilly** *shã-tee-yee* whipped & sweetened cream

–**crue** *krü* raw or unpasteurised cream
–**fouettée** *fwe-te* whipped cream
–**fraîche** *frehsh* naturally thickened cream, has a slightly sour tang
–**glacée** *gla-se* ice cream
–**de marrons** *der ma-rõ* sweetened chestnut purée used as a filling for desserts or served with **Chantilly** cream
–**pâtissière** *pa-tees-yehr* thick creamy pastry filling made of milk, eggs & flour served as a dessert or used to fill or cover cakes.

crème (la) *krehm* creamy soup mixed & thickened with cream or egg yolk
–**d'asperge** *das-pehrzh* cream of asparagus soup
–**de cresson** *der kreh-sõ* cream of watercress soup
–**de laitue** *der leh-tü* cream of lettuce soup, well seasoned
–**de légumes** *der le-güm* cream of vegetable soup
–**de volaille** *der vo-lay* cream of chicken soup

crème (la) *krehm* sweetened liqueur
–**de cacao** *der ka-ka-oh* chocolate-flavoured liqueur
–**de cassis** *der ka-sees* blackcurrant liqueur
–**de menthe** *der mãt* mint-flavoured liqueur

crêpe (la) *krehp* large, paper-thin pancake served with various fillings. Served with sugar, jam, fruits, or flamed as a dessert, or filled with meat, ham, smoked salmon, fish or cheese as an entrée or main course *(see* **galette**)
–**flambée** *flã-be* pancake flamed with brandy or other liqueur
–**Suzette** *sü-zeht* pancake with tangerine or orange sauce & brandy

crépine (la) *kre-peen* caul fat

crépinette (la) *kre-pee-neht* small sausage patty of ground pork, veal or poultry, seasoned with parsley, wrapped in caul fat, & served fried or grilled (sometimes flavoured with truffles)

cresson (le) *kreh-sõ* watercress

creuse (la) *krerz* type of oyster with a crinkly, tough shell

crevette grise (la) *krer-veht greez* tiny shrimp

crevette rose (la) *krer-veht rohz* small shrimp

croissant (le) *krwa-sã* flaky crescent-shaped roll, usually served for breakfast

croquant (le) *kro-kã* butter cookie or biscuit
–**de Bordeaux** *bor-doh* a crispy flat confection

croque-madame (le) *krok-ma-dam* grilled or pan-fried ham & cheese sandwich, topped with a fried egg

croquembouche (le) *kro-kã-boosh* grand dessert of cream puffs dipped in caramel & assembled into a large pyramid shape. The whole dessert is brushed with more caramel & elaborately decorated. A traditional dessert for weddings, birthdays etc.

croque-monsieur (le) *krok-mers-yer* grilled or pan-fried ham & cheese sandwich, sometimes covered with a mornay or **Béchamel** sauce, or dipped in egg & deep-fried

croquette (la) *kro-keht* thick patty or ball minced meat, fish, vegetable, rice or pastry breaded & deep fried or sautéed

crosne (le) *krohn* Chinese artichoke; small white root vegetable imported from Japan in the 19th century that tastes similar to Jerusalem artichoke

Crottin de Chavignol (le) *kro-tũ der sha-vee-nyol* goat's milk cheese shaped like a flattened ball (central France)

croustade (la) *kroo-stad* puff pastry shell filled with stewed fish, seafood, meat, poultry, mushrooms or vegetables

croûte (la) *kroot* crust; also a puff pastry case filled with various savoury foods; also the puff pastry that wraps some meat or fish when cooked **en croûte**

croûte, en *ã kroot* 'in crust'; food cooked enclosed in pastry

croûton (le) *kroo-tõ* a small piece of bread toasted or fried until crisp, used to garnish salads or soups
cru (le) *krü* growth; referring to a particular vineyard & its wine; also a system of grading wine, including **premier cru, grand cru** & **cru classé**
cru classé (le) *krü kla-se* vintage that has been given a basic classification
cru(e) *krü* raw
crudités (les, f) *krü-dee-te* selection of raw vegetables served sliced, grated or diced with dressing as an entrée
crustacé (le) *krü-sta-se* shellfish
cuillère (la) *kwee-yehr* spoon
cuire *kweer* to cook
cuisine (la) *kwee-zeen* cooking/kitchen
 –bourgeoise *boor-zhwaz* French home cooking of the highest quality
 –campagnarde *kã-pahn-yard* country or provincial cooking, using the finest ingredients & most refined techniques to prepare traditional rural dishes
 –minceur *mũ-serr (see* **nouvelle cuisine**)
 –des provinces *de pro-vũs* provincial cuisine; same as **cuisine du terroir**
 –du terroir *dü tehr-war (see* **cuisine campagnarde**)
cuisiner *kwee-zee-ne* to cook
cuisinier/cuisinière (le/la) *kwee-zee-nye/kwee-zee-nyehr* a cook
cuisse (la) *kwees* thigh, leg
 –de grenouilles *der grer-noo-y* frog's leg
cuit(e) *kwee(t)* cooked
 –au four *oh foor* baked
cul de veau *kü der voh* veal fillet or rump steak
cumin (le) *kü-mũ* cumin, caraway
Curaçao (le) *kü-ra-soh* liqueur made from orange peel, sugar & brandy
cure-dent (le) *kür-dã* toothpick
cuvée (la) *kü-ve* blend of wine from various vineyards in the making of Champagne; also refers to the vintage

D

darne (la) *darn* slice of a large raw fish, such as hake, salmon or tuna
datte (la) *dat* date
daube (la) *dohb* beef, poultry or game stewed in a rich wine-laden broth
daurade (la) *do-rad* sea bream
déjeuner (le) *de-zher-ne* lunch
délice (le) *de-lees* delicious, a delicacy; also often used to describe a dessert speciality of the chef
 –aux amandes *oh za-mãd* almonds delight dessert
demi *der-mee* half
 –glace (f) *glas* rich brown stock & **roux** sauce
 –sel (le) *-sehl* soft cream cheese – slightly salty
 –sec *-sehk* slightly sweet, of wine
demi (le) *der-mee* beer glass size, about 0.33L
dessert (le) *de-sehr* dessert
diablotin (le) *dya-blo-tũ* small hot appetiser, usually a sharp cheese purée, often with ground walnuts & a sauce; also a fruit fritter
dieppoise, à la *dye-pwaz* 'Dieppe style', soup generally consisting of fish, shrimp, mussels mushrooms, vegetables, herbs, & cream, cooked in cider; also fish (usually sole) poached in broth (Normandy)
digestif (le) *dee-zheh-steef* digestive; a drink served after a meal
dijonnaise, à la *dee-zho-nehz* 'Dijon style', dishes containing mustard or served with a mustard-based sauce (Burgundy)
dinde (la, f)/**dindon** (le, m) *dũd/dũ-dõ* turkey
 –aux marrons *oh ma-rõ* turkey stuffed with chestnuts, & sometimes bacon, chopped pork & an apple
dindonneau (le) *dũ-do-noh* young turkey
dîner (le) *dee-ne* dinner, supper

diplomate (le) *dee-plo-mat* trifle; sponge fingers steeped in milk or liqueur, put into a mould & filled with custard & candied fruits
dodine de canard (la) *do-deen der ka-nar* boned duck stuffed with forcemeat, rolled, cooked & served hot with a spicy sauce, or cold in slices with a mixed salad
domaine (le) *do-mehn* vineyard; used on a wine label, it indicates a wine of exceptional quality
dorade (la) *do-rad* sea bream
doré(e) *do-re* browned
dos *doh* back, meatiest portion of fish as in **dos de saumon**
doux/douce *doo(s)* mild; sweet; soft
dragée (la) *dra-zhe* almond or other nut confectionery in a chocolate & hard sugar-coating. Traditional sweet of weddings & baptisms. (Verdun, Lorraine)
Dubarry (la) *dü-ba-ree* cauliflower & cheese, browned in the oven
duchesse (la) *dü-shehs* dish of potatoes mashed with butter & egg yolk
dur(e) *dür* hard
duxelles (les, f) *dük-sehl* finely chopped mushrooms sautéed in butter with shallots or onions used as a seasoning or a sauce

E

eau (l', f) *oh* water
 –**minérale** *mee-ne-ral* mineral water
 –**du robinet** *dü ro-bee-ne* tap water
 –**de source** *der soors* spring water
eau-de-vie (l', f) *oh der vee* 'water of life', clear fruit or nut brandies
échalote (l', f) *e-sha-lot* shallot
écrevisse (l', f) *e-krer-vees* crayfish
 –**à la nage** *a la nazh* crayfish simmered in white wine, usually served with bread & butter as an entrée
églantine (l' f) *ehg-lã-teen* wild rose
églefin (l', m) *ehg-ler-fũ* haddock
émincé (l', m) *e-mũ-se* thinly sliced meat
Emmental (l', m) *e-mã-tal* cow's milk pressed & cooked cheese. It's brushed & has a golden yellow to brown rind. Originally produced in Switzerland. (Franche-Comté)
endive (l', f) *ã-deev* chicory (UK), endive (US)
 –**à la bruxelloise** *a la brü-sehl-waz* chicory/endive leaves rolled in a slice of ham, covered with cheese sauce & browned in the oven
entrecôte (l', f) *ã-trer-koht* rib steak
 –**Bercy** *behr-see* pan-broiled steak served with a butter sauce
 –**chasseur** *sha-serr* a pan-broiled steak with a brown sauce made of white wine, mushrooms & tomatoes
 –**marchand de vin** *mar-shã der vũ* steak poached in red wine, shallots & onions
 –**minute** *mee-nüt* minute steak; a small piece of steak quickly cooked
Entre-Deux-Mers (l', m) *ãtr-der-mehr* vast white wine producing region of the Bordeaux district
entrée (l', f) *ã-tre* the course before the **plat principal** (main course)
entremets (l', m) *ã-trer-meh* cream-based sweet or dessert
épais(se) *e-peh(s)* thick
épaule (l', f) *e-pohl* shoulder
 –**d'agneau** *da-nyoh* shoulder of lamb
 –**de mouton** *der moo-tõ* shoulder of mutton
éperlan (l', m) *e-pehr-lã* smelt (fish)
épice (l', f) *e-pees* spice
épinard (l', m) *e-pee-nar* spinach
Époisses de Bourgogne (l' f) *e-pwas der boor-gon-y* strong-smelling, fine-textured cheese washed in **marc** during ripening
escabèche (l', f) *ehs-ka-behsh* highly-seasoned marinade used to flavour & preserve small fish. The fish are fried or browned, marinated overnight in a broth made of onions, peppers, vinegar & spices, & served cold.

escalope (l', f) *ehs-ka-lop* thin boneless slice of meat, usually from the top round
–**viennoise** *vyen-waz* Wiener schnitzel; breaded veal **escalope** or cutlet
–**de veau** *der voh* thin boneless slice of veal
escargot (l', m) *ehs-kar-goh* snail
espadon (l', m) *ehs-pa-dõ* swordfish
espagnole, à l' *ehs-pan-yol* 'Spanish style', dishes generally including tomatoes, pimentos, capsicum, onion, garlic & rice *(see also* **sauce espagnole**)
estomac (l', m) *ehs-to-ma* stomach
estouffade (l', f) *ehs-too-fad* meat, usually beef or pork, stewed in wine with carrots & herbs (southern France)
estragon (l', m) *ehs-tra-gõ* tarragon
esturgeon (l', m) *ehs-tür-zhõ* sturgeon
étouffée/étuvée, à l' *e-too-fe/ e-tü-ve* food steamed or braised in a tightly sealed vessel with minimal liquid
extra-sec (l' m) *ehks-tra-sehk* very dry, of wine

F

faisan (le) *fer-sã* pheasant
fait(e) maison *feh(t) meh-zõ* home-made, of the house
faitout (or **fait-tout**) *feh-too* multipurpose pot or stew pot
farce (la) *fars* forcemeat/stuffing
farci(e) *far-see* stuffed
légumes- (les, m) *leh-güm-* stuffed vegetables cooked in oil
farine (la) *fa-reen* flour
faux-filet (le) *foh-fee-leh* beef sirloin
fenouil (le) *fer-noo-y* fennel
ferme (la) *fehrm* farm
feuilletage (le) *fer-y-tazh* puff pastry
feuilleté (le) *fer-y-te* puff pastry usually filled with fruit, cheese, mushrooms, meat, seafood or poultry
fève (la) *fehv* broad or Lima bean
fiadone (le) *fya-dohn* lemon-flavoured spongecake
ficelle (la) *fee-sehl* a long thin **baguette**; also a tender cut of meat, often beef or duck poached in rich broth
figue (la) *feeg* fig
–**de Barbarie** *der bar-ba-ree* prickly pear
–**de mer** *der mehr* ascidian or sea squirt; a potato-shaped 'clam' with a tough cellulose shell & iodine-rich yellow flesh
filet (le) *fee-leh* fillet of meat or fish
–**de bœuf** *der berf* beef fillet, tenderloin steak
–**mignon** *meen-yõ* a small delicately flavoured fillet cut of beef, veal or pork, usually grilled or pan fried
–**de sole aux amandes** *der sol ohz a-mãd* fillet of sole served with roasted almonds
film alimentaire (le) *feelm a-lee-mã-tehr* cling wrap
financier (le) *fee-nã-sye* **'banker's style'**, small rectangular sponge cake enriched with ground almonds & whipped egg whites, sometimes coated with cherry brandy or chocolate
financière, à la *fee-nã-syehr* food served with a rich dressing of pike dumplings, truffles, mushrooms, & **Madeira** wine, sometimes with olives & crayfish
fine de claire (la) *feen der klehr* greenish oyster raised in a **claire**
fines herbes (les, f) *feen zehrb* mixture of chopped fresh herbs consisting of tarragon, parsley, chervil & chives
flageolet (le) *fla-zho-leh* kidney bean
flamande, à la *fla-mãd* 'Flemish style', usually food with braised carrots, cabbage, turnips & sometimes bacon, potatoes or sausage, sometimes simmered in beer
flambé(e) *flã-be* dish with liqueur spooned or poured over it & ignited
flamiche (la) *flam-eesh* tart filled with leeks, eggs & cream, & sometimes pumpkin & **Maroilles** cheese (Picardy)

flan (le) *flã* open-top tart with various fillings; also a dessert made of baked custard flavoured with caramel
–**parisien** *pa-ree-zyũ* tart filled with a vanilla cream
fleischkechele (le) *flaysh-ke-sher-le* mixed grill (Alsace)
flétan (le) *fle-tã* halibut
florentine, à la *flo-rã-teen* 'Florence style', commonly dishes containing spinach & sometimes a cream sauce. **Steak florentine** is rubbed with olive oil & garlic, grilled & served with fresh lemon on the side. Also a flat cookie or biscuit with glazed fruit & a chocolate coating.
flûte (la) *flüt* similar to **baguette**
foie (le) *fwa* liver
–**gras** *gra* fatted goose or duck liver. The birds are force-fed to speed the fattening process. These livers are praised for their delicate flavour & rich, buttery texture. (south-west France, Strasbourg & Brittany)
fond (le) *fõ* stock; flavoured broth used as a base for sauces, or for moistening stews or braised meats
–**d'artichaut** *dar-tee-shoh* artichoke heart
fondant (le) *fõ-dã* icing kneaded to a smooth, soft paste which can be coloured or flavoured, & used as icing for cakes & **petits fours**; also a delicious chocolate cake variety
fondue (la) *fõ-dü* there are several different types of fondue. Generally it is a pot of melted cheeses, or hot oil or broth, that diners dip meat or bread in.
–**bourguignonne** *boor-geen-yon* bite-size pieces of beef cooked in boiling oil & dipped in a variety of sauces
–**chinoise** *sheen-waz* paper-thin slices of beef or sometimes fish, dipped in a rich chicken or meat broth, then in different sauces
–**chocolat** *sho-ko-la* fruits & pieces of cake dipped in hot melted chocolate
–**savoyarde** *sav-wa-yard* bread dipped in hot melted cheeses flavoured with white wine, garlic & cherry brandy, (Savoy)
forestière, à la *fo-reh-styehr* generally food sautéed with mushrooms & bacon, or with a **Cognac**-based sauce
Forêt-Noire (la) *fo-reh-nwar* black forest cake; chocolate cake sprinkled with cherry brandy & filled with sweetened whipped cream & poached cherries
fouetté(e) *fwe-te* whipped, whisked
fougazi *foo-ga-zee* big, flat, aniseed-flavoured biscuits (Corsica)
four (le) *foor* oven
fourchette (la) *foor-sheht* fork
Fourme d'Ambert (la) *foorm dã-behr* cow's milk blue cheese with a dark-grey bloomy rind spotted with yellow & red. Matured in cold, humid, well ventilated caves. (Auvergne)
frais/fraîche *freh/frehsh* fresh
fraise (la) *frehz* strawberry
–**des bois** *de bwa* wild strawberry
framboise (la) *frã-bwaz* raspberry; also raspberry liqueur
frangipane (la) *frã-zhee-pan* creamy filling made of butter, eggs & ground almonds or macaroons, generally used in puff pastry shells, cakes or **crêpes**
frappé(e) *fra-pe* chilled, iced
frappé (le) *fra-pe* syrup/liquid poured over crushed ice
friand (le) *free-yã* pastry stuffed with minced sausage meat, ham & cheese, or almond cream
friandise (la) *free-ã-deez* titbit, delicacy; also sweets or candy
fricadelle (la) *free-ka-dehl* small fried mincemeat patty or meatball
fricandeau (le) *free-kã-doh* veal fillet simmered in white wine, vegetables herbs & spices; also a pork pâté
fricassée (la) *free-ka-se* lamb, veal or poultry served in a thick creamy sauce, often with mushrooms & onions; also quickly pan-fried foods, sometimes with wild mushrooms

frit(e) *free(t)* fried
frites (les, f) *freet* chips, French fries
friture (la) *free-tür* deep-fried food, often fish like whitebait or smelts
froid(e) *frwa(d)* cold
fromage (le) *fro-mazh* cheese
–**blanc** *blã* cream cheese
–**de brebis** *der brer-bee* sheep's milk cheese
–**frais** *freh* fermented dairy product similar to curds or cottage cheese
–**à pâte molle** *a pat mol* soft cheese
–**à pâte demi-dure** *a pat der-mee dür* semi-hard cheese
–**à pâte dure** *a pat dür* hard cheese
–**à pâte persillée** *apat pehr-see-ye* veined cheese with greenish-blue streaks
–**pressé** *pat pre-se* pressed cheese
–**de tête** *der teht* brawn, head cheese (usually pork)
fromagerie (la) *fro-ma-zher-ree* cheese shop
Fronsac (le) *frõ-sak* Bordeaux region producing mainly red wine
fruit (le) *frwee* fruit
–**confit** *kõ-fee* candied or glazed fruit
–**glacé** *gla-se* candied or glazed fruit
–**rouge** *roozh* red or berry fruit (raspberry, strawberry etc)
–**sec** *sehk* dried fruit
–**de mer** *der mehr* seafood
fugasse (la) *fü-gas* lattice-shaped flat bread which may flavoured with orange or brandy, or brushed with olive oil & sprinkled with herbs or salt before baking
fumé(e) *fü-me* smoked
fumer *fü-me* to smoke
fumet (le) *fü-meh* aromatic broth used in soups & sauces

G

galantine (la) *ga-lã-teen* pressed cold meat, usually poultry, but pork or veal are also used, stuffed with forcemeat, served cold as an entrée
galette (la) *ga-leht* **crêpe** made with buckwheat flour; also flat plain cake of **brioche**-type dough or puff pastry, with a variety of fillings; also small short butter cookies
–**de pommes de terre** *der pom der tehr* potato **galette**
–**sarrasin** *sa-ra-zũ* buckwheat flour **crêpe**
gamba (les, f) *gã-ba* king prawns
garbure (la) *gar-bür* thick cabbage soup with salted pork, potatoes, vegetables, spices, herbs & sometimes **confit d'oie**. May be covered with bread slices & cheese, & browned in the oven. (Gascogne)
garni(e) *gar-nee* garnished
garniture (la) *gar-nee-tür* garnish; side dish; decoration
gâteau (le) *ga-toh* cake
–**basque** *bask* plain cake filled with **confiture** (usually cherry)
–**maison** *meh-zõ* home-made cake or chef's speciality
–**marbré** *mar-bre* marble cake; a cake with alternated layers of vanilla & chocolate batter
–**pithiviers** *pee-tee-vye* round, scalloped puff pastry case filled with **frangipane** cream
gaufre (la) *gohfr* waffle
gaufrette (la) *goh-freht* small crisp sweet wafer often served with ice creams
gayshelli (le) *ge-she-lee* sugared biscuits (Corsica)
gazeux(se) *ga-zer(z)* fizzy
gélatine (la) *zhe-la-teen* aspic or gelatin
gelée (la) *zher-le* aspic or fruit jelly
geler *zher-le* to freeze
gélinotte (la) *zhe-lee-not* hazel grouse; hazel hen; a game bird
genièvre (le) *zher-nyevr* juniper
génisse (la) *zhe-nis* heifer
génoise (la) *zhen-waz* very rich sponge cake, often eaten as is or used as the foundation for many other cake preparations

gentiane (la) *zhã-tyahn* gentian; a plant found in alpine areas whose bitter roots are used to flavour alcohol
gérant(e) (**le/la**) *zhe-rã(t)* manager at restaurant or hotel
gésier (le) *zhe-zye* gizzard, poultry entrails
gibelotte de lapin (la) *zhee-blot der la-pũ* rabbit stewed in wine sauce with bacon, potatoes, mushrooms, garlic, onion & herbs
gibier (le) *zheeb-ye* game
–**à plume** *a plüm* game bird
–**en saison** *ã seh-zõ* game in season
gigot (**le**) *zhee-goh* leg, generally of lamb or mutton
–**d'agneau** *da-nyoh* leg of lamb
gigue (la) *zheeg* haunch
–**de chevreuil** *der sher-vrer-y* haunch of venison
gingembre (le) *zhũ-*zhãbr ginger
girolle (la) *zhee-rol* boletus mushroom; same as **chanterelle** mushroom
glaçage (le) *gla-sazh* icing
glace (la) *glas* ice; ice cream
–**au chocolat** *oh sho-ko-la* chocolate ice cream
–**à la fraise** *a la frehz* strawberry ice cream
–**napolitaine** *na-po-lee-tehn* 'neapolitan ice cream', with several layers of different ice cream flavours
glacé(e) *gla-se* glazed/iced
glaçon (le) *gla-sõ* ice cube
gougère (la) *goo-zhehr* savoury pastry of **choux** paste flavoured with cheese, served as an appetiser or entrée; sometimes also made with ham & **Béchamel**
goujon (le) *goo-zhõ* gudgeon; freshwater fish related to carp
grain (le) *grũ* grain or cereal
graisse (la) *grehs* grease, fat or suet
–**animale** *a-nee-mal* animal fat
–**de canard** *der ka-nar* duck fat
–**d'oie** *dwa* goose fat
–**de porc** *der por* (pork) lard
–**végétale** *ve-zhe-tal* vegetable fat
–**de volaille** *der vo-lay* poultry fat
grand cru; grand vin (le) *grã krü; grã vũ* wine of exceptional quality
Grand Marnier (le) *grã mar-nye* orange liqueur
grand(e) *grã(d)* large, big
grande cuisine *grãd kwee-zeen* 'great cuisine' *(see* **haute cuisine**)
granité (le) *gra-nee-te* granita; granular textured fruit-flavoured water-ice or sorbet
gras/grasse *gra(s)* fat/plump
gras-double (le) *gra-doobl* tripe; may be cooked in water, moulded in a rectangular block, or cut in strips, & braised with tomatoes or onions
–**à la lyonnaise** *a la lee-o-nehz* tripe simmered in wine vinegar & onions
gratin (le) *gra-tũ* dishes cooked in the oven & browned with breadcrumbs or cheese forming a crust on the surface
–**dauphinois** *doh-feen-wa* sliced potatoes gratinéed in the oven with garlic, eggs, milk, cream & sometimes cheese
–**de homard** *der o-mar* pieces of lobster & other shellfish in a heavy sauce
gratinée (la) *gra-tee-ne* onion soup topped with toast & grated cheese (usually **Gruyère** cheese), browned in the oven
Graves (le) *grav* Bordeaux region especially renowned for its white & red wines
grecque, à la *grehk* 'Greek style', foods prepared with olive oil, onions, lemon, & sometimes with tomato, peppers or fennel added
grenadin (le) *grer-na-dũ* veal (or sometimes poultry) fillet, wrapped in a thin slice of bacon
grenouille (la) *grer-nooy* frog
–**cuisses de** *kwees der* frogs' legs
grillade (la) *gree-yad* mixed grill
grillé(e) *gree-ye* grilled
grillons (les, m) *gree-yõ* chunks of fatty pork or duck cooked until crisp
griotte (la) *gree-yot* morello cherry
grive (la) *greev* thrush

grondin (le) *grõ-dũ* gurnard (Mediterranean fish)

groseille (la) *groh-zehy* (red) currant

–**à maquereau** *a ma-kroh* gooseberry

Gruyère (le) *grü-yehr* cheese, originally from Switzerland. A moderate-fat cow's milk cheese with a rich, sweet & nutty flavour, prized for both out-of-hand eating & cooking. It has a golden brown rind & a firm, pale-yellow interior with well-spaced medium-size holes. The term is used generally to refer to an array of pressed **Gruyère** cheeses from areas such as Beaufort, Comté, etc, all rich in flavour & smooth in texture.

H

haché(e) *ha-she* minced, chopped

hachis (le) *ha-shee* minced meat, fish or chopped vegetables used to complete a preparation, or to make **fricadelles** or **croquettes**

–**Parmentier** *par-mã-tye* minced meat & mashed potatoes

haddock (le) *a-dok* haddock

–**fumé** *fü-me* smoked haddock

hareng (le) *a-rã* herring

–**fumé** *fü-me* smoked herring, kipper

haricot (le) *a-ree-koh* bean

–**blanc** *blã* white haricot or kidney bean

–**de mouton** *der moo-tõ* mutton & white haricot bean stew flavoured with onions, garlic, tomato purée & herbs; originally called **halicot de mouton**, a lamb stew without beans

–**rouge** *roozh* red kidney bean

–**de Soissons** *der swa-sõ* small white butter or Lima bean

–**vert** *a-ree-koh vehr* green bean, French or string bean

haute cuisine (la) *oht kwee-zeen* 'high cuisine', classic French style of cooking that originated in the spectacular feasts of French kings; typified by super-rich, elaborately prepared & beautifully presented multicourse meals

hélianthe (l' m) *el-yãt* sunflower

herbe (l', f) *ehrb* herb

hollandaise (la) *o-lã-dehz* emulsified oil & egg yolk sauce, flavoured with fresh lemon juice

homard (le) *o-mar* Atlantic lobster

–**à l'armoricaine/américaine** *ar-mor-ee-kehn/a-me-ree-kehn* lobster simmered in white wine, tomatoes, shallots, garlic, pepper, flamed in Cognac or whisky & served with a lobster coral (roe) sauce

–**Newburg** *ny-oo-boorg* lobster cut into sections, cooked in **Madeira** wine & served with creamy sauce

–**Thermidor** *tehr-mee-dor* lobster sautéed in butter, served in its shell with a white wine & **Béchamel** sauce flavoured with shallots, herbs, spices & mustard, sprinkled with cheese & browned

hongroise, à la *õ-grwaz* 'Hungarian stye', dish with paprika, or served with a paprika, onion & sour cream sauce

hors d'œuvre *or-dervr* appetisers

–**variés (les, m)** *var-ye* selection of appetisers

–**chauds (les, m)** *shoh* hot appetisers

huile (l, f) *weel* oil

–**d'arachide** *da-ra-sheed* groundnut or peanut oil

–**de colza** *der kol-za* rapeseed oil

–**de maïs** *der ma-ees* corn oil

–**de noix** *der nwa* walnut oil

–**de noisettes** *der nwa-zeht* hazelnut oil

–**d'olive** *do-leev* olive oil

–**de tournesol** *der toor-ner-sol* sunflower oil

–**de table** *der tahbl* 'table' or salad oil

huître (l', f) *weetr* oyster

–**de Belon** *der ber-lõ* round, flat & pinkish oyster

–**de claire** *der klehr* oyster farmed in marsh enclosures called **claire**

–**de Marennes** *der ma-rehn* greenish-coloured oyster (Atlantic Coast)

hure (l' f) *ür* brawn, head cheese (usually pork)
hysope (l' f) *ee-zop* hyssop; aromatic blue-flowered plant of the mint family

I

île flottante (l', f) *eel flo-tãt* dessert of egg whites floating on a custard surface, coated with caramel sauce
indienne, à l' *ũ-dyehn* 'Indian style', generally a dish flavoured with curry
infusion (l', f) *ũ-fü-zyõ* herbal tea

J

jalousie (la) *zha-loo-zee* latticed flaky pastry filled with almond paste & jam
jambon (le) *zhã-bõ* ham
 –de Bayonne *der bayon* fine raw, slightly salty ham (Basque Country)
 –de canard *der ka-nar* cured or smoke duck breast
 –chaud *shoh* baked ham
 –cru *krü* raw ham
 –fumé *fü-me* smoked ham
 –à l'os *a los* baked ham; on the bone
jambonneau (le) *zhã-bo-noh* ham knuckle
jardinière, à la *zhar-dee-nyehr* 'gardener's style', dish of cooked vegetables
jarret (le) *zha-reh* knuckle or shank
 –de veau *der voh* knuckle of veal
jeûner *zher-ne* to fast (not eat)
joue (la) *zhoo* cheek
 –de bœuf *der berf* meat cut from the cheek of a cow
jour, ... (du) *zhoor, ... (dü)* ... of the day; daily speciality
julienne (la) *zhü-lyehn* usually vegetables, sometimes ham or chicken breast, cut in long, fine strips, cooked in butter or served raw
Jura (le) *zhüra* this long strip, running parallel to the western Swiss border & Burgundy, offers white, red, rosé, golden & sparkling wine
jus (le) *zhü* gravy/juice
 –au *oh* dish served in meat drippings

K

kascher *ka-shehr* kosher
kir (le) *keer* white wine sweetened with **cassis**
 –royal *rwa-yal* Champagne with **cassis**
kirsch (le) *keersh* cherry **eau-de-vie** or brandy
kriek (le) *kreek* Belgian beer flavoured with cherries
kugelhopf/kougeloff (le) *kü-gerl-hopf/koo-gerl-hof* chocolate, almond & sultana cake (Alsace)

L

Laguiole (le) *lag-yol* variety of **Cantal** cheese
lait (le) *leh* milk
 –cru *krü* raw or unpasteurised milk used to make certain cheeses
 –fermenté *fehr-mã-te* sour milk
 –écrémé *e-kre-me* skimmed milk
laitance (la) *leh-tãs* soft roe
laitue (la) *leh-tü* lettuce
 –printanière *prũ-tan-yehr* spring lettuce
lamproie (la) *lã-prwa* lamprey eel
langouste (la) *lã-goost* spiny lobster, rock lobster (Mediterranean)
langoustine (la) *lã-goost-een* scampi, Dublin Bay prawn, langoustine
Langres (le) *lã-gr* smooth, pungent cheese from Champagne
langue (la) *lãg* tongue
 –de bœuf *der berf* ox tongue
 –de chat *der sha* 'cat's tongue', long thin biscuit, delicate & crumbly
Languedoc (le) *lãg-dok* region of the south-west, producing ordinary red & white table wine called **vins de pays**
lapereau (le) *la-per-roh* young rabbit
lapin (le) *la-pũ* rabbit
 –de garenne *der ga-rehn* wild rabbit
 –chasseur *sha-serr* rabbit sautéed in white wine with mushrooms & bacon
lard (le) *lar/beh-kon* bacon
 –fumé *fü-me* smoked bacon
 –maigre *mehgr* streaky bacon

lardon (le) *lar-dõ* bacon cube
laurier (le) *lor-ye* bay leaf
lavande (la) *la-vãd* lavender
légume (le) *le-güm* vegetable
–**sec** *sek* pulse, dried vegetable
légumes jardinière (les)*le-güm zhar-dee-nyehr* diced fresh vegetables (usually carrots, turnips, beans & cauliflower) with butter, chervil & cream
lentille (la) *lã-tee-y* lentil
levraut (le) *ler-vroh* young hare
levure (la) *ler-vür* yeast
–**de boulanger** *der boo-lã-zhe* baker's yeast
–**chimique** *shee-meek* baking powder
liaison (la) *lyeh-zõ* process of thickening a sauce, soup or stew, with **roux**, starch, liquid, egg yolks, & sometimes cream
lieu (le) *lyer* pollack, coley or coalfish related to cod
lièvre (le) *lyehvr* hare
–**en civet** *ã see-veh* jugged hare (hare stew)
limande (la) *lee-mãd* lemon sole, dab
–**meunière** *mer-nyehr* lemon sole sautéed in butter & garnished with lemon & parsley
limonade (la) *lee-mo-nad* lemonade (fizzy)
lingot (le) *lũ-go* type of haricot bean
Livarot (le) *lee-va-roh* pasteurised cow's milk cheese. Typically this assertively flavoured orange-red cheese has five strips of sedge which are wrapped around its plump & round shape. (Livarot, Normandy)
Loire (la) *lwar* the district extending over the vicinity of River Loire, producing fine red, white & rosé wine
longe (la) *lõzh* loin
–**de veau farcie** *der voh far-see* stuffed loin of veal
lorraine, à la *lo-rehn* 'Lorraine style', generally a dish garnished with red cabbage & potato croquettes, or bacon slices & **Gruyère** cheese.
Lorraine (la) *lo-rehn* region in north-east France producing wines of mostly minor importance
lotte (la) *lot* monkfish
loup de mer (le) *loo der mehr* sea bass
lyonnaise, à la *ly-o-nehz* 'Lyon style', dish generally including onions cooked golden brown, seasoned with wine, garlic & parsley

M

macaron (le) *ma-ka-rõ* macaroon; a meringue, biscuit or small cake made with almond paste
macédoine (la) *ma-seh-dwan* mixed & diced fruits, vegetables or even seafood
mâche (la) *mash* 'lamb's lettuce', wild lettuce with small round leaves – may be used for salads, or cooked as spinach
Mâconnais (le) *ma-kõ-neh* wine from the Mâcon region of Burgundy, which generally produces red wine
Madeira *(see* **madère**)
madeleine (la) *mad-lehn* small shell-shaped cake. Generally flavoured with lemon but also almonds or cinnamon.
madère (au) *ma-dehr* 'Madeira style', dishes served with a sauce flavoured with sweet **Madeira** (Portuguese fortified wine)
magret (le) *ma-greh* the breast meat from a fattened mallard or Barbary duck specially raised for **foie gras** *(see* **jambon de canard**)
maigre (au) *mehgr* lean, or without meat
maigre (le) *mehgr* meagre (type of fish)
maïs (le) *ma-ees* corn/maize
maison (de la) *meh-zõ* speciality of the restaurant
maître d'hôtel (le) *mehtr doh-tehl* head waiter
mandarine (la) *mã-da-reen* mandarine, tangerine
mange-tout (le) *mãzh-too* snowpea, mange-tout
maquereau (le) *ma-kroh* mackerel

marc (le) *mar* drink made from distilled grape skins & pulp left over after being pressed for wine. Different regions produce different variations. Some celebrated varieties are **marc de Champagne, marc de Bourgogne** (from Pinot Noir) & **marc du Jura**. A distillation of **marc du Jura** with the addition of unfermented grape juice becomes **marcvin du Jura.** Usually served after meals.

marcassin (le) *mar-ka-sũ* young boar

marchand de vin, à la *mar-shã der vũ* wine merchant; also 'wine merchant style', dish cooked with (red) wine

marché (le) *mar-she* market

marengo (la) *ma-rũ-goh* stewed chicken or veal served over toast & garnished with crayfish or shrimps, & sometimes fried eggs

margarine (la) *mar-ga-reen* margarine; invented in France in 1869

marinade (la) *ma-ree-nad* marinade; a highly flavoured liquid which may include wine or vinegar, oil, aromatic vegetables & herbs, that meat, fish or vegetables are steeped in to be flavoured & tenderised

mariné(e) *ma-ree-ne* marinated

marinière, à la *ma-ree-nyehr* 'mariner's style', usually mussels or other seafood simmered in white wine with onions parsley, thyme & bay leaves

marjolaine (la) *mar-zho-lehn* marjoram

marmelade (la) *mar-mer-lad* thick purée of fresh fruits stewed in sugar or compote; also marmalade

marmite (la) *mar-meet* pot

Maroilles (le) *mar-wal* semi-hard pungent cow's milk cheese with a red-brown washed rind (Picardy)

marron (le) *ma-rõ* chestnut *(see also* **châtaigne**)

–**glacé** *gla-se* candied chestnut

massepain (le) *mas-pũ* marzipan; almond paste; also a small pastry filled with ground almonds, sugar & egg whites, often iced with sugar or **praliné**

matelote (la) *mat-lot* fish stew (often eel) with wine, onions, shallots, garlic, & sometimes mushrooms

mauvais(e) *moh-veh(z)* bad

mayonnaise (la) *ma-yo-nehz* mayonnaise

médaillon (le) *me-da-yõ* small, round or oval cut of meat or fish

Médoc (le) *me-dok* Bordeaux region, producing highly renowned red wine

melba (la) *mel-ba* dishes created in celebration of Australian opera singer Dame Nellie Melba *(see* **pêche melba**)

melon (le) *mer-lõ* melon

menthe (la) *mãt* mint

menu (le) *mer-nü* generally means a set meal at a fixed price (**menu à prix-fixe**); *(see* **à la carte**)

–**de dégustation** *der de-gü-sta-syõ* tasting menu; special menu giving a small sample of several dishes

merguez (la) *mehr-gehz* spicy red sausage made from beef or mutton, originally from North Africa

meringue (la) *mer-rũg* meringue; egg whites whipped with sugar or syrup

merise (la) *mer-reez* wild cherries

merlan (le) *mehr-lã* whiting

merle (le) *merl* blackbird

merlu (le) *mehr-lü* hake

merluche (la) *mehr-lüsh* dried cod

merluchon (le) *mehr-lü-shõ* small hake

mérou (le) *me-roo* grouper

merveille (la) *mehr-veh-y* fried pastry shapes, sprinkled with sugar

mesclun (le) *mes-klũ* mixture of a half-dozen salad greens including rocket, lamb's lettuce, endive etc

meunière, à la *mer-nyehr* 'miller's wife's style', foods, usually fish, lightly sautéed in butter, usually with lemon juice & chopped parsley

–**meunière (la)** *mer-nyehr* sole sautéed in butter with lemon juice & parsley

–**normande** *nor-mãd* sole cooked with shrimps in a **court-bouillon**, served with a white creamy sauce flavoured with lemon (Normandy)

meurette (la) *mer-reht* red wine sauce
michette (la) *mee-sheht* savoury bread stuffed with cheese, olives, onions & anchovies (Nice)
miel (le) *myehl* honey
mignon (le) *meen-yõ* small piece of tenderloin of beef, pork or veal
mijoté(e) *mee-zho-te* simmered
milanese, à la *mee-la-nehz* 'Milan style', foods dipped in egg, breadcrumbs, & sometimes Parmesan cheese, fried in butter or baked **au gratin**
millas (le) *mee-las* corn flour & goose fat cake eaten with a meat course
–**de Bordeaux** *der bor-doh* custard & cherry tart
mille-feuille (le) *meel-fer-y* '1000 leaves', flaky pastry layered with custard or thick cream filling
Mimolette (la) *mee-mo-leht* Edam-like bright orange cheese that can be aged up to 36 months
mique (la) *meek (see* **millas**)
mirabelle (la) *mee-ra-behl* small yellow plum, used in tarts as well as liqueurs & plum brandy (Alsace, Lorraine)
mirepoix (le) *meer-pwa* cubed vegetables (onions, carrots, celery) cooked together & added to sauces
miroton (le) *mee-rotõ* slices of precooked beef, usually leftovers, simmered with onions, often served as stew
mode, à la *mod* 'of the fashion', often means made according to a local recipe *(see also* **bœuf à la mode**)
moelle (la) *mwal* bone marrow
mojette (la) *mo-zheht* haricot bean
moka (le) *mo-ka* combination of coffee & chocolate; also a **savoie** cake flavoured with coffee
mont-blanc (le) *mõ blã* canned chestnut purée with or without a meringue base, topped with crème **Chantilly**
Morbier (le) *mor-bye* pressed cheese with a distinctive grey line of ash through its middle (Jura)
morceau (le) *mor-soh* morsel or piece
morille (la) *mo-ree-y* morel mushroom, a wild mushroom, with a honeycomb cap & hollow stem, possessing a wonderful earthy flavour
Mornay (la) *mor-ne* **Béchamel** sauce with **Gruyère** cheese, sometimes enriched with egg yolks. Used mainly with fish & vegetable dishes.
morue (la) *mo-rü* cod
moules (les, f) *mool* mussels
–**marinière** *ma-ree-nyehr* mussels with onions in white-wine sauce flavoured with parsley, thyme & bay leaves
moule (la) *mool* cake tin
mousse (la) *moos* set sweet or savoury ingredients, generally lightened with whipped egg whites or sometimes cream, blended & folded together. May be served hot or cold.
mousseline (la) *moos-leen* fine purée or forcemeat lightened with whipped cream; also a variation of **hollandaise** sauce made with whipped cream
mousseron (le) *moos-rõ* blewit; fleshy wild mushroom
mousseux (le) *moo-ser* sparkling; also sparkling wine
moustachole (le) *moo-sta-shol* bread with big sugar crystals on top (Corsica)
moût (le) *mooh* must; juice pressed from grapes before it is fermented
moutarde (la) *moo-tard* mustard
mouton (le) *moo-tõ* mutton
mulet (le) *mu-leh* mullet
Munster (le) *mũ-stehr* strong, pungent but delicious cow's milk cheese of orange-red colour, sometimes sprinkled with caraway seeds (Alsace)
mûre (la) *mür* blackberry
muscade (la)) *müs-kad* nutmeg
Muscadet (le) *müs-ka-deh* white wine from the Loire region
muscat (le) *mü-ska* type of grape; also the name of a sweet dessert wine, the most renowned from **Roussillon**

museau (le) *mü-zoh* muzzle or snout; also pork brawn, head cheese
myrtille (la) *meer-tee-y* bilberry or European blueberry

N

Nantais (le) *nã-teh* region of the Loire especially renowned for its **Muscadet** white wine
nature *na-tür* plain
navarin (le) *na-va-rũ* mutton or lamb stew with vegetables & herbs
–**de mouton** *der moo-tõ* mutton stew with vegetables & herbs
navet (le) *na-veh* turnip
neige (la) *nehzh* 'snow', stiff beaten egg white
Neufchâtel (le) *nerf-sha-tehl* soft creamy cow's milk cheese with a bloomy rind that comes in many shapes & sizes (Normandy)
Niçoise, à la *nees-waz* 'Nice style', foods cooked with wine, black olives, onions & often garlic, anchovies, tomatoes & herbs *(see also* **salade niçoise**)
Noilly Prat (le) *nwa-yee prat* a French vermouth
noir(e) *nwar* black
noisette (la) *nwa-zeht* hazelnut; also a round, choice, boneless cut of lamb or venison
–**d'agneau** *da-nyoh* boneless round piece of lamb taken from the loin or rib, may be rolled in a slice of bacon
noix (la) *nwa* nut, walnut
–**du Brésil** *breh-zeel* brazil nut
–**de coco** *der ko-koh* coconut
–**de muscade** *der müs-kad* nutmeg
–**de veau** *der voh* choice round cut of veal leg topside
normande, à la *nor-mãd* 'Norman style', usually a dish of meat, shellfish or vegetables, served with cream. May be flamed with **Calvados** brandy, served with a cream sauce or with apples. Also an oven-roasted leg of lamb.
note (la) *not* bill or check (restaurant)
nougat (le) *noo-ga* nougat; confectionery made from sugar, egg whites & honey mixed with nuts (South-East France); also a vanilla ice cream with almonds, hazelnuts & candied fruits
nougatine (la) *noo-ga-teen* darker candy than **nougat**, made of caramel syrup & ground almonds. May be rolled into thin sheets & formed into cups or bowls to serve as a vessel for other candy or fruit. Also a **génoise** sponge cake filled with **praliné** cream, decorated with almonds or hazelnuts.
nouilles (les, f) *noo-y* noodles
–**fraîches** *frehsh* fresh noodles
nourriture (la) *noo-ree-tür* food, nourishment
nouvelle cuisine (la) *noo-vehl kwee-zee*n food prepared & presented to emphasise the inherent textures & colours of the ingredients; features rather small portions served with light sauces

O

œuf (l', m) *erf (er) (plural)* egg
–**au bacon** *beh-kon* bacon & eggs
–**brouillé** *broo-ye* scrambled egg
–**à la coque** *a la kok* soft-boiled egg
–**dur** *dür* hard-boiled egg
–**farci** *far-see* stuffed egg
–**frit** *free* fried egg
–**en gelée** *ã zher-le* an egg lightly poached & served in aspic
–**au jambon** *oh zhã-bõ* ham & eggs
–**au lait** *oh leh* custard, served cold
–**mollet** *mo-leh* medium-soft egg
–**à la neige** *a la nehzh* sweet meringue puffs poached in milk, chilled, then drizzled with caramel & served with a **crème anglaise**
–**sur le plat/au plat** *sür ler pla/oh pla* fried egg
–**poché** *po-she* poached egg
–**de poisson** *der pwa-sõ* roe, fish egg

–**à la poêle/poêlé** *a la pwal/pwa-le* pan-fried egg
–**Rossini** *ro-see-nee* egg with truffles & **Madeira** wine
oie (l', f) *wa* goose
oignon (l', m) *on-yō* onion
oiseau (l', m) *wa-zoh* bird
–**sans tête** *sā teht* 'headless bird', thin veal or beef slice rolled around or stuffed with sausage meat, bacon or ham
olive (l', f) *o-leev* olive
–**farcie** *far-see* stuffed olive
–**noire** *nwar* black olive
–**verte** *vert* green olive
omble chevalier (l', m) *ōbl sher-val-ye* char, a trout-like fish (Savoy)
ombre (l' m) *gray-ling*
omelette (l', f) *om-leht* omelette; pan-cooked beaten eggs, with a variety of fillings or toppings
–**basquaise** *bas-kehz* omelette with green and red peppers/capsicums (Basque Country)
–**à la confiture** *kō-fee-tür* jam omelette, served as dessert
–**aux coquilles Saint-Jacques** *oh ko-keey sū-zhak* omelette with scallops
–**aux crevettes** *krer-veht* omelette with shrimps
–**aux fines herbes** *feen zehrb* omelette with parsley, chervil & chives
–**flambée** *flā-be* sweet omelette, flamed, usually with cherry brandy
–**au foie de volaille** *fwa der vo-lay* omelette with chicken liver
–**aux fruits de mer** *frwee der mehr* seafood omelette
–**au jambon** *zhā-bō* ham omelette
–**jardinière** *zhar-deen-yehr* omelette with diced vegetables
–**aux lardons** *oh lar-dō* omelette with diced bacon
–**au fromage** *oh fro-mazh* omelette with grated cheese
–**nature** *na-tür* plain omelette
–**norvégienne** *nor-vezh-yehn* baked Alaska; sponge cake soaked with brandy, topped with moulded ice cream, covered with meringue, browned in the oven, & served before the ice cream melts
–**Parmentier** *par-mā-tye* potato omelette
–**aux pointes d'asperges** *oh pwūt d'as-pehrzh* omelette with asparagus tips
–**provençale** *pro-vā-sal* omelette with garlic, tomato, olives & olive oil
–**aux rognons** *oh ro-nyō* omelette with kidneys
–**aux tomates** *oh to-mat* omelette with tomatoes
–**aux truffes** *oh trüf* omelette with truffles
onglet (l', m) *ō-gleh* prime cut of beef
orange (l', f) *o-rāzh* orange
orange pressée (l', f) *o-rāzh pre-se* freshly squeezed orange juice
oreille (l', f) *o-reh-y* ear
organe (l' m) *or-gahn* organ
orge (l', m) *orzh* barley
origan (l', m) *o-ree-gā* oregano
ormeau (l', m) *or-moh* abalone
ortolan (l', m) *or-to-lā* garden bunting (a small game bird)
os (l', m) *os* bone
–**à moelle** *a mwal* marrow-bone
oseille (l', f) *oh-zehy* sorrel, bitter leafy green herb
Ossau-Iraty (l' m) *o-ssoh ee-ra-tee* a ewe's-milk cheese (Basque Country)
oursin (l', m) *oor-sū* sea urchin

P

pain (le) *pū* bread; also a loaf of bread weighing 400g
–**d'avoine** *dav-wan* oat bread
–**azyme** *a-zeem* unleavened bread
–**biologique** *byo-lo-zheek* organic bread
–**bis** *bees* brown bread
–**blanc** *blā* white bread

–de **campagne** *der kā-pan-y* country loaf of bread
–**aux céréales** *oh se-re-al* grain bread
–**au chocolat** *oh sho-ko-la* flat **croissant** filled with chocolate
–**complet** *kō-pleh* wholemeal/wholewheat bread
–**à discrétion** *a dee-skre-syō* bread served free of charge
–**d'épices** *de-pees* gingerbread
–**de froment** *der from-ā* wheat bread
–**grillé** *gree-ye* toast
–**de gruau** *der grü-au* fine wheaten bread
–**de levain** *der lev-ū* chewy yeast bread
–**noir** *nwar* black bread, pumpernickel; very dark rye bread
–**au pavot** *pa-voh* bread with poppy seeds
–**de seigle** *der sehgl* rye bread
–**de seigle noir** *der sehgl nwar* dark rye bread or pumpernickel
–**de son** *der sō* bread with bran
–**à volonté** *a vo-lō-te* bread at no extra charge

palmier (le) *pal-myeh* sweet pastry shaped like a heart or a palm leaf
palourde (la) *pa-loord* medium-sized clam
pamplemousse (le) *pā-pler-moos* grapefruit
pan-bagnat (le) *pā ban-ya* small round bread loaves, split or hollowed out, soaked with olive oil & filled with onions, vegetables, anchovies & black olives (Nice)
panaché (le) *pa-na-she* shandy (beer & lemonade)
panade (la) *pa-nad* bread soup, simple peasant fare (Jura)
panais (le) *pa-neh* parsnip
pané(e) *pa-ne* coated in breadcrumbs; breaded
panisse (la) *pa-nees* pancake or patty of chickpea flour fried & served with certain meat dishes (Provence)
pannequet (le) *pan-keh* a large, paper-thin pancake with a sweet or savoury filling, rolled or folded into quarters
papier (le) *pa-pye* paper
–**aluminium** *a-lü-mee-nyom* aluminium foil
–**paraffiné** *pa-ra-fee-ne* waxed, greaseproof paper

papillote (la) *pa-pee-yot* dish cooked encased in greaseproof paper or foil; also paper crowns for adorning crown roast, chicken drumsticks etc
parfait (le) *par-feh* ice cream dessert, often served in a tall glass, & sometimes with custard, fruit, nuts & liqueur
Paris-Brest (le) *pa-ree-brehst* ring-shaped cake of **choux** pastry filled with butter cream, decorated with flaked almonds & icing sugar
Parmentier (la) *pa-mā-tye* any dish containing potatoes
pastèque (la) *pas-tehk* watermelon
pastis (le) *pas-tees* puff pastry cake filled with apples or prunes marinated in **Armagnac** brandy, served cold or slightly warm (Gascony); also an aniseed-flavoured drink drunk as an aperitif & always mixed with water
patate douce (la) *pa-tat doos* sweet potato
pâte (la) *pat* paste; pastry; batter; dough; crust
–**d'amande** *da-mād* almond paste; marzipan
–**à baba** *a ba-ba* enriched yeast dough mixed with currants, baked & soaked with a rum or cherry brandy syrup
–**à beignets** *a behn-yeh* doughnut or fritter batter
–**brisée** *bree-ze* shortcrust pastry, pie crust
–**à chou(x)** *a shoo* **choux** pastry, a very light egg-based pastry
–**à crêpes** *a krehp* **crêpe** batter
–**feuilletée** *fer-y-te* puff pastry

–à frire *a freer* frying batter
–à génoise *a zhen-waz* very rich sponge cake batter sometimes flavoured with zest, vanilla, liqueur or almonds
–levée *ler-ve* dough
–sucrée *sü-kre* sweet, shortcrust pastry for tarts & tartlets
–à pizza *a pee-dza* pizza dough

pâté (le) *pa-te* potted meat; thick paste, often pork. Sometimes called **terrine**.
–de campagne *der kã-pan-y* strongly flavoured **pâté** of a variety of minced pork cuts & liver, mixed with shallots, onions, **Armagnac** & herbs
–du chef *dü shehf* chef's own recipe **pâté**
–en croûte *ã kroot* meat, fish, or vegetable forcemeat in a pastry case
–de foie gras *der fwa gra* goose or duck liver paste
–maison *meh-zõ* **pâté** made according the restaurant's own recipe

pâtes (les, f) *pat* pasta/noodles
–fraîches *frehsh* fresh pasta/noodles

pâtisserie (la) *pa-tees-ree* pastries, cakes & other sweetmeats; also the place where they are sold

paupiette de veau (la) *poh-pyeht der voh* thin slice of veal stuffed & rolled

pavé (le) *pa-ve* thickly cut steak

paysanne, à la *pe-ee-zan* 'peasant style', dish containing various vegetables & wine, or assorted chopped vegetables, usually used to garnish a **potage**, soup or an omelette

pêche (la) *pehsh* peach
–flambée *flã-be* peach poached in syrup & usually flamed in brandy
–Melba *mel-ba* poached peach halves served with vanilla ice cream, topped with raspberry sauce & flaked almonds; by chef Auguste Escoffier in honour of Australian opera singer Nellie Melba
–de vignes *der veen-y* wild peach that grows in vineyards

perche (la) *pehrsh* perch

perdreau (le) *pehr-droh* young partridge

perdrix (la) *pehr-dree* partridge

Périgourdine, à la *peh-ree-goor-deen* 'Perigourd style', dish containing truffles & sometimes **foie gras**

Pernod (le) *pehr-noh* type of **pastis**

persil (le) *pehr-seel* parsley

persillade (la) *pehr-see-yad* mixture of chopped parsley & garlic, added to recipes at the end of cooking

pet-de-nonne (le) *peh-der-non* 'nun's fart', small deep fried fritter or **choux** pastry, served hot with sugar or with fruit **coulis**

Pétillant(e) *pe-tee-yã(t)* slightly sparkling

petit(e) (le/la) *per-tee(t)* small

petit *per-tee*
–beurre *-berr* small buttery biscuit/cookie
–cuillère *kwee-yehr* teaspoon
–déjeuner *-de-zher-ne* breakfast
–four *foor* small decorated cake, served on buffets or at the end of meals
–monnaie *mo-neh* small change
–pain *pũ* bread roll
–peu *per* a little bit, a piece
–pois *pwa* pea
–salé (au chou) *sa-le (oh shoo)* salted pork (with cabbage)
–suisse *swees* a mild-flavoured double-cream cheese

pétoncle (le) *pe-tõkl* queen/bay scallop

pibale (la) *pee-bal* alevin or small eel, generally fried

pichet (le) *pee-sheh* earthenware wine jug; jug; pitcher

pied (le) *pyeh* foot, trotter
–bleu *bler* blue & white medium-sized mushroom
–de mouton *der moo-tõ* sheep's foot; also a meaty cream-coloured mushroom
–de porc *der por* pigs' trotter

pigeon (le) *pee-zhõ* pigeon

pigeonneau (le) *pee-zho-noh* squab, young pigeon
pignon (le) *pee-nyō* pine nut/kernel
pilaf (le) *pee-laf* rice & onions cooked in stock, served with shellfish, poultry, kidneys, minced meat, or fish
piment (le) *pee-mã* pimento, small red pepper; also allspice
Pineau de Charentes (le) *pee-no der sha-rãt* an **AOC** distillation of unfermented grape juice & **eau de vie** usually drunk as an **apéritif** (Charentes, Cognac)
pintade (la) *pũ tad* guinea fowl
piperade (la) *pee-per-rad* scrambled eggs with green & red peppers, garlic, tomatoes & ham (Basque Country)
piquant(e) *pee-kã(t)* hot; sharp; spicy
pissaladière (la) *pee-sa-la-dyehr* tart or 'pizza'; thick crust covered with puréed onions & garlic & flavoured with anchovies & black olives (Provence)
pissenlit (le) *pee-sã-lee* dandelion
pistache (la) *pees-tash* pistachio nut
–**en pistache** *ã pees-tash* dish prepared with garlic (rare)
pistou (le) *pee-stoo* pesto; basil & garlic pounded together with a mortar & pestle; *(see also* **soupe au pistou**)
plat (le) *pla* plate/dish
–**du jour** *dü zhoor* speciality of the day
–**principal** *prũ-see-pal* main course or dish
plateau de fromage (le) *pla-toh der fro-mazh* cheese board or platter
pleurote (la) *pler-rot* pleurotus; mild white mushroom with tender flesh
plie (la) *plee* plaice, also called **carrelet**
pluvier (le) *plü-vye* plover (small game bird)
poché(e) *po-she* poached
pochouse (la) *po-shooz* freshwater fish stew (Burgundy)
poêle (la) *pwal* frying pan
poêlé(e) *pwa-le* pan-fried
poêlon (le) *pwa-lō* casserole dish
–**en terre cuite** (le) *ã tehr kweet* earthenware casserole dish
point à *pwũ* medium-well done meat, usually still pink
–**d'asperge** (la) *das-pehrzh* asparagus tip
poire (la) *pwar* pear
–**Belle-Hélène** *behl-e-lehn* poached pears with vanilla ice cream & chocolate sauce
–**flambée** *flã-be* pear poached in syrup & flamed with brandy
–**Melba** *mehl-ba* pear with vanilla ice cream & raspberry sauce
poiré (le) *pwa-re* perry (pear cider)
Poire William (la) *pwar wee-lee-am* pear-based **eau-de-vie**
poireau (le) *pwa-roh* leek
pois (le) *pwa* pea
–**cassé** *ka-se* split pea
–**chiche** *sheesh* chickpea
poisson (le) *pwa-sō* fish
–**d'eau douce** *doh doos* freshwater fish
–**de mer** *der mehr* saltwater fish
–**de rocher** *der ro-sher* rock fish
poissonnerie (la) *pwa-son-ree* fish shop, fishmonger,
poitrine (la) *pwa-treen* breast; meat from the chest area
–**d'agneau** *da-nyoh* breast of lamb
–**de bœuf** *der berf* beef brisket
–**de mouton** *der moo-tō* breast of mutton
–**de porc** *der por* pork belly
–**de veau** *der voh* breast of veal
poivre (le) *pwavr* pepper
à la- *a la-* dish served with black pepper or pepper sauce
–**blanc** *blã* white pepper
–**de Cayenne** *der ka-yehn* cayenne pepper
–**noir** *nwar* black pepper
poivron (le) *pwav-rō* capsicum or sweet pepper
Pomerol (le) *pom-rol* Bordeaux region producing red wines
pomme (la) *pom* apple
–**au four** *oh foor* baked apple
–**beignet** *behn-yeh* apple fritter

pomme de terre (la) *pom der tehr* potato
–**allumette** *a-lü-meht* matchstick chips or French fries
–**à l'anglaise** *a l'ā-glehz* steamed or boiled potatoes
–**Anna** *a-na* thinly sliced potatoes baked in butter in a casserole
–**bouillies** *boo-yee* boiled potatoes
–**chips** *sheeps* crisps or potato chips
–**dauphinoise** *doh-feen-waz (see* **gratin dauphinois**)
–**duchesse** *dü-shehs* deep-fried mashed potato, butter & egg yolk fritter
–**au four** *foor* baked potatoes
–**frites** *freet* chips/French fries
–**gratinées** *gra-tee-ne* oven-browned potatoes with grated cheese
–**au lait** *leh* creamed potatoes
–**mousseline** *moos-leen* mashed potatoes with egg yolks & cream
–**nature** *na-tür* boiled/steamed potato
–**nouvelle** *noo-vehl* new potato
–**en purée** *püre* potatoes mashed with butter, nutmeg & hot milk or cream
–**en robe des champs/en robe de chambre** *ā rob de shā/der shābr* baked or jacket potato
–**sautée** *soh-te* sautéed potato
–**vapeur** *va-perr* steamed potato
Pommeau (le) *po-moh* **Calvados** strengthened by adding cider must or wort & drunk as an **apéritif**
Pont-l'Evêque (le) *pō-l'e-vehk* soft & runny cow's milk cheese with holes, strong & pungent in taste (Normandy)
porc (le) *por* pork or pig
porto (le) *por-toh* port
Port-Salut (le) *por-sa-lü* soft, creamy, pressed, mild & yellow cheese (Loire)
potage (le) *po-tazh* usually a thickened soup of puréed vegetable base
–**à l'ail** *a l'ay* garlic soup
–**de betterave** *der beh-trav* beetroot soup or borscht
–**bonne femme** *bon fam* 'good wife', garnish for meat or fish of bacon, potatoes, onions & mushrooms
–**au chou** *oh shoo* cabbage soup
–**Crécy** *kre-see* carrot soup
–**crème** *krem* cream soup
–**cressonnière** *kre-son-yehr* watercress soup
–**cultivateur** *kül-tee-vaterr* soup made with mixed vegetables & bacon or pork
–**Dubarry** *dü-ba-ree* cream of cauliflower
–**du jour** *dü zhoor* soup of the day
–**Parmentier** *par-mā-tye* potato soup
–**puré** *pü-re* **consommé** thickened with a purée of vegetables, meat or fish
–**Saint-Germain** *sū-zhehr-mū* split-pea soup
–**soissonnais** *swa-so-neh* butter bean soup
–**tortue** *tor-tü* turtle soup
–**velouté** *ver-loo-te* **potage purée** to which **velouté** has been mixed
pot-au-feu (le) *po-toh-fer* beef, root vegetable & herb stockpot. Traditionally, the stock is served as an **entrée** & the meat & vegetables are served as a main course.
potée (la) *po-te* meat (usually pork) & vegetables cooked in an earthenware pot
–**lorraine** *lo-rehn* pork braised with sausages & bacon, cabbage, leeks, turnips, potatoes & haricot beans
–**auvergnate** *o-ver-nyat* hearty soup-stew of cabbage, pork & potatoes
potimarron (le) *po-tee-ma-rō* variety of squash, gourd
potiron (le) *po-tee-rō* pumpkin
pouding (le) *poo-deeng* pudding
poudre (la) *poodr* powder
poularde (la) *poo-lard* pullet, fattened chicken – generally a female chicken younger than one year old.
–**à la demi-deuil** *a der-mee-der-y* fattened chicken with truffles inserted under the skin, simmered in a broth with vegetables & herbs
poule (la) *pool* hen for boiling

poulet (le) *poo-leh* chicken
–**basque** *bask* chicken cooked with tomatoes, peppers & white wine
–**de Bresse** *der bress* chicken; the best in France (Franche-Comté)
–**chasseur** *sha-serr* chicken sautéed in white wine with mushrooms, shallots & bacon
–**en cocotte** *ā ko-kot* chicken cooked in an earthenware casserole dish with white wine, mushrooms, bacon, garlic & parsley
–**à l'estragon** *a l'eh-stra-gō* chicken cooked in white wine & tarragon, served with a creamy tarragon sauce
–**froid** *frwa* cold chicken
–**fermier** *fehr-mye* free-range chicken
–**de grain** *der grū* corn-fed chicken
–**marengo** *ma-rū-goh* chicken sautéed in olive oil, white wine, tomatoes, garlic, shallots, & mushrooms, may be garnished with crayfish & eggs
–**au pot** *oh poh* whole chicken filled with giblets, ham & bread, stewed with vegetables. The broth & meat are served separately as for **pot-au-feu**.
–**au riz** *oh ree* stewed chicken served with rice cooked in the broth flavoured with grated cheese, butter &, sometimes, mushrooms & peas
–**rôti** *roh-tee* roast chicken
poulpe (le) *poolp* octopus
pourboire (le) *poor-bwar* tip or gratuity
poussin (le) *poo-sū* very young chicken
praire (la) *prehr* clam
pralin (le) *pra-lū* ground caramelised almonds or hazelnuts used as filling or flavouring for sweets
praline (la) *pra-leen* almonds, sometimes flavoured with coffee or chocolate, & with a sugar coating
praliné (le) *pra-lee-ne* mixture of chocolate & ground **praline**; also **praline**-flavoured ice cream
pré-salé (le) *pre-sa-le* lamb pastured in the salty meadows of the Atlantic or the English Channel
premier cru *prer-myeh krü* high-quality wines from specific vineyards
presse (la) *prehs* utensil for pressing, pureeing, or for extracting juice
primeur (la) *pree-merr* spring or early vegetable or fruit
printanière, à la *prū-ta-nyehr* dish often prepared or served with fresh spring vegetables
prix (le) *pree* price
–**fixe** *feeks* at a fixed price *(see* **menu** & **à la carte**)
produits de la mer (les, m)*pro-dwee der la mehr* seafood
profiterole (la) *pro-fee-trol* small ball of **choux** pastry with savoury or sweet fillings
–**au chocolat** *oh sho-ko-la* a **profiterole** filled with vanilla ice cream & covered with melted chocolate
provençale, à la *pro-vā-sal* 'Provence style', dish usually cooked with olive oil, tomatoes, garlic, onions, olives, sweet peppers, & various herbs
Provence (la) *pro-vās* France's most ancient wine-producing region, though most wines produced here now are ordinary
provisions (les, f) *pro-vee-zyō* provisions or food supplies
prune (la) *prün* plum
pruneau (le) *prü-noh* prune, dried plum
pruneaux fourrés (les, m) *prü-noh foo-re* prunes usually stuffed with cream
prunelle (la) *prü-nel* sloe (small, sour blue-black fruit)
pudding (le) *poo-deeng* pudding
puits d'amour (le) *pwee da-moor* small puff pastry shell filled with custard or jam & sprinkled with sugar
pur(e) *pür* pure
purée (la) *pü-re* preparation of mashed or strained pulped fruits or vegetables, fish or other food; can be used for soup, forcemeat or mousse
purée de marrons (la) *pü-re der ma-rō* chestnut purée

Q

qualité (la) *ka-lee-te* quality
quatre-quarts (le) *kat-kar* 'four quarters', cake made of equal parts of butter, sugar, eggs & flour, usually flavoured with vanilla, lemon, cocoa or candied fruits
quenelle (la) *ker-nehl* oval-shaped dumpling of fish or meat, forcemeat, egg & flour, often served poached
 –de brochet *der bro-sheh* pike dumpling
quetsche (la) *kwehtsh* plum **eau-de-vie** or brandy (Alsace, Lorraine)
queue (la) *ker* tail
 –de bœuf *der berf* oxtail
 –d'écrevisse *de-krer-vees* crayfish tail
 –de homard *der o-mar* lobster tail
quiche (la) *keesh* open-top tart with meat, fish or vegetable filling, baked with beaten eggs & cream
 –lorraine *lo-rehn* bacon & cheese quiche

R

râble (le) *rabl* saddle; the unseparated loin from the ribs to the legs of, usually, rabbit or hare
raclette (la) *rak-leht* hot melted cheese scraped from a block of cheese placed in front of a vertical grill & served with potatoes & gherkins (Savoy)
radis (le) *ra-dee* radish
ragoût (le) *ra-goo* stew of meat, poultry or fish &/or vegetables
raie (la) *reh* skate/ray
raifort (le) *reh-for* horseradish
raisin (le) *reh-zū̃* grapes
 –de Corinthe *der ko-rū̃t* currant
 –sec *sehk* raisin
 –de Smyrne *der smeern* sultana
ramequin (le) *ram-kū̃* ramekin or small baking dish
rascasse (la) *ras-kas* scorpion fish; grotesque but delicious fish essential in **bouillabaisse** (Mediterranean)
ratafia (le) *ra-ta-fia* liqueur obtained by infusing fruit in alcohol rather than by distillation
ratatouille (la) *ra-ta-too-y* vegetable 'stew'; tomatoes, zucchini, eggplant, sweet peppers & onions flavoured with garlic, herbs, & olive oil, served either hot or cold with lemon juice
ravigote (la) *ra-vee-got* cold spicy vinegar sauce enriched with parsley, tarragon, chervil, capers & onions, served as a vinaigrette or with grilled fish, brawn or hard-boiled eggs
raviole (la) *rav-yol* French-style ravioli; pasta dough dumplings filled with meat, with cheese or a green vegetable forcemeat (Provence) or balls of spinach & cheese (Savoy)
Reblochon (le) *rer-blo-shō̃* soft, mild cheese, pale cream in colour (Savoy)
réchauffé(e) *re-shoh-fe* reheated, warmed up
reine, à la *rehn* 'queen's style', a dish with poultry
reine-claude (la) *rehn-klohd* greengage (type of plum)
religieuse (la) *rer-lee-zhyerz* double-decker **choux** pastry puffs, filled with coffee or chocolate flavoured custard & coated with icing very vaguely resembling a nun as its name implies
rémoulade (la) *re-moo-lad* classic sauce made by combining **mayonnaise** with mustard, capers, chopped gherkins, herbs & anchovies, served chilled with grated celery, or as an accompaniment to cold meat or seafood
repas (le) *rer-pa* meal
rhubarbe (la) *rü-barb* rhubarb
Ricard (le) *ree-kar* type of **pastis**
rillettes (les, f) *ree-yeht* coarsely shredded, spiced potted meat, covered with a layer of lard & spread cold on toast; usually of pork, although goose, rabbit, poultry & even fish can be used.
rillons (les, m) *ree-yō̃* chunks of fatty pork or duck cooked until crisp

ris de veau (les, m) *ree der voh* sweetbreads
rissole (la) *ree-sol* fried or baked pastry turnover filled with a savoury filling of meat, poultry or vegetables
riz (le) *ree* rice
–**à l'impératrice** *a l'ũ-pe-ra-t*rees rich, moulded custard with rice & candied fruit, topped with a fruit sauce
–**rouge de Camargue** *roozh der kamarg* red rice grown in the Camargue delta (Provence)
Robert (la) *ro-behr* garlic, white wine, vinegar, mustard & herb sauce
rognon (le) *ron-yõ* kidney
–**en brochette** *ã bro-sheht* kidneys grilled on a spit & served with cooked tomatoes
–**de veau** *der voh* veal kidneys
romarin (le) *ro-ma-rũ* rosemary
Roquefort (le) *rok-for* world-famous ewe's milk blue-veined cheese – it's strong, piquant & salty (Languedoc)
rosbif (le) *ros-beef* roast beef; also a pejorative term for a Briton similar to the English 'frog' for a French person
rosette de Lyon (la) *roh-zeht der lyõ* large pork sausage (like salami)
rôti (le) *roh-tee* roast
rouelle de veau (la) *rwehl der voh* slice of veal, cut across the leg
rougail (le) *roo-gay* purée of eggplant, tomatoes & cod flavoured with spices & chilli, served hot or cold with grilled meat or fish (Creole)
rouget (le) *roo-zheh* mullet
–**barbet** *bar-beh* red mullet or goatfish
rouille (la) *roo-y* thick **aïoli** sauce. Bread or potatoes are mixed with dried chilli, garlic, fish broth & olive oil. Traditionally served with **bouillabaisse** or fish soup. (Provence)
roulade (la) *roo-lad* slice of meat or fish rolled around stuffing or a rolled-up vegetable soufflé
roulé(e) *roo-le* rolled
roulé (le) *roo-le (see* **roulade**)
Roussillon (le) *roo-see-yõ* region of southern France producing wine similar in character to that of the **Languedoc**; a speciality is **vin doux naturel**
roux (le) *roo* mixture of flour, butter, milk, water, broth or other liquid used to thicken white or brown sauces
rutabaga (le) *rü-ta-ba-ga* swede or rutabaga

S

sabayon (le) *sa-ba-yõ* creamy dessert, beaten eggs, sugar & wine or liqueur, flavoured with lemon juice, served slightly warm or chilled; also a frothy wine-based sauce served with seafood (originally Italian)
sablé (le) *sab-le* rich shortbread biscuit/cookie
safran (le) *sa-frã* saffron
saignant(e) *sehn-yã(t)* rare (meat)
Saint Émilion (le) *sũ- te-mee-lyõ* Bordeaux region producing famous red wine
Saint Marcellin (le) *sũ mar-ser-lũ* soft white goat's milk (Lyon)
Saint Maure de Touraine (le) *sũ mohr der too-rehn* creamy, mild cheese (Loire)
Saint Nectaire (le) *sũ nehk-tehr* pressed, pink or reddish, semi-hard cow's milk cheese produced in the same region & with the same milk as **Cantal** cheese. Maturing takes place in old wine cellars excavated in volcanic rock. (Auvergne)
Saint Raphaël (le) *sũ-ra-fa-ehl* quinine-flavoured **apéritif**
Saint-Pierre (le) *sũ-pyehr* John Dory fish
saisi(e) *seh-zee* seared
salade (la) *sa-lad* salad; also lettuce
–**composée** *kõ-po-zeh* mixed salad
–**de fruits** *der frwee* fruit cocktail
–**aux gésiers** *oh zhe-zye* curly endive served with preserved poultry gizzards

–**niçoise** *nees-waz* salad of tomatoes, green beans, hard-boiled eggs, olives, anchovies, capers & potatoes, & sometimes cucumber, green pepper (capsicum), lettuce &/or tuna
–**russe** *rüs* 'Russian', cooked vegetables in mayonnaise, with boiled eggs
–**de tomates** *der to-mat* tomato salad
–**verte** *vehrt* green salad
salé(e) *sa-le* salted
Salers Haute Montagne (le) *sa-lehrs oht mõ-tany* variety of **Cantal** cheese
Salers (le) *sa-lehrs* among the bitterest of all **apéritifs** in France, made from the bitter root of the wild gentian plant
salmis (le) *sal-mee* game or poultry partially roasted, then simmered in wine
salpicon (le) *sal-pee-kõ* a variety of diced savoury or sweet ingredients, held together by a sauce, a cream or a syrup binding, used as a garnish or stuffing
salsifis (le) *sal-see-fee* salsify or oyster plant
sandre (le) *sãdr* pike-perch, a large freshwater fish
sang (le) *sã* blood
sanglier (sauvage) (le) *sã-glee-ye (so-vazh)* (wild) boar
sanguette (la) *sã-get* **boudin** sausage – often flat – made from rabbit, duck or goose blood (Périgord)
sans glace *sã glas* without ice
sapin (le) *sa-pũ* fir/fir tree
sarcelle (la) *sar-sehl* teal (wild duck)
sardine (la) *sar-deen* sardine
sarrasin *sa-ra-zũ* buckwheat
sarriette (la) *sa-ree-yeht* savoury (herb)
sauce (la) *sohs* sauce
–**à l'américaine/armoricaine** *a la-me-ree-kehn/lar-mo-ree-kehn* lobster based sauce, simmered with lobster coral (roe) & white wine
–**béarnaise** *be-ar-nehz* bearnaise sauce; the most notable of all the **hollandaise** sauce variations, made with a white wine & vinegar reduction flavoured with shallots & tarragon
–**Béchamel/béchamel** *be-sha-mehl* milk-based sauce thickened with a **roux**, generally used as a base for more complex sauces, though it may be used alone for binding
–**Bercy** *behr-see* butter sauce with white wine & shallots
–**beurre blanc** *berr blã* emulsified white sauce made of a vinegar & white wine reduction, blended with softened butter & shallots. It's a tricky sauce that may be stabilised by a touch of cream. It is flavoured in many ways for fish, vegetables & poultry dishes.
–**beurre noir** *berr nwar* browned butter sauce, sometimes flavoured with capers, lemon juice & parsley
–**bigarade** *bee-ga-rad* brown sauce generally of oranges, sugar & vinegar
–**bordelaise** *bor-der-lehz* brown sauce made of a red wine reduction, with shallots & herbs. Some versions include slices of bone marrow added at the end of cooking. Usually served with pan-fried or grilled red meats. Also a **Bordeaux** white wine sauce with shallots, thyme & herbs, served with fish or shellfish.
–**bourguignonne** *boor-geen-yon* Burgundy red wine sauce with mushrooms, herbs, onions & spices, usually served with soft-boiled or poached eggs, poultry or meats
–**chasseur** *sha-serr* white wine sauce with mushrooms, shallots, tomato purée & herbs, usually served with chicken, rabbit or veal **escalope**
–**Colbert, à la** *kol-behr* butter sauce flavoured with parsley, lemon, & tarragon, served with grilled meats & fish
–**demi-glace** *der-mee glas* rich brown sauce of beef stock lightened with **consommé**
–**diable** *dyabl* hot, spicy sauce with white wine, herbs, & cayenne pepper

–**diplomate** *dee-plo-mat* rich, buttery white sauce with lobster & sometimes truffles & Cognac

–**espagnole** *ehs-pan-yol* this is the foundation of most brown sauces, also used when simmering meat. A rich brown beef or veal stock thickened with a brown **roux**, flavoured with browned bacon or ham, onions, diced vegetables, shallots & herbs, strained through very fine muslin after a long, slow cooking.

–**financière** *fee-nã-syehr* rich **Madeira** wine sauce, with truffles, mushrooms, cooked ham, olives & herbs; may be served with sweetbreads, poultry breast & **quenelles**

–**aux fines herbes** *oh feen zehrb* white wine sauce with **fines herbes**

–**gribiche** *gree-beesh* cold sauce made of oil, lemon juice, hard-boiled egg yolks, herbs, capers & mustard

–**hollandaise** *o-lã-dehz* the most basic of the egg & oil emulsified sauces with fresh lemon juice

–**lyonnaise** *lyo-nehz* classic preparation of sautéed onions, white wine & **demi-glace** (rich brown sauce), strained before serving with meat or poultry

–**madère** *ma-dehr* brown **Madeira** wine sauce with bacon, onions, shallots & herbs, served with giblets, poultry, ham or vegetables

–**Mornay** *mor-neh* **Béchamel** sauce with **Gruyère** cheese, sometimes enriched with egg yolks. Mainly used for fish & vegetable preparations.

–**Nantua** *nã-tü-a* sauce of freshwater crayfish, butter & cream

–**normande** *nor-mãd* white sauce with butter, cream, eggs & mushrooms in a fish stock base

–**piquante** *pee-kãt* sharp vinegar & white wine sauce with shallots, gherkins & herbs, usually served with pork

–**au raifort** *oh reh-for* horseradish sauce made with milk, cream & bread

–**ravigote** *ra-vee-got* cold spicy vinegar sauce enriched with herbs, capers & onions, served as a vinaigrette or with grilled fish, brawn or hard-boiled eggs

–**à la reine** *a la rehn* cream & chicken sauce

–**rémoulade** *re-moo-lad* classic sauce combining **mayonnaise** with mustard, capers, chopped gherkins, herbs & anchovies, served chilled with grated celery, or as an accompaniment to cold meat, fish or shellfish

–**Robert** *ro-behr* reduction of white wine & broth flavoured with herbs, mustard & garlic

–**suprême** *sü-prehm* thick sauce with cream & mushrooms in a chicken stock base, served with poultry or vegetables such as asparagus or artichoke

–**Soubise** *soo-beez* white sauce with puréed onions

–**tartare** *tar-tar* **mayonnaise**-based sauce with egg, white wine, olive oil, honey, Worcestershire sauce, chives, gherkins, capers & herbs, served hot with meat, poultry or grilled fish

–**tortue** *tor-tü* 'turtle sauce', wine reduction sauce, with ham, onions, carrots, basil, herbs & tomatoes, originally served with turtle, but now may accompany foods such as calf's head or brains, & cold fish

–**veloutée** *ver-loo-te* veal, poultry or sometimes fish stock-based white sauce often used as a base for other more complex sauces

–**verte** *vehrt* **mayonnaise** base with spinach, tarragon, chervil & herb **purée**

–**vinaigrette** *vee-neh-greht* sauce commonly used to dress salads, made of oil, vinegar & herbs. Shallots, mustard & hard-boiled eggs may also be added.

saucisse (la) *soh-sees* sausagec
–**de Francfort** *der frãk-for* frankfurter
–**de Strasbourg** *der straz-boor* knackwurst
–**de Toulouse** *der too-looz* mild pork sausage
saucisson (le) *soh-see-sõ* large sausage usually air-dried & eaten cold
–**à l'ail** *a lay* garlic sausage served warm
–**chaud** *sho* a fresh sausage often boiled
–**de Lyon** *der lyõ* confusingly, can be a long air-dried pork sausage flavoured with garlic & pepper or a boiling sausage similar to **saucisson à l'ail** eaten with potato salad
–**sec** *sehk* air-dried sausage (like salami)
sauge (la) *sohzh* sage
saumon (le) *soh-mõ* salmon
–**fumé** *fü-me* smoked salmon
sauté (le) *soh-te* sautéed, lightly browned in hot butter, oil or fat
Sauternes (le) *soh-tehrn* Bordeaux region noted for its sweet white wine
sauvage *soh-vazh* wild
savarin (le) *sa-va-rũ* ring-shaped sponge cake soaked with a rum syrup & filled with custard or whipped cream, & fresh or poached fruits
Savoie (la) *sav-wa* Savoy, the alpine district producing primarily dry, light & often slightly acid white wine along with good red, rosé & sparkling wine
savoie (la) *sav-wa* light, airy cake made with beaten egg whites
scarole (la) *ska-rol* escarole, a leafy vegetable similar to chicory
sec/sèche *sehk/sehsh* dry
séché(e) *seshe* dried
seiche (la) *sehsh* cuttlefish
sel (le) *sehl* salt
–**de Guérande** *der ge-rãd* sea salt, best available in France
selle (la) *sehl* saddle; the unseparated loin from the ribs to the legs of an animal
–**d'agneau** *da-nyoh* saddle of lamb
–**de chevreuil** *der sher-vrer-y* saddle of venison
semoule (la) *ser-mool* semolina
serveur/serveuse (le/la) *sehr-verr/sehr-verz* waiter
service (le) *sehr-vees* service (charge)
–**compris** *kõ-pree* 'service included', (often abbreviated as s.c. at the bottom of the bill) service charge is built into the price of each dish. Pay the total at the bottom.
–**en sus** *en süs* service charge is calculated after the food & drink ordered is added up. Pay the total at the bottom.
–**non compris** *nõ kõ-pree (see* **service en sus**)
serviette (la) *sehr-vyeht* serviette/napkin
sésame (le) *se-zam* sesame
sirop (le) *see-roh* fruit syrup or cordial served mixed with water, soda or with carbonated mineral water
socca (la) *so-ka* thin **crêpe**-like snack made from chickpea flour & olive oil (Nice)
soissons (haricots) (les, m) *swa-sõ* large butter beans
soja (le) *so-zha* soya bean
sole (la) *sol* sole
–**dieppoise** *dyep-waz* sole cooked with shrimps, mussels, cider, cream, vegetables, & herbs (Normandy)
solette (la) *soh-let* baby sole
sommelier (le) *so-mer-lye* wine waiter
sorbet (le) *sor-beh* sorbet; crushed ice made from fruit juice or flavoured water, often with beaten egg whites
soubise (la) *soo-beez* dish served with creamed onion purée & rice
soufflé (le) *soof-le* beaten egg whites folded through a heavy, flavoured egg yolk sauce or custard, & baked in moulds until puffed & browned. Can be flavoured with various foods such as ham, poultry, crab, vegetable or fruit purée, chocolate, or cheese.
–**au fromage** *oh fro-mazh* cheese soufflé
–**à la reine** *a la rehn* soufflé with poultry or minced meat

soupe (la) *soop* soup – generally thick & hearty
- **–au chou** *oh shoo* cabbage soup
- **–au cresson** *oh kreh-sõ* watercress soup
- **–à l'oignon** *lon-yõ* onion soup
- **–à l'oignon gratinée** *lon-yõ gra-tee-ne* classic onion soup sprinkled with grated cheese & then browned in the oven
- **–au pistou** *oh pee-stoo* soup with basil, vegetables, vermicelli noodles, olive oil, garlic, herbs & Parmesan cheese (Provence)
- **–de poisson** *der pwa-sõ* fish soup
- **–aux poivrons** *oh pwav-rõ* soup made with capsicums (peppers)

souper *soo-pe* supper

spéciale (la) *spes-yal* top-quality oyster

spécialité (de la maison) (la) *spes-ya-lee-te (der la meh-zõ)* the speciality of the house

steak (le) *stehk* steak
- **–frites** *freet* minute steak with chips/French fries
- **–haché** *ha-she* minced steak, hamburger mince
- **–au poivre** *oh pwavr* pepper steak; meat broiled (grilled) and covered with crushed peppercorns, often flamed in brandy
- **–tartare** *tar-tar* steak tartare; raw minced beef served with raw onion, egg yolk, capers & parsley, served with many seasonings that can be anything from Worcestershire sauce to Tabasco

sucre (le) *sükr* sugar
- **–glacé** *gla-se* icing sugar
- **–vanillé** *va-nee-ye* vanilla sugar

sucré(e) *sü-kre* sweetened

suprême de volaille (le) *sü-prehm der vo-lay* boned chicken breast with creamy sauce

sur commande *sür ko-mãd* to your special order

Suze (la) *süz* bitter **apéritif** based on the **gentiane** plant

T

table d'hôte (la) *tabl doht* meal at a set price & hour

taboulé (le) *ta-boo-le* tabouli, Lebanese salad of softened or cracked bulghur wheat with parsley & mint, tomatoes & onions, seasoned with olive oil & lemon juice

tanche (la) *tãsh* tench (freshwater fish)

tapenade (la) *ta-pee-nad* savoury spread or dip of puréed olives, anchovies, capers, olive oil & lemon eaten with bread or hard-boiled eggs

tartare, à la *tar-tar* 'Tartar style', food crumbed & broiled, served with a piquant sauce *(see also* **sauce tartare, steak tartare**)

tarte (la) *tart* flan, tart
- **–aux fraises** *oh frehz* strawberry tart
- **–flambée** *flã-be* thin layer of pastry topped with cream, onion, bacon & sometimes cheese or mushrooms & cooked in a wood-fired oven.
- **–aux fruits** *oh frwee* fruit tart, the ultimate French **pâtisserie**
- **–aux pommes** *oh pom* apple tart
- **–à l'oignon** *a lon-yõ* onion tart
- **–aux poires** *oh pwar* pear tart
- **–Tatin** *ta-tũ* type of tart with pastry baked on top of fruit (usually apples) that has been caramelised atop the stove first & inverted after baking.

tartelette (la) *tar-ter-leht* small tart

tartiflette (la) *tar-tee-fleht* dish of potatoes, **Reblochon** cheese & sometimes bacon baked in the oven & served piping hot (Savoy)

tartine (la) *tar-teen* slice of bread with any topping or garnish, such as butter, jam, honey, cream cheese etc

tasse (la) *tas* cup

tastevin (le) *tast-vũ* small shallow wine-tasting cup

tendron (le) *tã-drõ* cut of meat from the end of ribs to the breastbone
- **–d'agneau** *da-nyoh* lamb **tendron**

–**de bœuf** *der berf* beef **tendron**
–**de mouton** *der moo-tõ* mutton **tendron**
–**de veau** *der voh* veal **tendron**

terrine (la) *teh-reen* preparation of meat, poultry, fish or game, baked in a ceramic dish called a terrine, & served cold

tête (la) *teht* head
–**de veau** *der voh* calf's head, usually used in **fromage de tête**

thé (le) *te* tea
–**au citron** *oh see-trõ* tea with lemon
–**au lait** *oh leh* tea with milk
–**nature** *na-tür* plain tea (without milk)

thon (le) *tõ* tuna

thym (le) *tũ* thyme

tian (le) *tee-yã* mousse-like gratins of eggplant; vegetables; goat's cheese cooked in a small earthenware dish

timbale (la) *tũ-bal* meat, fish, or seafood stew with sauce cooked in a pastrycase; also rice or pasta with vegetables, cooked in a round or cup-shaped mould, served with sauce

tisane (la) *tee-zan* herbal tea; same as **infusion**
–**de camomille** *der ka-mo-meey* camomile tea
–**de menthe** *der mãt* mint tea
–**de tilleul** *der tee-yerl* tea made with dried linden blossoms)

tomate (la) *to-mat* tomato

tomme (la) *tom* various cheeses made from cow's, goat's or ewe's milk. Usually a speciality of mountainous regions, the most common **tomme** is a cow's milk mild pressed cheese with a greyish crust. (Savoy)
–**de Cantal** *der kã-tal* **tomme** cheese from the **Cantal** district (Auvergne)
–**Corse** *kors* semi-hard, granular raw ewe's milk cheese (Corsica)
–**de chèvre** *der shehvr* harder variety of goat's cheese, best from the Pyrenees
–**de Savoie** *der sav-wa* outstanding cheese made from either raw or pasteurised cow's milk

topinambour (le) *to-pee-nã-boor* Jerusalem artichoke

tortue (la) *tor-tü* turtle

Touraine (la) *too-rehn* renowned district in the Loire producing varying types of wine

tournedos (le) *toor-ner-doh* thick round slice of beef fillet
–**Rossini** *ro-see-nee* **tournedos** garnished with **foie gras** & truffles, served with **Madeira** wine sauce

tourte (la) *toort* sweet or savoury pie

tourteau (le) *toor-toh* large crab

tourtière (la) *toor-tyehr* sweet or savoury pie

tout compris *too kõ-pree* from **prix tout compris**; all-inclusive price

traiteur (le) *treh-teur* caterer or delicatessen selling prepared dishes

tranche (la) *trãsh* slice
–**napolitaine** *na-po-lee-tehn* ice cream, usually made with three differently flavoured layers

tranché(e) *trã-she* sliced

travers (le) *tra-vehr* spare rib

tripes (les, f) *treep* tripe
–**à la mode de Caen** *a la mod der kã* tripe simmered with cider, leeks & carrots

Triple Sec (le) *treepl sehk* an orange-flavoured brandy

trompette de la mort (la) *trõ-peht-der-la-mor* 'trumpet of death', wild dark grey or black mushroom with a hollow, funnel-shaped cap. It has a robust flavour & may be used to flavour sauces or soups.

troquet (le) *tro-keh* bistro, tavern, café or small restaurant

truffe (la) *trüf* truffle
–**en chocolat** *ã sho-ko-la* melted chocolate enriched with butter, cream & egg yolks, rolled into small balls & covered with cocoa. Can be flavoured with vanilla, coffee, whisky or rum.

–**diamants noirs** *dya-mã nwar* black diamond truffles (Périgord)
truite (la) *trweet* trout
–**au bleu** *oh bler* a very fresh trout poached in a **court-bouillon** broth of vinegar, white wine, vegetables & herbs
–**aux amandes** *oh za-mãd* trout cooked & topped with almonds
tuile (la) *tweel* 'tile', fragile, wing-like almond biscuit
turbot (le) *tür-boh* turbot

V

vache (la) *vash* cow
vacherin (le) *vash-rũ* mellow cheese (Savoy, Jura); also a meringue shell filled with whipped cream, ice cream, & candied fruits or roasted almonds. Sometimes an ice cream dessert served like a cake slice.
vanille (la) *va-nee-y* vanilla
vapeur (la) *va-perr* steam
–**à la** *a la* steamed
varié(e) *var-ye* assorted
veau (le) *voh* veal
–**blanquette** *blã-keht* veal stewed in white sauce enriched with cream, vegetables, & often mushrooms
–**escalope** *ehs-ka-lop* thin, boneless slice of veal, usually from the top round
–**paupiette** *poh-pyeht* a thin slice of veal stuffed & rolled
velouté (le)*ver-loo-te* soup, usually prepared with vegetables, shellfish or fish purée, thickened with cream, egg yolks & butter *(see also* **sauce veloutée**)
velouté de perdrix (le) *ver-loo-te der pehr-dree* classic thickened partridge soup
venaison (la) *ver-neh-zõ* venison
vendange (la) *vã-dãzh* grape harvest, vintage
–**tardive** *tar-deev* late harvest, usually producing sweet grapes & wine
verdure (la) *vehr-dür* green vegetables
vert-pré (le) *vehr-pre* garnish of watercress (& sometimes potatoes)
viande (la) *vyãd* meat
–**hachée** *ha-she* minced meat
–**séchée** *se-she* dried beef served in paper-thin slices as **hors d'œuvre**
–**froide** *frwad* cold meat
Vichy (le) *vee-shee* garnish of carrots; also a brand of mineral water
viennoiserie (la) *vyen-waz-ree* baked goods like croissants & brioches
vin (le) *vũ* wine
–**blanc** *blã* white wine
–**chambré** *shã-bre* wine at room temperature
–**doux** *doo* sweet, dessert wine
–**doux naturel** *doo na-tü-rehl* red or white wine made from Muscat grapes to which a neutral spirit has been added before fermentation begins
–**mousseux** *moo-ser* sparkling wine
–**ordinaire** *or-dee-nehr* table wine
–**de pays** *der pe-ee* reasonable quality & generally drinkable wine
–**rosé** *roh-ze* rosé; also pink when referring to **Champagne**
–**rouge** *roozh* red wine
–**sec** *sehk* dry wine
–**de table** *der tabl* table wine; very cheap lower-quality wine
vin délimité de qualité supérieure (VDQS) (le) *vũ de-lee-mee-te der ka-lee-te sü-per-yerr* good regional wines; the second rank of French quality control
vin jaune (le) *vũ zhohn* sweet yellow wine from the Jura
vinaigre (le) *vee-nehgr* vinegar
–**balsamique** *bal-sa-meek* wonderfully fragrant Italian vinegar made from the juice of Trebbiano grapes, heated & aged in wooden barrels. The resulting vinegar is deep rich brown with a sweet-&-sour flavour. The best is expensive.

vinaigrette (la) *vee-neh-greht* dressing made of vinegar, oil, herbs, onions or garlic, & sometimes mustard or eggs
violet (le) *vyo-leh* ascidian or sea squirt; a potato-shaped 'clam' with a tough cellulose shell & iodine-rich yellow flesh
violette (la) *vjo-leht* violet
volaille (la) *vo-la-y* poultry, fowl
vol-au-vent (le) *vo-loh-vã* round puff-pastry cases filled with a mixture of sauce & meat, poultry, seafood or vegetables, often with dumplings or mushrooms added
VSO (le) *ve ehs o* 'very special old'; indicates that a **Cognac** has been aged 25 years
VSOP (le) *ve ehs o pe* 'very special old pale'; indicates that a Cognac has been aged 30 years

W

waterzoï (le) *wa-tehr-zoy* chicken or sometimes fish poached, cooked with shredded vegetables (especially leeks), & served with a sauce of broth, cream & egg yolks (northern France)

X

Xérès (le) *gze-rehs* sherry

Y

yaourt (le) *ya-oort* yoghurt
 –**à boire** *a bwar* yoghurt drink
 –**brassé** *bra-se* thick creamy yoghurt
 –**maigre** *mehgr* low-fat yoghurt

Z

zeste (le) *zehst* zest
ziminu (le) *zee-mee-nü* seafood soup, not unlike **bouillabaisse** (Corsica)

Photo Credits

Greg Elms Front cover, p1, p5, p8, p9 top, bottom right, p10, p11, p13, p14, p15, p21, p22, p27, p28, p29, p31, p32, p34, p36, p39, p40, p41, p43, p46, p47, p48, p50, p51 right, p52, p53, p57, p60, p61, p64, p65, p67, p68, p69, p70, p71, p72, p73, p75, p90, p91, p93, p95, p96, p97, p99, p100, p101, p103, p104, p107, p108, p109, p110, p113, p114, p117 top right, bottom left, p125, p129, p135, p136, p143, p144, p149, p153, p157, p161, p165, p172, p179, p186, p187, p188, p189, p191, p192, p196, p199, p201 bottom left, p202, p203, p204, p205, p206, p207, p213, p214, p215, p216, p217, p218, p219, p221, p223, p225, p226, p227, p228, back cover.

Brenda Turnnidge p12, p45, p187 top right, p201 top right, p209, p210, p211, p231.

Simon Bracken p24, p187 bottom right, p198, p201 bottom right, p222.

Jean-Bernard Carillet p19, p37, p51 left, p175, p193, p201 top right.

Steve Davey p94, p117 top left, bottom right, p118, p122.

Julia Wilkinson p9 bottom left, p16, p63.

John King p76.

Lee Foster p84, p87.

Sally Dillon p44, p182.

Frances Linzee Gordon p140.

Jean Robert p166.

John Elk III p132.

Katherine Widing p98.

Rob Flynn p187 top left.

A

B

C

D

E

F

G

H

I

INDEX

J

K

L

M

N

O

P

Y

Z

Maps

Boxed Text

Recipes

More World Food Titles

Brimming with cultural insight, the World Food series takes the guesswork out of new cuisines and provide the ideal guides to your own culinary adventures. The books cover everything to do with food and drink in each country – the history and evolution of the cuisine, its staples & specialities, and the kitchen philosophy of the people. You'll find definitive two-way dictionaries, menu readers and useful phrases for shopping, drunken apologies and much more.

The essential guides for travelling and non-travelling food lovers around the world, look out for the full range of World Food titles including:

Italy, Morocco, Mexico, Thailand, Spain, Vietnam, Ireland, Turkey, New Orleans & Hong Kong.

World Food
ITALY
World Food
MOROCCO
World Food
MEXICO
World Food
THAILAND
World Food
SPAIN
World Food
VIETNAM
World Food
IRELAND
World Food
TURKEY
World Food
NEW ORLEANS

Out to Eat Series

Lonely Planet's Out to Eat series takes its food seriously but offers a fresh approach with independent, unstuffy opinion on hundreds of hand-picked restaurants, bars and cafes in each city. Along with reviews, Out to Eat identifies the best culinary cul-de-sacs, describes cultural contexts of ethnic cuisines, and explains menu terms and ingredients.

Updated annually, new Out to Eat titles include:
Melbourne, Paris, Sydney, London and San Francisco.

Planet Talk

Our FREE quarterly printed newsletter is full of tips from travellers and anecdotes from Lonely Planet guidebook authors. Every issue is packed with up-to-date travel news and advice, and includes:

- a postcard from Lonely Planet co-founder Tony Wheeler
- a swag of mail from travellers
- a look at life on the road through the eyes of a Lonely Planet author
- topical health advice
- prizes for the best travel yarn
- news about forthcoming Lonely Planet events
- a complete list of Lonely Planet books and other titles

To join our mailing list, residents of the UK, Europe and Africa can email us at go@lonelyplanet.co.uk; residents of North and South America can do so at info@lonelyplanet.com; the rest of the world can email talk2us@lonelyplanet.com.au, or contact any Lonely Planet office.

The Lonely Planet Story

Lonely Planet published its first book in 1973 in response to the numerous 'How did you do it?' questions Maureen and Tony Wheeler were asked after driving, bussing, hitching, sailing and railing their way from England to Australia. Written at a kitchen table and hand collated, trimmed and stapled, *Across Asia on the Cheap* became an instant local bestseller.

Eighteen months in South-East Asia resulted in their second guide, *South-East Asia on a Shoestring*, which they put together in a backstreet Chinese hotel in Singapore in 1975. The 'yellow bible', as it quickly became known to backpackers around the world, soon became the guide to the region. It has sold well over ¾ million copies and is now in its 10th edition, still retaining its familiar yellow cover.

Today there are over 400 titles, including travel guides, walking guides, language kits & phrasebooks, travel atlases & maps, diving guides, restaurant guides, first time travel guides, condensed guides, illustrated pictorials and travel literature. The company is the largest independent travel publisher in the world.

The emphasis continues to be on travel for independent travellers. Tony and Maureen still travel for several months of each year and play an active part in the writing, updating and quality control of Lonely Planet's guides.

They have been joined by over 120 authors and over 400 staff at our offices in Melbourne (Australia), Oakland (USA), London (UK) and Paris (France). Travellers themselves also make a valuable contribution to the guides through the feedback we receive in thousands of letters each year and on our web site.

The people at Lonely Planet strongly believe that travellers can make a positive contribution to the countries they visit, both through their appreciation of the countries' culture, wildlife and natural features, and through the money they spend. In addition, the company makes a direct contribution to the countries and regions it covers. Since 1986 a percentage of the income from each book has been donated to ventures such as famine relief in Africa; aid projects in India; agricultural projects in Central America; Greenpeace's efforts to halt French nuclear testing in the Pacific.

Lonely Planet Offices

Australia
PO Box 617, Hawthorn, Victoria 3122
☎ 03-9819 1877
fax 03-9819 6459
email:talk2us@lonelyplanet.com.au

USA
150 Linden St, Oakland, CA 94607
☎ 510-893 8555 TOLL FREE: 800 275 8555
fax 510-893 8572
email: info@lonelyplanet.com

UK
10a Spring Place, London NW5 3BH
☎ 020-7428 4800
fax 020-7428 4828
email: go@lonelyplanet.co.uk

France
1 rue du Dahomey, 75011 Paris
☎ 01 55 25 33 00
fax 01 55 25 33 01
email: bip@lonelyplanet.fr